A Complete Guide to MONEY AND YOUR BUSINESS

Robert E. Butler and Donald Rappaport
Partners
Price Waterhouse

New York Institute of Finance

Library of Congress Cataloging-in-Publication Data

Butler, Robert E.
A complete guide to money and your business.

Includes index.
1. Business enterprises—Finance—Handbooks, manuals, etc. I. Rappaport, Donald. II. Title.
HG4027.3.B88 1986 658.1'5 85-32094
ISBN 0-13-160276-4

This publication is designed to provide accurate and authoritative information in regard to the subject matter covered. It is sold with the understanding that the publisher is not engaged in rendering legal, accounting, or other professional service. If legal advice or other expert assistance is required, the services of a competent professional person should be sought.

From a Declaration of Principles Jointly Adopted by a Committee of the American Bar Association and a Committee of Publishers and Associations

A Division of Simon & Schuster, Inc.
70 Pine Street, New York, NY 10270

Printed in the United States of America

10 9 8 7 6 5 4 3 2 1

New York Institute of Finance
(NYIF Corp.)
70 Pine Street
New York, New York 10270

Contents

Chapter 3:
Historical Analysis: A Case Study in Planning, *21*

Chapter 4:
Preparing the Business Plan: Documenting the Strategic and Tactical Objectives, *44*

Chapter 5:
The Narrative Support, *52*

Chapter 6:
Documenting the Assumptions and Developing Operational Plans, *69*

Chapter 12:
Financing a Going Concern: Sources of Funds, *161*

Chapter 13:
Banks, Creditworthiness, and You, *182*

Preface

TO THE ENTREPRENEUR AND BUSINESS MANAGER

Out of the great mass of literature on starting and operating a small business, we have condensed in this book the essentials in the financial and administrative areas. We have mined the experiences of enough of small businesses to indicate what those essentials are. The book is designed especially to provide the entrepreneur and the manager of a small business with a discussion of these essentials and with practical examples from a variety of industries.

Entrepreneurs and managers of family businesses are down-to-earth executives. They must make most of the decisions and perform many of the operations, particularly in the financial area. They do not have the large staffs of specialized professionals a giant corporation can command, and yet even the simplest business organization requires most of the financial tools, forms, and skills that medium and large organizations need to survive.

Small businesses must be properly planned and financed. Their goods or services must be properly made, delivered, and marketed. The experiences of thousands of small or newly started businesses attest, however, to the need to understand and learn how to perform the financial essentials. Entrepreneurs may be excellent salespeople and able to market their products superbly, but if they have not properly financed their businesses, they will fail. The lack of adequate financing and financial management is the reason most often given for the failure of small businesses. Entrepreneurs may be fine engineers or software programmers, but if they cannot control their companies, they will go under. They must know all the essential aspects of financing and of financial management, not just one or two.

Almost half of the wealth of America comes from small businesses with sales of $1 to $15 million, and these enterprises generate a commensurate percentage of the jobs in America's private, nonagricultural work force. This book is dedicated to the entrepreneurs and managers of these businesses. May they survive and flourish!

Robert E. Butler
Donald Rappaport

What the Entrepreneur Needs to Know

As an entrepreneur, you start with a marketable product or service. You go to the bank for money, get some friends to invest, and hire some people to come to work with the business by showing them the prototype of the widget or the service and demonstrating its unique usefulness or appeal.

You start making the widgets in a basement or garage and then go around to get initial orders. The first widgets "fly out" of the stores, and you know the product is a hit. You go back and get some more money, buy an old factory, and with the team—"all for one and one for all"—start turning them out like crazy. You and your team work 20-hour days. You and a couple of friends become salespeople. Your marketing efforts cause the orders to pour in even faster. You rev up your manufacturing. You hire more people. Suddenly, one day, you're sitting there, the orders are pouring in, and you're broke. You don't know where the money for the next payroll is coming from. You've reached the first major crisis in business. . . .

The entrepreneur or manager of a small business represents the bulwark of free enterprise in this country. Yet small businesses are characterized by such a high degree of volatility during start-up and growth that their success rates are strikingly low. Nearly 50% of all new ventures fail during the first year of operations, 80% within the first four years. Or to look at it another way, although nearly 500,000 new businesses are started each year, nearly 400,000 fail.

This book will help you "beat the odds."

Although the specific reasons for failing are varied, the underlying theme is that the entrepreneur or owner/manager did not change management style as the business grew and encountered new problems. As a business grows, your knowledge of management techniques and procedures must increase. This book describes just how these techniques can be developed and formalized.

Neither the problems nor the solutions are new. A wealth of material on the subject is available in textbooks and offered in business courses. In fact, so much information is available that it is a problem in itself because, among the many scarce resources with which an entrepreneur must deal, time is perhaps the scarcest of all. This book abstracts from both the academic literature and the practical experience of the authors the tools, techniques, and pieces of information that are most critical. This information is presented in a way that is easy to understand and implement. In essence, we are dealing with the fundamental measure of value in business—money: how to get it, how to manage it, and how to keep it.

Your job as a manager is to be responsible for and to perform four major functions: planning, organizing, directing, and controlling. If you fail in any one of these functions, your business is not profitable and cannot achieve its potential. You operate in six major areas: your environment, your resources, your organization, your plans, your controls, and your information. You face a series of *environments* in attempting to build your business; you have various human and capital *resources,* some scarce, some less so, that you can use in your business; and ultimately you must *plan, organize,* and *control* the use of these resources.

What This Book Will Do for You

This book strips away all but the crucial fundamentals and tells you how to go about your basic objectives of building your business and making it profitable. Part I, "The Business Plan—A Basic Tool," deals with your first concern—raising capital or money. This part helps you to better understand the many dimensions of your business, as well as help you to demonstrate its possibilities to others, so that you can secure the kind of financing you need. Part I also shows you in detail how to put together a complete financing package for a retail distribution company, including a balance sheet forecast, an income statement forecast, and a cash flow forecast.

Part II, "Getting the Money," shows you where money to finance businesses generally comes from, how to prepare a business plan for a retailing, service, or light manufacturing company, how to choose a commercial bank, how to make yourself creditworthy so that you can tap these sources, where the major sources are for borrowing to start a business, where to get money for buying assets and equipment, where to get money for working capital, and where money is available for special situations.

Part III, "How to Manage Your Financial Resources," identifies the balance sheet and income statement items that make up your financial resources and gives you techniques for managing each of them. Part III also looks at the way these individual balance sheet and income statement items interact in the overall operation of your business. It shows you how to use the techniques of ratio analysis and break-even analysis to measure your company's performance and to steer it toward more profitable operations. Finally, it shows you how to use your capital—both long- and short-term—more effectively.

Part IV, "Controlling Your Business," shows you how to protect and conserve your resources. Having brought in and earned the money and having learned to manage it, you can learn to keep it. This part discusses the objectives of controlling cash, accounts receivable, inventory, investments, fixed assets, accounts payable, and payroll. A self-assessment questionnaire is provided for each of these items to help you evaluate how well you are controlling the item. Part IV goes on to indicate, clearly and concisely, how to minimize your risks of loss of resources through fraud or error and highlights a comprehensive control framework for the major financial areas of your business.

Your Business—Its Life Cycle

A small or growing business has been defined as one with sales from $250,000 to $15 million or more, depending on the nature of the business. For example, a wholesale distribution business can often support a substantially higher level of sales with the same staff as a modest-sized manufacturing company.

This book is for the business, whatever its size, that has fewer members on the management team than functions to be performed. This means that some members of management—often you, the owner, founder, or entrepreneur—have to perform more than one function. Human nature being what it is, people naturally gravitate toward what they do well and away from what they do less well or simply do not enjoy. In such businesses, one or more critical business functions will often receive less than the attention they require. You may have too many hats to wear and too few people to wear them.

Small and growing businesses have an almost predictable life cycle, the way people do. They move through stages similar to the various human stages of childhood, adolescence, the career period, the midlife crisis, the fifties plateau, and the mature years. Each period has its attendant triumphs and problems.

Trying to Do Everything Yourself

Let's say that you reach that crisis described at the beginning of this chapter. The business is doing very well, but you're broke.

Now you sit down and start to think. What went wrong? Why didn't you see you were running out of working capital? You are also noticing a major change in everybody's attitude. The bank wants to see more figures on your business, wants you to make business projections. Your "all-for-one-and-one-for-all" buddies don't want to continue working 20-hour days, and they'd like to see some compensation that is commensurate with their efforts. A few of them have turned out to be not that bright, and you aren't sure how to get rid of them before they ruin the business. Others have turned out to be powerhouses. They want to run the business their way, not your way, and you don't quite know how to tell them you are the boss. You suddenly realize that you don't really know how to do everything, and you're going to have to do some delegating. You're going to have to trust others with some pretty important tasks, and yet you've got to keep track of what they're doing while you continue to sell widgets. You don't know quite how to do this. You need help.

There are three ways you can go. You can buy help. You can see what you can do yourself with all you've learned in the past year. Or you can go on the way you're going and hope for the best.

The first way has major possibilities. You can hire qualified professionals to be part of your management team, or you can use outside experts on a part-time basis to supplement your expertise. The second way uses your experience and knowledge in the art of managing, but if you are a great salesperson but know less than you ought to know about the techniques of finance or production, you're in trouble. The third way almost guarantees that you will be out of business and in the bankruptcy court within six months.

You may have survived the first crisis of growth. You were lucky and bought assistance that has helped you meet the growth challenges and weather that crucial passage. Everything seems to be going along fine now. You have moved to a new order of running a business—using the art of managing to plan, organize, administer, and control. For a while, all is well. Then one day someone else with a better product or an improved version of your product comes to market, and you realize that you face a major challenge. You have come to the midlife crisis in the life cycle of your small business.

You realize now that you need either a new or improved product to survive; you need something that can weather the storm. You've got to study the market more carefully, invest in research, and test new products for the future. And you realize also that you must take a careful, more cost-conscious look at your widget if it is to be competitive. Making it has become more costly; the cost of materials has gone up. The scheduling leaves a lot to be desired. The union wants a raise. You've got a lot of people around, and the paperwork and accounting are getting too complicated. The government wants more information from you. The company is paying a lot of taxes, and you need someone to look at your personal tax situation. You need help.

Again, you have three ways to go. You can get professional assistance, you can rethink your problems and make some changes, or you can go on the way you have been and hope for a return to the noncompetitive past—"the good old days." Hoping for the good old days again is dreaming—and dreamers often awake to harsh realities too late. Going it alone, using all you've learned, gives you an even chance. Getting the right kind of help increases the odds in your favor. Even so, as a small business president, you need all the luck you can get because the business at this stage would have trouble surviving even one bad season. The time spans for analyzing costs and prices and for taking corrective action are still too short for comfort.

Again you use sound judgment, and you've gotten the right kind of help. You've worked out a new product. You've retained an expert to tell you how other small successful companies have organized themselves. A specialist in marketing has done an analysis and given you a realistic picture of which way and how far to go with your present product. A supplier's engineer has helped you work to improve production efficiency. Your accountant has provided assistance in improving the general accounting systems, developing a cost accounting system, and structuring financial reports. Costs are now under control, and the organization is "lean."

Meanwhile, you have come up with another product worth testing. You retain an advertising and public relations agency to develop marketing programs and to improve the company's image. The old friends who could hardly tie their shoelaces are gone. A few of the brilliant friends who wanted to run the company have also left, but some of them have settled in and accommodated themselves to working in an organization. An expert in compensation plans and personnel has been hired.

The test results of the new product are in, and it looks like a winner. The first year of full production ends, and to your relief and joy, you find that you have had the best year in the history of the company. You have passed the midlife crisis. The five-year projections indicate expansion and profitability. The business has become a truly stable and able company.

There will, of course, be other problems, other dangers, other booms and slumps, but the crucial times of your small business have been weathered and the business is on its way to becoming a medium-sized company with new kinds of challenges and opportunities.

Money and Your Business has been designed to help you through your business life cycle, to help you do better the things you already do well, and to help you know what parts of your business need your attention before they become areas of crisis. You will hear in this book the voices of other businesspeople who have faced the same challenges you face, and you will see how they successfully met them.

I

THE BUSINESS PLAN—A BASIC TOOL

The first part of the book presents and illustrates the development of a formal business plan. A *business plan* is a document that is prepared by the management and that summarizes for readers independent of the business, presumably bankers or investors, the nature of the business, its historical activities, (if any), and its goals and objectives.

A business plan consists of five major components:

1. A historical analysis of the business, showing its financial performance over a period of years.
2. A statement of the purpose or mission of the business, a description of its goals or objectives, which may relate directly to the goals and objectives of the entrepreneur, and the development of a series of action steps, which over a period of years are designed to enable the business to reach its goals or objectives.
3. A narrative description of the business, its market, its competition, its location, its management, and its personnel.

4. An operating plan or budget, which takes the form of a forecast of operating results, financial position, and cash flow of the company for one to three years into the future.
5. An indication of the amount and possible source of financing required by the business.

A business plan is prepared most often at the direct request of a banker or other potential investor in the business. In a start-up situation, a business plan is essential to obtain capital for running the business. Also, a business plan is often required to obtain additional capital for on-going operations even when the investor has the historical results of the company to consider in deciding whether to invest. Therefore, developing a sound business plan is fundamental to getting the money to run the business.

The preparation of a business plan has other benefits that are often overlooked:

- It forces the entrepreneur to think about how the business will develop and grow. This process reveals weaknesses in the logic behind the goals and objectives of the business.
- Preparing a forecast of operating results and financial position, a major component of the business plan, in a format consistent with the financial statements of the company, forces the entrepreneur to take a realistic view of the profit potential of the business.
- Once prepared, that forecast represents an objective against which the entrepreneur can measure the progress of the business toward its goals. Comparison of actual results to the budget can highlight for the entrepreneur significant variances. Either the business is doing better than expected (in which case the expectations may be revised upward), or the actual results are less than expected (in which case corrective action is justified).

With all these good reasons to prepare a business plan, it is perhaps surprising that more companies do not make use of such a plan as an important management tool.

THE PURPOSE OF THIS PART

The purpose of this part is fourfold:

1. To encourage the development and use of business planning in the small to medium-sized business.
2. To discuss and surmount some common obstacles to business planning.

3. To describe the components of a typical business plan.
4. To illustrate those components with a case study.

This part contains nine chapters:

Chapter 1 discusses some of the more commonly encountered obstacles to planning in the small business. Often these obstacles are merely excuses for not doing a professional job of management. In other cases the obstacles are very real. The chapter describes ways to overcome these obstacles and reinforces the value of business planning by highlighting the major reasons for planning.

Chapter 2 provides a detailed definition of the business planning process. Its purpose is to translate the technical jargon used to describe business planning into terms that make sense and that are easy to relate to any business. This chapter presents an outline or table of contents of a formal business plan.

Chapter 3 introduces a case study that is used throughout the part to illustrate the business planning process. This case study, a retail fuel oil distributorship, is used because it is a relatively easy business to understand, and yet it is in a market that is subject to severe shock due to changes in the worldwide oil situation. The environment is one in which entrepreneurs must be especially sure to plan in order to survive. Your business may be altogether different, but the principles of business planning illustrated in this case study are the same regardless of the nature of your business. This chapter provides a detailed historical analysis of the Lucky Fuel Oil Company and presents a series of financial statements and schedules that are intended to establish the basis for developing the operating plans for the company. They illustrate the type of analysis that may be productive for your business.

Chapter 4 begins the business planning process for Lucky Fuel Oil by defining the statement of purpose, the goals, and objectives of the business, along with the action steps that the entrepreneur (Peter O'Henry) intends to take to build the business and to achieve his *personal* goals.

Chapter 5 provides additional insights into the planning process by presenting a series of detailed questions. These should be answered in order to adequately describe to someone independent of the business the nature of its market, competition, location, management, personnel, and the use of any additional outside funding required.

Chapter 6 describes and illustrates the process of defining and documenting a series of detailed assumptions about the financial results anticipated for the business within the next year. The culmination of this process is the preparation of a month-by-month forecast of operating results and the financial position of the company. The process is illustrated by means of the case study.

Chapter 7 defines the difference between a forecast of financial results and a cash flow forecast, and it illustrates the preparation of a cash flow forecast using the Lucky Fuel Oil Company as an example.

Chapter 8 illustrates the use of the financial forecast to perform an analysis of how "sensitive" the business is in terms of its profitability and cash flow to changes in the underlying assumptions used to prepare the original forecast. This chapter also discusses the use of the forecast to test alternative strategies for the growth of the business or to plan a course of action to reduce costs if the anticipated levels of sales do not materialize.

Chapter 9 provides a summary and conclusion to the part and emphasizes the reasons to plan that are offered by recognized experts in the management of small businesses.

In sum, this first part of the book is a comprehensive treatment of business planning presented in an easy-to-understand form that is illustrated in enough detail to provide a model for the development of a business plan for any business.

1

Obstacles to Planning in a Small Business

When confronted with the concept of business planning, very few entrepreneurs reject it out of hand. Yet, many small businesses have no operating budgets, no formal tactical plans, no formal statements of business purpose. In short, they have no plans and no planning process.

Why not?

OVERCOMING THE EXCUSES FOR NOT PLANNING

The explanations (or perhaps the excuses) for not planning are many and varied. The Conference Board, an organization that studies groups of businesses, once asked more than 200 businesses (large and small) to describe the obstacles to successful planning. The results are provided in Figure 1.1. Other experience has shown that the obstacles listed in that figure can be combined into five categories:

FIGURE 1.1
Obstacles to Successful Planning (Percentage of Respondents)

Total Response by Obstacle	*Obstacles*	*By Size of Business*			*By Type of Bus.*	
		Small	*Medium*	*Large*	*Mfg.*	*Non-mfg.*
%		%	%	%	%	%
58	Insufficient time to plan	68	54	53	63	49
54	Economic uncertainties	57	60	46	60	43
42	Political uncertainties	32	49	45	43	41
40	Industry uncertainties	43	49	31	45	31
39	Problems in reconciling short- and long-term goals	41	41	35	44	28
29	Difficulty in setting objectives	16	35	35	27	34
26	Difficulty in measuring effectiveness	16	29	32	28	23
25	Poor attitudes of planners	21	21	33	24	27
25	Reluctance to forego immediate benefits	29	26	20	28	19
24	Poor input information	21	28	24	27	20
23	Excessive expectations	14	28	27	24	22
23	Difficulties with planning procedures	21	28	21	22	26
22	Communication, organization, and personnel problems	22	15	27	16	31
18	Improper definition of corporate planning	16	16	22	16	23
18	Insufficient commitment by top management	8	24	21	17	19
100	Percentage response	100	100	100	100	100
(209)		*(63)*	*(68)*	*(78)*	*(135)*	*(74)*

Reprinted with permission, from G. T. Caldwell, *Corporate Planning in Canada: An Overview*, Canadian Study No. 38 (Ottawa: The Conference Board in Canada, 1975), p. 22.

1. *Time*: "There isn't enough time to plan."
2. *Past Success*: "I have been successful in the past without planning; I don't see why I should start now."
3. *Uncertain Future*: "The future is too uncertain. Things are changing too fast to be able to develop an accurate plan."
4. *Apprehension*: "I don't want others to know what my plans are." (Translation: "I don't want to see what the plans tell me.")
5. *Know-How*: "I simply don't know how."

Although these obstacles are not without substance, they can be overcome. Let's look at each of them.

Time

There is no question that developing a good plan for your business takes time. All the people who will be called upon to accomplish the plan—that is, the key members of the management team—must participate in its development. But the time expended need not be great. In general, putting together a workable plan should not take more than 80 hours. So, to figure the total time, multiply 80 hours times the number of people you wish to have involved to arrive at a rough estimate of the total time it will require. Remember, not all the team members need to participate in the planning process all the time. Specific parts of the plan can be delegated and then considered by the group when complete. So the actual time spent may be less than the aggregate of the estimates for the individuals involved. Once an initial plan has been prepared, maintaining and revising the plan should consume only a few hours a month.

After reaching a decision to plan, perhaps the most difficult part of the planning itself is taking the first step—which should be to set aside a specific time to plan. Many entrepreneurs who have been successful at planning *have begun by spending a weekend with the management group at a hotel or retreat away from the pressures and interruptions of the day-to-day affairs of the business.* During this weekend, they discuss, define, and agree on the future direction of the business and what each individual's responsibilities are to move the company in that direction.

Whether or not you decide to use a separate facility, you can make certain that the time spent will be productive by preparing *an agenda* for the meetings. Also prepare a series of instructions that clearly tell the participants what you expect them to do. *Design forms* to capture the vital planning information. And, if you can, *prepare a preliminary statement of the goals and objectives of the business,* as you see them, to use as a starting point.

Make certain that the members of the management group come *prepared* to participate. Encourage them to do so and call upon them to participate in or even to lead the discussions in their areas of responsibility.

When it comes to the preparation of financial statement forecasts, consider using one of the many automated systems available through timesharing, a microcomputer (personal computer), or minicomputer to assist in accumulating the numbers and testing the impact of changes in the assumptions.

The only positive response to the obstacle of not having enough time to plan is to make the time.

Past Success

Many entrepreneurs enjoy repeated success without ever formulating a detailed business plan. Yet a startling statistic confronts all entrepreneurs: 50% of all new ventures fail in the first year, 80% in the first four years. To put it into perspective, the odds are 4:1 against being successful in a new business after four years.

A major cause of business failure is the lack of management skill. But, if you can put together and use a business plan, you probably have the management skill to be successful. (Potential investors will be looking for this evidence of management skill.) Business planning can help you change the odds of success in your favor.

Another reason to consider business planning, even if you have been successful in the past without it, is that *your business may be facing a changing environment.* What worked in the past might not always work in the future. For example, there are only a few areas of the country where heating oil is not a critical factor in the household budget. The retail suppliers of home heating oil have faced a rapidly changing environment over the past several years:

- Let's say that OPEC escalates crude oil prices.
- Refiners have traditionally passed these price increases on to the retail fuel oil dealers and through them to the consumer.
- In addition, suppliers have tightened their credit terms by insisting on payment within ten days of delivery in some cases. Retail dealers are unable to pass these terms through to the consumer.
- With price increases, consumers generally take measures to conserve fuel or to convert to another fuel. Both measures serve to reduce volume, forcing a struggle among dealers to retain volume.
- Finally, a rapid escalation in prices tends to increase dealers' needs for lines of credit to finance receivables from their customers. For example, if dealers had to borrow $250,000 three years ago to finance receivables and inventory, they might require $750,000 for the same volume of business. With the increased cost of money, this increased borrowing has had a serious impact on profits.

Dealers who in the past managed on intuition alone are finding it difficult to survive. Those with adequate plans can justify to their bankers the need for additional capital. And they can explore the possible effects of their decisions by using their plans rather than having to implement their decisions and then waiting to see if they are successful.

Past success might not continue in the future for another reason: the growth of business. Figure 1.2 shows the typical growth pattern of a small business. The curve in the chart represents the *rate of growth.*

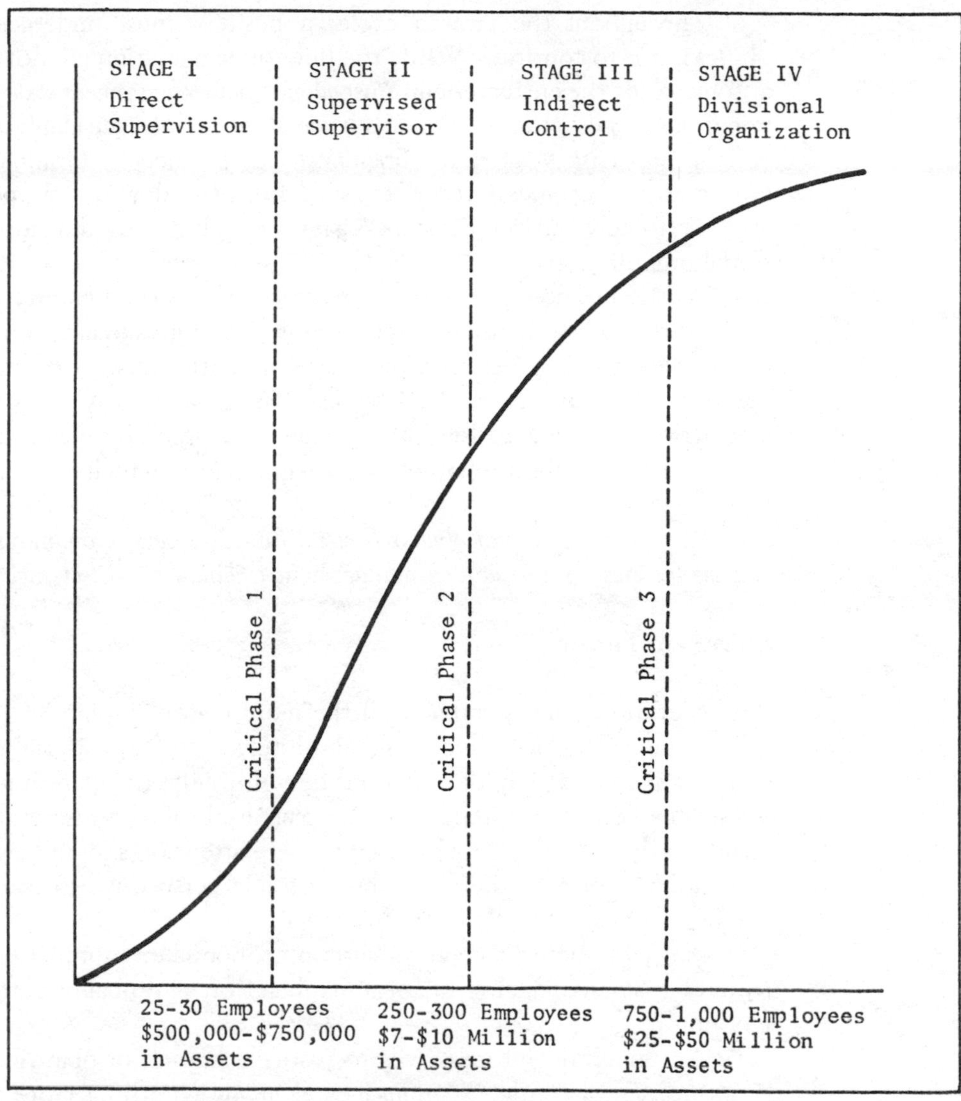

FIGURE 1.2
Stages of Organizational Growth and Their Critical Phases

In the initial stage, the rate of growth is low. It takes time for the business to catch on, to become known. Once it does catch on—if it is successful—it grows at a fairly rapid rate. Ultimately, it becomes difficult to sustain the rapid rate of growth. For example, a $5 million business can double in size more easily than a $50 million business. So the growth rate levels off.

Throughout the growth cycle, a business must undergo critical phases if it is to continue. While the lines of demarcation are not precise, at some point the entrepreneur must *adopt a new management style, moving from a mode of direct supervision to a mode of supervising individuals who will, in turn, supervise those who work directly at production.* Gradually, the entrepreneur becomes further removed from the day-to-day operations and has to rely on indirect supervision and ultimately develop a divisional organization.

As the business grows, *the entrepreneur must evolve into an administrator* or relinquish the management reins to a professional administrator in order to pursue other entrepreneurial activities inside or outside the company. In either case, the business owner has to rely less on direct interaction and more *on using information to manage.* This means developing better financial information, an integral part of which is the business plan.

Past success may not always portend future success. Conditions change and the business grows, and so management techniques must change.

Uncertain Future

An uncertain future is actually all the more reason to plan.

A plan does not have to be absolutely accurate, especially if it is your first plan or a plan for a new business. Initially, the planning process is as valuable to the company as the plan itself. Comparisons of actual results to the plan not only highlight where attention should be given to changing the plan in the future but also add perspective to the process itself.

Many businesses face an uncertain economic environment, and all things considered, facing uncertainty head on is probably better than ignoring it.

An uncertain future serves to justify a branch of planning called "contingency planning." *Contingency planning* is nothing more than an organized, prearranged method of changing the direction of the business or retrenching in the face of less-than-hoped-for results. As an example, if you project sales of $10 million but during the year sales look as though they will reach only $6 million, you should have *an organized plan* for reducing your staff, your labor force, inventories, receivables, and so on to bring costs into line with expected sales.

A business plan provides a mechanism for interpreting uncertainty.

Apprehension

Apprehension about planning is often expressed as a reluctance to let others (employees) know very much about the business. Yet it can be a way of expressing a more deep-seated apprehension about what the plan will reveal. Remember that the employees of a business often have as much at stake (a source of income, a vested pension, favorable working conditions) as the entrepreneur and the other investors. In addition, having a fully disclosed plan ensures that your associates and your employees are all heading in the right direction.

Know-How

Since the lack of know-how is perhaps the most substantive obstacle to planning, *it is the purpose of the remainder of this part to help you over this hurdle.*

REASONS TO PLAN

This chapter has explored some of the frequently mentioned obstacles to planning:

- Not enough time.
- Past success without planning.
- An uncertain future.
- Apprehension about what the plan will reveal.
- A lack of planning know-how.

Some of these obstacles are more perceived than real, and others have some substance. If you are serious about business planning, this part of the book can help you over the last hurdle (know-how) by providing an outline of a business plan and comprehensive illustration of its development.

In the same survey that revealed these obstacles, the Conference Board explored the perceived benefits of planning. The responses are found in Figure 1.3. Some further reasons to plan include:

- It is difficult to control the growth of your business without a plan.
- It is a means of anticipating what is ahead in order to have enough time to do something about it.
- It is an excellent tool to establish *preventive* and *detective* controls over a business.
- Your banker may very likely insist upon it.

FIGURE 1.3
Perceived Benefits of Corporate Planning (Percentage of Respondents)

Total Response by Benefit	*Perceived Benefits*	*By Size of Business*			*By Type of Bus.*	
		Small	*Medium*	*Large*	*Mfg.*	*Non-mfg.*
%		%	%	%	%	%
54	Provides organized approach to management	60	46	56	56	51
34	Helps set targets and objectives	38	35	28	39	24
24	Reveals areas of opportunity and uncertainty	24	21	28	29	16
17	Helps in the process of resource allocation	19	19	14	18	16
17	Forces greater management discipline	13	25	13	22	8
16	Useful guide to corporate operations	13	19	17	19	12
13	Aids in the evaluation of progress and performance	16	10	13	14	11
12	Forces future thinking	13	12	10	10	15
11	Encourages positive action rather than reaction	3	13	14	10	11
9	Helps improve communications	8	12	8	10	7
100 *(209)*	Percentage response	100 *(63)*	100 *(68)*	100 *(78)*	100 *(135)*	100 *(74)*

Reprinted with permission, from G. T. Caldwell, *Corporate Planning in Canada: An Overview*, Canadian Study No. 38 (Ottawa: The Conference Board in Canada, 1975), p. 20.

2
Definition of Business Planning

Let's work out some definitions that will be used consistently throughout the remainder of the book.

In its most basic terms, business planning involves developing and documenting answers to the following five questions:

1. Where is your business now?
2. Where do you want your business to go?
3. How are you going to get there?
4. What is that going to cost?
5. Where is the money going to come from?

These questions are cumbersome to refer to in their entirety. So, over time, a shorthand way to refer to each question or component of business planning has evolved. These shorter terms are discussed in the following several paragraphs.

WHAT DOES BUSINESS PLANNING INVOLVE?

1. *Where is the business now?* This question really has no constructive answer in a start-up situation. For a going concern, however, the question can be answered in some detail using historical analyses of markets, competition, personnel, and financial results. A comprehensive historical analysis of the financial results of a small business is presented in Chapter 3. This question will be referred to as *historical analysis* throughout the book.

2. *Where do you want your business to go?* Developing an answer to this question is referred to as *strategic planning.* Although this term smacks of the theoretical or academic, consider that "strategy" simply means an overall set of goals or objectives. A strategy is also a mission or a statement of purpose. Therefore, it is important to have a clearly defined strategy, goal, or mission so that you can make sure that the activities of your business are productive—that is, designed to move the business in the direction you wish it to go.

In many small businesses, it is equally important to investigate your motives for being in business. The business is really a means to an end for you. For example, the following could be your strategic objectives:

- To run a ($5-, $10-, $25- . . . , $50-million) business.
- To build a business and sell it in order to become financially independent.
- To build a business to create an annuity for your family.
- To build a business that will grow at (10%, 20%, . . . 200%) per year.

The entrepreneur is motivated by a desire to run the show, to make the decisions, or to see an idea through to its successful implementation. It is important for you to recognize your motivation for getting into business because, as the business grows, the nature of your function may change in a way that is inconsistent with your personal objectives.

Strategic objectives are most often stated in terms of the business. For example, according to Lucien Rhodes of *Inc.* magazine, "one small business in the appliance rental field has as a statement of purpose: 'to serve every consumer television and appliance rental market in the United States that equitably benefits our customers, employees, and stockholders.' "* This is a fairly elaborate statement and illustrates why you should consider the goals or objectives of your business. *The statement in the illustration provides a focal point for all subsequent decisions and leads*

*Lucien Rhodes, "He Learned You Can't Do It Alone," *Inc.*, Vol. 2, No. 3, March 1980, p. 44.

naturally to the development of action steps—that is, the ways in which that entrepreneur's goals will be accomplished.

Look at the statement carefully; pick it apart:

1. It clearly defines the nature of the business as TV and appliance *rentals,* not sales.
2. It identifies the market as the United States. This is perhaps optimistic but may not be in light of the other qualifying aspects of the statement. For example, it does not mean that every part of the United States is a marketplace for the business; it says that the business is concerned with *rental* markets only.
3. The statement is further qualified by the condition that entry into a new market (and, presumably, remaining in an old market) must provide equal benefit to *customers, employees,* and *investors*. Therefore, underlying any decision to enter a new market, to leave an old market, or even to stay with an existing market will be made only in light of the impact on the customers, employees, and investors.

Equitable treatment of customers might mean comparable pricing policies or only opening up a new market when the company can provide adequate service.

Equitable treatment of employees might mean not moving so quickly into new markets as to require frequent moves by the sales force. It could mean analyzing the market so that the company avoids making a move into markets that, if unsuccessful, would jeopardize the jobs of the employees hired to serve the market.

Equitable treatment of investors might mean analyzing each new market or product to assure that it will contribute to rather than detract from the earnings of the business and, thereby, the investors' financial interests.

Documenting the objectives of the business, its statement of purpose, is not very time-consuming, but it *provides a valuable focus for further decisions.* It is important that the strategic objectives of the company be defined in writing and accepted by the management group so that everyone is working toward the same goal.

3. *How are you going to get there?* If the answers to question two can be referred to as the strategic objectives of the business, then the answers to this question may be referred to as "tactics," a process that is referred to in this book as *tactical planning*. In military terms, if the strategic objective is to take the hill, then the tactics might include an air strike, a frontal assault, and a pincer movement from the flanks. In business terms, tactical planning, or tactics, are the action steps that will be taken to reach the strategic goals or objectives of the company.

Some sample tactical objectives in the example of the TV and appliance rental firm might be to:

- Hire five more salespeople.
- Open three new offices or retail locations.
- Acquire a new manufacturing facility.
- Do more advertising (raise the advertising budget by 25%).
- Develop three new products.
- Acquire two companies in the (same, related, unrelated) businesses.
- Automate the production of goods and information.
- Establish and monitor sales or production quotas.
- Reduce inventories or costs by 10%.

Most entrepreneurs do strategic and tactical planning, although it may often be informal and known only to themselves. This book makes a major recommendation to you: Make your tactical planning process formal. Put the strategic and tactical plans of your company in writing, and get everyone to agree to them.

Quantify your tactical objectives wherever possible. As in the preceding example, specify the number of salespeople as well as the costs associated with hiring and supporting them. Document your expectations for their contribution in terms of sales and profits, and weigh them against the cost. Evaluate any advertising dollars to be spent with regard to the expected increase in sales, and quantify and document the cost/benefit trade-offs of automation.

Once you have your tactical plans prepared and implemented, you can measure the results. Some companies compare their budgets to actual financial results, but few assess the actual results of tactical decisions although the process is exactly the same and as, if not more, important. Strategic and tactical objectives for Lucky Fuel Oil are developed and illustrated in Chapters 4 and 5.

4. *What is accomplishing the strategic and tactical plans going to cost?* After you have defined and documented your company's strategic and tactical plans, translate them into dollars and cents for the next year or two of operations. This process, which is the subject of the bulk of this part of the book—Chapters 6, 7, and 8—is referred to as *operational planning* or *budgeting*. Budgets are familiar to most entrepreneurs; they are often the only formal, documented plan that a company will have.

In the business planning process, operational plans or budgets are simply the expression of the tactical objectives in financial terms. For example, if your business has four products and operates in ten areas of the country, you can estimate the sales of each product in each market, multiply each such sale by an estimated selling price, and add the totals to arrive at an estimated sales figure for the company. This process can be used for each element of cost as well. For example, how many employees will it take to make and sell the products, how much material, how much overhead, and what will these cost? These assumptions can be varied to include as much or as little detail as desired. When all revenue and cost items are combined, you can arrive at an estimated profit for the year.

You can extend the process of developing detailed assumptions and applying them to your business to include estimates of the assets and liabilities of the business. You can use still other assumptions to estimate how cash will flow into and out of the business. All these concepts are developed in detail in the chapters that follow.

The outcome of this process should be a series of financial statement forecasts. These may simply be the historical results of the company extrapolated into the future, or they may be a forecast of future results based on a detailed set of assumptions that may or may not relate directly to the company's historical results. In either case, these financial statement forecasts should consist of:

1. Income statements.
2. Balance sheets.
3. Cash flow forecast.

All three parts of the financial statement forecast should give information for one year by the month and for two years by the quarter.

5. *Where is the money going to come from?* After you have prepared your operating plans or budgets, including a forecast of cash flow from the business, the result may show a need for additional cash, either in total or at one or more intervals throughout the years involved in the forecast. A *financing plan* is a set of assumptions regarding the sources of those funds. Funds may be obtained by borrowing from private or public investors, or they may be generated by the business itself.

Once an initial financial statement forecast and cash flow forecast are prepared and indicate a need for funds, you can make assumptions about the best source of those funds and the cost of those funds to the business. Enter these assumptions into the original forecasts, and prepare new forecasts.

OUTLINE OF A BUSINESS PLAN

Business planning has been defined to include the consideration of the *strategic* and *tactical* plans of the business, the preparation of *operating plans* or *budgets,* taking the form of financial statement forecasts, and the development of a *financing plan*. These components of a business plan are best combined into a formal document, the outline of which is given in Figure 2.1. The remaining chapters of Part I illustrate the preparation of the components of the Outline of a Business Plan.

FIGURE 2.1
Outline of a Business Plan

Cover Sheet

1. Name of the business
2. Names of the principals
3. Address of the business
4. The phone number of the business

Table of Contents
Historical Analysis—for Established Businesses Only (See Chapter 3)

1. Historical Financial Statements:
   (a) Income Statements—for the past two to three years
   —by division, department, or profit center, if relevant
   —by product
   (b) Balance Sheets—for the past two to three years
2. Tax Returns—for the past two to three years
3. Ratio Analysis (See Chapters 3 and 24)
   Liquidity ratios
   Leverage ratios
   Turnover ratios
   Profitability ratios
   Trading ratios
4. Break-even Analysis (See Chapters 3 and 25)
   Margin Analysis (See Chapter 3)

Strategic and Tactical Plans (See Chapter 4)

1. Formal Statement of Business Purpose
2. Strategic Objectives of the Business
3. Tactical Objectives

The Narrative Support (See Chapter 5)

This provides detailed information about the business, including:

The Description
The Market(s)
The Competition
The Location(s)
The Management
The Personnel
The Application of Any Expected Funding

FIGURE 2.1 (Cont.)
Outline of a Business Plan

Operational Plans (See Chapters 6 and 7)

1. Detailed Assumptions
2. Income Statement Forecast
3. Balance Sheet Forecast
4. Cash Flow Forecast
5. Financing Plan

Sensitivity Analysis (See Chapter 8)

This demonstrates the impact on the financial forecasts and cash flow as a result of changes in the underlying assumptions.

Supporting Documents

Management's personal resumes
Personal financial statements and
financial commitments of the owners and principals
Credit reports
Leases
Contracts
Market analyses
Letters of reference

CONCLUSION

Business planning involves finding answers to the following questions:

- Where is your business now?
- Where do you want it to go?
- How are you going to get there?
- What is it going to cost?
- Where is the money going to come from?

Business planning encompasses strategic, tactical, and operational planning or budgeting and often includes the preparation of a financing plan. Strategic planning helps everyone in the management group to focus on the goals and objectives of the business. Tactical planning lays out the specific steps that must be taken in order to reach the strategic goals and objectives. Operational planning is the translation of the tactical plans into financial terms. The *most realistic* operational plan should be adopted as a budget, which can be used to monitor the progress of the company throughout the year and to highlight areas for management scrutiny. (Note: The use of a budget as a major *control feature* in a small business is discussed in Chapter 1 of Part IV.) The financing plan is the means of considering the sources and respective costs of funds required to run the business.

The business planning process, which is described and illustrated in detail in the remaining chapters, is similar in concept to the thought process any entrepreneur would go through in developing a plan to start or build a business. The real difference is in the level of documentation and, possibly, the comprehensiveness of the resulting plan. Thus, business planning forces an objective, critical, and, it is hoped, unemotional look at your business in its entirety. It can become an operating tool. And it can provide a comprehensive and consistent means for communicating your ideas to others, most notably to bankers or other investors.

3

Historical Analysis: A Case Study in Planning

We have discussed some obstacles to planning in the small business environment and have provided a definition of the business planning process.

This chapter introduces a case study. It illustrates how an actual company used a series of historical analyses to determine where the business stood and to set the stage for how it would plan to face an uncertain operating environment. As described in Chapter 2 and indicated in Figure 2.1, this historical analysis of a company is an integral part of the business plan.

The actual company selected for this case study is a fuel oil dealer located in Massachusetts. The name of the business has been changed for use as an example to Lucky Fuel Oil, and the owner's name has been changed to Peter O'Henry.

Although the fuel oil business may be different from your industry, the techniques used by O'Henry to plan for his company's future that are illustrated in this chapter and the chapters that follow provide you with a practical example of the use of basic business planning tools. The emphasis throughout the case example is to (1) understand the historical framework in which a company operates and (2) plan for the most likely future events.

CURRENT OPERATING ENVIRONMENT

At first glance, the fuel oil business in recent years may appear to be a good industry to call your own. Haven't oil prices been increasing dramatically? Haven't major oil companies been reporting huge profits? Doesn't the fuel oil dealer merely pass through to the consumer any cost increases incurred? Consider, however, the following list of current or potential problems facing this very small portion of the oil industry:

1. *Size*. Most fuel oil dealers are small, independent businesses with a handful of delivery trucks. Individually, they have almost no influence with the major oil suppliers.
2. *Conservation*. With the escalation of crude oil prices by OPEC several years ago, the government and consumers have campaigned vigorously to influence consumers to use less fuel oil.
3. *Credit terms*. Major suppliers have tightened credit terms to payment within ten days of delivery, whereas retail fuel oil dealers have been unable to pass these terms through to the consumer.
4. *Conversion from oil*. Natural gas has emerged as a fierce competitor of fuel oil.
5. *Tenuous supply*. The availability of fuel oil is subject to political (Iran) and economic events (boycotts) totally beyond the influence of a small dealer.
6. *Volatile prices*. Dramatic swings in supply price, mostly upward, can be expected.
7. *Highly seasonal business*. A fuel oil dealer may expect to sell two-thirds of his annual gallonage in the winter months between November and March.
8. *Weather*. An unseasonably warm winter is bad news for a fuel oil dealer.
9. *Need for short-term credit*. With the foregoing factors, the need to finance receivables from customers has doubled or tripled in recent years.
10. *Consumer price resistance*. Consumers do not have unlimited resources. If a dealer tries to pass on all price increases, consumers may switch dealers or may simply be unable to pay their heating oil bills on a current basis.

11. *Competition*. Conservation and conversion to alternate sources of energy have reduced volume, forcing a struggle for survival among remaining dealers to retain their market share.

Faced with these problems, the fuel oil dealer is not in an enviable position.

HISTORICAL ANALYSIS (WHERE IS THE BUSINESS NOW?)

The first step O'Henry took to prepare a business plan was to answer the question of where the business is now by carefully analyzing his past performance. He assembled the following package of financial results that covered the past three years:

	Figure Number
Volume summary—gallons	3.1
Summary income statement	3.2
Detailed income statement—in dollars	3.3
Detailed income statement—as a percentage of sales	3.4
Operations by profit center:	
East	3.5
West	3.6
Burner Service	3.7
LPG (liquid propane gas)	3.8
Balance sheet—in dollars	3.9
Balance sheet—as a percentage of sales	3.10

Each of the figures is presented in this section, with sample observations that O'Henry made at the time he analyzed the schedules.

Note: The schedules that are presented in this chapter are, for the most part, income statements (statements of operations) and balance sheets (statements of financial position). An income statement shows the cumulative revenues and expenses for a business over a period. In most of the examples, the period is a year. A balance sheet is a "snapshot" of the financial position of the business at a point in time. In the case of the figures in the chapter, that point is the last day of the fiscal years of the business in the case study—March 31.

In some cases, the schedules present an income statement for a profit center. A profit center is simply a subset of the business. In the Lucky Fuel Oil Company, the major profit centers are two divisions, an East Oil Division and a West Oil Division. There are also profit center

FIGURE 3.1
Lucky Fuel Oil Company
Three-Year Volume Summary (in Gallons)

	19X1	*19X0*	*19X9*
No. 2, Kerosene, and Diesel	4,642,118	4,867,785	3,421,498
No. 4, 5, and 6 Heavy Oil	3,744,237	3,871,603	1,210,226
LPG	381,894	389,955	382,523
Gasoline	281,346	194,410	—
Total Gallonage	9,049,595	9,323,753	5,014,247
Annual Volume Increase (Decrease)	(274,158)	4,309,506	1,962,589
Percentage Increase (Decrease)	(6.3%)	85.9%	64.3%
Net Profit Before Tax	$ 132,250	$ 152,371	$ 64,766

income statements for certain lines of business—for example, Burner Service and Liquid Propane Gas (LPG). A profit center differs from a cost center by having revenues, as well as expenses, directly associated with it. A cost center is a subdivision of a company that has only costs (expenses) that can be directly associated with or allocated to it.

The schedules have certain other characteristics. One is the combination of statistics with financial information in the same schedule. Some schedules show gallons sold as well as revenues and expenses. These statistics have been developed in order to present certain line items of the financial statement in terms of cents per gallon. Other schedules show the line items as a percentage rather than a dollar amount. Finally, some schedules have more detail as to expense line items than do others.

You can use all these techniques to make the historical information you develop for your business more meaningful. Remember that one purpose of analyzing historical performance is to provide a framework for planning.

When you read this business plan, it is as though you were actually looking over the shoulder of Peter O'Henry as he prepares it.

Figure 3.1 shows that O'Henry's business consists of several fuel-related products. Total gallonage increased by nearly 86% during 19X0, due to acquisitions. Due to conservation and conversion, his gallonage declined slightly in 19X0. Gasoline was the only product that displayed an increase in volume during 19X1. Gasoline was added as a countercyclical product line, having its sales peak during the summer rather than the winter months.

FIGURE 3.2
Lucky Fuel Oil Company
Summary Income Statement

	12 Months Ending March 31		
	19X1	*19X0*	*19X9*
Sales (Net)	$6,964,581	$4,323,700	$2,426,378
Cost of Sales	5,999,303	3,511,158	1,872,494
Gross Profit Margin	965,278	812,542	554,884
Operating Expenses			
Depreciation	84,200	45,600	43,961
Interest	62,345	45,273	24,635
Other	693,898	586,960	436,868
Operating Profit/Loss	124,835	134,709	48,420
Other Income (Expense)			
Interest	3,198	12,063	10,004
Miscellaneous	4,217	5,599	6,342
Income Before Taxes	132,250	152,371	64,766
Income Taxes	39,675	35,040	8,000
Net Income	$ 92,575	$ 117,331	$ 56,766

Figure 3.2 indicates that although gallonage decreased in 19X1, net sales increased compared to 19X0. Higher prices accounted for the growth in net sales. *Gross profit margin* advanced strongly over the three years, and *operating profit* dropped in 19X1. *Operating expenses* increased significantly in that year and should be monitored more closely in the future. Interest expense increased by approximately 50% in 19X0. Overall, the approximately 19% increase in gross profit (19X0–19X1) was reduced to a 21% decrease in net income by higher operating expenses and taxes and by the fact that interest income dropped dramatically from $12,000 to $3,000 due to lower levels of cash for short-term investments.

The detailed income statement in Figure 3.3 reveals where some of the increased operating expenses were incurred. In addition to a large increase in interest expense, depreciation nearly doubled due to a recent acquisition, and professional fees almost tripled in 19X1 compared to 19X0. On the positive side, supplies and rent, both comparatively small amounts, actually declined in 19X1.

Figure 3.4 restates the detailed income statement as a *percentage of sales*. This commonly used analytical technique can offer new insight into a financial statement. For example, O'Henry may have been sur-

FIGURE 3.3
Lucky Fuel Oil Company
Detailed Income Statement (In Dollars)

	12 Months Ending March 31		
	19X1	*19X0*	*19X9*
Sales (Net)	$6,964,581	$4,323,700	$2,426,378
Cost of Sales	5,999,303	3,511,158	1,872,494
Gross Profit Margin	965,278	812,542	553,884
Operating Expenses			
Officer salaries	36,800	34,120	30,320
Salaries and wages	297,422	275,369	207,153
Contract labor	37,864	24,861	9,863
Health insurance	13,712	11,962	9,758
Auto and truck expense	88,491	68,044	52,621
Depreciation	84,200	45,600	43,961
Insurance (general)	28,711	28,144	17,883
Bad debts	22,413	19,897	8,528
Supplies	19,912	22,944	15,037
Professional fees	29,869	10,073	19,093
Rent	3,294	3,514	1,252
Interest	62,345	45,273	24,635
Other	115,410	88,032	65,360
Total	840,443	677,833	505,464
Operating Profit/(Loss)	$ 124,835	$ 134,709	$ 48,420

prised to see that his healthy gross profit *dollars* actually represented a decline from 22.8% to 13.9% of sales over the three-year period. Clearly, he was not as successful in passing supply price increases on to the consumer as he thought.

As a percentage of sales, these inflated operating expenses did not look so bad. Only depreciation and professional fees actually increased as a percentage of sales from 19X0 to 19X1. O'Henry realized the danger in considering only dollars of income and expense or only the percentage income statements, and reviewed both the actual dollars and percentage figures together. In this way he could quickly focus on those items that were showing rapid dollar changes or that were disproportionate to the level of sales. (Later in this chapter the point is made that some expenses are relatively fixed—that is, they don't vary directly with changes in sales. Looking at dollars and percentages helps to highlight which items are fixed and to place their variation into perspective.)

FIGURE 3.4
Lucky Fuel Oil Company
Detailed Income Statement
(As a Percentage of Sales)

	12 Months Ending March 31		
	19X1	*19X0*	*19X9*
Sales (Net)	100.0%	100.0%	100.0%
Cost of Sales	86.1	81.2	77.2
Gross Profit Margin	13.9	18.8	22.8
Operating Expenses			
Officer salaries	0.5	0.8	1.2
Salaries and wages	4.3	6.4	8.5
Contract labor	0.5	0.6	0.4
Health insurance	0.2	0.3	0.4
Auto and truck expense	1.3	1.6	2.2
Depreciation	1.2	1.1	1.8
Insurance (general)	0.4	0.7	0.7
Bad debt expense	0.3	0.4	0.4
Supplies	0.3	0.5	0.6
Professional fees	0.4	0.2	0.8
Rent	0.1	0.1	0.1
Interest expense	0.9	1.0	1.0
Other	1.7	2.0	2.7
Total	12.1	15.7	20.8
Operating Profit/(Loss)	1.8%	3.1%	2.0%

To analyze results more effectively, O'Henry had divided his company into four profit centers several years ago. By analyzing the results of operations for each profit center, he hoped to be able to commit resources in the future to those segments of his business that offered the highest return. Figures 3.5, 3.6, 3.7, and 3.8 are analyses of the four profit centers.

O'Henry was aware that more than 90% of his sales dollars came from the East and West Oil Divisions (Figures 3.5 and 3.6). The West Oil Division had been acquired at the end of fiscal 19X9 and provided the business with a substantial volume of heavy oil and some additional sales of No. 2 home heating oil, diesel fuel, and kerosene.

The conversion to a cents-per-gallon basis (just another way of representing the operating results of the company) showed that the East Oil Division (Figure 3.5) operating profit per gallon, before a corporate

FIGURE 3.5
Lucky Fuel Oil Company
Analysis of Operations by Profit Center
East Oil Division: No. 2, Diesel, Kerosene, and Gasoline

	12 Months Ending March 31		
	19X1	*19X0*	*19X9*
Sales (Net)	$2,933,374	$1,787,093	$1,217,303
Cost of Sales	2,526,056	1,471,631	960,517
Gross Profit Margin	407,318	315,462	256,786
Oil Delivery Expenses	198,563	129,964	94,002
Oil Operating Income	$ 208,755	$ 185,498	$ 162,784
Conversion to Cents per Gallon Basis:			
Gallons	3,422,841	3,457,701	2,514,946
Sales	0.857	0.517	0.484
Cost of Sales	0.738	0.426	0.382
Gross Profit Margin	0.119	0.91	0.102
Oil Delivery Expenses:			
Salaries	0.18	0.14	0.16
Auto and truck	0.06	0.04	0.05
Depreciation	0.07	0.05	0.06
Gasoline & diesel fuel	0.17	0.07	0.04
Other	0.10	0.07	0.06
Total	.058	0.37	0.37
Oil Operating Profit per Gallon Before Corporate Overhead Charge	.061	0.54	0.65

overhead charge, had decreased from 6.5 to 6.1 cents per gallon between 19X9 and 19X1. The West Oil Division (Figure 3.6) showed slight increases in heavy oil operating profit before a corporate overhead charge and significant increases in light oil profit per gallon although the gross margin on light oil was a bit below that of the East Oil Division (11.9 cents vs. 11.3 cents). This should have an impact on his tactical planning; O'Henry should seek to increase his margins in the West Oil Division.

The Burner Service segment (Figure 3.7), somewhat of a necessary

FIGURE 3.6
Lucky Fuel Oil Company
Analysis of Operations by Profit Center
West Oil Division: No. 2, Heavy Oil, Diesel, and Kerosene

	12 Months Ending March 31			
	19X1		*19X0*	
Sales	$3,431,152		$2,019,688	
Cost of Sales	3,122,348		1,791,648	
Gross Profit Margin	308,804		228,040	
Oil Delivery Expenses	90,810		78,875	
Oil Operating Income	$ 217,994		$ 149,165	
Heavy Oil Volume (Gallons)	3,744,237	Gal.	3,871,603	Gal.
Light Oil Volume (Gallons)	1,500,623	Gal.	1,604,494	Gal.

Conversion to Cents per Gallon Basis.

	19X1		*19X0*	
	Heavy	*Light*	*Heavy*	*Light*
Sales	58.2¢	83.1¢	31.9¢	48.8¢
Cost of Sales	54.6	71.8	28.9	42.0
Gross Profit Margin	3.6	11.3	3.0	6.8
Oil Delivery Expenses	1.7	1.7	1.4	1.4
Oil Operating Profit Before Corporate O/H Charge	1.9¢	9.6¢	1.6¢	5.4¢

evil, continued to lose money, and the LPG Division (Figure 3.8) showed healthy gross profit margins up to 25.3% in 19X1.

The balance sheet for Lucky Fuel Oil (Figure 3.9) shows that accounts receivable have nearly *doubled* in three years, as have current liabilities. The ability to finance these receivables through banks is obviously a critical success factor for the business, and O'Henry should do everything possible to retain that ability.

Long-term debt has not increased dramatically. The financing needs related to seasonal working capital (inventories and receivables) are clearly short-term requirements. Financing for expansion or acquisition of fixed assets would more appropriately be done by long-term debt. (See Part II, "Getting the Money," for a detailed discussion of this concept.)

FIGURE 3.7
Lucky Fuel Oil Company
Analysis of Operations by Profit Center
Burner Service

	12 Months Ending March 31		
	19X1	*19X0*	*19X9*
Sales and Revenues (parts, new system, labor)	$291,862	$275,000	$206,975
Cost of Sales (raw materials only)	145,923	118,149	82,139
Gross Profit Margin	145,939	157,551	124,836
Burner Service Expenses	170,862	170,214	135,431
Operating Income (Loss)	($24,923)	($12,663)	($10,595)
Conversion to Percentage Basis:			
Sales and Revenues	100.0%	100.0%	100.0%
Cost of Sales	50.0	49.9	39.7
Gross Profit Margin	50.0	57.1	60.3
Burner Service Expenses			
Salaries	37.2	39.8	43.1
Salaries—overtime	3.1	4.1	3.6
Auto and truck	3.2	3.3	1.6
Depreciation	3.2	3.3	4.3
Supplies	2.7	2.7	2.8
Gasoline and diesel fuel	1.3	.8	2.8
Other	7.8	7.7	7.2
Total	58.5	61.7	65.4
Service Operating Profit/(Loss) Before Corporate Overtime Charge	(8.5%)	(4.6%)	(5.1%)

FIGURE 3.8
Lucky Fuel Oil Company
Analysis of Operations by Profit Center
LPG Division

	12 Months Ending March 31		
	19X1	*19X0*	*19X9*
Sales	$268,193	$215,281	$198,424
Cost of Sales	171,376	125,262	125,462
Gross Profit Margin	96,817	90,019	72,962
LPG Delivery Expenses	25,983	22,044	26,162
Operating Income	$ 70,834	$ 67,975	$ 46,800
LPG Volume: Gallons	381,894	389,955	382,523
Conversion to Cents/ per/Gallon Basis:			
Sales	70.2¢	55.2¢	51.9¢
Cost of Sales	44.9	32.1	32.8
Gross Profit Margin	25.3¢	23.1¢	19.1¢

FIGURE 3.9
Lucky Fuel Oil Company
Statement of Financial Condition (Balance Sheet)

	March 31		
Assets	*19X1*	*19X0*	*19X9*
Cash	$ 115,411	$ 111,461	$ 101,169
Accounts Receivable, Net	918,803	758,621	528,012
Inventory	125,204	104,443	81,157
Total Current	1,159,418	974,525	710,338
Fixed Assets, Gross	809,468	685,284	550,922
Accumulated Depreciation	(324,479)	(240,479)	(194,879)
Fixed Assets, Net	484,989	440,805	356,043
Cash Value (Life Insurance)	—	—	—
Total Assets	1,644,407	$1,419,330	$1,066,381
Liabilities and Net Worth			
Notes Payable (Bank)	$ 226,000	$ 100,000	$ 135,000
Current Portion (L-T-D)	88,200	92,959	21,000
Accounts Payable (Trade)	456,416	443,531	325,674
Accounts Payable (Other)	8,242	6,477	57,948
Accrued Expenses and Taxes	38,211	36,200	7,798
Total Current Liabilities	817,069	679,167	547,420
Long-Term Debt	398,800	404,200	300,329
Total Liabilities	1,215,869	1,083,367	847,749
Capital Stock	50,620	50,620	50,620
Retained Earnings	377,918	285,343	168,012
Total Net Worth	428,538	335,963	218,632
Total Claims on Assets	$1,644,407	$1,419,330	$1,066,381

FIGURE 3.10
Lucky Fuel Oil Company
Statement of Financial Condition (Balance Sheet)
Accounts as a Percentage of Total Assets

	March 31		
Assets	*19X1*	*19X0*	*19X9*
Cash	7.0%	7.9%	9.5%
Accounts Receivable, Net	55.9	53.4	49.5
Inventory	7.6	7.4	7.6
Total Current	70.5	68.7	66.6
Fixed Assets, Gross	49.2	48.2	51.7
Accumulated Depreciation	(19.7)	(16.9)	(18.3)
Fixed Assets, Net	29.5	31.3	33.4
Cash Value (Life Insurance)	—	—	—
Total Assets	100.0%	100.0%	100.0%

Liabilities and Net Worth			
Notes Payable (Bank)	13.7%	7.0%	12.6%
Current Portion (L-T-D)	5.4	6.5	2.0
Accounts Payable (Trade)	27.8	31.2	30.5
Accounts Payable (Other)	.5	.5	5.5
Accrued Expenses and Taxes	2.3	2.6	.7
Total Current Liabilities	49.7	47.8	51.3
Long-Term Debt	24.3	28.5	28.2
Total Liabilities	74.0	76.3	79.5
Capital Stock	3.0	3.6	4.7
Retained Earnings	23.0	20.1	15.8
Total Net Worth	26.0	23.7	20.5
Total Claims on Assets	100.0%	100.0%	100.0%

Finally, Figure 3.10 expresses balance sheet accounts as a percentage of total assets. This reinforces the fact that receivables are the major asset and that accounts payable and short-term debt are the major liabilities.

SEASONAL FACTORS

The fuel oil business is highly seasonal, as one might expect. O'Henry analyzed his previous years' sales statistics and prepared the following schedule:

Month	Percentage of total gallons consumed this month	
September	3.5%	
October	6.8	
November	10.2	58.6 (November–March)
December	13.6	
January	16.5	
February	15.8	
March	12.7	
April	7.8	
May	5.4	
June	2.8	
July	2.4	
August	2.5	
Total	100.0%	

About 60% of O'Henry's gallonage is sold between December and March. During this period he experiences both his peak financing requirements and peak labor needs. He realized that diversification, where practical, into less seasonal or counter-cyclical products should be considered as an additional tactical objective. LPG and gasoline, for example, are products sold mostly in the summer months.

Mr. O'Henry was aware of the importance of maintaining flexibility in labor hiring to coincide with his peak seasonal needs. One alternative he employed was to hire local individuals who worked at counter-cyclical jobs, such as a lawn care service, or as lifeguards.

Finally, the need to *maintain and coordinate short-term lines of credit during the winter months was critical.* To help Lucky Fuel Oil in this regard, O'Henry believed his business plan would be his best ally.

RATIO ANALYSIS

Another tool that O'Henry used to analyze the historical performance of his company was ratio analysis. By examining the relationships between selected income statement and balance sheet accounts, he hoped to learn more about where potential areas of improvement existed. The five types of ratios he analyzed were:

- Liquidity ratios.
- Leverage ratios.
- Turnover ratios.
- Profitability ratios.
- Trading ratios.

(A detailed discussion of the nature of these ratios and how they are calculated is in Part III, "How to Manage Your Financial Resources.")

Liquidity ratios measure the firm's ability to meet its maturing short-term obligations. According to the balance sheet (Figure 3.9) at March 31, 19X1, Lucky has current liabilities (due within one year) of $817,069. Can these obligations be satisfied?

An asset that is readily convertible into cash is called a *liquid* asset. A complete analysis of Lucky's liquidity position would require the use of a cash budget. By relating the amount of cash and other current assets of the company to its current liabilities, however, liquidity ratio analysis provides a fast and simple gauge of the company's liquidity.

For fuel oil dealers, all current assets including inventory are "liquid." Accordingly, the liquidity analysis may be performed by using two ratios: the current ratio and the quick ratio. The *current ratio* is computed as follows:

$$\text{Current ratio} = \frac{\text{Current assets}}{\text{Current liabilities}}$$

Current assets normally include cash, marketable securities, accounts receivable, and inventory. *Current liabilities* normally include accounts payable, short-term notes payable, current maturities of long-term debt, and accrued expenses.

The current ratio indicates the extent to which the claims of short-term creditors are covered by assets that are expected to be converted to cash in a period roughly corresponding to the maturity of those claims.

The *quick ratio* is a subset of the current ratio and is equal to *cash and accounts receivable* only, divided by current liabilities. It represents the ratio of the assets that can be converted to cash very quickly, divided by current obligations.

Generally, the higher the current and quick ratios, the greater the "cushion" between current obligations and a firm's ability to pay them. However, the composition and quality of current assets is a critical factor in the final interpretation of a company's liquidity. (This is discussed further in Part III, Chapter 24.) Lucky's current and quick ratios are calculated in Figure 3.11. In Lucky's case both ratios are acceptable, but there really isn't a very large "cushion." What is significant is the slight decline in both ratios since 19X0. There is now only $1.42 of current assets for every $1.00 of current liabilities and $1.26 of cash and accounts receivable for every $1.00 of current liabilities.

Leverage ratios measure the relative stake that the owner (entrepreneur) has in the business as compared to the outside creditors. The implications of these ratios are as follows:

1. By raising funds through debt (leverage), the owner gains the benefit of maintaining control of the firm with a *limited personal financial risk.*

	LUCKY FUEL OIL RATIO TRENDS CHART								
	Ratio Date	3/81/87	3/81/88	3/81/89			Ind	Goal	Comments
LIQ	Current	1.30	1.43	1.42				1.5	ACCEPTABLE
	Quick	1.15	1.28	1.26					
LEV	Debt-to-Worth	3.88	3.22	2.84					REASONABLE
	Cash Earnings-to Current Maturity	4.81	1.75	2.00					
TURNOVER	AR Turnover	4.59	5.70	7.57					IMPROVING
	Days Sales O/S	78	63	48					IMPROVING
	Inventory T/O	23.1	33.8	47.9					IMPROVING
	Days Stock	15.6	10.6	7.5					
	Payables T/O	7.1	9.2	14.7					
	Days Payables	50.7	39.1	24.5					
PROFITABILITY	Pretax Return on Assets	6.1%	10.7%	8.0%				12.0%	
	Pretax Return on Net Worth	30%	45%	31%					
	Pretax Profitability	2.7%	3.5%	1.9%				4%	
	Gross Margin	22.8%	18.8%	13.9%					DECLINING, DANGER
	Operating Expenses	20.8%	15.7%	12.1%					
	Interest Expenses	1.0%	1.1%	.89%					
	Depreciation Expense	1.8%	1.1%	1.2%					
TRAD	Sales/Working Capital	14.9%	14.6%	20.4%					
	Sales/Total Assets	2.3	3.0	4.2					IMPROVING

FIGURE 3.11
Lucky Fuel Oil Ratio Trends Chart

2. Outside creditors look to the *equity* or *net worth* (owner-supplied funds and retained profits) to provide a margin of safety for their investment in the company. If the owner has provided only a small portion of the total financing, the risks associated with the business are mainly borne by the creditors.
3. If the company earns more (income) on the money it borrows than it pays to use it (interest), the return to the owner(s) is *magnified* and, accordingly, it makes sense to borrow.
4. Leverage cuts both ways. If the return on funds employed (income) is *less* than the cost of borrowing those funds (interest), then the difference must be absorbed by earnings from nonborrowed funds. Therefore, decisions about the use of leverage (degree) must balance higher expected returns against increased risks.

The most often used measure of leverage is the *debt-to-worth ratio,* which is computed as follows:

$$\text{Debt-to-worth ratio} = \frac{\text{Total liabilities}}{\text{Net worth}}$$

This ratio is most often used by creditors from either the trade or, more particularly, financial institutions. The ratio attempts to measure the investment that outside creditors have in your business for every dollar of equity. Theoretically, creditors prefer a low ratio. Owners prefer a higher one, either to magnify their earnings potential or because raising new equity involves giving up some degree of control.

Traditionally, creditors have felt that excessive leverage may encourage irresponsibility on the part of the owner. In such an instance, the personal stake of the owner can become so small that only successful speculative activity can yield a substantial percentage of return, but failure in the activity will bring only a moderate loss because the owner's investment is now so small.

Another leverage ratio is:

$$\frac{\text{Net income} + \text{Noncash charges (e.g., depreciation} + \text{amortization)}}{\text{Current maturities of long-term debt}}$$

Cash-to-debt-ratio

In essence, this ratio measures whether or not the business generates enough cash to cover current maturities of long-term bank loans. A ratio less than 1 means that the company has a potential cash bind. Figure 3.11 indicates that Lucky Fuel Oil has a reasonable amount of debt compared to owner's equity and is generating more than enough cash to cover current maturities, although the ratios have declined since 19X9.

Turnover ratios measure how effectively a company is managing its financial resources. (A detailed discussion of financial resource management is the subject of Part III.)

Three sets of turnover ratios are significant: receivables turnover, inventory turnover, and accounts payable turnover. In each case, the ratios can be expressed in terms of a number of *turns* (e.g., 7.5 turns, 47.9 turns, 14.7 turns) *and* in terms of a *number of days* an item (receivable, inventory, or payable) is *outstanding* (e.g., 48 days, 7.5 days, 24.5 days). These turnover ratios are calculated as follows:

$$\text{Receivables turns} = \frac{\text{Annual sales (\$)}}{\text{Average monthly receivable balance (\$)}}$$

$$\text{Inventory turns} = \frac{\text{Annual purchase (cost of sales) (\$)}}{\text{Average monthly inventory balance (\$)}}$$

$$\text{Payables turns} = \frac{\text{Annual purchases and operating expenses (\$)}}{\text{Average monthly accounts payable balance (\$)}}$$

Each ratio can be converted to a number of days outstanding by dividing 360 by the number of turns, as follows:

$$\text{Days outstanding} - \text{receivables} = \frac{360}{\text{Receivables turns}}$$

$$\text{Days outstanding} - \text{inventory} = \frac{360}{\text{Inventory turns}}$$

$$\text{Days outstanding} - \text{payables} = \frac{360}{\text{Payables turns}}$$

Figure 3.11 shows these ratios for Lucky Fuel Oil are improving. This means Peter O'Henry is collecting his receivables more rapidly, is holding his inventory down to reasonable levels, and is paying his payables promptly.

Profitability ratios measure the rate of return the business is providing on invested capital and also the relationship of certain major areas of expense to total sales. Three main ratios that measure returns on capital are:

$$\text{Pre-tax return on assets} = \frac{\text{Net income before taxes (\$)}}{\text{Total assets (\$)}}$$

$$\text{Pre-tax return on net worth} = \frac{\text{Net income before taxes (\$)}}{\text{Net worth (\$)}}$$

$$\text{Pre-tax profitability} = \frac{\text{Net income before taxes (\$)}}{\text{Net sales (\$)}}$$

The other profitability ratios include:

$$\text{Gross margin percentage} = \frac{\text{Operating margin (\$)}}{\text{Net sales (\$)}}$$

$$\text{Operating expense percentage} = \frac{\text{Operating expenses (\$)}}{\text{Net sales (\$)}}$$

$$\text{Interest expense percentage} = \frac{\text{Interest expense (\$)}}{\text{Net sales}}$$

$$\text{Depreciation expense percentage} = \frac{\text{Depreciation expense (\$)}}{\text{Net sales}}$$

Figure 3.11 shows these ratios for Lucky Fuel Oil. The ratios of significance are the three ratios that measure return on capital. These are not at the desired levels and are declining. Likewise, Peter O'Henry's gross margin is declining.

Finally, *trading ratios* simply show the level of sales in relation to working capital and total assets. As shown in Figure 3.11, these ratios are on the increase due largely to escalating prices, not to greater volume.

Note: Peter had been unable to find relevant industry data with which to compare his ratios. He believed that a comparison of his own business from one year to the next was a good measure of progress. He planned to review these ratios on a quarterly basis, using comparable data from the past three years.

The conclusion that Peter drew from his analysis was that inflation in the price of oil was driving up his dollar sales even though his gallons sold had remained about the same over the past two years. This inflationary increase was reflected in an increase in his *trading ratios* and a decline in his *ratios of expenses to sales.*

The *turnover ratios* indicated he was doing a better job of managing his financial resources. His *liquidity* and *leverage ratios* likewise indicated a responsible level of debt to equity. His *declining gross margin* and *declining profitability ratios* signalled a need *to control operating expenses* and *to pass on increases in the price of fuel oil.*

BREAK-EVEN ANALYSIS

Wishing to analyze further the historical performance of his business, O'Henry used break-even analysis. He had heard of this analytical tool and often wondered at what point he had covered his fixed and variable costs and begun to make a profit. Put another way, how much fuel oil did he have to sell just to break even?

Break-even analysis is basically an analytical technique for studying the relationships among fixed costs, variable costs, and profits. (A detailed discussion of this technique is in Part III, "How to Manage Your Financial Resources," Chapter 25.

Before proceeding, it is important to understand some basic definitions of the key elements found in the break-even formula, namely:

- Fixed costs.
- Variable costs.
- Relevant range.
- Contribution margin.

Fixed costs are those costs that remain constant in total regardless of changes in the level of activity. This definition must be tempered somewhat to include the *relevant range* concept, which implies that there is a relevant range of sales volume throughout which a company's fixed costs (plant and equipment depreciation, insurance, certain maintenance costs, executive salaries, rent, lease obligations, etc.) will remain approximately the same. However, outside either the upper or lower boundary of this range, these fixed costs will either increase dramatically or can be reduced.

As a simple illustration, assume that a small fuel oil dealer can sell a minimum of 750,000 gallons annually with one delivery truck. Also assume that the truck costs $20,000 and is depreciated over five years, and that it is the only fixed cost. The fixed costs associated with the depreciation of the truck are $4000 ($20,000 ÷ 5) annually (using straight-line depreciation) within the relevant range of activity, which is 1 to 750,000 gallons.

As soon as that dealer finds that he is capable of selling 1 million gallons, he is going to need a second truck, which will increase the fixed costs to $8000 ($20,000 + $20,000 = $40,000 ÷ 5) a year within the relevant range of 750,000 to 1,000,000, gallons. The lower limit of the relevant range is now considered to be 750,000 (rather than 1,000,000) because it is assumed that should the dealer's volume decline and be expected to stay below the 750,000-gallon level, he would react by selling one of his trucks, thus reducing his fixed costs to $4000 per year.

If a cost changes directly in proportion to changes in activity, it is variable. Therefore, product costs—for example, those of #2 home heating oil, kerosene, gasoline, and heavy oil—are clearly variable costs.

Thus far, we have seen that costs may be either fixed or variable in nature and that *it is an important prerequisite to break-even analysis to be able to correctly identify each.* Unfortunately, in reality, costs are not always clearly fixed or variable. Some costs may contain both fixed and variable elements. These kinds of costs are referred to as either *mixed* or *semivariable* costs.

As an example, a dealer may incur an auto and truck expense of

$12,000 at a volume level of one million gallons, whereas at the level of 2.5 million gallons, the cost would increase to only $13,000 (Chapter 25 describes how to separate mixed costs into their fixed and variable components.) Once costs have been assigned, the break-even point may be calculated by using a formula. The level of operations at which there is no profit and no loss is determined as follows:

$$\text{Break-even point} = \frac{\text{Total fixed costs}}{\text{Contribution margin per gallon}}$$

Contribution margin is the selling price less total variable costs. When you subtract from sales the variable costs associated with making those sales, the balance may be channeled toward paying your fixed costs and yielding a profit. *Contribution margin* differs from the *gross profit margin* because it considers only the variable portion of *all* operating expenses. The gross profit margin is simply the difference between *sales* and *cost of goods* sold. Thus it does not include any other operating expenses, fixed or variable.

Peter O'Henry identified the various components of the break-even formula for Lucky Fuel Oil as follows:

	19X1 Data
Sales	$6,964,581
Less: Variable expenses	6,492,417
Contribution margin	$ 472,164
Contribution margin per gallon ($472,164 ÷ 9,049,595)	$0.0521752
Fixed expenses	$ 379,589
Break-even $\frac{\$379,589}{\$.0521752}$ =	7,275,276 gallons

To answer his original question, O'Henry has to sell 7,275,276 gallons of fuel oil to break even.

With the break-even point determined, various "what if" questions can be analyzed. For example, if Peter's goal is to earn $200,000 profit, what volume level would be required? This can be calculated by adding the profit goal to the fixed expenses and dividing by the contribution margin per gallon:

$$\frac{\$379,589 + \$200,000}{\$0.0521752} = 11,108,515 \text{ gallons}$$

Is this amount in the relevant range within which the costs will behave as outlined? Probably. What if Peter's goal is a $250,000 profit?

$$\frac{\$379{,}589 + \$250{,}000}{\$.0521752} = 12{,}066{,}825 \text{ gallons}$$

Is this amount within the relevant range? Maybe.

MARGIN ANALYSIS

In break-even analysis, the focus was on fixed costs and trying to cover them with a contribution margin, the dollar value of which grows with increased sales volume. Thus far, volume and sales growth have been emphasized. There is, however, a second side of the formula that must be examined as well, namely, *reducing variable costs per unit in order to increase the contribution margin per unit*. Analyze the overall picture with respect to cost behavior in the fuel oil business. In the discussions on break-even analysis, the following identifications of costs were made:

Variable costs (including taxes)	$6,492,417	94.5%
Fixed costs	379,589	5.5%
Total costs	$6,872,006	100.0%

One can quickly appreciate the importance of variable costs in the fuel oil business because they represent 94.5% of total costs. Of course, the major variable cost is the cost of product, which for Lucky represented 90% of these types of expenses. If any of these variable costs could be reduced even by a small amount, the *contribution margin* would be increased and the number of gallons O'Henry would need to sell to break even and to guarantee a profit would be lower.

In the end, much of this historical analysis focuses on margins. However, one further look at margins may prove worthwhile when viewed from a historical perspective with an appreciation for both conservation and inflation. Look at the effects of conservation on the East Oil Department's No. 2 Home Heating Oil business since 19X1 (Figure 3.12). Look at this erosion of annual contribution per customer (from a needed 20¢/gal. to an actual 14.94¢/gal.). The erosion is likely to be caused by two factors:

1. Inflation.
2. Conservation.

How much of the erosion can be attributed to each of these factors?

FIGURE 3.12
Use of No. 2 Oil

	12 Months Ending March 31	
	19X1	*19X9*
Total No. 2 customers	1,287	2,293
Total sales of No. 2 (gallons)	2,208,919	2,426,175
Average annual consumption per customer	1,576 gal.	1,058 gal.
Margin in 19X9 required to match the 19X1 contribution	—	20.0¢
Average annual contribution per customer	$124	$158
19X1 contribution per customer in 19X1 dollars	$212[a]	
Average annual margin per gallon	7.85¢	14.94¢

[a]Assumes average annual inflation of 8%.

The factor for an annual inflation rate of 8% over the seven years is 1.713. By multiplying the 19X1 margin of 7.85 cents by this factor, we arrive at 13.45 cents, the 19X9 margin that is necessary to keep pace with inflation. Since this adjusted 19X1 margin of 13.45 cents is less than Lucky's actual 19X9 margin of 14.94 cents by 0.0149 cents, Peter kept pace with inflation.

To analyze the 19X9 annual contribution per customer more clearly, consider the following:

Adjusted 19X1 margin	$212
Conservation (518 gallons × 0.1345)	− 70
Increase in per gallon margin (1058 gallons × 0.0149)	16
Average annual contribution per customer	$158

In this simplified example, although O'Henry has approximately kept pace with inflation, conservation efforts have eroded his annual contribution per customer. What can he do to deal with this problem?

1. Develop more volume spread among more customers.
2. Develop new products.

CONCLUSION

This chapter has presented a series of detailed analyses aimed at discovering just how the Lucky Fuel Oil business operates, where it stands, and what factors require attention in order for the business to grow and prosper. The techniques illustrated include:

- Divisional and product line financial statements.
- Financial results expressed as percentages as well as cents per gallon.
- Financial ratio analysis.
- Break-even analysis.
- Contribution margin analysis.

The remaining chapters use much of this information to construct the strategic, tactical, and operating plans for Lucky Fuel Oil.

4

Preparing the Business Plan: Documenting the Strategic and Tactical Objectives

This chapter describes and illustrates the documentation of strategic and tactical objectives, which, as described in Chapter 2, are an integral part of a business plan. The illustration is again the Lucky Fuel Oil Company. A review of Chapter 2 will reveal that Lucky is facing a difficult business environment. The company's supplier is tightening up credit and has raised prices dramatically in response to increased crude oil prices. Because the price increases have been frequent and substantial, and because heating oil has become a major factor in the household budget of Lucky's customers, Lucky has been unable to demand the same kind of payment terms that the supplier has demanded of Lucky. These factors have several implications for Lucky.

First, Peter O'Henry has to be careful that, to the extent possible, the price increases are passed on to his customers. If he does not pass on the increases and attempts to maintain a constant differential (or gross profit margin) between the cost he pays for the product and what he charges his customers, eventually he will not have enough money left to pay his drivers and office help, to pay his utility bills, his salesmen, and his other expenses, and to leave a profit. Therefore, Peter has to make sure he maintains his gross profit margin to assure that he will make enough money to stay in business.

Second, Peter has to be concerned that his customers do not switch to other suppliers or reduce their use of heating oil through conservation, conversion to gas, or using supplementary wood stoves for heat. Otherwise, his total gallonage will fall below his break-even level.

Third, even if Peter monitors his gross profit margin, is aware of his fixed costs and his break-even point, calculates everything correctly, sets his price appropriately, and bills his customers on a current basis, there is often a delay in how fast they pay him. Therefore, even if he makes all his calculations properly, he might still be in trouble if his customers do not pay him promptly. This means that he will have to borrow from the bank in order to have enough cash to pay his suppliers and to meet his payroll and his other bills until he is paid by his customers. If he has to borrow substantial amounts, the interest cost is another factor to be considered in his pricing decision.

Peter found these factors difficult to cope with and to coordinate without an *organized and formal* approach. So, he set about to construct his business plan. He began his business planning process by first defining his own strategic objectives and then the objectives for his business.

PETER'S PERSONAL OBJECTIVES

Peter's own objectives had always been clear. He had worked for years as a member of middle management for one of the major oil companies. He had worked at the corporate headquarters in New York, had been transferred to the field in Houston, had audited drilling locations on Alaska's North Slope, and had managed a storage terminal in Chelsea (Boston), Massachusetts. Peter assessed his managerial strengths and weaknesses. He *knew the heating oil business,* having been deeply involved in the supply side. He had a *sound business background* by virtue of his education and his work experience; he had a college degree in economics and had been directly responsible for the profitable operations of the terminal in the Boston area.

Some of the drawbacks to his position with a major oil company were that he did not really share in the profit of the business the way he might had he owned a business himself. He was subject to the possibility of frequent transfers, which he found disruptive to his family. He found the large corporate environment to be a very political climate, one that he found detracted from, rather than added to, his enjoyment of his work.

Peter had decided to become his own boss, to build a business that he could point to with pride as his accomplishment, one that would provide a livelihood for himself and his family. And, since he had two children, he wished to build a business in which he could involve them if they were interested. Finally, Peter liked the Boston metropolitan area as a place to live and had decided to search for a business there in order to establish a permanent residence. Therefore, he had purchased Lucky Fuel Oil Company because of *his objectives:*

- To be his own boss.
- To build a business of his own.
- To provide a comfortable living for his family.
- To escape the corporate environment.
- To live where he wanted.
- To provide an annuity for his children.

PETER'S STRATEGIC OBJECTIVES FOR HIS BUSINESS

As Peter thought about the matter, he began to formulate strategic objectives for the business. These are discussed in the next several paragraphs.

Profit Objectives

Peter realized that his business must be profitable if he was to accomplish his personal objectives. Historically, the business had generated profits of between 2% and 4% before taxes, when compared to sales, and between 6% and 10% before taxes, when compared to total assets. Peter also looked at his return on his net worth (his investment in his business). Because of his relatively modest investment, his return on net worth was quite high (31%). As he acquired new companies, which required more cash up front, his return on net worth would decrease. Since he planned some acquisitions in the near future, he did not know how much he could realistically expect as a return on net worth, but he decided to set his goal at 25%. He decided that his primary focus would be on the first two profitability measures, return on sales and return on assets, as his guides. *He set as his goals a steady 4% return on sales and 12% return on assets.*

He also decided he should use profits before, rather than after, taxes as his measure of profits. Since the business had carry-forward losses that had served to reduce its tax liability in the past, they would cause historical *after*-tax profit numbers not to be comparable to similar current numbers. Furthermore, there had been some recent activity in Congress to ease the tax burden for small companies, which would mean that the historical results would no longer be comparable. In a few years, when things settled down, he believed he could begin to look at *after*-tax numbers. For the time being, pre-tax numbers were a reasonable basis for setting his goals.

Growth

Peter realized that given his customers' current conservation efforts he would have to have an active marketing program just to *retain* his current level of gallons sold. And, although continued profits would help him to accomplish his personal goals of being his own boss, living where he wanted, and providing for his family, if he wanted to provide room for his children in the business, he would have to make the business grow.

He set his objective as an annual 2% growth in gallons sold. He used gallons as the measure of growth because, with the recent price increases, his base of sales dollars had continued to grow dramatically, although his gallonage had stayed about the same or had declined.

Other Objectives

Peter believed that his profit and growth objectives, if accomplished, would serve to help him attain his personal goals. He believed that he had three other groups of individuals to consider in addition to himself and his family: his customers, his employees, and his community.

Regarding his customers, Peter set as his objectives the following:

- To provide adequate fuel on a timely basis.
- To provide emergency service to assure that his customers would have warm homes.
- To provide routine maintenance to assure that his customers' equipment worked well.
- To provide insulation and burner conversion service (conversion to more efficient burners). Even though this served to reduce consumption by his customers, Peter saw conservation as inevitable and believed he would be wise to be involved in the conservation effort, both to retain his customers and to pick up some additional revenue.

Regarding his employees, Peter adopted the following as objectives:

- To pay them a decent wage.
- To provide good fringe benefits.
- To provide steady employment.

Regarding his community, Peter adopted as objectives the following:

- To employ local people whenever possible.
- To support local civic activities.

PETER'S STATEMENT OF BUSINESS PURPOSE

Peter decided to formulate all these objectives into a single mission statement or statement of business purpose, which read:

> *The purpose of this business is to provide adequate fuel and service to homes and businesses in the greater Boston metropolitan area at a price that is competitive, yet enables this business to survive and prosper, both to support its employees and to provide an acceptable return to its owners.*

PETER'S TACTICAL PLANS FOR THE BUSINESS

Now that Peter had a clear focus on his strategic objectives (where he wanted to go), he decided to document his tactical plans (how he was going to get there). What specific activities was he going to pursue in order to accomplish his strategic goals? To grow he was going to need (1) an active marketing program, and (2) an active acquisition program. To be profitable, he was going to need (1) to manage the financial resources and obligations of the business carefully, and (2) to reduce costs wherever possible.

These overall tactical objectives had subsidiary objectives. For example, as part of his marketing program he believed he needed to do the following:

- Hire another salesperson.
- Establish goals or quotas for the salespeople.
- Develop an incentive compensation scheme to encourage the salespeople to achieve their quotas.
- Monitor new residential construction as a source of new customers.
- Find out from realtors when potential customers were moving into his market area.

To establish an acquisition program, O'Henry first had to decide if he wanted to acquire additional fuel oil distributors or to diversify by acquiring counter-cyclical businesses. Then, he had to establish some goals for those acquisitions. For example, they should be in his market area and should have a sound customer base. And they should have a reason to sell out (such as an entrepreneur seeking to retire, or a business in difficult financial circumstances). He also had to establish some financial criteria for those businesses and to begin to line up financing sources. As a start, he decided he would discuss his program with his banker.

To manage the business more effectively, he had to consider in depth exactly how he was currently managing his *financial resources* and his *financial obligations*.

His financial resources included:

1. *Cash*—the money he had in the bank.
2. *Accounts receivable*—what was owed to the business by his customers.
3. *Inventory*—the resources of the business tied up in his stock of raw product.
4. *Fixed assets*—those resources tied up in bricks and mortar, machinery, and equipment.

These financial resources were supported by Peter's financial obligations. To protect his resources, Peter had to manage his obligations effectively. These obligations consisted of:

1. *Accounts payable*—money he owed his suppliers.
2. *Notes payable*—money he owed his bank.
3. *Net worth*—money he had invested in the business. This represented the portion of the business he really owned.

Peter realized that *sales* helped to increase his financial resources and that the *cost of his sales* used up his resources. Therefore, the net increase to his financial resources was the difference between the resources provided from sales and other sources and resources expended in producing the sales. (Detailed discussions of the effective management of these specific resources for any business are in Part III, "Managing Your Financial Resources.")

Peter decided to investigate the possibility of buying or building a larger storage facility as a way of reducing his product cost. He believed he could stabilize the price of his product somewhat by buying in larger quantity at a reasonable price and storing it rather than always having to buy at the current market price. Peter also planned to encourage his customers to fill their tanks in the summer when the price was more favorable for them.

At this point, Peter believed he had established a reasonable set of strategic and tactical objectives. Figure 4.1 illustrates the interaction of these two separate levels of objectives.

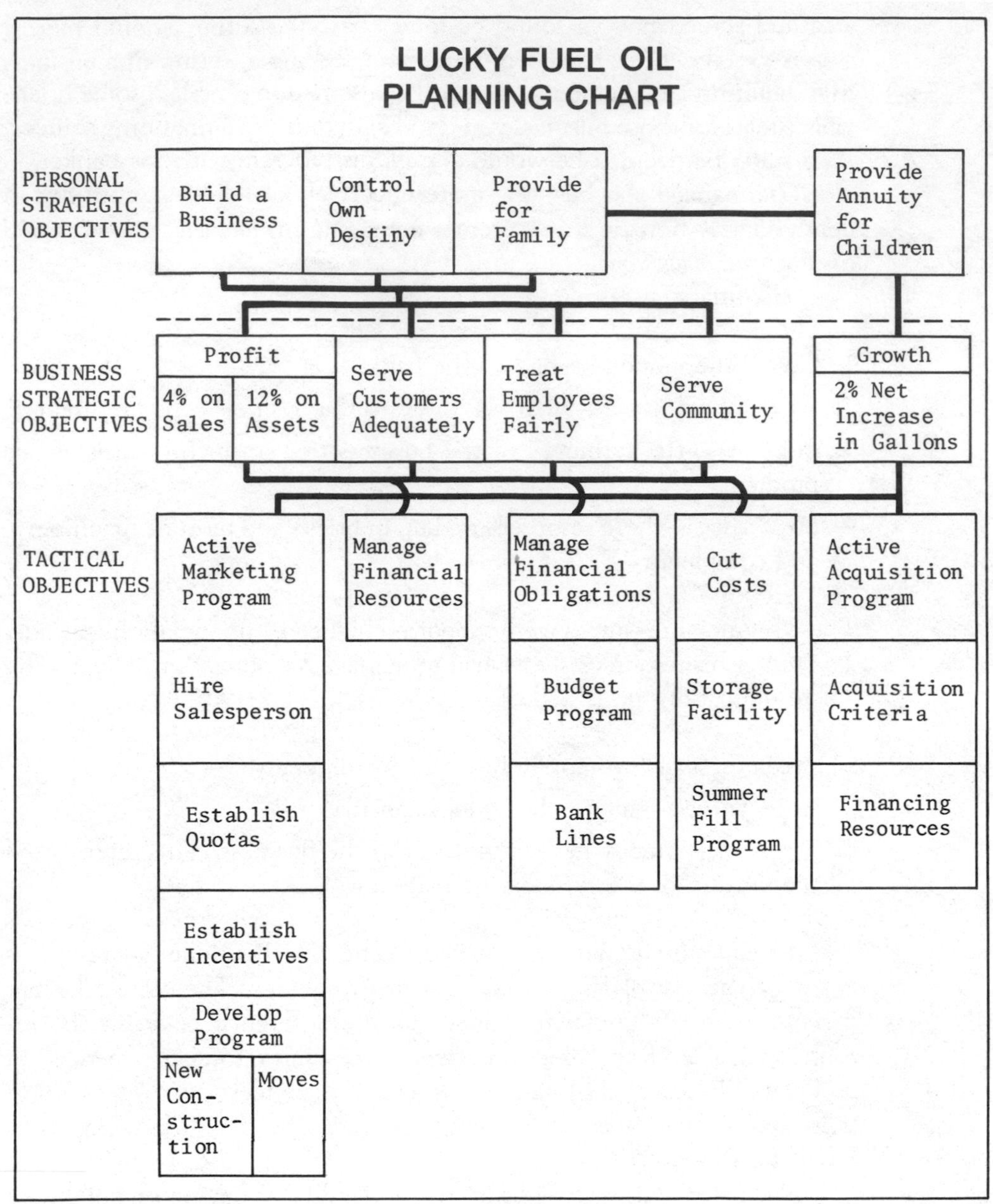

FIGURE 4.1
Lucky Fuel Oil Planning Chart

CONCLUSION

In giving thought to the business planning process, Peter had formulated his own strategic objectives, which had led to the purchase of Lucky Fuel Oil. He had analyzed the historical activity of his company and had then developed a series of strategic and tactical plans for the business that were consistent with his personal goals. These would satisfy the second section of the outline of a business plan.

At this point, therefore, he had answered the questions:

- Where am I now?
- Where do I want to go?
- How am I going to get there?

What remained was to develop the formal narrative support for the business plan and to translate his tactical objectives into financial terms—that is, to answer the question, "What is it going to cost to accomplish the strategic and tactical plans?"

5
The Narrative Support

Chapter 3 introduced Lucky Fuel Oil by showing its prior three years of results. Chapter 4 explored Peter O'Henry's reasons for acquiring the business and developed a series of strategic and tactical plans for the business. This chapter is a continuation of Chapter 4. It defines and illustrates the narrative support for a formal business plan. The chapter discusses what ought to be considered in the following aspects of any business:

- Its description.
- Its market.
- Its competition.
- Its location.
- Its management.
- Its personnel.

When the purpose of the plan is to obtain financing, the business plan should also include a description of how the expected funding is to be used.

The chapter takes the form of a series of questions. Developing answers to the questions and documenting them in writing serves several purposes:

1. It forces you to think in detail about the strengths and weaknesses of your business.
2. It helps you to complete the analysis of tactical objectives.
3. It provides a means for others to understand your business and its need for funds.

DESCRIPTION OF THE BUSINESS

The purpose of describing the business is to provide the reader of your business plan with background information that may be useful in evaluating the remainder of the narrative. The answers to the questions that follow will provide a detailed description of the business.

1. What type of business is this?
   Merchandising.
   Manufacturing.
   Distribution.
   Service.
2. What products (services) does it offer?
3. What is the business's status?
   Start-up.
   Takeover.
   Expansion.
4. What is the form of organization of the business?
   Proprietorship.
   Partnership.
   Subchapter-S corporation.
   Corporation.
5. How long has the business been operating?
6. What seasonal factors affect the business, if any?
7. What are the strengths of the business? What makes it successful?
   Management.
   Skilled personnel.
   Unique product/process.

FIGURE 5.1
Description of the Business
Lucky Fuel Oil Company

The Lucky Fuel Oil Company, organized as a corporation, is a distributorship serving retail and wholesale markets. The company offers petroleum products for the heating of residential, industrial, and municipal space (end-users). It offers the same products and gasoline and diesel fuel on a wholesale basis to other distributors. Liquified propane gas (LPG) is offered to restaurants for cooking and to seasonal homes for cooking and heat. Lucky offers replacement heating units and boilers, a full range of energy-saving equipment, and to a lesser extent home appliances. The company offers service on the products it sells and on the heating units of the customers to whom distillates are sold. The business is greatly affected by seasonal factors. Its heating products are sold principally in December, January, and February. LPG and gasoline are sold primarily in the summer months.

The business, Lucky Fuel Oil Company, was founded more than 35 years ago. Until his death in 1963, the founder, E.L. Smith, actively managed the business. Ownership and management succeeded to his only son, Don Smith, who before his father's death, participated minimally in the business. Lack of industry expertise on the part of the son resulted in poor operating results. Profits soon turned to losses, and equity was eroded. Realizing that he was unable to run the business successfully, Smith offered the business for sale. Peter O'Henry, through his industry contacts, heard of this offering and acquired the assets of the company in 1971. Realizing that a strong equity base would subsequently serve as a springboard for growth, O'Henry concentrated on building the equity of his business in the early 1970s. Principally, his efforts were directed toward improving the profitability of the existing organization. Concurrently, he eliminated the payment of dividends and kept his own salary to a minimum level. In 1977 he determined that he had the capital and the management skill required to acquire other dealers and to diversify his product line.

The success in this business can be attributed for the most part to Peter O'Henry's ability to manage his company well. However, this sound management goes hand-in-hand with the company's ability to provide service to the customer and to assure that an adequate supply of product is always available.

The greatest limitation on this business is the buying market. Through conversion to alternative heating sources, the number of available buyers is actually dwindling. Conservation of gasoline limits growth in this area as well. Growth through acquisition is also limited since other dealers have strategic goals similar to Peter's and are unwilling to sell their businesses.

Constant source of supply.

Good service.

8. What are the limitations on the business?

Capital.

Management resources.

Personnel.

Questions 1 through 6 are factual in nature. The remaining questions, 7 and 8, are subjective in that they require you to identify the factors or characteristics of your organization that have made or will make it successful. These critical success factors are your perceptions of what makes your organization better or stronger than a similar organization in the marketplace. Critical success factors are skilled craftsmanship, attention to detail, or perhaps the ability to provide fast turnaround on customer orders. In some cases, the critical success factor can also be a limitation on the business. For instance, the ability to provide skilled craftsmanship may be limited by your ability to hire sufficient skilled craftsmen. The process of identifying the critical success factors requires you to pinpoint the reasons why a customer would turn to your business instead of that of a competitor or why your business distinguishes itself in an industry.

Figure 5.1 is the description of the business for the Lucky Fuel Oil Company. The description is brief and to the point. The description of the business needs to be only as long as is necessary to state its purpose and to disclose those factors that make it successful.

THE MARKET

The purpose of defining the market is to affirm that the strategic and tactical goals of the company are realistic. If your business presently covers the existing market and the market is not expandable, then it will be difficult to expand your business. Most small businesses don't have a lion's share of the market so that growth in market share is always theoretically possible. The constraining factor may be the competition. Understanding the market may be crucial in order to beat the competition.

You should answer the following questions about your market.

1. Who or what is your target market?
2. Can this market be segmented, and if so, how?
3. What is the size of your target market?
4. What share of the market do you have?
5. What is the growth (historical, potential) of this market?
6. What is the growth potential of your market share?
7. How do you maintain and increase your market share:
   How do you satisfy your current customers' needs?

How do you attract new customers?

What do you offer that no one else does?

8. Do your pricing policies help or hurt you in the marketplace?
9. What have your historical sales been by product/service?

   Numbers of units.

   Dollars of sales.

   Percentage of total sales.
10. What does each product/service cost you to sell?
11. What have your profits been by product/service?
12. What are your current sales goals by product/service?

    Number of units.

    Dollars of sales.

    Percentage of total sales.

The first eight questions seek to find out how much you know about the market you face. Clear and concise answers to these questions will demonstrate a well-thought-out approach to your business. Questions 9, 10, and 11 will serve to put the answers to the first eight questions into perspective. If the historical experience of the business, summarized as responses to questions 9, 10, and 11, does not support your responses to the first eight questions, it is likely that these first eight responses will be discounted by the reader of your business plan unless you provide also a convincing analysis of how the situation has changed. Question 12 is an introduction to financial statement forecasts (the subject of Chapter 6). Once the analysis of the market is complete, the last step is to formulate sales goals for the next one to three years. It is helpful to present this analysis by product or service line and by units as well as by dollars.

Figure 5.2 is the description of the market for Lucky Fuel Oil.

THE COMPETITION

Implicit in the consideration of your business's market share is the discussion of your competition. If your market is nationwide, then it is important to consider your national competitors. If, like Lucky Fuel Oil, your market is local, then the focus naturally should be limited to the local competition. Answer the following questions in order to define your competition:

1. At present, who are your major competitors? (List the three to five nearest or the largest.)

FIGURE 5.2
The Market
Lucky Fuel Oil Company

Lucky's target market is the users of fuel oil, heavy oil, or kerosene primarily as heating products. These same consumers represent Lucky's market for heating unit service and heating related equipment sales. Lucky also markets to the users of gasoline, diesel, and liquid propane gas. This market can be segmented as follows:

Product	*Market*
Fuel oil	Residences, small businesses, other fuel oil dealers
Kerosene	Residences
Heavy oil	Industry, municipal units
Equipment units	The above users of heating products
Gasoline and diesel	Gas stations, construction companies, marinas, dealerships for diesel-powered cars
LPG	Restaurants, seasonal homes

The target market in consuming units is approximately as follows:

Product	*Number of consuming units*
Fuel Oil	10,000 residences, small businesses, and other fuel oil dealers
Kerosene	1000 residences
Heavy oil	20 industrial plants and municipal units
Equipment	10,000 residences and small businesses
Gasoline and diesel	75 gas stations, marinas, construction companies, and car dealerships
LPG	2000 seasonal homes and restaurants

It is believed that Lucky currently controls approximately 30% of its identified target markets. Due to the nature of the products and services, growth is limited largely to acquiring competing fuel distributors or to attracting customers away from competitors. Peter O'Henry believes that through an aggressive acquistition campaign over the next seven years he will control approximately 60% of his target market.

Lucky Fuel is characterized as one of the higher priced product dealers in the area. This perception appears neither to help nor to hinder O'Henry in the marketplace. He satisfies his existing customers by providing a supply of product and competent service to assure uninterrupted heating comfort. His equipment line meets the recent consumer demand for energy-saving system enhancements. All of Lucky's products are backed by good service. Lucky's diversified line of petroleum products is able to attract individuals/businesses seeking a single supplier for their multiple petroleum product needs (e.g., the owner of a resort hotel who requires fuel oil for heat and hot water and LPG for the restaurant grill).

FIGURE 5.2 (Con't)

A summary of the most recent year's sales by dollars and by product is:

	Sales Dollars	*Sales Gallons*	*Sales as Percentage of the Total Dollar*
Fuel oil	$3,482,290	3,910,032	50%
Kerosene	374,988	467,380	5%
Diesel	139,291	266,190	2%
Heavy oil	2,159,020	3,744,237	31%
Gasoline	208,937	281,346	3%
LPG	268,193	381,894	4%
Appliance	40,000	—	—
Burner service	291,862	—	5%
Total	$6,964,581	9,049,595	100%

Cost of goods sold and gross profit percentages by product line are as follows:

	Sales %	*Cost of Goods Sold %*	*Gross Profit %*
Fuel oil	100%	83.2%	16.8%
Kerosene	100%	82.8%	17.2%
Diesel	100%	88.5%	11.5%
Heavy oil	100%	93.8%	6.2%
Gasoline	100%	95.9%	4.1%
LPG	100%	63.9%	36.1%
Appliances	100%	79.8%	20.2%
Burner service	100%	50.0%	50.0%
Average	100%	79.7%	20.3%

Projected 19X2 volume by product:

	Sales Dollars	*Gallons*	*Sales Dollars as Percentage of Total*
Fuel oil	$ 5,589,665	4,178,000	53%
Kerosene	683,167	464,000	6%
Diesel	326,900	268,000	3%
Heavy oil	2,419,073	3,744,000	23%
Gasoline	796,369	580,000	8%
LPG	476,291	380,000	4%
Appliances	37,000	—	—
Burner service	325,000	—	3%
	$10,653,463	9,528,000	100%

2. How large are they compared to your business?
   Sales in dollars.
   Number of employees.
   Number of locations.
   Number of customers.
3. Are their businesses:
   Steady?
   Increasing?
   Decreasing?
4. How are they similar/dissimilar to your business?
5. Where do you believe you have a business advantage?
   Product.
   Price.
   Service.
   On-time delivery.
6. Where are their:
   Strengths?
   Weaknesses?
7. What have you learned by observing them?

These questions will guide you to focus on your competition, to learn from them, and to seek ways to make your product or service distinctive.

Figure 5.3 presents Lucky's analysis of its competition.

THE LOCATION

The location of a business is often critical to its success. Many computer companies have developed in the Silicon Valley in Southern California and in the Boston, Massachusetts, metropolitan area because of the need for a ready supply of engineers and computer scientists graduating from the local colleges and universities. Other industries spring up close to a source of raw materials or labor or close to a market outlet. Hence the location of businesses which support drilling rigs (exploration companies, rig leasing companies) are located in the oil fields of the Southwest, for example. Even for a small manufacturing or service business, location is often an important factor due to the cost of transportation of goods and services to its customers. The following questions will focus your attention on location and define its relevance to your business.

FIGURE 5.3
The Competition
Lucky Fuel Oil Company

Competition is provided by the following companies in the region:

- Higgins Oil
- Starlight Oil
- General Oil

To a lesser extent, competition is provided by the eight "rack buyers" selling in Lucky's territory. A rack buyer is typically a one-man operation; the owner of the truck delivers the fuel and provides service as necessary. A rack buyer usually obtains his supply from a larger retailer, such as Lucky.

Of Lucky's major competitors, both Higgins and Starlight deliver less volume than Lucky. The volume of General Oil approximates that of the Lucky Fuel Oil Company. Overall, it appears that Lucky and General each controls 30% of the market, with Higgins and Starlight controlling 15% and 20% respectively. All three competitors offer heating oil, kerosene, and equipment service and sales. The heavy oil market in the area appears to be split between Lucky and General. Of these four companies only Lucky offers gasoline, diesel, and LPG. Unlike Lucky Fuel, each of the other competing businesses is owned/managed by a descendant of the founder. In a tradition-bound area such as this, O'Henry is regarded as an outsider. Peter has done much to overcome his newcomer status by taking an active part in community affairs. None of the owners of the competing businesses has Peter's managerial experience and background.

In diversifying his product line into the gasoline, diesel, and LPG markets, Peter has developed an edge over his competitors. As mentioned earlier, individuals with multi-petroleum product needs are attracted to Lucky as a single supplier. In general, it appears that Lucky's competitors have done little to shore up or compensate for their shrinking fuel oil volumes.

1. What are the characteristics of your present location?

   Physical characteristics/size.

   Cost.

   Owned.

   Leased.

   Operating costs.

2. How does this location affect your business?

   Proximity to markets.

   Proximity to supplies of:

   —raw materials.

   —labor.

Figure 5.4
The Location
Lucky Fuel Oil Company

All operations are directed from a central location, a two-story 20-year-old wooden frame building. This building also houses the company's parts and equipment inventory. Within a two-mile radius of this headquarters, are four fuel storage tanks providing a total storage capacity of 250,000 gallons. The location provides sufficient space for parking the company's fleet of 7 fuel delivery trucks and 6 service vans. The net asset value of the property owned by the business is $484,989. The annual operating costs at the existing volume level are $840,443.

Although Lucky Fuel Oil Company is situated in a semi-rural region, this location is in the relative center of the fuel-consuming communities and resort areas. Product is delivered to the business from the large bulk storage plants in Boston. There is a sufficient supply in this area of the semiskilled labor required by Lucky. The local banks and the larger banks in Boston serve as a source of capital for Lucky Fuel Oil.

Because industrial development in the area has been limited and much of the economy is supported by tourism, labor is plentiful, particularly during the winter months. Delivery costs, however, tend to be higher for Lucky than for a dealer operating in a larger metropolitan area. Given an equal customer base, it is likely that there is a greater geographic dispersion among the customers of the rural dealer than among those of the metropolitan dealer. Therefore, a delivery driver must travel more miles to deliver the same quantity of oil than does his metropolitan counterpart.

No major changes in the existing location are anticipated in the near future. The existing capacity can sufficiently absorb further acquisitions. Furthermore, an acquisition may include trucks or storage tanks.

—capital.

Operating costs.

3. What major changes do you anticipate in your location in the near future?

   Renovation costs.

   Additional or replacement facilities (larger, smaller).

   Move to a different location.

The first question establishes certain facts about the location. Questions 2 and 3 identify the relationship between your business and your location. Question 4 is intended to provide input to the financial statement forecasts. If major changes in the location of the business are anticipated, such as a move or an expansion into other regions, the estimated costs and benefits to the business should be built into the forecasts of capital requirements.

Figure 5.4 presents Lucky Fuel's analysis of its location.

THE MANAGEMENT

The definition of the management of a business is crucial to its business plan, whether the plan is to be used to obtain capital for a start-up situation or for the purchase of a business by a new owner. It is slightly less important in an on-going business seeking additional capital only because the potential investors have the track record of current management as a guide. In the start-up case, it is the characteristics of the management group that largely form the basis for a decision to invest. In the on-going business, it is the historical financial results.

The following questions must be considered in analyzing the management of a small business.

1. What is the personal history of the principals?

   Age.

   Educational background.

   —formal.

   —informal.

   General abilities.

   Business background.

   —management.

   —other.

   Health.

   Outside interests.
2. What related work experiences do the principals have?

   Operational.

   Managerial.

   Demonstrated expertise.
3. What are the duties and responsibilities of the principals?

   Organization chart.

   Job descriptions.

   Decision-makers.

   Appropriate delegation.

   Authority commensurate with responsibility.
4. Has the loss of a key member of management been considered from:

   A tax planning point of view?

   A management succession point of view?
5. Is there a written succession plan?
6. What is the compensation package for the management group?

7. What other resources are available to the business?
   Lawyer.
   Accountant (CPA).
   Tax counsel.
   Consultants (marketing, systems, etc.).
   Trade association.
8. Who is on the board of directors?
   Inside representation.
   Outside representation.

Questions 1 through 5 provide background and demonstrate the thought process that went into the formation of the management team. Question 6 provides input to the financial statement forecasts and also provides perspective on the willingness of the management team to sacrifice personal wealth to build the business. This item is likely to be more important in a new venture than in an on-going enterprise. It may be useful for the entrepreneur and other members of the management team who are also investors to indicate their *personal* financial commitments. With this information, the reader of the business plan can evaluate management's level of commitment to the business and their staying power should the business not grow as rapidly as hoped or fall on hard times.

Questions 7 and 8 seek to determine the other resources available to the business. Often a small business will have fewer people in the management group than functions to be performed. If some of these functions can be provided by outside resources or members of the board, this provides added strength to the management group.

Figure 5.5 presents Lucky's analysis of its management team.

THE PERSONNEL

In most manufacturing and distribution businesses and in all service businesses, availability of qualified personnel is critical to the success of the business. Answers to the following questions will demonstrate the extent to which the entrepreneur has considered this aspect of the business.

1. What is your current personnel complement?
   Number of people.
   Skills.
   Seasonal factors.

Figure 5.5
Management
Lucky Fuel Oil Company

Currently in his mid-forties, Peter O'Henry was born in Providence, Rhode Island. In the family tradition, Peter attended Providence Country Day School and on graduation was admitted to Brown University. Unlike his father and two elder brothers, on completion of his undergraduate studies, Peter chose not to pursue a career in the legal profession. Instead, he accepted a position on the corporate staff of a major oil company.

Peter O'Henry's employment with this major oil company exposed him to a number of challenging projects and assignments. Over the years his responsibilities included financial analysis at the corporate headquarters in New York, systems implementation in Houston, and project auditing at various drilling locations on Alaska's North Slope. In his last position with the company, he was given operational responsibility for a major fuel storage plant (terminal) where he managed 175 employees and dealt with a union. In each capacity, Peter O'Henry was judged successful by his superiors.

An avid sportsman, Peter enjoys alpine skiing, trout fishing, and golf. He is active in the community. He sponsors Little League baseball teams and a soccer team, and he chairs the cancer research fund-raising drives. He holds memberships in the Rotary Club and the Agawam Hills Country Club. He enjoys excellent health.

All major decisions at Lucky Fuel Oil are made by Peter O'Henry as chief executive officer. For example, he handles all product pricing decisions. The day-to-day operational decisions, such as route scheduling, are made by his fuel department and service department managers. Decisions such as hiring and termination are made by Peter O'Henry on recommendations by the department managers. In addition to their operational duties, the department managers are responsible for the upkeep and control of the company assets assigned to their departments. Administrative and bookkeeping duties are assigned by Peter to the office personnel. Peter is seeking to hire a controller to head up the accounting and office management functions. Although Peter employs one salesman, he personally contacts major customer leads.

To develop ties to the community, Peter employs local lawyers and CPAs as necessary for professional services. For programming assistance for his minicomputer system, he uses a regional systems software house that has a strong reputation in the fuel oil industry. Until recently, when his peak short-term borrowing needs grew substantially, all of Peter's banking was done with a local commercial bank. He continues to use the local commercial bank but also maintains a short-term borrowing line with a major commercial bank in Boston.

Peter is currently working with an estate-planning advisor. He is interested in providing for succession of his business to his two children. A written succession plan will be prepared on completion of the estate planning project. The outstanding shares of Lucky Fuel Oil Company are held by Peter and his wife, Joan. No dividends are currently paid in an attempt to build equity in the company. Peter draws an annual salary $39,000. The board of directors of the Lucky Fuel Oil Company currently consists of Peter O'Henry, his wife, and his brother, Thomas. Outside representation on the board is provided by partners from O'Henry's CPA and law firms.

2. What is your expected turnover?
   Retirement.
   Normal turnover.
3. What will be your personnel needs one to three years from now?
   Number of people.
   Skills.
4. Are such people available in the job market?
5. Will it be necessary to train them? If so, how?
6. What will the compensation package need to be?
   By skill level.
   By job class.
7. Do your personnel know:
   What they are supposed to do (job descriptions)?
   When?
   How?
   Their prospects for advancement?
8. Do you have periodic performance evaluations?

Figure 5.6 provides Peter O'Henry's assessment of his personnel needs.

USE OF THE EXPECTED FUNDS

The last item in the narrative support for a business plan, if such a plan is prepared in support of a request for funds, is a description of the way in which those funds are going to be used. Potential investors or bankers want to be certain that the funds are going to be used in an appropriate fashion. Clearly, the use of invested funds solely to increase the compensation of management is inappropriate. Often, bankers prefer to loan money to support tangible assets (buildings and equipment) because they can see their investment and have something to attach if the business turns sour. This is not to say that funds will not be invested to support receivables or inventories during seasonal peaks—that is, for ordinary working capital. Clearly, they will. (Part II, "Getting the Money," discusses various sources of funds for each of these particular uses.) The following questions will help you to describe the use of expected funding.

1. What is the purpose of this loan or investment?
   What financial resources are to be funded?

   or

   What items are to be acquired?

FIGURE 5.6
The Personnel
Lucky Fuel Oil Company

Position	*Name*	*Tenure*
President	P. O'Henry	11 years
Controller/Office Manager	Vacant[a]	
Fuel Department Manager	Ken Brown	15 years
Service Department Manager	Ed Reneau	8 years
Salesman	Andrew Shelton	4 years
Secretary to President	Linda Snow	2 years
Credit Clerk	Rosemary Force	6 years
Bookkeeper (disbursements)	Mary Thornley	10 years
Asst. Bookkeeper (cash receipts)	Hazel Jones	4 years

[a]Newly created position.

In addition, the company employs seven delivery drivers and six servicemen. During the summer months three of the deliverymen are temporarily laid off. Turnover at Lucky Fuel Oil Company is minimal. The annual lay-offs are anticipated by the deliverymen, and all of them return to Lucky in the fall.

Wages paid to drivers are considered fair and competitive in relation to those offered by other distributors in the area. Both the delivery drivers group and the service department are unionized; thus, the men are paid in accordance with a contract. The service and fuel department managers are paid a salary. The service manager also receives compensation for overtime. Wages for clerical employees are slightly above average in reward for their long service. As mentioned earlier, in a continuing effort to build equity in the company Peter O'Henry limits his salary to $39,000 per year. All employees are evaluated annually, at which time wage increases are granted if it is felt they are deserved.

It is the responsibility of each of the department managers to train new hires to his department. However, since much of the growth of the organization has occurred through acquisition, the need to hire inexperienced personnel has been minimal. Typically, Lucky meets its increased manpower needs by hiring the experienced personnel of the newly acquired company.

—Who are the suppliers?

—What are the makes or models?

—What are the costs?

What are the related support costs (installation, etc.)?

2. How will the loan or investment help to enhance the profitability of your business?

Figure 5.7 is a description of how the funds are to be used at Lucky Fuel Oil.

FIGURE 5.7
Application of Expected Funding
Lucky Fuel Oil Company

During the fiscal year April 1, 19X1 to March 31, 19X2, Lucky Fuel Oil will require funding for capital expenditures of $84,200.

Capital expenditures consist of:	
1 Magnum VII burster machine to separate copies of EDP printouts	$ 1,200
1 Ford pickup truck to replace a fully depreciated service truck	10,000
Acquisition of a competing business consisting of:	
400,000 gallons of No. 2 home heating oil @ 12½¢/gallon	50,000
300,000 gallons of gasoline @ 7⅔¢/gallon	23,000
	$84,200

Remaining funding is to provide working capital (for accounts receivable and inventory) to the business during the months of September through March. This business experiences a substantial build-up in its accounts receivable balance during these months of heavy fuel use because the cost of fuel oil deliveries outstrips the customers' ability to pay on a timely basis. As a result, receivable payments are extended, forcing the company to carry its customers for a period. To meet its own obligations on a timely basis, the company requires a short-term influx of cash, which builds over the period until it reaches a peak in February (estimated to be $785,345). In March, as the heating season comes to a close, deliveries taper off, and customer payments on receivables exceed the additions to their outstanding balances. This provides excess cash to the business that is used to reduce the short-term debt. In the past, this debt has been repaid in full by June, and it is anticipated that the same repayment schedule will operate in the prospective year.

CONCLUSION

This chapter has described and illustrated the major components of the narrative support for a business plan. The areas of concern involve:

- A description of the business.
- The market.
- The competition.
- The location.
- The management.
- The personnel.
- The application of the expected funding.

Each area is defined through the development of answers to a series of questions. When answered, these questions should provide any reader with insight into the strengths and weaknesses of the business, indicate the level of forethought and management skill involved in the business, and provide certain financial input to the financial statement forecasts. This narrative support for the business plan provides the link between the tactical plans and the operating plans of the company.

The intent of this chapter has been to illustrate the concept of a narrative support for the business plan. In your plan you might wish to develop the narrative in each area in much greater detail. The point is to make the business plan as complete and informative as possible.

6

Documenting The Assumptions And Developing Operational Plans

The historical results of the business have been analyzed, the strategic and tactical plans of Peter O'Henry and his business have been documented, and the narrative support for the business plan has been prepared. Various pieces of statistical information found to be of value (various ratios, costs per gallon, etc.) have been developed, and the format for a set of management reports has been devised that derives directly from the historical financial statements. The next step is to develop a set of operational plans that take the form of a set of financial statement forecasts. To create such forecasts, it is necessary first to make a series of assumptions about each major line item in the company's historical financial statements and then to use those assumptions to project that line item into the future. This chapter describes and illustrates that process.

DEFINING YOUR ASSUMPTIONS

Choosing an Appropriate Level of Detail

The process of preparing projections can be carried out at various levels of detail. As an example, Peter O'Henry could define as an assumption that his total sales in dollars would grow at 2% for the next five years; this is in fact one of his strategic objectives. As an alternative, he could develop his assumptions about sales dollars at a more detailed level. For example, he could make assumptions about the gallons he expects to sell by product type and by division. Then, he could estimate the selling price by product, by division, and even by month during the year. In this latter instance, the process of defining the assumptions would take more time and would still result in a forecast of sales, but when he was finished Peter would have a plan that would correspond closely to the way his business operates. Also, he would be able to analyze his actual results if they varied from his plan in order to determine if any unfavorable variances were caused either by a lack of volume of a particular product in a particular division or because he failed to set a high enough sales price. Thus, *the development of detailed assumptions can aid in the analysis of the business and can pinpoint areas for corrective action*. Also, as will be discussed in Chapter 8, this added flexibility enables you as an entrepreneur to explore the results of changes to your business *without actually making those changes*. This is called "sensitivity analysis" or analyzing "what would happen, if. . . ." Therefore, *the more detail you can build into your operating plan or budget, the better it will serve you in your management of your business*.

Documenting Your Assumptions

Regardless of the level of detail at which you choose to develop your assumptions, it is important to make a written record of them. This documentation will provide a handy reference source to use to investigate variances or to modify your operating plans in the future.

The way in which you document your assumptions is a matter of personal choice. You may simply list them sequentially on a report pad, or you may wish to develop a standard form. Having a form is an advantage because it provides consistency and formality in the way in which the assumptions are written. In addition, it can serve to remind you to document *all* the relevant characteristics of the assumptions. A third benefit of a properly constructed form is that it can save time by allowing you simply to fill in the blanks. Figures 6.1 and 6.2 are sample forms that you may wish to use in completing your assumptions.

At the top right-hand corner of Figure 6.1, "Detailed Assumption Form," you can enter your company, division, department, and product line codes or names. The form has space in which you can indicate who prepared it, who reviewed it, and when those actions took place. As indicated by the check boxes, you can use the form to describe either budget assumptions or changes in manpower. The body of the form has space in which you can list the chart of account number(s) of the item for which the assumption is to be developed, the item description, and the basis of the assumption. If you use the form for an explanation of manpower changes, you can omit the account code or you can use the account code of the item against which the salary or wage of the employee added or removed will be charged or credited.

Assumptions will often have a specific time sequence. For example, sales may be seasonal, the work force may increase or decline with the sales level, or some expenses such as insurance premiums may be a periodic rather than a regular monthly occurrence. The form shown in Figure 6.2 can reflect when items of income or expense will be received or incurred. You can also use it to schedule certain balance sheet items such as when you will acquire fixed assets, when you will pay major bills, or when you will receive financing. You can also use this form to develop detailed assumptions about staffing levels.

For the purpose of this chapter, Peter has employed a mechanized financial planning system available to him through a timesharing network. As a result, many of his detailed assumptions are stored in the system and printed out as schedules to support his financial statement forecasts. The use of such a system, although more expensive initially than manual calculations (although this point is debatable), is far more efficient in the long run because a change in assumption requires only a single change to the system. The system will then generate all the revised reports and underlying schedules automatically. Therefore, if Peter uses the system as a management tool, as is suggested in Chapter 8, he can save a great deal of manual effort in the future. Furthermore, with the system in place, all future planning will require a minimum amount of manual effort.

In sum, it is important to document your planning assumptions. Whether you use these forms, others you design personally, or none at all, do not fail to *keep a record of the items you considered as you developed your plan*.

LUCKY FUEL OIL'S ASSUMPTIONS

O'Henry decided that he would develop his assumptions at a very detailed level. In part, he wished to do this because he wanted his plan to be as accurate as possible (although he realized that no one can predict the future with certainty). In addition, he wanted to be able to determine how sensitive his business would be to some of these assumptions once he

FIGURE 6.1
Detailed assumption form.

DETAILED ASSUMPTION FORM

Prepared by ______________________ Date ______________ Company ______________

Reviewed by ______________________ Date ______________ Division ______________

Department ______________

Product Line ______________

☐ Budget Assumptions ☐ Explanation of Manpower Changed

A/C	Description/Position	Explanation

FIGURE 6.2
Manpower budget assumption form.

MANPOWER BUDGET ASSUMPTION FORM

Reviewed by ______________________ Date ______________ Division ______________

Department ______________

Product Line ______________

☐ Head Count
☐ Salary $

Position	Prior Year	Apr	May	June	July	Aug	Sept	Oct	Nov	Dec	Jan	Feb	Mar

had constructed his plan. By developing detailed assumptions, he figured he could change minor components and see what the impact would be on his bottom line. For example, if his assumptions included gallons by product and both selling prices and costs of sales for each product, he could vary his gross margins by product and assess the impact on his after-tax profits (the bottom line). He would also be able to compare his detailed plans by product line to his actual results by product line to pinpoint where he was doing better or worse than he had expected.

One final procedural note: Peter began by developing assumptions about his revenues and expenses (his income statement). With this information, he could then construct a balance sheet forecast. And with forecasts of both sets of statements, he could figure out his cash flow. This last point is discussed in detail in Chapter 7. Now look at Peter's assumptions item by item.

INCOME STATEMENT ASSUMPTIONS

Sales

Peter began the process of developing assumptions by considering his most important financial statement item: *sales*. Because he had good historical information on his sales by product, he decided he would develop his assumptions along detailed product lines, as follows:

- No. 2 home heating oil.
- Kerosene.
- Diesel fuel.
- Gasoline.
- LPG.
- Heavy oil (Nos. 4, 5, 6).
- Burner service sales.
- Appliance sales.

In 19X1, Peter had the following sales by product:

No. 2 home heating oil	3,910,032 gallons
Kerosene	467,380 gallons
Diesel fuel	266,190 gallons
Gasoline	281,346 gallons
LPG	381,894 gallons
Heavy oil (Nos. 4, 5, 6)	3,744,237 gallons
Burner service sales	$291,862
Appliance sales	$40,000

He knew that it would be unlikely to have much natural sales growth. Therefore, as one of his tactical objectives (discussed in Chapter 4) he decided to acquire a small competitor who had a business of 300,000 gallons of gasoline and 400,000 gallons of No. 2 home heating oil. He figured he would retain only about 70% of the home heating oil portion of this business, in part because of normal attrition and in part because he would weed out slow payers. The gasoline sales would probably be retained largely intact. Therefore, he set as his estimates for total sales, including the acquisition:

No. 2 home heating oil	4,178,000 gallons
Gasoline	580,000 gallons

He placed his estimates for kerosene and diesel fuel very close to his actual results for the current year. He figured that his business in kerosene might decline slightly and that his diesel business might pick up. His estimates for the ensuing year were:

Kerosene	464,000 gallons
Diesel	268,800 gallons

Because the number of cabins for rent in his market area had not increased, he figured his LPG sales would be flat:

LPG	380,000 gallons

Because there had not been much commercial development in his market area (the area was already fairly well developed), Peter figured his sales of heavy oil would be about the same in the ensuing year:

Heavy oil (Nos. 4, 5, 6)	3,744,000 gallons

Because of greater interest in conservation, he estimated that his burner service revenues might increase:

Burner service revenues	$325,000

Finally, he figured his appliance sales would be level:

Appliance sales	$37,000

Clearly, these were not a major portion of his business.

Time-Phased Sales

Now that Peter had figured what his product sales might be in total, he decided that it would be helpful to spread them out, month-by-month, over the course of the year because there were great seasonal fluctuations that would have an impact on his need for working capital. He decided to use his historical statistics regarding seasonality. He spread the total sales by product by calculating the ratio of each month's sales during 19X1 by product to his total 19X1 sales for that product and multiplying the resulting ratio by the estimated total sales for the first year of the projection. For example, if he sold 13.6% of his No. 2 home heating oil in December 19X1, he could multiply that ratio (0.136) by 4,178,000 (estimated total gallons) and arrive at his estimate of 568,208 gallons for December 19X2. (As a practical matter and to the extent possible, Peter took into consideration the estimates of whether it would be a severe or a mild winter and whether the spring or fall was to be abnormally hot or cold both when he established his total gallonage and when he allocated it by month.) Peter completed this analysis for each product line. The results are given in Figure 6.3.

Cost of Sales

Once O'Henry had completed his sales analysis, he could slot in the estimated cost of each product. By multiplying number of gallons by cost, he could arrive at cost of sales. (For burner service and appliance sales he simply estimated cost of sales based on historical ratios of costs to sales. The cost of gasoline includes an estimate of state taxes.) This information is included in Figure 6.3 as well.

It is important to recognize that because Peter had developed his sales assumptions by month, he could enter a *different estimate for the unit cost per gallon for each month.* As can be seen in Figure 6.3, this is an important consideration because each month's estimate is different for virtually all of his products because the supply price tends to vary with world supply and demand and because the variations are substantial. If Peter had simply made a broad estimate of sales dollars and cost of sales dollars, *without this detail,* when he compared his actual results to his estimates *it would be difficult for him to pinpoint the cause of any variances.* With the details, he will be able to ascertain whether his gallonage, unit price, unit cost, or seasonal factor estimates differed from actual.

Gross Margin

Peter knew that to generate enough money from his product sales to cover his remaining expenses and generate a profit he had to maintain a constant gross margin (the difference between his selling price and his cost of sales).

FIGURE 6.3

Lucky Fuel Oil Company

Monthly Sales and Cost of Sales Assumptions

	April 19X1	*May 19X1*	*June 19X1*	*July 19X1*	*August 19X1*	*September 19X1*	*October 19X1*	*November 19X1*	*December 19X1*	*January 19X2*	*February 19X2*	*March 19X2*	*12-Month Total*
No. 2 Home Heating Oil													
Gallons sold	325,884	255,612	116,984	100,272	104,450	146,230	284,104	426,156	568,208	689,370	660,124	530,606	4,178,000
Unit cost per gallon	0.82	0.90	0.95	1.00	1.05	1.10	1.15	1.20	1.25	1.30	1.35	1.40	
Average gross margin	0.12	0.12	0.12	0.12	0.12	0.13	0.13	0.13	0.14	0.14	0.14	0.14	
Average selling price	0.94	1.02	1.07	1.12	1.17	1.23	1.28	1.33	1.39	1.44	1.49	1.54	
Gross Sales	$306,331	$230,173	$125,124	$112,305	$122,206	$179,863	$363,653	$566,787	$789,809	$992,693	$983,585	$817,133	$5,589,663
Cost of Sales	267,225	203,051	111,135	100,272	109,672	160,853	326,720	511,387	710,260	896,181	891,167	742,848	5,030,772
Gross Margin	39,106	$ 27,073	$ 14,038	$ 12,033	$ 12,534	$ 19,010	$ 36,934	$ 55,400	$ 79,549	$ 96,512	$ 92,417	$ 74,285	$ 558,891
Kerosene													
Gallons sold	33,872	22,272	8,352	4,176	4,176	15,312	30,624	38,976	71,456	91,872	81,664	61,248	464,000
Unit cost per gallon	0.92	1.00	1.05	1.10	1.15	1.20	1.25	1.30	1.35	1.40	1.45	1.50	
Average gross margin	0.14	0.14	0.14	0.14	0.14	0.15	0.15	0.15	0.15	0.15	0.15	0.15	
Average selling price	1.06	1.14	1.19	1.24	1.29	1.35	1.40	1.45	1.50	1.55	1.60	1.65	
Gross Sales	$ 35,904	$ 25,390	$ 9,939	$ 5,178	$ 5,387	$ 20,671	$ 42,874	$ 56,515	$107,184	$142,402	$130,662	$101,059	$ 683,166
Cost of Sales	31,162	22,272	8,770	4,594	4,802	18,374	38,280	50,669	96,466	128,621	118,413	91,872	614,294
Gross Margin	$ 4,742	$ 3,118	$ 1,169	$ 585	$ 585	$ 2,297	$ 4,594	$ 5,846	$ 10,718	$ 13,781	$ 12,250	$ 9,187	$ 68,872
Diesel Fuel													
Gallons sold	12,000	24,000	24,000	28,000	28,000	24,000	20,000	28,000	16,000	20,000	16,000	28,000	268,000
Unit cost per gallon	0.85	0.93	0.97	1.03	1.07	1.13	1.18	1.23	1.28	1.33	1.37	1.43	
Average gross margin	0.07	0.07	0.07	0.07	0.07	0.07	0.07	0.07	0.07	0.07	0.07	0.07	
Average selling price	0.92	1.00	1.04	1.10	1.14	1.20	1.25	1.30	1.35	1.40	1.44	1.50	
Gross Sales	$ 10,980	$ 23,880	$ 25,080	$ 30,660	$ 32,060	$ 28,680	$ 24,900	$ 36,260	$ 21,520	$ 27,900	$ 23,120	$ 41,860	$ 326,900
Cost of Sales	10,140	22,200	23,400	28,700	30,100	27,000	23,500	34,300	20,400	26,500	22,000	39,900	308,140
Gross Margin	$ 840	$ 1,680	$ 1,680	$ 1,960	$ 1,960	$ 1,680	$ 1,400	$ 1,960	$ 1,120	$ 1,400	$ 1,120	$ 1,960	$ 18,760

FIGURE 6.3 (Con't)

	April 19X1	May 19X1	June 19X1	July 19X1	August 19X1	September 19X1	October 19X1	November 19X1	December 19X1	January 19X2	February 19X2	March 19X2	12-Month Total
Heavy Oil													
Gallons sold	269,568	217,152	123,552	67,392	119,808	164,736	321,984	374,400	535,392	569,088	539,136	441,792	3,744,000
Unit cost per gallon	0.55	0.56	0.57	0.58	0.59	0.60	0.61	0.62	0.63	0.64	0.64	0.64	
Average gross margin	0.03	0.03	0.03	0.03	0.03	0.03	0.03	0.03	0.03	0.03	0.03	0.03	
Average selling price	0.58	0.59	0.60	0.61	0.62	0.63	0.64	0.65	0.66	0.67	0.67	0.67	
Gross Sales	$156,349	$128,120	$ 74,131	$ 41,109	$ 74,281	$103,784	$206,070	$243,360	$353,359	$381,289	$361,221	$296,001	$2,419,073
Cost of Sales	148,262	121,605	70,425	39,087	70,687	98,842	196,410	232,128	337,297	364,216	345,047	282,747	2,306,753
Gross Margin	$ 8,087	$ 6,515	$ 3,707	$ 2,022	$ 3,594	$ 4,942	$ 9,660	$ 11,232	$ 16,062	$ 17,073	$ 16,174	$ 13,254	$ 112,320
Gasoline (Commercial)													
Gallons sold	36,540	33,640	53,360	48,140	65,540	48,140	48,140	38,860	60,320	41,180	45,820	60,320	580,000
Unit cost per gallon	1.06	1.10	1.15	1.20	1.25	1.30	1.35	1.35	1.40	1.45	1.45	1.50	
State tax	0.13	0.13	0.13	0.13	0.13	0.13	0.13	0.13	0.13	0.13	0.13	0.13	
Average gross margin	0.05	0.06	0.06	0.06	0.06	0.07	0.07	0.07	0.07	0.07	0.07	0.08	
Average selling price	1.11	1.16	1.21	1.26	1.31	1.37	1.42	1.42	1.47	1.52	1.52	1.58	
Gross Sales	$ 40,559	$ 39,022	$ 64,566	$ 60,656	$ 85,857	$ 65,950	$ 68,359	$ 55,181	$ 88,670	$ 62,594	$ 69,646	$ 95,306	$ 796,369
Cost of Goods Sold	38,732	37,004	61,364	57,768	81,925	62,582	64,987	52,461	84,448	59,711	66,439	90,480	757,903
Gross Margin	$ 1,827	$ 2,018	$ 3,202	$ 2,888	$ 3,932	$ 3,370	$ 3,370	$ 2,720	$ 4,222	$ 2,883	$ 3,207	$ 4,826	$ 38,466
LPG													
Gallons sold	26,220	30,780	31,920	40,660	43,700	33,060	28,120	25,080	28,880	30,780	31,920	28,880	380,000
Unit cost per gallon	0.82	0.84	0.87	0.89	0.91	0.92	0.93	0.94	0.95	0.96	0.97	0.98	
Average gross margin	0.33	0.33	0.33	0.33	0.34	0.34	0.34	0.34	0.34	0.35	0.35	0.35	
Average selling price	1.15	1.17	1.20	1.22	1.25	1.26	1.27	1.28	1.29	1.31	1.32	1.33	
Gross Sales	$ 30,153	$ 36,013	$ 38,304	$ 49,605	$ 54,625	$ 41,656	$ 35,712	$ 32,102	$ 37,255	$ 40,322	$ 42,134	$ 38,410	$ 476,291
Cost of Sales	21,500	25,855	27,770	36,187	39,767	30,415	26,152	23,575	27,436	29,549	30,962	28,302	347,470
Gross Margin	$ 8,653	$ 10,158	$ 10,534	$ 13,418	$ 14,858	$ 11,241	$ 9,560	$ 8,527	$ 9,819	$ 10,773	$ 11,172	$ 10,108	$ 128,821
Burner Service													
Burner Service Sales	$ 9,750	$ 26,000	$ 32,500	$ 26,000	$ 22,750	$ 29,250	$ 32,500	$ 29,250	$ 32,500	$ 32,500	$ 32,500	$ 19,500	$ 325,000
Cost of Sales	4,387	11,700	14,625	11,700	10,237	13,162	14,625	13,162	14,625	14,625	14,625	8,775	146,248
Gross Margin	$ 5,363	$ 14,300	$ 17,875	$ 14,300	$ 12,513	$ 16,088	$ 17,875	$ 16,088	$ 17,875	$ 17,875	$ 17,875	$ 10,725	$178,752

FIGURE 6.3 (Con't)

	April 19X1	May 19X1	June 19X1	July 19X1	August 19X1	September 19X1	October 19X1	November 19X1	December 19X1	January 19X2	February 19X2	March 19X2	12-Month Total
Appliance Gross Sales													
Appliance Sales	$ 6,000	$ 1,000	$ 5,000	$ 7,000	$ 4,000	$ 1,000	$ 1,000	$ 5,000	$ 2,000	$ 2,000	$ 1,000	$ 2,000	$ 37,000
Cost of Sales	5,040	840	4,200	5,880	3,360	840	840	4,200	1,680	1,680	840	1,680	31,080
Gross Margin	$ 960	$ 160	$ 800	$ 1,120	$ 640	$ 160	$ 160	$ 800	$ 320	$ 320	$ 160	$ 320	$ 5,920
Summary													
Gross Sales	$596,027	$509,549	$374,693	$332,514	$401,167	$470,855	$775,068	$1,024,456	$1,432,297	$1,681,699	$1,643,869	$1,411,269	$10,653,463
Cost of Sales	526,450	444,527	321,688	284,188	350,551	412,069	691,515	921,883	1,292,612	1,521,083	1,489,494	1,286,605	9,542,665
Gross Margin	$ 69,577	$ 65,022	$ 53,004	$ 48,325	$ 50,616	$ 58,786	$ 83,552	$ 102,574	$ 139,686	$ 160,616	$ 154,375	$ 124,664	$ 1,110,798

In Peter's case, he considered his cost of sales simply his cost of product. In a manufacturing company, cost of sales includes material, labor, and overhead associated with manufacturing a product. In either case, gross margin is the amount left over to cover selling, distribution, general, and administrative expenses and to generate a profit.

In the prior year, Peter's average gross margins by product were as follows:

No. 2 home heating oil	11.7¢/gallon
Kerosene	13.8¢/gallon
Diesel fuel	7.0¢/gallon
Gasoline	5.0¢/gallon
LPG	25.3¢/gallon
Heavy oil (Nos. 4, 5, 6)	3.6¢/gallon
Burner service	50%
Appliance sales	16%

Peter hoped he could increase his margins in some cases. He planned for the following average gross margins:

No. 2 home heating oil	12.6¢/gallon
Kerosene	14.5¢/gallon
Diesel fuel	7.0¢/gallon
Gasoline	6.6¢/gallon
LPG	33.9¢/gallon
Heavy oil (Nos. 4, 5, 6)	3.0¢/gallon
Burner service:	55%
Appliance sales	16%

He knew he would have to phase in these increases over the course of the year, but he wanted them to take effect during the period of his peak sales if possible. He slotted these margins into his assumption schedule, Figure 6.3, and by adding his estimated margins to his cost of sales, he *arrived at his estimated selling prices.*

With this information, Peter could calculate his forecast of sales, cost of sales, and gross margins by product in terms of dollars. A major portion of his forecast was complete.

Remember the following important points about these forecasts.

1. The forecast results are not going to come true unless Peter takes action. He must periodically raise his selling prices as indicated in the figure in order to attain his margins.

2. He has to monitor his actual margins against those planned and make appropriate corrections.
3. He has to be careful that he doesn't price himself out of the market by his attempt to raise his margins. By monitoring his actual gallons sold, he should detect if he is losing customers.

The plans won't come true simply because they have been created. They have to be monitored, and corrective actions must be taken periodically. For example, if Peter's home heating oil customers won't accept $1.54 per gallon, Peter will have to drop his margin on this product and try to make up the difference somewhere else, either by raising his margins on other products still further or by cutting costs so that he doesn't need such high margins. (One other point about margins. It should be clear that it is advantageous to concentrate your sales efforts on those products that have the highest gross margins.)

Compensation and Related Expenditures

Peter decided to calculate his salaries and wages by the following detailed components:

- Drivers' wages.
- Service wages.
- Clerical wages.
- Management salaries.

In addition, he decided to estimate the components of related benefits and expenses. By doing this, he would have the detailed information against which he could compare his actual expenses to highlight major variances or areas in need of management control. In addition, he would be able to explore changes to these detailed assumptions on a prospective basis to determine what the impact of changes might be. His detailed assumptions are as follows:

Drivers' wages. Peter planned to employ four drivers during the spring and summer months (April through September) when business is slow. He planned to increase the number to seven drivers from October to March. He currently pays his drivers $7.00 an hour and has just negotiated a two-year contract with the drivers' union for a pay increase to $8.20 an hour starting in December. Peter expects to incur overtime in August in order to fill his customers' tanks before fall, in January and February when it is particularly cold, and in March in order to fill the tanks before summer. According to his contract, Peter pays time and a half for hours in excess of 40 per week. He planned to give his seven drivers a bonus of $500 each in February, once the season was almost over. This was not part of his contract, and Peter planned to wait to see how the season would turn out before committing to the bonus. He had managed to pay the bonus in the past and believed it created goodwill with the drivers and that as a result they were more apt to be diligent in their work.

He used the previous year's actual drivers' *hours* to estimate his wages for the ensuing year:

Month	Number of Drivers	Estimated Hours/Person Regular	Overtime	Rate/Hour	+	Overtime and Bonus	=	Total Wages[a]
April	4	176		$7.00				$ 4,920
May	4	168		7.00				4,731
June	4	176		7.00				4,911
July	4	155		7.00				4,352
August	4	169	37	7.00		+$1,554	=	6,277
September	4	165		7.00				4,625
October	7	160		7.00				7,840
November	7	170		7.00				8,322
December	7	180		8.20				10,369
January	7	159	44	8.20		+$3,788	=	12,934
February	7	160	62	8.20		+$8,888	=	18,045
March	7	176	22	8.20		+$1,894	=	11,980
								$99,307

[a]May not foot due to rounding of the hours.

Service wages. Because they are more highly skilled than the drivers, Peter pays his servicemen $9.30 an hour. Although they are unionized, their contract has just been settled and extended for two years. As with the drivers, Peter pays his servicemen time and a half for overtime (over 40 hours per week). He planned to pay the servicemen a $500 bonus in March if the year turned out well and he could afford the money. Peter retains six servicemen year round. In the summer, they work a bit less than normal and in the winter a bit more. In August, they work quite hard in order to clean and service customers' burners in preparation for the fall and winter. Peter used the hours worked in the previous year to estimate service wages.

Clerical wages. Peter employs four individuals—a secretary, a bookkeeper and her assistant, and a credit clerk—to run the office, to operate the computer, to prepare bills, to collect cash, to post the books, and to generate management reports. These individuals have been with the company anywhere from 2 to 10 years. He currently pays $4.15 an hour on the average to these four individuals and planned to increase these wages to an average of

Month	Number of Servicemen	Estimated Hours/Person Regular	Overtime	Rate/Hour	+	Overtime and Bonus	=	Total Wages[a]
April	6	131		$9.30				$ 7,345
May	6	131		9.30				7,313
June	6	140		9.30				7,813
July	6	142		9.30				7,955
August	6	167	35	9.30		+$2,930	=	12,272
September	6	154		9.30				8,607
October	6	161		9.30				9,005
November	6	158		9.30				8,859
December	6	173		9.30				9,681
January	6	165		9.30				9,207
February	6	176		9.30				9,872
March	6	175	11	9.30		+$3,920	=	13,711
								$111,640

[a]May not foot due to rounding of the hours.

$4.50 an hour in October. Generally, the clerical force works a 37½-hour week but incurs some overtime in August to bill for service calls and again in February to clean up outstanding bills at the end of the heating season. Therefore, using the previous year's hours, he calculated clerical wages as follows:

Month	Number of Employees	Estimated Hours/Person	Rate per Hour	Total Wages[a]
April	4	151	$4.15	$ 2,504
May	4	151	4.15	2,504
June	4	151	4.15	2,504
July	4	151	4.15	2,504
August	4	229	4.15	3,798
September	4	150	4.15	2,504
October	4	150	4.50	2,706
November	4	150	4.50	2,706
December	4	150	4.50	2,706
January	4	153	4.50	2,750
February	4	179	4.50	3,214
March	4	150	4.50	2,706
				$33,106

[a]May not foot due to rounding of the hours.

Management salaries. Peter employs two supervisors, one for fuel oil delivery and one for the service operations and office administration. His fuel department manager, Ken Brown, has been with the company 15 years and earns $33,000 a year. The service department manager, Ed Reneau, has been with Peter only eight years and earns a base salary of $25,000. Because he is on call during the heating season to respond to emergency situations and to schedule servicemen, Reneau also earns overtime. At the end of the year in March, Peter planned to review the service operations. If Ed was on budget, Peter planned to pay a $1000 bonus. Peter has one salesman, Andrew Shelton, to whom he pays a base salary of $19,200. Peter planned to raise this salary to a base of $21,600, or $1800 a month, in August. In addition, Peter planned to pay Andrew a commission of 2¢ on every gallon that he could bring into the company. Peter estimated that Andrew would bring approximately 300,000 gallons of fuel oil and gasoline into the company and, consequently, estimated his commissions at $6000. Peter planned to pay these commissions on a periodic basis—$2500 in August, $2500 in February, and the final $1000 in March.

In accordance with his tactical plan, Peter planned to hire a second salesperson at $15,600 a year as a base salary. If by August the salesperson had demonstrated a capacity to sell for the business, Peter planned to raise the salary to a base of $18,000 a year. As with his first salesperson, Peter planned to pay the second one a commission on the basis of 2¢ a gallon and expected the person to generate sales of 200,000 gallons over the course of the year. Therefore, he planned to pay this individual $1500 in commission in August, $1500 in February, and $1000 in March.

Month	*Peter*	*Fuel Department Manager*	*Service Manager*	*Salesperson No. 1*	*Salesperson No. 2*	*Total*
April	$ 3,000	$ 2,750	$ 2,214	$ 1,600	$ 1,300	$ 10,864
May	3,000	2,750	2,214	1,600	1,300	10,864
June	3,000	2,750	2,536	1,600	1,300	11,186
July	3,000	2,750	2,214	1,600	1,300	10,864
August	3,000	2,750	2,446	4,300	3,000	15,496
September	3,000	2,750	2,136	1,800	1,500	11,186
October	3,000	2,750	2,194	1,800	1,500	11,244
November	3,000	2,750	2,194	1,800	1,500	11,244
December	3,000	2,750	2,194	1,800	1,500	11,244
January	3,000	2,750	2,194	1,800	1,500	11,244
February	3,000	2,750	2,446	4,300	3,000	15,496
March	6,000	2,750	3,182	2,800	2,500	17,232
	$39,000	$33,000	$28,164	$26,800	$21,200	$148,164

Payroll taxes. Peter estimated payroll taxes, including state, federal, and federal unemployment taxes, to be 7.9% of his total payroll. He planned to pay these taxes monthly.

Workmen's compensation. Peter planned to pay workmen's compensation quarterly when he was billed. In the past he had found this to be approximately 2.2% of his total payroll.

Related benefits and expenses. Included in this category of expenses are Peter's life insurance and the life insurance plan for his employees, medical insurance for Peter and his employees, and the union pension obligations.

Peter is billed $4100 on an annual basis for his life insurance premium. Group life for his employees is $5280/year, and he pays this monthly ($440 a month).

Peter's own medical insurance amounts to $2040/year, or $170 a month. The contract for his employees was renewed in June. Currently, it is running $847 a month but is expected to go to $961 a month to reflect increased costs of hospitalization.

Peter could determine all the above costs either through invoices he had already received or by contacting his insurance agent directly.

The pension obligation is $510 a month through June and will increase to $550 a month in July.

All the expenses discussed in the foregoing paragraphs are summarized in Figure 6.4.

Operating Expenditures Run Through Accounts Payable

In addition to compensation and related benefits, Peter anticipated a series of monthly expenditures for items that he would purchase on credit (that is, they would flow through accounts payable in one month and then be paid in the next month.) These included the following:

- Auto and truck expenses.
- Gasoline and diesel fuel.
- Repairs and maintenance.
- Supplies.
- Advertising.
- Dues and subscriptions.
- Uniforms and laundry.
- Telephone and utilities.
- Professional fees.

FIGURE 6.4

Lucky Fuel Oil Company

Forecast of Compensation and Related Expenditures

	April 19X1	*May 19X1*	*June 19X1*	*July 19X1*	*August 19X1*	*September 19X1*	*October 19X1*	*November 19X1*	*December 19X1*	*January 19X2*	*February 19X2*	*March 19X2*	*12-Month Total*
Wages, Salaries, and Taxes:													
Drivers' Wages (Union)	$ 4,920	$ 4,731	$ 4,911	$ 4,352	$ 6,277	$ 4,625	$ 7,840	$ 8,322	$10,369	$12,934	$18,045	$11,980	$ 99,307
Service Wages (Union)	7,345	7,313	7,813	7,955	12,272	8,607	9,005	8,859	9,681	9,207	9,872	13,711	111,640
Clerical Wages	2,504	2,504	2,504	2,504	3,798	2,504	2,706	2,706	2,706	2,750	3,214	2,706	33,106
Management Salaries	10,864	10,864	11,186	10,864	15,496	11,186	11,244	11,244	11,244	11,244	15,496	17,232	148,164
Payroll Taxes	2,025	2,008	2,087	2,087	2,990	2,127	2,433	2,459	2,686	2,855	3,684	3,605	30,985
Workmen's Compensation	1,604	—	—	1,604	—	—	1,604	—	—	1,604	—	—	6,416
Related Benefits and Expenses:													
Life Insurance—Officer	—	—	—	—	4,100	—	—	—	—	—	—	—	4,100
Life Insurance—Group	440	440	440	440	440	440	440	440	440	440	440	440	5,280
Medical Insurance—Officer	170	170	170	170	170	170	170	170	170	170	170	170	2,040
Medical Insurance—Group	847	847	961	961	961	961	961	961	961	961	961	961	11,304
Pension Costs	510	510	510	550	550	550	550	550	550	550	550	550	6,480
Total Compensation and Related Expenses	$31,229	$29,387	$30,582	$31,428	$47,054	$31,170	$36,953	$35,711	$38,807	$42,715	$52,433	$51,355	$458,822

Auto and truck expenses. Peter estimated these expenses on the basis of his fiscal 19X0 expenses plus 10%, as an estimate of increased cost of maintenance.

Gasoline and diesel fuel. These he based on fiscal 19X1 plus 20%. (The cost of fuel is greater during September through March when the delivery schedule is the heaviest.)

Repairs and maintenance. Since it was difficult for Peter to anticipate when repairs would be needed, he decided to establish a budget of $9600 spread evenly over the 12 months. This represented a 10% increase in cost over fiscal 19X1. To this he added $4,000 in July to repair the roof and paint his office building and to paint his storage tanks.

Supplies. This was a minor item in Peter's budget. He estimated it to be $3000, or $250/month.

Advertising. Peter planned to increase his advertising eight times over what he had spent in 19X1. His advertising expenditures included sponsoring local community activities and a float in the Memorial Day parade. In addition, he planned a series of energy-saving tips to be broadcast on a local radio station. The intent was to encourage customers to convert to new, more efficient burners. Although this would result in additional reductions in the volume of business due to the increased efficiency of the burners, Peter believed it would result in some goodwill and might attract new customers. He had worked out a $30,000 advertising plan with a local agency and arranged to pay for their services on a monthly basis at $2500 a month.

Dues and subscriptions. These expenses represented dues to the New England Fuel Institute, which supported training courses for O'Henry's service people, provided management education courses, and represented retail fuel oil dealers in Washington. The dues were based on sales and came to $2200, payable quarterly.

Uniforms and laundry. Peter rented uniforms from a laundry and uniform rental service. These costs averaged $550 a month.

Telephone and utilities. These costs were based on the previous year plus 10%.

Professional fees. These costs related to attorney's fees and accountant's fees. Peter expected these fees to be about the same as last year, or $2000 a month. He generally paid his accountant each month to avoid a big payment during his busy season when cash might be tight.

FIGURE 6.5

Lucky Fuel Oil Company

Forecast of Other Accounts Payable–Type Operating Expenditures

	April 19X1	*May 19X1*	*June 19X1*	*July 19X1*	*August 19X1*	*September 19X1*	*October 19X1*	*November 19X1*	*December 19X1*	*January 19X2*	*February 19X2*	*March 19X2*	*12-Month Total*
Auto and Truck	$ 3,950	$ 3,950	$ 3,950	$ 3,950	$ 3,950	$ 3,950	$ 3,950	$ 3,950	$ 3,950	$ 3,950	$ 3,950	$ 3,950	$ 47,400
Gasoline and Diesel Fuel	3,000	3,000	3,000	3,000	3,000	3,200	3,900	6,000	8,900	9,400	9,400	6,700	62,500
Repairs and Maintenance	800	800	800	4,800	800	800	800	800	800	800	800	800	13,600
Supplies	250	250	250	250	250	250	250	250	250	250	250	250	3,000
Advertising	2,500	2,500	2,500	2,500	2,500	2,500	2,500	2,500	2,500	2,500	2,500	2,500	30,000
Dues and Subscriptions	—	—	550	—	—	550	—	—	550	—	—	550	2,200
Uniforms and Laundry	550	550	550	550	550	550	550	550	550	550	550	550	6,600
Telephone and Utilities	1,250	1,250	1,250	1,250	1,250	1,250	1,250	1,250	1,250	1,250	1,250	1,250	15,000
Professional Fees	2,000	2,000	2,000	2,000	2,000	2,000	2,000	2,000	2,000	2,000	2,000	2,000	24,000
Total Purchases	$14,300	$14,300	$14,850	$18,300	$14,300	$15,050	$15,200	$17,300	$20,750	$20,700	$20,700	$18,550	$204,300
Monthly A/P-Type Purchases	$14,300	$14,300	$14,850	$18,300	$14,300	$15,050	$15,200	$17,300	$20,750	$20,700	$20,700	$18,550	$204,300
Monthly A/P-Type Disbursements	$18,211	$14,300	$14,300	$14,850	$18,300	$14,300	$15,050	$15,200	$17,300	$20,750	$20,700	$20,700	$206,161

The costs just discussed are summarized in Figure 6.5. At the bottom of the schedule, Peter assumed that whatever he incurred in accounts payable would be paid (disbursed) in the subsequent month. This would keep his average days/payables at approximately 30 days.

Operating Expenditures Not Run Through Accounts Payable

During the year, Peter incurred several expenses that he did not run through accounts payable. Generally, these expenses were paid upon presentation of the bill or occurred at regular intervals and could be estimated and planned for. They included:

- Contract labor.
- Corporate insurance.
- Licenses and permits.
- Property taxes.
- Postage.
- Rent.
- Contributions.
- Travel and entertainment.

Contract labor. Peter's business was of a size to require data processing to schedule deliveries and to handle his billings. He decided that he would expand his use of data processing to include accounts payable, cash disbursements, general ledger/financial reporting, and business planning. He had negotiated an agreement with a contract programming staff and had asked them for an estimate of their time charges over the year. They expected to be paid monthly to provide themselves with working capital and to receive larger payments on a quarterly basis whenever they were expected to provide major project deliverables.

Corporate insurance. Peter had worked out his insurance needs with his insurance broker and had agreed to pay 30% of the cost in the first two months of the year and to spread the remainder equally over the rest of the year, $2450 a month.

Licenses and permits. Since Peter owned several delivery and service vehicles, his licenses, registrations, motor vehicle taxes, and highway use taxes were substantial. The licenses and registrations were renewed throughout the year on the anniversary of the purchase of the equipment. The highway use tax was paid regularly, and the tax on the motor vehicles was paid in February. Rather than calculate each individual item, Peter estimated the monthly amounts at $400. The annual taxes were easier to calculate, and he estimated these to be $5600.

Property taxes. Peter had storage facilities in two neighboring towns. Each town in which he owned property had a different tax year. As a result, he estimated that his taxes would be paid as follows:

August	$4,000
September	1,500
October	1,000

Postage. This was estimated at $500 monthly.

Rent. Peter leased storage space for his service parts and appliance inventories. This amounted to $400 a month under his old lease and was payable through June. Starting in July, his new lease called for a rental of $425 a month.

Contributions. Peter estimated his contributions at $200 a month. In addition, he planned to sponsor a Little League and a soccer team for which he would provide the uniforms. He estimated these to cost $1800, and he would order them in February. Finally, he planned to send $5000 to his alma mater in March for a major capital improvement program they planned to conduct over the winter and for which Peter was a fund-raising team captain.

Travel and entertainment. Peter estimated his travel and entertainment as a standard amount each month. This was easier than trying to anticipate what the actual charges might be and when they might be incurred. Peter belonged to the country club and played golf with his commercial customers from time to time. In addition, he attended industry conventions and incurred the expense of business lunches and other miscellaneous travel. These expenses he estimated to be $1100 a month.

All the foregoing expenses are summarized in Figure 6.6.

Other Expenses

In addition to the items already discussed, Peter incurred certain other expenses; as follows:

- Depreciation.
- Interest.
- Bad debt expense.

Interest expense and *bad debt expense* are discussed later in conjunction with an estimate of Peter's needs for short-term debt and the calculation of his average monthly accounts receivable balance.

FIGURE 6.6
Lucky Fuel Oil Company
Forecast of Non–Accounts Payable Operating Expenditures

	April 19X1	*May 19X1*	*June 19X1*	*July 19X1*	*August 19X1*	*September 19X1*	*October 19X1*	*November 19X1*	*December 19X1*	*January 19X2*	*February 19X2*	*March 19X2*	*12-Month Total*
Contract Labor	$ 5,500	$1,000	$1,400	$ 5,300	$ 1,000	$1,500	$ 5,300	$1,000	$2,000	$ 5,700	$ 1,400	$ 1,500	$ 32,600
Corporate Insurance	5,800	4,900	2,450	2,450	2,450	2,450	2,450	2,450	2,450	2,450	2,450	2,450	35,200
Licenses and Permits	400	400	400	400	400	400	400	400	400	400	6,000	400	10,400
Property Taxes	—	—	—	—	4,000	1,500	1,000	—	—	—	—	—	6,500
Postage	500	500	500	500	500	500	500	500	500	500	500	500	6,000
Rent	400	400	400	425	425	425	425	425	425	425	425	425	5,025
Contributions	200	200	200	500	200	200	200	200	200	200	2,000	5,000	9,300
Travel and Entertainment	1,100	1,100	1,100	1,100	1,100	1,100	1,100	1,100	1,100	1,100	1,100	1,100	13,200
Total Monthly Disbursements	$13,900	$8,500	$6,450	$10,675	$10,075	$8,075	$11,375	$6,075	$7,075	$10,775	$13,875	$11,375	$118,225

For *depreciation expense* related to his building, storage tanks, vehicles, and office equipment, O'Henry used straight-line depreciation. The estimated useful lives were as follows:

Office equipment	10 years
Trucks	7 years
Storage tanks	20 years
Building	30 years

Because O'Henry anticipated buying some additional computer equipment and an additional service truck, an addition to his storage tanks, and possibly an acquisition, he expected his depreciation expense to increase during the year.

Income Tax Expense

Once all other items of income and expense were estimated and combined, the bookkeeper determined net pretax income for the fiscal year. Next, income tax expense was calculated on this pretax amount, using federal and state income tax statutes. Federal taxes were computed as follows:*

	19X1	*19X2*	*19X3 and later years*
1st $25,000 of net income	17%	16%	15%
2nd $25,000	20%	19%	18%
3rd $25,000	30%	30%	30%
4th $25,000	40%	40%	40%

There was a tax of 46% for all net income greater than $100,000.

After the income tax amount for the *year's* estimated earnings was computed, the bookkeeper determined the effective tax rate for the Lucky Fuel Oil Company. The effective tax rate was obtained by dividing income tax expense for the year by total pretax income. In Lucky's case, the effective rate was 29%.

On a monthly basis, pretax operating losses were netted against pretax earnings. When this netting process produces a positive balance, that is, an earnings position, the effective tax rate is applied to the balance to obtain income tax expense for the month. The net pretax earnings shown in Figure 6.14 do not become positive until January, at which time income taxes are reflected in the schedule.

*These figures reflect rates prevailing before the tax legislation of late 1986. The point here, obviously, is that applicable tax rates must be taken into consideration.

BALANCE SHEET ASSUMPTIONS

So far, Peter had developed detailed assumptions for every line item in his income statement. In order to get the most benefit out of his planning process, he decided to create a monthly balance sheet as well. To do this, he had to estimate each line item in his balance sheet.

Cash

Estimating your cash balance is straightforward. You should seek to have very little cash that is not required to be in your checking account by virtue of any compensating balance agreements with your bank. Any excess cash should be used to pay off short-term debt or should be invested on a short-term basis.

In Peter's case, he had to maintain $50,000 in compensating balances according to his loan agreement. He adopted this as his cash balance estimate.

Short-Term Investments

Peter did not contemplate having much extra cash, so he considered that short-term investments would be zero for the year. (In Chapter 8, Peter investigates the cash flow from his business. Only after that analysis could he estimate the timing and extent of any excess cash during the year.)

Accounts Receivable

To estimate his accounts receivable, Peter needed four pieces of information:

1. His opening balance of accounts receivable (the balance at the end of his current fiscal year).
2. His estimated monthly sales to credit customers. (These are additions to his receivable balance and can be obtained from his schedule of estimated sales by product, Figure 6.3.) For simplicity, he assumed that all his sales were made on a credit basis.
3. An estimate of how many sales would prove to be uncollectible (bad debt).
4. An estimate of his monthly collections. (These, of course, reduced his receivable balance.)

Peter could readily obtain the first two items—the first from his year-end financial statements, the second from Figure 6.3.

Peter's historical experience had shown that his uncollectible sales ran 0.5% of sales from April to September when it was warm and decreased to 0.3% during the fall and winter months when customers were fearful of having their deliveries stopped for nonpayment. Peter could also rely on historical experience regarding his collections. This experience showed him the following:

In:		
	30 days	30% of his A/R balance was collected,
	60 days another	40% was collected,
	90 days another	20% was collected,
	120 days another	9% was collected,
	150 days the final	1% was collected.

By applying his estimate of uncollectible receivables against his estimated monthly sales, he arrived at an estimate of total *future collections*. By applying his collection percentages against the estimate of total future collections, he estimated how much would be collected each month. Then he took his opening balance in A/R, added his estimated sales, subtracted his estimated collections, and found his ending A/R balance for the month. This ending balance became the beginning balance for the next month. Figure 6.7 illustrates how Peter estimated his monthly balance in accounts receivable.

Inventories

To estimate his inventory balance at the end of each month, Peter first estimated his gallon sales by product and by month on the basis of his historical experience. Then, for each product, he inserted a desired ending inventory by month. These inventory levels increased during the winter months to reflect greater usage and the need to have reserves should a supply shipment be delayed. Once he had inserted his desired ending inventory in gallons where applicable, he subtracted his opening inventory at the beginning of the month. The difference represented his estimated purchases for the month. He multiplied these by his estimate of his unit cost, which he figured would grow from $0.82 a gallon to $1.40 by the end of March.

He performed this analysis for each type of product and used the results to arrive at Figure 6.8. Since diesel fuel is three parts No. 2 home heating oil and one part kerosene, there is no separate category for diesel fuel. Its components are part of the estimates for No. 2 and kerosene. Also note that for heavy oil, gasoline, and appliances Peter anticipated no inventories.)

Figures 6.8 and 6.9 summarize the dollar values of all opening inventories, product purchases, and costs of goods sold. The result is the estimated total inventory balance at the end of each month for the company as a whole.

FIGURE 6.7

Lucky Fuel Oil Company

Forecast of Receivable Collections and Accounts Receivable Balances

	April 19X1	*May 19X1*	*June 19X1*	*July 19X1*	*August 19X1*	*September 19X1*	*October 19X1*	*November 19X1*	*December 19X1*	*January 19X2*	*February 19X2*	*March 19X2*	*12-Month Total*
Monthly Sales (including tax)	$600,777	$513,922	$381,629	$338,772	$409,687	$477,113	$781,326	$1,029,508	$1,440,139	$1,687,052	$1,649,825	$1,419,111	$10,728,861
Less: Uncollectible (0.005% of sales/0.003% of sales)	3,004	2,570	1,908	1,694	2,048	2,386	2,344	3,089	4,320	5,061	4,949	4,257	37,630
Future Collections	597,773	511,352	379,721	337,078	407,639	474,727	778,982	1,026,419	1,435,819	1,681,991	1,644,876	1,414,854	10,691,231
Schedule of Collections													
First month: 1-30 days (30%)	179,332	153,406	113,916	101,123	122,292	142,418	233,695	307,926	430,746	504,597	493,463	424,456	
Second month: 31-60 days (40%)	343,000	238,109	204,541	151,888	134,831	163,056	189,891	311,593	410,568	574,328	672,796	657,950	
Third month: 61-90 days (20%)	201,916	169,421	119,555	102,270	75,944	67,416	81,528	94,945	155,796	205,284	287,164	336,398	
Fourth month: 91-120 days (9%)	80,320	96,884	75,400	56,030	46,022	34,175	32,337	36,687	42,725	70,108	92,378	129,224	
Fifth month: 121-150 days (1%)	7,500	10,480	12,791	9,000	6,829	6,213	3,877	3,848	4,640	5,060	8,324	10,565	
Total Monthly Collections	812,068	668,300	526,203	420,311	385,918	413,278	541,328	754,999	1,044,475	1,359,377	1,554,125	1,558,593	10,038,975
Projection of Month End Accounts Receivable Balances													
Accounts Receivable—Beginning	960,102	745,807	588,859	442,377	359,144	380,865	442,314	679,968	951,388	1,342,732	1,665,346	1,756,097	960,102
Add: Month's Sales	597,773	511,352	379,721	337,078	407,639	474,727	778,982	1,026,419	1,435,819	1,681,991	1,644,876	1,414,854	10,691,231
Less: Month's Collections	812,068	668,300	526,203	420,311	385,918	413,278	541,328	754,999	1,044,475	1,359,377	1,554,125	1,558,593	10,038,975
Accounts Receivable—Ending	$745,807	$588,859	$442,377	$359,144	$380,865	$442,314	$679,968	$ 951,388	$1,342,732	$1,665,346	$1,756,097	$1,612,358	$ 1,612,358

FIGURE 6.8

Lucky Fuel Oil Company
Monthly Product Purchase Assumptions

	April 19X1	*May 19X1*	*June 19X1*	*July 19X1*	*August 19X1*	*September 19X1*	*October 19X1*	*November 19X1*	*December 19X1*	*January 19X2*	*February 19X2*	*March 19X2*	*12-Month Total*
No. 2 Home Heating Oil a													
+Projected Sales													
(incl. diesel) Gals.	344,884	243,612	134,984	121,272	125,450	164,230	299,104	447,156	580,208	704,370	672,124	551,606	4,379,000
+Desired Ending Inv.	55,000	37,000	43,000	50,000	63,000	62,000	41,000	36,000	77,000	82,000	64,000	73,000	
−Beginning Inv.	73,000	55,000	37,000	43,000	50,000	63,000	62,000	41,000	36,000	77,000	82,000	64,000	
=Purchase for the Month (Gals.)	316,884	255,612	140,984	128,272	138,450	163,230	278,104	442,156	621,208	709,370	654,124	560,606	
Unit Cost	0.82	0.90	0.95	1.00	1.05	1.10	1.15	1.20	1.25	1.30	1.35	1.40	
Dollar Purchases for the Month	$259,845	$203,051	$133,935	$128,272	$145,372	$179,553	$319,820	$530,587	$776,510	$922,181	$883,067	$784,848	$5,267,042
Kerosene													
+Projected Sales													
(incl. diesel) Gals.	36,872	28,272	14,352	11,176	11,176	21,312	35,624	45,976	75,456	96,872	85,664	68,248	531,000
+Desired Ending Inv.	35,000	24,000	24,000	19,000	16,000	18,000	17,000	17,000	22,000	23,000	21,000	11,000	
−Beginning Inv.	11,000	35,000	24,000	24,000	19,000	16,000	18,000	17,000	17,000	22,000	23,000	21,000	
=Purchases for the Month (Gals.)	60,872	17,272	14,352	6,176	8,176	23,312	34,624	45,976	80,456	97,872	83,664	58,248	
Unit Cost	0.92	1.00	1.05	1.10	1.15	1.20	1.25	1.30	1.35	1.40	1.45	1.50	
Dollar Purchases for the Month	$ 56,002	$ 17,272	$ 15,070	$ 6,794	$ 9,402	$ 27,974	$ 43,280	$ 59,769	$108,616	$137,021	$121,313	$ 87,372	$ 689,884
LPG													
+Projected Sales													
(incl. diesel) Gals.	26,220	30,780	31,920	40,660	43,700	33,060	28,120	25,080	28,880	30,780	31,920	28,880	380,000
+Desired Ending Inv.	9,600	4,000	5,600	5,100	11,300	11,900	9,900	9,400	12,400	8,300	12,000	11,100	
−Beginning Inv.	11,000	9,600	4,000	5,600	5,100	11,300	11,900	9,900	9,400	12,400	8,300	12,000	
=Purchases for the Month (Gals.)	24,820	25,180	33,520	40,160	49,900	33,660	26,120	24,580	31,880	26,680	35,620	27,980	
Unit Cost	0.82	0.84	0.87	0.89	0.91	0.92	0.93	0.94	0.95	0.96	0.97	0.98	
Dollar Purchases for the Month	$ 20,352	$ 21,151	$ 29,162	$ 35,742	$ 45,409	$ 30,967	$ 24,292	$ 23,105	$ 30,286	$ 25,613	$ 34,551	$ 27,420	$ 348,052
Heavy (No Inventory)													
Projected Gallons	269,568	217,152	123,552	67,392	119,808	164,736	321,984	374,400	535,392	569,088	539,136	441,792	3,744,000
Unit Cost	0.55	0.56	0.57	0.58	0.59	0.60	0.61	0.62	0.63	0.64	0.64	0.64	
Dollar Purchases for the Month	$148,262	$121,605	$ 70,425	$ 39,087	$ 70,687	$ 98,842	$196,410	$232,128	$337,297	$364,216	$345,047	$282,747	$2,306,753
Gasoline (No Inventory)													
Projected Gallons	36,540	33,640	53,360	48,140	65,540	48,140	48,140	38,860	60,320	41,180	45,820	60,320	580,000
Unit Cost (includes tax)	1.06	1.0	1.15	1.20	1.25	1.30	1.35	1.35	1.40	1.45	1.45	1.50	
Dollar Purchases for the Month	$ 38,732	$ 37,004	$ 61,364	$ 57,768	$ 81,925	$ 62,582	$ 64,989	$ 52,461	$ 84,448	$ 59,711	$ 66,439	$ 90,480	$ 757,903

FIGURE 6.8 (Con't)

	April 19X1	May 19X1	June 19X1	July 19X1	August 19X1	September 19X1	October 19X1	November 19X1	December 19X1	January 19X2	February 19X2	March 19X2	12-Month Total
Burner Service & Installation													
+Projected Cost of Sales	$ 4,307	$ 11,700	$ 14,625	$ 11,700	$ 10,237	$ 13,162	$ 14,625	$ 13,162	$ 14,625	$ 14,625	$ 14,625	$ 8,775	$ 146,250
+Desired Ending Inv.	44,300	51,800	46,800	42,000	40,400	50,500	46,500	51,200	52,800	52,600	49,600	46,500	
−Beginning Inv.	42,200	44,300	51,800	46,800	42,000	40,400	50,500	46,500	51,200	52,800	52,600	49,600	
Dollar Purchases for the Month	$ 6,487	$ 19,200	$ 9,625	$ 6,900	$ 8,637	$ 23,262	$ 10,625	$ 17,862	$ 16,225	$ 14,425	$ 11,625	$ 5,675	$ 150,550
Appliances (No Inventory)													
+Projected Cost of Sales	$ 5,040	$ 840	$ 4,200	$ 5,880	$ 3,360	$ 840	$ 840	$ 4,200	$ 1,680	$ 1,680	$ 840	$ 1,680	$ 31,080

a No. 2 and kerosene projected sales reflect volume necessary to meet projected diesel fuel sale, i.e., 40,000 gallons of diesel fuel sales would require 30,000 gallons of No. 2 and 10,000 gallons of kerosene.

FIGURE 6.9
Lucky Fuel Oil Company
Monthly Inventory Balance Assumptions

	April 19X1	*May 19X1*	*June 19X1*	*July 19X1*	*August 19X1*	*September 19X1*	*October 19X1*	*November 19X1*	*December 19X1*	*January 19X2*	*February 19X2*	*March 19X2*
Inventory—Beginning of Month	$125,204	$133,476	$109,072	$111,164	$107,419	$161,661	$133,613	$ 102,353	$ 100,853	$ 163,033	$ 166,797	$ 140,186
Add: Product Purchases	534,722	420,123	323,780	280,443	364,793	424,021	660,255	920,113	1,355,062	1,524,847	1,462,883	1,280,223
Equals: Goods Available	659,926	553,599	432,852	391,607	472,212	545,682	793,868	1,022,466	1,455,645	1,687,880	1,629,680	1,420,409
Less: Cost of Sales	526,450	444,527	321,688	284,188	350,551	412,069	691,515	921,883	1,292,612	1,521,083	1,489,494	1,286,605
Inventory—End of Month	$133,476	$109,072	$111,164	$107,419	$121,661	$133,613	$102,353	$ 100,583	$ 163,033	$ 166,797	$ 140,186	$ 133,804

Fixed Assets

As mentioned in the earlier discussion of depreciation, Peter planned to acquire some EDP equipment in May, make some improvements to his storage tanks (tank farm) in June, purchase a pickup truck for his service department in August, and use some of his capital for an acquisition in September. These capital additions are summarized in Figure 6.10 and represent increases to fixed assets with corresponding cash outflows in the months indicated.

Accounts Payable—Trade

Peter's calculation of his estimated accounts payable balance began with his calculation of his product payments. Earlier in these discussions, it was indicated that his suppliers had tightened their credit terms. In fact, he was on a ten-day payment schedule for No. 2 oil and kerosene and a 15-day schedule for his other products. To estimate his monthly disbursements for product, he separated his product types into two groups based on their relative payment schedules.

On a ten-day disbursement schedule, at the end of the month roughly a third of the purchases (10 days ÷ 30 days) would be outstanding, which means that two thirds would have been paid. For convenience, Peter rounded these factors to 70% and 30% and applied them to the current month's purchases and the preceding month's purchases. The results are reflected in Figure 6.11. Using May as an example, Peter expected to disburse the remaining 30% of April's purchases ($315,847 × 0.30 = $94,754) and 70% of May's purchases ($220,323 × 0.70 = $154,226) for a total of $248,980.

For the products with 15-day payment terms, roughly half (15 days ÷ 30 days) of the month's purchases would be paid for during the month, and the other half would be paid for in the next month.

Peter added his two sets of anticipated product purchases and product disbursements together (the two sets of totals at the bottom of Figure 6.11). Combining this information with his estimates of other accounts payable–type operating expenditures (from Figure 6.5) and his opening accounts payable balance (plus or minus any other miscellaneous accruals), he compiled an estimate of his ending accounts payable balance for each month (Figure 6.12).

Notes Payable—Bank

In any planning process, the item used to balance the balance sheet in the financial statement forecast is generally short-term debt or notes payable. This is because many businesses require some outside funding, and rather than trying to guess how much will be required, it is often more accurate to

FIGURE 6.10
Lucky Fuel Oil Company
Capital Expenditure Assumptions

	April 19X1	May 19X1	June 19X1	July 19X1	August 19X1	September 19X1	October 19X1	November 19X1	December 19X1	January 19X2	February 19X2	March 19X2	12-Month Total
Capital Expenditures													
Burster Machine		$1,200											$ 1,200
Acquisition—No. 2 Oil						$50,000							50,000
Gasoline			$23,000										23,000
Pickup Truck					$10,000								10,000
		$1,200	$23,000		$10,000	$50,000							$84,200

FIGURE 6.11

Lucky Fuel Oil Company

Monthly Product Expenditure Assumptions

	April 19X1	*May 19X1*	*June 19X1*	*July 19X1*	*August 19X1*	*September 19X1*	*October 19X1*	*November 19X1*	*December 19X1*	*January 19X2*	*February 19X2*	*March 19X2*	*12-Month Total*
Product Purchase													
(15-day terms):													
No. 2	$259,845	$203,051	$133,935	$123,272	$145,372	$179,553	$319,820	$530,587	$ 776,510	$ 922,181	$ 883,067	$ 784,848	$5,267,042
Kerosene	56,002	17,272	15,070	6,794	9,402	27,974	43,280	59,769	108,616	137,021	121,313	87,372	689,884
Total Purchases	315,847	220,323	149,005	135,066	154,775	207,527	353,100	590,356	885,126	1,059,202	1,004,380	872,220	5,956,926
Disbursement Schedule:													
First Month (70%)	221,093	154,226	104,303	94,546	108,342	145,269	254,170	413,249	619,588	741,441	703,066	610,554	4,169,847
Second Month (30%)	273,600	94,754	66,097	44,701	40,520	46,433	62,258	108,930	177,107	265,538	317,761	301,314	1,799,013
Total 10-day disbursements	494,693	248,980	170,400	139,247	148,862	191,702	316,428	522,179	796,695	1,006,979	1,020,827	911,868	5,968,860
Product Purchases													
(21-day average terms):													
LPG	20,352	21,151	29,162	35,742	45,409	30,967	24,292	23,105	30,286	25,613	34,551	27,420	348,052
Heavy oil	148,262	121,605	70,425	39,087	70,687	98,842	196,410	232,128	337,297	364,216	345,047	282,747	2,306,753
Gasoline	38,732	37,004	61,364	57,768	81,925	62,582	64,989	52,461	84,448	59,711	66,439	90,480	757,903
Burner parts	6,487	19,200	9,625	6,900	8,637	23,262	10,625	17,862	16,225	14,425	11,625	5,675	150,550
Appliances	5,040	840	4,200	5,880	3,360	840	840	4,200	1,680	1,680	840	1,680	31,080
Total Purchases	218,875	199,800	174,776	145,378	210,018	216,493	297,156	329,757	469,936	465,645	458,502	408,002	3,594,339
Disbursement Schedule:													
First Month (50%)	109,438	99,900	87,388	72,689	105,009	108,247	148,578	164,878	234,968	232,823	229,251	204,001	1,797,170
Second Month (50%)	90,999	109,438	99,900	87,388	72,689	105,009	108,247	148,578	164,878	234,968	232,823	229,251	1,684,168
Total 15-day disbursements	200,437	209,338	187,288	160,077	177,698	213,256	256,825	313,456	399,846	467,791	462,074	433,252	3,481,338
Total Monthly Product Purchases	534,722	420,123	323,780	280,444	364,793	424,020	660,256	920,113	1,355,062	1,524,847	1,462,882	1,280,222	9,551,265
Total Monthly Product Disbursements	$695,130	$458,318	$357,688	$299,324	$326,560	$404,957	$573,253	$835,635	$1,196,541	$1,474,769	$1,482,900	$1,345,121	$9,450,197

FIGURE 6.12
Lucky Fuel Oil Company
Monthly Forecast of Accounts Payable Balance

	April 19X1	*May 19X1*	*June 19X1*	*July 19X1*	*August 19X1*	*September 19X1*	*October 19X1*	*November 19X1*	*December 19X1*	*January 19X2*	*February 19X2*	*March 19X2*	*12-Month Total*
Accounts Payable—Beginning	$456,416	$296,007	$257,812	$223,905	$205,025	$243,258	$262,321	$349,824	$ 433,801	$ 592,322	$ 642,399	$ 622,381	$4,585,471
Add: Product Purchases	534,722	420,123	323,780	280,444	364,793	424,020	660,256	920,113	1,355,062	1,524,847	1,462,882	1,280,222	9,551,265
Add: Other A/P Purchases	14,300	14,300	14,850	18,300	14,300	15,050	15,200	17,300	20,750	20,700	20,700	18,550	204,300
Less: Product Disbursements	695,130	458,318	357,688	299,324	326,560	404,957	573,253	835,635	1,196,541	1,474,769	1,482,900	1,345,121	9,450,197
Less: Other A/P Disbursements	18,211	14,300	14,000	14,850	18,300	14,300	15,050	15,200	17,300	20,750	20,700	20,700	203,961
Add/Less: Other Misc. Accruals	3,910		(549)	(3,450)	4,000	(750)	350	(2,601)	(3,450)	49	2,151	(340)	
Accounts Payable—End of Month	$296,007	$257,812	$223,905	$205,025	$243,258	$262,321	$349,824	$433,801	$ 592,322	$ 642,399	$ 622,381	$ 557,483	$4,686,538

develop all the assumptions regarding income, expenses, balance sheet items, and cash flow and to determine what will be required to balance the balance sheet. If it turns out that the balancing item should be on the asset side, this signifies that excess cash will be *provided* by the business. The balancing item should be called short-term investments. If the balancing item is on the liability side, it means that the business will need additional funds. In this case, the item should be called short-term debt, or notes payable–bank.

In Chapter 7, the analysis of cash flow from the business is discussed in detail, and the derivation of this balancing number and its position in the financial statement forecast will become clearer.

Accrued Expenses

Accrued expenses includes sales commissions, salaries, and wages that are due but unpaid at the end of the month, and payroll taxes.

Accrued Income Taxes

To estimate the liability for income taxes to be incurred in the projection year, the bookkeeper uses projected income tax expense as calculated in the income statement. The bookkeeper assumes that 80% of the income tax expense of the coming fiscal year will be paid in that year and that the remaining 20% will be paid in the following year. Estimated payments are assumed to take place in the fourth, sixth, ninth, and twelfth months of the fiscal year. To determine the amounts of the payments in months 4, 6, 9, and 12, the bookkeeper annualizes the tax expense amount on the basis of year-to-date operating results and applies the pro rata factor (0.20, 0.40, 0.60, or 0.80) to this amount to obtain intended payments to date. The difference between the intended payments to date and the actual cumulative payments to date represents the amount of the payment to be made.

Unpaid income taxes of the year prior to the projection year are reflected as paid in the fourth month of the projected fiscal year.

Long-Term Debt

Peter's last major set of assumptions related to long-term debt. For each month, Peter subtracted his principal payments from the outstanding principal balance of his existing long-term debt. Then he separated the balance into the current portion, the amount he expected to pay within 12 months, and a long-term portion, the remainder.

Finally, as a way of estimating his interest expense, he multiplied his *monthly* interest factor by the remaining principal balance. These assumptions are summarized in Figure 6.13.

FIGURE 6.13

Lucky Fuel Oil Company

Forecast of Long-Term Debt and Interest

	April 19X1	*May 19X1*	*June 19X1*	*July 19X1*	*August 19X1*	*September 19X1*	*October 19X1*	*November 19X1*	*December 19X1*	*January 19X2*	*February 19X2*	*March 19X2*	*12-Month Total*
Total Long-Term Debt (at Beginning of month)	$487,000	$475,110	$463,220	$451,330	$439,440	$427,550	$455,660	$443,770	$431,880	$419,990	$408,100	$396,210	$487,000
Less: Principal Payments	11,890	11,890	11,890	11,890	11,890	11,890	11,890	11,890	11,890	11,890	11,890	11,890	142,680
Total Long-Term Debt (at end of month)	$475,110	$463,220	$451,330	$439,440	$427,550	$455,660	$443,770	$431,880	$419,990	$408,100	$396,210	$384,320	$384,320
Current Portion	88,200	88,200	88,200	88,200	88,200	88,200	88,200	88,200	88,200	88,200	88,200	88,200	88,200
Long-Term Portion	386,910	375,020	363,130	351,240	339,350	367,460	355,570	343,680	331,790	319,900	308,010	296,120	296,120
Interest on Long-Term Debt	$ 4,276	$ 4,169	$ 4,062	$ 3,955	$ 3,848	$ 4,101	$ 3,994	$ 3,887	$ 3,780	$ 3,673	$ 3,566	$ 3,459	$ 46,769

Net Worth

Peter's net worth consists of his capital account (the amount that he put into the business originally) and his retained earnings. His retained earnings are the accumulation of net income from the business for the years it has been in operation. Figure 6.15 shows that the retained earnings in the balance sheet forecast changes each month by the amount of the net income or loss reflected in the income statement forecast, Figure 6.14.

FINANCIAL STATEMENT FORECASTS

Once Peter had developed all his assumptions, he was able to combine the data into a forecast that took the form of his income statement and his balance sheet—Figures 6.14 and 6.15 respectively.

These statements are referred to as a financial forecast to distinguish them from financial projections. The difference is that a financial forecast (like a weather forecast) is an estimate of *the most likely* occurrence. Projections, on the other hand, are generally considered to be a series of *possible outcomes* rather than the most likely set. Since Peter's intent was to make his assumptions as realistic as possible, he considered his output as a *forecast* and one that *he could adopt as an operating budget.*

Look at the forecast for the Income Statement (Figure 6.14). Notice that the *cumulative* profit (loss) before taxes is a loss for the *first nine months* of the year. Only in January does it turn to a profit. It would not take very much in the way of a decrease in business or failure to control costs or a failure to maintain gross profit margins for the business to wind up with a loss for the year. This is no doubt true for many cyclical or seasonal business. Yet, *this* fact *emphasizes the need for developing an operating plan or budget*. This plan benefited Peter in four ways:

1. It enabled him to anticipate what his operating results were likely to be so that *he could take steps to improve those results while there was time for his actions to have an impact.*
2. By creating a plan like this, *Peter could use the details of the plan to monitor his operations on a month-to-month basis.*
3. *Peter could use the plan to project the impact of changes to his business* by simply factoring those changes into his plan rather than implementing the changes and waiting to see the results.
4. Finally, and perhaps most important, *this plan allowed Peter to sleep better at night because he knew he had some measure of control* over his business.

FIGURE 6.14

Lucky Fuel Oil Company

Income Statement Forecast: April 30, 19X1 through March 31, 19X2

	April 19X1	May 19X1	June 19X1	July 19X1	August 19X1	September 19X1	October 19X1	November 19X1	December 19X1	January 19X2	February 19X2	March 19X2	12-Month Total
Gross Sales	$596,027	$509,549	$374,693	$332,514	$401,167	$470,855	$775,068	$1,024,456	$1,432,297	$1,681,699	$1,643,869	$1,411,269	$10,653,463
Cost of Sales	526,450	444,527	321,688	284,188	350,551	412,069	691,515	921,883	1,292,612	1,521,083	1,489,494	1,286,605	9,542,664
Gross Profit Margin	69,577	65,022	53,004	48,325	50,616	58,786	83,552	102,574	139,686	160,616	154,375	124,664	1,110,799
Operating Expenses:													
Compensation & Related Expenses	31,229	29,387	30,582	31,428	47,054	31,170	36,953	35,711	38,807	42,715	52,433	51,355	458,822
Auto and Truck	3,950	3,950	3,950	3,950	3,950	3,950	3,950	3,950	3,950	3,950	3,950	3,950	47,400
Gasoline and Diesel Fuel	3,000	3,000	3,000	3,000	3,000	3,200	3,900	6,000	8,900	9,400	9,400	6,700	62,500
Repairs and Maintenance	800	800	800	800	800	800	800	800	800	800	800	800	13,600
Supplies	250	250	250	250	250	250	250	250	250	250	250	250	3,000
Advertising	2,500	2,500	2,500	2,500	2,500	2,500	2,500	2,500	2,500	2,500	2,500	2,500	30,000
Dues and Subscriptions	—	—	550	—	—	550	—	—	550	—	—	550	2,200
Uniforms and Laundry	550	550	550	550	550	550	550	550	550	550	550	550	6,600
Telephone and Utilities	1,250	1,250	1,250	1,250	1,250	1,250	1,250	1,250	1,250	1,250	1,250	1,250	15,000
Professional Fees	2,000	2,000	2,000	2,000	2,000	2,000	2,000	2,000	2,000	2,000	2,000	2,000	24,000
Contract Labor	5,500	1,000	1,400	5,300	1,000	1,500	5,300	1,000	2,000	5,700	1,400	1,500	32,600
Corporate Insurance	5,800	4,900	2,450	2,450	2,450	2,450	2,450	2,450	2,450	2,450	2,450	2,450	35,200
Licenses and Permits	400	400	400	400	400	400	400	400	400	400	6,000	400	10,400
Property Taxes	—	—	—	—	4,000	1,500	1,000	—	—	—	—	—	6,500
Postage	500	500	500	500	500	500	500	500	500	500	500	500	6,000
Rent	400	400	400	425	425	425	425	425	425	425	425	425	5,025
Contributions	200	200	200	500	200	200	200	200	200	200	2,000	5,000	9,300
Travel and Entertainment	1,100	1,100	1,100	1,100	1,100	1,100	1,100	1,100	1,100	1,100	1,100	1,100	13,200
Depreciation Expense	6,473	6,483	6,667	6,667	6,747	7,147	7,147	7,147	7,147	8,040	8,040	8,040	85,741
Interest Expense	4,276	6,852	4,483	3,481	3,331	4,025	2,752	7,154	9,845	13,882	17,528	18,241	98,333
Bad Debt Expense	2,634	2,634	2,634	2,634	2,634	2,634	2,534	2,634	2,634	2,634	2,634	2,634	31,608
Total Operating Expenses	72,812	68,156	65,666	73,185	84,141	68,101	76,061	76,021	86,258	98,746	115,210	110,195	997,029
Operating Profit (Loss)	(3,235)	(3,133)	(12,661)	(24,860)	(33,524)	(9,314)	5,008	26,553	53,428	61,870	39,166	14,470	113,768
Income Taxes	—	—	—	—	—	—	—	—	—	17,472	11,380	4,204	33,056
Net Profit After Tax	($ 3,235)	($ 3,133)	($12,661)	($24,860)	($33,524)	($ 9,314)	$ 5,008	$ 26,553	$ 53,428	$ 44,398	$ 27,786	$ 10,266	$ 80,712
Cumulative Net Profit (Loss) Before Tax	($ 3,235)	($ 6,368)	($19,029)	($43,889)	($77,413)	($86,727)	($81,719)	($ 55,166)	$ 1,738	$ 60,132	$ 99,298	$ 113,768	

FIGURE 6.15

Lucky Fuel Oil Company

Balance Sheet Forecast: April 30, 19X1 through March 31, 19X2

	March 19X1	*April 19X1*	*May 19X1*	*June 19X1*	*July 19X1*	*August 19X1*	*September 19X1*	*October 19X1*	*November 19X1*	*December 19X1*	*January 19X2*	*February 19X2*	*March 19X2*
Assets													
Cash	$ 115,411	$ 50,000	$ 50,000	$ 50,000	$ 50,000	$ 50,000	$ 50,000	$ 50,000	$ 50,000	$ 50,000	$ 50,000	$ 50,000	$ 50,000
Savings & C.D.s		—	—	47,370	51,750	7,614	—	—	—	—	—	—	—
Accounts Receivable—gross		787,921	633,479	487,588	406,984	429,556	492,106	731,840	1,003,737	1,395,644	1,718,571	1,809,857	1,666,417
Allowance for doubtful accounts		(42,114)	(44,620)	(45,211)	(47,840)	(48,691)	(49,792)	(51,872)	(52,349)	(52,912)	(53,225)	(53,760)	(54,059)
Accounts Receivable—net	918,803	745,807	588,859	442,377	359,144	380,865	442,314	679,968	951,388	1,342,732	1,665,346	1,756,097	1,612,358
Inventory	125,204	133,476	109,072	111,164	107,419	121,661	133,619	102,353	100,583	163,033	166,797	140,186	133,804
CURRENT ASSETS	1,159,418	929,283	747,931	650,911	568,313	560,140	625,933	832,321	1,101,971	1,555,765	1,882,143	1,946,283	1,796,162
Fixed assets—gross		809,124	810,324	833,324	833,324	843,324	893,324	893,324	893,324	893,324	893,324	893,324	893,324
Accumulated depreciation		330,952	337,435	344,101	350,768	357,514	364,661	371,808	378,954	386,101	394,141	402,181	410,220
Fixed assets—net	484,989	478,172	472,889	489,223	482,556	485,810	528,663	521,516	514,370	507,223	499,183	491,143	483,104
TOTAL ASSETS	$1,644,407	$1,407,455	$1,220,820	$1,140,134	$1,050,869	$1,045,950	$1,154,596	$1,353,838	$1,616,341	$2,062,989	$2,381,326	$2,437,426	$2,279,266
Liabilities and Net Worth													
Notes payable—bank	$ 226,000	$ 157,831	$ 24,791	$ —	$ —	$ —	$ 73,049	$ 192,170	$ 356,740	$ 600,538	$ 821,307	$ 869,545	$ 798,227
Current Maturity: L.T. Debt.	88,200	88,200	38,200	88,220	88,200	88,200	88,200	88,200	88,200	88,200	88,200	88,200	88,200
Accounts payable—trade	456,416	296,007	257,813	223,905	205,025	243,258	262,321	349,324	433,801	592,322	642,399	622,381	557,483
Accounts payable—other	8,242	8,242	8,242	8,242	8,242	8,242	8,242	8,242	8,242	8,242	8,242	8,242	8,242
Accrued expenses		15,436	15,059	17,623	13,513	15,775	13,513	13,513	12,307	15,097	12,608	13,212	15,097
Accrued income taxes	38,211	29,525	29,525	29,525	—	—	—	—	—	—	18,358	30,048	6,936
CURRENT LIABILITIES	817,069	595,242	423,630	367,495	314,980	355,475	445,325	651,449	899,290	1,304,399	1,590,228	1,630,432	1,473,896
Long-term debt	398,800	386,910	375,020	363,130	351,240	339,350	367,460	355,570	343,680	331,790	319,900	308,010	296,120
TOTAL LIABILITIES	1,215,869	982,152	798,650	730,625	66,220	694,825	812,785	1,007,019	1,242,970	1,636,189	1,910,128	1,938,442	1,770,016
Capital stock	50,620	50,620	50,620	50,620	50,620	50,620	50,620	50,620	50,620	50,620	50,620	50,620	50,620
Retained earnings	377,918	374,683	371,550	358,889	334,029	300,505	291,191	296,199	322,752	376,180	420,578	448,364	458,630
TOTAL NET WORTH	428,538	425,303	422,170	409,509	384,649	351,125	341,811	346,819	373,372	426,800	471,198	498,984	509,250
TOTAL LIABILITIES & NET WORTH	$1,644,407	$1,407,455	$1,220,820	$1,140,134	$1,050,869	$1,045,950	$1,154,596	$1,353,838	$1,616,341	$2,062,989	$2,381,326	$2,437,426	$2,279,266
NET WORKING CAPITAL	$ 342,349	$ 334,041	$ 324,301	$ 283,416	$ 253,333	$ 204,665	$ 180,608	$ 180,872	$ 202,681	$ 251,366	$ 291,915	$ 315,851	$ 322,266

ENHANCEMENTS TO THE FORECASTS

Although financial statement forecasts are satisfactory for control of the business at the top level, it would be beneficial to develop forecasts of operating results for each division similar to the statements of actual results discussed in Chapter 3 and shown in Figures 3.5 to 3.8. In this way, management control could be extended to the individual divisions as well as to the company as a whole.

CONCLUSION

This chapter has explained and illustrated the process of identifying and documenting the key assumptions that support the development of a financial forecast or a set of financial projections. The illustrations have purposely been presented in some detail, both to demonstrate the methodology of developing assumptions and to reinforce the value of an in-depth analysis of your business. Developing your plans at this level of detail should increase your knowledge of your business and provide you with useful data to monitor and control actual results. *The process of developing an operating plan or budget is as important as the result.*

The next chapters discuss the extension of this analysis to determine the *cash flow* from the business and the use of the plan to perform *sensitivity analyses* to test management assumptions.

7

Cash Flow Forecast

In the preceding chapter, detailed assumptions were developed to form the basis for a financial forecast of operating results and a month-by-month balance sheet forecast for Lucky Fuel Oil. The forecast of operating results indicated a nine-month period of operating losses and a three-month period of operating profits. This chapter draws a distinction between cash flow and operating results and determines the amount of the cash flow from operations. Both the financial statement forecasts developed in Chapter 6 and the cash flow forecast developed in this chapter are an integral part of the operating plans of a company and should be included in your business plan.

THE DIFFERENCE BETWEEN INCOME AND CASH FLOW

Anyone who has been in business for more than a month rapidly comes to know the difference between income and cash flow. The discussions in Chapter 6 point to many of those differences. Because of current accrual accounting practices, net income differs from cash flow most often as a result of the following:

- Sales for credit (accounts receivable).
- Purchases for credit (accounts payable).
- Accrued income or expense (earned or incurred but not paid).
- Prepaid income or expense (paid but not earned or incurred).
- Payments on debt principal (reflected as a reduction of the debt liability and not as an expense).
- Capital expenditures (reflected as additions to fixed assets and not as expenses).
- Dividends (reflected as a reduction of owner's equity or net worth and not as an expense).
- Taxes—state and federal (incurred with every transaction but generally paid only quarterly).
- Depreciation and amortization (noncash expenses).

In essence, net income and cash flow differ due to: (1) the difference between the *timing* of receipts and payments by customers or by the business and when the transactions relating to those receipts and payments are reflected as income or expense in the financial statements; (2) the fact that some cash expenditures are not reflected as *expenses* in the financial statements; or (3) because some items reflected as expenses in the financial statements are not *current* cash expenditures.

Whatever the reasons for these differences, the fact remains that they exist. Even if the financial forecast of a business indicates that the business will show a *profit*, this does not rule out the possibility that the business will run into a *cash flow problem* and be unable to meet current obligations as they come due. One way to spot a potential cash flow problem is through the analysis of liquidity ratios (the current ratio or quick ratio) and the analysis of the leverage ratio by comparing cash to current maturities of long-term debt. Both sets of ratios were discussed in Chapter 3 and illustrated in Figure 3.11. Better management of financial resources with a view toward increasing cash flow is also the basis for Part III, "Managing Your Financial Resources."

DEVELOPMENT OF A CASH FLOW FORECAST

There are two ways to develop a cash flow forecast. One way is to estimate cash receipts from sales; cash payments for payroll, purchases of materials, and other operating expenses; and cash payments on debt principal, capital expenditures, and short-term borrowings. These were calculated in Figures

FIGURE 7.1
Lucky Fuel Oil Company
Cash Flow Forecast: April 30, 19X1 through March 31, 19X2

Sources of Cash	*April 19X1*	*May 19X1*	*June 19X1*	*July 19X1*	*August 19X1*	*September 19X1*	*October 19X1*	*November 19X1*	*December 19X1*	*January 19X2*	*February 19X2*	*March 19X2*
Net Income	($ 3,235)	($ 3,133)	($ 12,661)	($ 24,860)	($ 33,524)	($ 9,314)	$ 5,008	$ 26,553	$ 53,428	$ 44,398	$ 27,786	$ 10,266
Depreciation	6,473	6,483	6,666	6,667	6,746	7,147	7,147	7,146	7,147	8,040	8,040	8,039
Increase in Liabilities												
Accounts Payable Trade					38,233	19,063	87,003	84,477	158,521	50,077		
Accrued Income Taxes	6,750									17,472	11,380	
Accrued Expenses			2,564		2,262				2,790		604	1,885
Long-Term Debt						28,110						
Decrease in Assets:												
Cash	65,411											
Accounts Receivable	171,768	154,442	145,891	80,604								143,440
Allowance for Doubtful Accounts	1,228	2,506	591	2,629	851	1,101	2,080	477	563	313	535	299
Inventory		24,404		3,745			31,266	1,770			26,611	6,382
Fixed Assets (net of change in depreciation)	344											
Total Sources	248,939	184,702	143,051	68,785	14,568	46,107	132,504	120,423	222,449	120,300	74,956	170,311
Increase in Assets:												
Accounts Receivable					22,572	62,550	239,734	271,897	391,907	322,927	91,286	
Inventory	8,272		2,092		14,242	11,958			62,450	3,764		
Fixed Assets		1,200	23,000		10,000	50,000						
Decrease in Liabilities:												
Accounts Payable Trade	160,409	38,194	33,908	18,880							20,018	64,898
Accrued Income Taxes				29,525								22,205
Accrued Expenses		337		679		2,262		1,206		2,489		
Long-Term Debt	11,890	11,890	11,890	11,890	11,890		11,890	11,890	11,890	11,890	11,890	11,890
Total Uses	180,571	51,661	70,890	64,405	58,704	126,770	251,624	284,993	446,247	341,070	123,194	98,993
New Cash Flow	$ 68,168	$133,041	$ 72,161	$ 4,380	($ 44,136)	($ 80,633)	($119,120)	($164,570)	($243,798)	($220,770)	($ 48,238)	$ 71,318
Cumulative Cash Flow	$ 68,168	$201,209	$273,370	$277,750	$233,614	$152,951	$ 33,831	($130,739)	($374,537)	($595,307)	($643,545)	($572,227)
Beginning Balance Short-Term Debt (March 31,1981)	(226,000)											
Cumulative Short-Term Debt	($157,832)	($ 24,791)				($ 73,049)	($192,164)	($356,739)	($600,537)	($821,307)	($869,545)	($798,227)
Cumulative Short-Term Investments			$ 47,370	$ 51,750	$ 7,614							

6.4 through 6.8 and Figures 6.10, 6.11, and 6.13. If these inflows and outflows are added and subtracted, the difference is net cash flow.

Another way to approach the calculation of cash flow uses the forecast of financial operations and the balance sheet forecast produced at the end of Chapter 6 (Figures 6.14 and 6.15). In Figure 7.1, the cash flow for Lucky Fuel Oil is calculated beginning with *net income* (always a source of cash) and adding and subtracting items that represent additional *sources* or *uses* of cash.

Traditionally, the first items added to net income are *depreciation, amortization,* and other *noncash charges.* Since these are expenses (items subtracted from net sales to arrive at net income) that *do not* require a current cash expenditure, they are considered a *source* of cash.

The next source of cash is any *increase in liabilities.* Since a liability is a promise to pay in the future, any increase in liabilities serves to conserve or save cash by substituting a promise to pay for the payment itself. Hence, an increase in accounts payable, accrued expenses, and short- or long-term debt is a source of cash for use in the business. By the same token, *a decrease in an asset* of the business is a source of cash. Since a reduction in accounts receivable is generally a result of customers paying their bills, it is a source of cash. Likewise, a reduction in inventory or even fixed assets generally results from the sale of these items and, therefore, is a source of cash.

It is more difficult to understand how a reduction in the company's *cash* balance can be a *source* of cash. Keep in mind that a source of cash means a source of cash *used* in the *business*. If you remove money from a savings account to pay some bills, that *reduction in your cash balance* is a *source of cash* for your current operations. Similarly, if you put some money into savings, you have removed it from current operations; hence it is a *use* of cash. In sum, sources of cash are the following:

- Net income from operations.
- Noncash charges.
- Decreases in assets.
- Increases in liabilities.

Uses of cash are simply the opposite of sources of cash. They derive from the following:

- All losses from operations.
- Increases in assets.
- Decreases in liabilities.

If your accounts receivable balance increases, this means that fewer customers have actually paid for their purchases and you have had to use your own cash to extend them credit. If inventories and fixed assets increase, you have *used* your cash to acquire other assets.

If your balance in accounts payable, accrued expenses, short- or long-term debt *decreases*, you have *used* your cash to pay off your creditors.

The difference between your sources and uses of cash is going to be either positive (a net source of cash) or negative (a net use of cash). If your business results in a net source of cash in any month, you should be able to put the extra cash into short-term investments. If your business is a net user of cash, you will have to borrow that money either short-term or long-term from a bank, finance company, friends and relatives, or the public.

Figure 7.1 has been constructed in the manner just described. Net income or loss for each month has been entered, and noncash charges have been added. Increases in liabilities and decreases in assets have been added to arrive at total sources. Increases in assets and decreases in liabilities have been combined to arrive at total uses. The difference between total sources and total uses is net cash flow; it may be positive or negative. The figure shows that Lucky Fuel Oil has positive cash flow from April through July, because accounts receivable from the previous heating season are collected during that period. Receivables begin to build in August and extend through February when the cycle begins to reverse itself. Note that the *cumulative* cash flow is positive through October.

At the bottom of the schedule, the balance of short-term debt at March 31, 19X1 has been appended. It has been decreased by net positive cash flow under the theory that it would be wise to reduce debt and its associated interest expense if the business has excess cash.

During June, July, and August, the business has generated enough cash to totally pay off short-term debt and still provide an excess. That excess is invested by O'Henry in short-term investments. In September, the business has a net negative cash flow, and he must return to the bank for funds. His short-term debt needs reach $869,545 in February, a staggering amount for a business with only $10 million in forecast sales.

By extending his cash flow forecast for another year, Peter fully expects and can demonstrate that he should be able to pay off this loan by June or July of 19X2. This is by no means a certainty, and Peter must be careful to monitor his actual results versus his assumptions and to assess the impact of changes in those assumptions on a current basis to assure that the forecast results can be achieved. His current tactical plans to stimulate sales and to monitor receivables should help him to achieve his forecast results. If not, he may have to take a different set of steps to improve his results or reduce his operating expenses. As a practical matter, Peter can test different tactics using his forecasts to simply change the assumptions, performing the calculations and reviewing the results.

This process, referred to as *sensitivity analysis*, is discussed in greater length in the next chapter.

This schedule, which is the culmination of the operational planning process, demonstrates the value of and the real need for planning, especially in this industry. Because the industry is volatile, it is unlikely that Peter would have guessed his financing needs accurately as he began the year. If he did not, he would have had to spend valuable time, which could be better spent managing his business, trying to secure the funds he needed to finance his operations.

The final and perhaps the most compelling argument for the development of a business plan is the fact that it is unlikely in this example that a bank would loan Peter $869,545 without a formal document to demonstrate both the *need for the money* and *how he would pay it back.*

COST OF THE "CREDIT GAP"

To put the picture a bit more in perspective, Figure 7.2 calculates the cost of what is referred to as the "credit gap," that is, the net interest cost on the difference between cumulative short-term borrowings and short-term cash investments. The outstanding amounts at the end of each month are multiplied by an estimated prime rate, factored for the length of time the balance is likely to be outstanding. Although it is true that short-term investments may not be invested at the prime rate and that the balance at the end of a month is not necessarily representative of the amount that was outstanding during the month, the calculation represents a close approximation.

The point is that Peter is spending nearly as much as his business earns each year on interest expense. If he could find ways to increase his cash flow, it would serve to reduce this major expense of the business.

PLANNING IN A SERVICE BUSINESS

The planning problems that a service business owner faces sometimes appear to be completely different from those in merchandising or manufacturing. Some are, in fact, different, while others are essentially the same.

Problems that all kinds of businesses encounter are, for example, financing work in process and coping with seasonal workloads. In merchandising or manufacturing, work in progress entails buying equipment, keeping inventories, and waiting for receivables. In the service industry, it means making payroll and awaiting receivables. Similarly, seasonal work can spell layoffs in a smokestack business, but, in a service firm, how do you lay off highly skilled or professional employees (such as draft engineers or accountants)?

FIGURE 7.2
Cost of the Credit Gap

	Short-Term Debt	Short-Term Investments	Number of Days in Month ÷ 365	Estimated Prime Rate	Interest Expense (Income)
April	$157,832		8.22%	9.50	$ 1,235
May	24,791		8.49%	9.50	200
June		$47,370	8.28%	9.00	(353)
July		51,750	8.49%	9.75	(428)
August		7,614	8.49%	10.00	(65)
September	73,049		8.22%	10.50	631
October	192,169		8.49%	10.75	1,754
November	356,739		8.22%	10.75	3,152
December	600,537		8.49%	11.00	5,608
January	821,307		8.49%	11.50	8,019
February	869,545		7.67%	11.75	7,837
March	798,227		8.49%	12.00	8,132
Total Cost of Financing the Credit Gap					$35,722

The service industry, however, does own a unique set of problems, particularly:

- Dealing with payroll's relentless drain on cash.
- Setting profitable billing rates.
- For the professional in private practice, remaining current.
- Maintaining the same high level of service while the company grows.

Making Payroll

At least twice a month, the payroll must be paid, but too often clients do not pay until the job is finished. For example, most lawyers take damage suits while basing their fees on a percentage of the award. Court calendars, not to mention the Courts of Appeal, are so backed up that it is often years before the client sees any money at all. The staff, both clerical and professional, must be paid during this period, not to mention the mortgage on the summer home of the senior partner of the firm. Again, the solution is usually to finance this problem with partners' capital—the most expensive money there is—simply because there is no neat schedule of aged receivables, as there is elsewhere in business.

How expensive is partner capital? Since this source of funds participates both in income and future growth, there is no fixed interest rate. However, return on equity figures are available for various industries and they run from 25% to even 100% in such high-risk industries as closely held broker/dealers. Clearly, partners should be the last source of funds.

Setting Billing Rates

Billing rates are the equivalent of selling prices. In either case, there are two questions to answer: First, what do we need to make a profit? Second, what will the market bear?

The service industries have been particularly lax in this area. Often a "magic formula" arises in an industry and everyone lives by it. In the following case study, the billing rates are set at two and a half times the hourly rate of the employee using 2,000 hours per year as the estimated billable hours. This is not typical of a medium-sized accounting firm. However, as we get into the case, it becomes clear that this approach does not work.

Staying Current

Professionals face the special problem of remaining current. For the medical arts, it is new discoveries; for accountants and lawyers, the constantly changing laws, not to mention court opinions; for the engineer, daily improvements in methods and technological advance are the rule. Ensuring that the quality of service is maintained presents a personnel problem not found in other industries.

Maintaining Service

In the small organization, the "I-can-do-it-better" syndrome bogs senior persons down in production rather than making use of them in planning. In the medium-sized organization, the training and retention of good people constitute an often overwhelming burden. Making a good producer a partner is often the only way to retain him or her. This, of course, is a terribly expensive means of maintaining staff. Further, you do not get rich billing your own time. At any billing rate, the real profits in the service field come from billing the time of others. For the large firm, quality control is usually the longest mile, during which supervision often breaks down.

As in any industry, expansion and growth in the service industry requires organizational structure, which is usually dictated by specialization. Corporate law firms are a good example. On staff are specialists in SEC law, state civil law, federal antitrust law, and other areas. Specialization applies also to accounting, medicine, broker/dealers, and the like.

In most service companies, each department head reports to a management committee, which coordinates the various departments and product lines. In the following case study, a new department is established to handle a new specialty. Since the department involves auditing, it is planned to begin as a subdepartment under the audit partner to provide guidance and supervision. The plan is to eventually (in this case, four to five years hence) have an independent department with its own partner in charge.

CASE STUDY

History of the Business

Ten years ago, Bob Gordon and John Hacker combined their individual practices to form the current firm. Both men were managers with Big 8 firms before starting their own practices.

Bob is considered to be an expert in tax planning, and at first most of his business came from this area of expertise. As his practice grew, he received more and more business in the area of small and medium-sized industrial companies needing accounting services, especially in the area of systems development.

While with Big 8, John developed a reputation for installing computerized accounting systems "that worked," as he put it. He had always considered "going Big 8" out of school as a training ground, and after being promoted to manager began to look for a business opportunity.

Bob and John were members of the same Rotary chapter, and with Bob's practice growing beyond his ability to handle the work (both from a time and expertise point of view), the formation of the partnership was a natural.

Currently, there are two junior partners, both hired out of school. One of the junior partners is responsible for all audit work and the other for nonaudit responsibilities. In addition, four others are part of the professional staff, and there are four clerical employees.

The Market

The market for the type of accounting services provided by Gordon & Hacker has been expanding. With the proliferation of government intervention and the ever more complicated tax code, the profession as a whole has enjoyed remarkable growth. For Gordon & Hacker, the growth has been even higher than the industry. Two of their clients, one in the financial services industry, have experienced a period that can best be described as a *breakout*. These clients have been recommending a steady stream of new prospects, and along with the firm's ability to retain old clients, income has steadily been rising.

Four years ago, the state passed a new code with regard to divorces called *equitable distribution*. In divorce, the parties are entitled to an equitable distribution of the assets acquired during marriage. This has been a boon to several medium-sized accounting firms that specialize in business valuation work. These firms have either been hired by one of the parties or appointed by the courts to value the business of a party to a divorce. This value is then used during the division of assets.

Gordon & Hacker has not been involved in this market. At a recent party marking the opening of a new law office in town, Bob met an old friend who had recently been appointed to the bench. The judge mentioned that in the county, only one CPA firm was interested in divorce evaluations. He noted that the firm has been appointed over 700 times in the last four years and was severely backlogged. Recently, he had asked the firm that does his personal tax return if they were interested, and the answer was a flat no. The reason was collection time. The courts were backed up between 12 and 18 months in hearing cases. However, even after fees were awarded, it was often more months of waiting since inevitably both parties had run up large attorney bills as well as large accounting fees.

Bob gave a typical "CPA" answer to the question of whether his firm was interested, "I'll have to study the situation."

Competition

The competition with regard to the existing practice is extensive. Hundreds of small and medium-sized accounting practices in the county serve thousands of small and medium-sized businesses. To date there has been no real price competition. Most competition is based first on contracts and then on quality. Gordon and Hacker have done well, but there is little time to rest on their laurels.

With regard to the proposed new business, there is virtually no competition. However, the reason for this lack of competition may simply be that the business is not profitable.

Location

The firm is located two miles from the county courthouse. More importantly, this county and the four surrounding counties are among the nation's highest net worth counties. Also, the divorce rate in the area is among the nation's highest.

The office is only 22 miles from the state border and the neighboring state has introduced equitable distribution legislation, which is expected to pass. Both Bob and John are licensed in the other state to practice as individuals; so licensing the firm should be no problem.

Management

While Bob and John carry more than 50% of the voting power of the firm, Sarah Gold (junior audit partner) and Bill Welch (junior client services partner) have traditionally participated in firm management meetings.

A meeting was called to discuss the possibilities of entering the divorce evaluation field.

Bill noted that the AICPA's booklets on continuing professional education offered about 40 hours of study on business evaluations. This answered two questions: (1) Should we as professionals be doing this type of work (if national was educating us to do it, the answer must be yes)? (2) Where would we get the expertise to perform such evaluations?

Sarah made the observation that the AICPA was also "pushing" courses on personal financial planning. The pitch was two-pronged: First, who better than the CPA to do financial planning for their clients? Second, financial planning would be a nonseasonal business. She remarked that divorce evaluation work could lead to financial planning work. She had several friends who had received large cash settlements from their husbands as equitable distribution for the value of the husband's business interests. As a result, these women were in real need of financial planning to handle their newly acquired responsibilities. She noted that being involved with the divorce could lead to also doing the post-divorce financial planning, a further expansion of the business.

It was agreed that Bill and Sarah would jointly work up a net income and cash flow forecast for the potential new venture. The following information was obtained prior to preparing the projections:

1. The judge stated that he would probably be able to direct about two cases per month for the first year, assuming, of course, that the court found our work to be competent.

2. Two local attorneys who dealt with the firm's clients were questioned on their needs. Both made the same comment: "The need is there not only to evaluate the business, but to audit the books." In most cases, where they represented a nonworking spouse, their client made all sorts of claims about the misuse of company funds. They both felt that our fees could be justified by disclosing that certain closely held businesses were far more valuable than the books would lead one to believe, because many personal expenses were being put through the books. They felt that, between them, they could send us another 24 cases in the first year with 10% growth after that.

3. We spoke with Sam Gross of the CPA firm of Gross and Gross, the firm that is admittedly the front runner in the business. Sam told us he was "team teaching" a one-day seminar in Philadelphia on the subject

of being examined and cross-examined in court when presenting business evaluations. He stated that anticipating courtroom actions was one of the hardest problems his staff had to overcome. He was pleased to give us some statistics on the work he had done. He noted that on court-appointed cases, the evaluations, including a reasonable review of the books and records, was running about 60 hours on average. On cases directed by attorneys, the average was close to 100 hours per case. He said a lot of that time was "hand holding," that is, chasing false leads where one spouse felt the other was abusing the closely held business. Most of that amounted to nothing, but it took up a lot of time.

He noted that his average collection period was 14 months from the time they started the case to the time of collection. On the court-appointed cases, the ultimate bad debts were running 10%. He stated that some of those cases involved families with very modest assets, and therefore, the parties simply could not afford the fees.

Sarah asked him whether the business had led to any financial planning business. He replied that his firm did not do that sort of work and had decided not to get into it.

4. It was decided that two additional staff would be hired. The first a new college graduate at $20,000 per year, and the second a young CPA with four years audit experience on the staff of a larger firm. His starting salary would be $40,000. Initially he would report to Sarah, but it was hoped that he could be groomed for partner in four to five years. He would be responsible for all phases on the new business, especially expansion of the business as more judges and attorneys heard of the services in the area.

It was further decided that Sarah would concentrate on expanding into the financial planning area. She and one of the staff people would begin taking courses on the subject.

At the next partners' meeting, Sarah and Bill provided the following income and cash flow analysis:

PROJECTED NET INCOME
First Full Year of Divorce Evaluation

Billings:	
Court-appointed, 24 cases @ 60 hours each = 1,440 hours	
720 hours @ $50	$ 36,000
720 hours @ $25	18,000
Attorney-appointed, 24 cases @ 100 hours each = 2,400 hours	
1,200 hours @ $50	60,000
1,200 hours @ $25	30,000
Gross billings	$144,000
Less bad debts, 10% of court-appointed	5,400
Net billings	$138,600

Expenses:		
Nonbillable supervision		
(250 hours @ $75)	$18,750	
Staff salaries	60,000	
Payroll taxes and other benefits	12,000	
Allocated computer expenses	4,000	
Allocated occupancy costs	12,000	
Allocated office support	10,000	116,750
Projected net income		$ 21,850

The billing rates per hour were computed using the firm's traditional formula of 2½ times an hourly rate assuming 2,000 hours of billable time. The billing was divided equally between the anticipated two new employees.

An important component of this projection is to include 250 hours of Sarah's time for unbillable supervision at her regular billing rate. Her regular rate is used since, if she were not supervising this project, she would in fact be billing clients. The project, to be considered financially successful, must be able to cover this cost. Further, including this time disciplines Sarah on the use of her time. She must plan to spend time here and not just squeeze it in. Since, obviously, her time is limited, this may force her to reschedule her regular client load to more junior personnel.

Note also that the senior partners have not budgeted time to the project. This is a sign of healthy expansion. The senior partners should be involved with marketing and planning, not with day-to-day operations, if the firm is to grow.

Since it is anticipated that fourteen months will pass before collections will begin, the $136,208 ($116,750 × 14/12) will be required to support the start-up of the department. Further, one month's salary and benefits will be needed for the new staff to take courses and get organized—an additional $6,000.

To be on the safe side, Sarah and Bill recommended that $150,000 of funds be earmarked to start.

"Wonderful!" exclaimed Bob. No wonder there is no competition. Using 12% (the current rate at the bank for short-term financing), the future value of $150,000 fourteen months from now is $172,400. The projected return of $21,850 on the $172,400 investment would only be 13%.

Bob noted that the firm could easily borrow $172,400 from the bank. That amount would be needed so interest payments could be made monthly during start-up. However, a return of 25% before interest expense was the rock bottom return he would require before approving the project.

Sarah and Bill went back to the drawing board. A 25% return on $172,400 would require a bottom line of $43,100. Sarah noted that there was little room to move on billable time. Generally the firm expected each staff member to bill 1,880 hours annually (47 weeks at 40 hours per week), leaving five weeks for vacation, sick leave, holidays, and continuing education. Already the plan called for 3,840 hours billable from two people resulting in 80 hours planned overtime.

The only answer had to be billing rates. The amount of additional income needed to meet the goal of 25% return was $21,250 ($43,100 – $21,850). For 3,840 billable hours this would mean $5.53. Since the firm did not bill in cents, an increase of $6 per hour to $56 and $31 per hour would be required. The extra "pennies" should also cover the problem of bad debts on court-appointed work.

The next question was would the market bear these rates? This was easily addressed. The average court-appointed bill would be $2,610 (30 hours @ $56 and 30 hours @ $31). Bill called the judge's clerk and asked if an average bill of $2,610 was in the ballpark with the other firms the court was using? The response, "That's more than reasonable" struck the right chord.

The two attorneys were contacted, and an average bill of $4,350 on each case did not seem to cause great concern. One of the attorneys even stated that collection should not be a problem since the courts have generally ordered the husband to pay the accounting fees for the business evaluation. From his understanding, the bills were generally paid by the companies being evaluated. From his experience, husbands were more inclined to pay the accountant before the wife's attorney.

Based on all this, Bill and Sarah prepared the following evaluation:

PROJECTED NET INCOME
First Full Year of Divorce Evaluation

Billings:	
Court-appointed, 24 cases @ 60 hours each = 1,440 hours	
720 hours @ $56	$ 40,320
720 hours @ $31	22,320
Attorney-appointed, 24 cases @ 100 hours each = 2,400 hours	
1,200 hours @ $56	67,200
1,200 hours @ $31	37,200
Gross billings	$167,040
Less bad debts, 10% of court-appointed	6,264
Net billings	$160,776

Expenses:		
Nonbillable supervision		
(250 hours @ $75)	$18,750	
Staff salaries	60,000	
Payroll taxes and other benefits	12,000	
Allocated computer expenses	4,000	
Allocated occupancy costs	12,000	
Allocated office support	10,000	116,750
Projected net income before interest expense		$ 44,026
Interest expense, 12% on $172,400		20,668
Projected net income		23,338

"Now we are getting somewhere," said Bob: No partner capital involved, planned supervision, and a respectable bottom line. What made the figures even more impressive is that no "fudging" was done for the expected 10% growth and the expansion of the personal financial planning business.

Sarah then addressed the problem of paying off the $172,400 of bank debt. She noted that, if the note were converted to a ten-year note at 12% the monthly payments for principal and interest would be $2,473.44. Rounding this to $2,500, this would reduce the net income to a cash flow of $14,026 ($30,000 of bank payments, less $20,688 of interest, leaving principal payments in the first year of $9,312).

John Hacker asked, "What would a five-year pay-down do to cash flow?"

Sarah responded, "The monthly payments would be $3,834.94. Let's say $3,900. In that case annual payments would be $46,800, less the interest of $20,688 in the first year, requiring about $26,112 of principal payments in the first year. That, of course, would create a negative cash flow at least in the earlier years before the projected 10% annual growth."

"Here comes the 'fudge'?" laughed Bob. "Let's go with the five-year note. I know the bank will have no problem with five years and ten may give the loan committee some pause. I know this will cause some partner capital to be used, but that is what the bank looks for anyway."

"We all agree?" questioned John. The nods were there. "OK Sarah, this one is yours. I think you should take it from here."

Sarah was chosen to handle the project, rather than Bill, because she was the one who linked this project to the next field of growth, personal financial planning, and she would most likely push this additional area.

CONCLUSIONS

This chapter has defined the difference between net income and cash flow, and it has described how cash flow may be calculated. Knowledge of cash flow is fundamental to a small business because a lot is riding on the ability of the business to meet its current obligations in a timely manner. The illustration using Lucky Fuel Oil is dramatic because the numbers are large relative to the size of the business since the industry is experiencing a severe readjustment. The Gordon & Hacker case is perhaps less dramatic, but it points up the different needs of the service firm.

Your business may not have the same cash flow needs or be quite as volatile. Nevertheless, the principles behind the planning process remain valid. Much can be learned about your business by developing an operating plan, regardless of the level of detail at which that development takes place.

The next chapter illustrates how the plan, once constructed, can be used to test possible changes in the business.

8

Sensitivity Analysis

In the preceding chapters, the emphasis was placed on developing a business plan, including a statement of business purpose, strategic and tactical objectives, an operating plan or budget, and a cash flow statement. The reasons given for the development of the plan were (1) that it provides a handy way to communicate with outsiders about the business and (2) that it focuses the activities of all those involved with the business in a consistent direction. Another benefit of the process of developing the operational plan is that *the plan can be used to test alternative tactics for the business in order to assess the impact of those tactics without having to implement them.*

It is the purpose of this chapter to illustrate this process, which is referred to as *sensitivity analysis.*

The intent of sensitivity analysis is to test how "sensitive" the business is to changes in its sales, cost of sales, gross margins, operating expenses, or any other similar factors. An operating plan or income statement and balance sheet forecasts and cash flow analysis are developed using many detailed assumptions. *Any one of those assumptions or any combination of them can be changed, and the impact on the financial statement forecasts can be ascertained.*

COMPUTERIZING THE PLANNING PROCESS

Anyone who has gone through a planning process as comprehensive as the one described here knows that testing the impact of alternative assumptions can be a laborious process if done manually. Fortunately, there are time-sharing systems, microcomputers, and minicomputers that provide easy-to-operate planning software with which it is possible to computerize the production of all or most of the schedules described in Chapters 6 and 7. With a computerized system, the process of testing assumptions is as simple as entering the one or more factors (assumptions) that have changed, running the system, and reviewing the results. Processing such changes on a manual basis is extremely time-consuming and limits the number of alternatives that can be explored.

TESTING ALTERNATIVE SCENARIOS

A review of Figure 6.14 shows that *after taxes*, Peter O'Henry anticipates net income (profits after taxes) of $80,712, somewhat less than the $92,575 he earned in 19X1, and certainly less than the $117,331 he earned in 19X0. It is not surprising that he might be interested in investigating realistic ways of improving his profit picture. Peter decided to do this by exploring three different scenarios, as follows:

> *Scenario* A: What would happen if he was able to achieve an additional moderate increase in his gross margin on middle distillates and gasoline from 12.6 cents a gallon to 13.1 cents a gallon? (In his operating plan, he had already planned an increase in his gross margin from 11.7 cents a gallon, his actual margin in 19X1, to 12.6 cents a gallon.)
>
> *Scenario* B: What would happen if he was able to achieve a significant increase in his gross margin from 12.6 cents a gallon to 13.6 cents a gallon?
>
> *Scenario* C: What would happen if he was able to improve his cash collections on his accounts receivable?

Sensitivity analysis can be used not only to explore what will happen if certain positive actions are taken but also to explore the impact on the business if certain planned events do not materialize. As an example, Peter decided to explore what would happen if he did *not* achieve the level of gasoline sales he had included in his forecast by constructing the following scenario:

Scenario D: What would happen if his planned gasoline gallonage was not achieved? For example, if instead of selling 580,000 gallons as forecast, he could sell only 455,000 gallons, what would be the result?

Scenario Results

For each scenario, Peter entered the changed assumptions and worked through the calculations. The results are summarized in Figure 8.1.

FIGURE 8.1
Lucky Fuel Oil Company
Sensitivity Analysis

	Average Gross Margin per Gallon	*Extended Gross Margin*	*Net Profit Before Taxes*	*Peak Borrowings*
Scenario A:				
Moderate Margin Increases				
Middle Distillates and Gasoline	13.1¢	$719,000		
LPG	33.9¢	128,000		
Heavy Oil	3.0¢	112,000		
Burner Service	55%	178,000		
Appliance Sales	16%	6,000	$148,000	$852,000
Scenario B:				
Significant Margin Increases				
Middle Distillates and Gasoline	13.6¢	744,000		
LPG	33.9¢	128,000		
Heavy Oil	3.0¢	112,000		
Burner Service	55%	178,000		
Appliance Sales	16%	6,000	$176,000	$837,000
Scenario C:				
Improve Cash Collections				
Middle Distillates and Gasoline	12.6¢	691,000		
LPG	33.9¢	128,000		
Heavy Oil	3.0¢	112,000		
Burner Service	55%	178,000		
Appliance Sales	16%	6,000	$141,000	$525,000
Scenario D:				
Gasoline Gallonage Not Achieved				
Middle Distillates and Gasoline	12.6¢	676,000		
LPG	33.9¢	128,000		
Heavy Oil	3.0¢	112,000		
Burner Service	55%	178,000		
Appliance Sales	16%	6,000	$105,000	$866,000

Scenario A. Under this scenario, Peter increased the margin he hoped to achieve on middle distillates (No. 2 home heating oil and kerosene) and gasoline from 12.6 cents a gallon to 13.1 cents a gallon. All other average gross margins remained the same. As stated earlier, it is not necessary that only one assumption be changed at a time. All assumptions can be changed at once if so desired. In the example, only one assumption has been changed—in part for simplicity and in part to illustrate the *sensitivity* of the business to that single assumption.

The result of this moderate change in the gross margin for middle distillates and gasoline is to generate a profit *before taxes* of approximately $148,000. This increased profit comes from two sources. First, since an increase in the gross margin is really an increase in the selling price to the consumer, there is no corresponding increase in cost. Therefore, all the increase (to the extent it is realized) becomes additional profit. So, the bulk of the increase in pre-tax profits from $113,000 to $148,000 is due to the increased margin.

Second, since there are increased profits, cash flow is increased (remember in Chapter 7 it was determined that *net income* is a chief source of cash flow). With increased cash flow, overall borrowings are decreased. Notice that in Figure 8.1 peak borrowings have decreased from the $869,000 of the original forecast to $852,000. The level of borrowings over the whole year is reduced as a result of the increased cash flow from the increase in gross margin. This decrease in borrowings results in a decrease in *interest expense*. The combination of this decrease in expense and the increase in the gross margin on middle distillates and gasoline accounts for the increase in net profit before taxes reflected in Figure 8.1.

Scenario B. In this scenario, the increase in gross margin on middle distillates and gasoline is a full 1 cent a gallon, from 12.6 to 13.6 cents a gallon. As might be expected, the results are similar to the results from Scenario A and for the same reasons. The increased margin results in additional profit before taxes. This has the impact of increasing cash flow and, thereby, reducing the need for borrowing. Peak borrowings are reduced from the $869,000 of the original forecast to $837,000. Again, the whole level of borrowings during the year is reduced due to the additional cash flow. The combination of reduced borrowings and increased profits caused by the increased margin raises estimated net profit before taxes to $176,000 versus $113,000 in the original forecast.

Scenario C. Under this set of assumptions, Peter is seeking to test the impact of an improvement in his cash collections. In the original forecast, Peter estimated that for every $1.00 of sales 30 cents was received in the first succeeding month; 40 cents in the next succeeding month; 20 cents the next month; 9 cents the next month; and the last 1 cent in the fifth month after the sale (see Figure 6.7). Under this alternative set of assumptions, out of every $1.00 of sales Peter hoped to collect 40 cents in the first succeeding month; 44 cents in the second month; and 6 cents, 9 cents, and 1 cent in each succeeding month thereafter. The impact of this change is dramatic, as is illustrated in Figure 8.1. Collections of receivables are a source of cash, as discussed in Chapter 7. The faster the collections, the less money that must be borrowed during the year. Figure 8.1 shows that peak borrowings have decreased to $525,000 from $869,000 in the original forecast. Average borrowings over the year have declined by over $100,000 a month. The result is to increase profits from $113,000 to $141,000 as a result of a substantial decrease in interest expenses. It is important to understand that this $28,000 increase in profits is a direct result of *better management of accounts receivable*.

There are some additional impacts of this improved management of receivables. Since Peter has to raise only $525,000 at most under this scenario, he will probably have an easier time convincing his banker to make the loan than if he had to borrow $869,000. Hence, he can spend more time working at managing the business rather than negotiating a loan. Another less tangible benefit of this scenario, if Peter can accomplish it, is that it will demonstrate Peter's management ability clearly to his banker. This should serve to increase the banker's confidence in Peter's ability to pay back the loan.

So far, all the scenarios have dealt with improvements to the business. Being realistic, however, Peter decided to explore the impact on his business if certain of his assumptions did not materialize. In *Scenario D*, he explored the impact of a *reduction* in gasoline sales from 580,000 gallons to 455,000 gallons. The results are shown in Figure 8.1. With lower sales, Peter would also have lower cost of sales. Likewise, his need to borrow would be reduced slightly due to the lower level of sales. Despite the reduced cost of sales and lower interest expense due to reduced borrowings, Peter still loses the gross margin on the lost gasoline sales. The net result is to lower his prospective profits from $113,000 before taxes to $108,000.

CONTINGENCY PLANNING

So far, this chapter has dealt with the exploration of single changes in the assumptions underlying the operating plan for Lucky Fuel Oil. Most of these changes have stemmed from a desire to improve the profits of the business. Only Scenario D explored the impact of a failure to achieve one of the underlying assumptions.

Contingency planning may be thought of as a subset of sensitivity analysis. The intent of contingency planning is to find a way to retrench or reduce costs if more than a few of the hopeful assumptions about the business do not materialize. For example, assume, as in Scenario D, that expected gasoline sales are not achieved, *and* that No. 2 home heating oil gallonage drops by 20%. In this circumstance, Peter O'Henry ought to have a contingency plan for reducing his operating costs by taking one or more of the following steps:

- Letting one or more drivers go.
- Letting one or more servicemen go.
- Selling one or more delivery or service trucks.
- Cancelling certain discretionary expenses such as his community contributions or his new computer systems.

Rather than respond haphazardly to a decline in business, *contingency planning allows an ordered or structured plan for reducing the size of the business*. As callous as it may sound, Peter should evaluate each employee and decide which ones would be the first to go in an economic downturn. He should also reexamine his expenses and decide, if he has to cut back, which items he would cut. He can explore the impact of these changes by running them through his operational planning process.

CONCLUSION

One purpose of this chapter has been to illustrate the concept of *sensitivity analysis*. The objective of such an analysis is to ascertain the extent to which profits are affected by (are sensitive to) changes in operating assumptions. The benefit of sensitivity analysis using an operating plan is that the impacts can be determined prospectively. This is a vast improvement over a trial-and-error method in which the impacts can be judged only *after* a change has been made.

The chapter suggests that a computerized planning system will not only aid in the initial preparation of the operating plan or budget but will enable the user to explore many more alternatives than would be possible on a manual basis.

Finally, a planning system will enable the user to establish a formal *contingency plan* in order to ascertain with relative certainty the impact of changes to reduce the size of the business in response to an economic downturn.

II
GETTING THE MONEY

Part II will be of interest to you whether you are just embarking on your own business and need seed money or whether you are already in business. You will learn of the experiences of entrepreneurs who went out to get money for various purposes. A commercial banker will tell you what a bank generally looks for in a borrower and a borrowing relationship. Part II discusses the following subjects:

- *Financing a start-up situation.*
- *General guidelines for financing a going concern.*
- *Sources of funds for financing a going concern.*
- *Funds available for special situations, such as disaster loans or agricultural loans.*
- *Choosing your commercial bank.*
- *Making yourself creditworthy.*
- *Understanding the fundamentals of loan documentation.*

In Chapter 9 is a self-assessment checklist designed to test your awareness of various aspects of getting the money. The checklist will help you to identify those areas covered in Part II on which you may wish to focus.

Part II is based on the assumption that you have already developed a business plan that provides you with the appropriate documents you will need to present to a prospective lender in applying for credit. More important, in the process of developing a business plan, you will have determined the purpose, amount, and kind of financing necessary for your business.

The business plan, which includes a financing proposal, gives a description of your business, the market for your products or services, the rationale for the location, identification of the management and other personnel, and the way the business is to be financed. It is the major tool by which you will be able to construct an intelligent procedure for getting the money. It indicates to you and to anyone who reads it the reason for your going into business in the first place, and especially why you have chosen a particular business. Second, it indicates how much financing you have to generate and how your business may become successful and make a profit. It is an essential tool that shows you how much you need to put into the new business, that can also induce family or friends to share in the enterprise, and that is a tool to help make yourself creditworthy for debt financing.

Chapter 10 discusses financing a start-up situation. Chapters 11 and 12 discuss financing a going concern. Chapter 13 discusses other financing topics, such as how to choose a bank, what you should know about loan documentation, and making yourself creditworthy.

9

Self-Assessment Checklist: Getting the Money

Can you answer "yes" to the following questions? If you cannot, refer to the page numbers listed to the right of each question to find the answer.

Do you know:	*Yes*	*No*	*If not, refer to:*
☐ Where most entrepreneurs get start-up capital?			Chapter 10, "Financing a Start-up Situation," page: 137
☐ What the difference is between equity financing and debt financing?			
☐ Why you need equity capital before you can obtain debt?			
☐ What steps you should take in getting money?			
☐ What are the advantages and disadvantages of equity (as opposed to debt) financing?			

Do you know:	*Yes*	*No*	*If not, refer to:*
☐ Where you can obtain equity financing?			
☐ Where an entrepreneur can borrow start-up funds?			
☐ What are the requirements of these various financing organizations: • banks?			
• SBA?			
• SBICs and MESBICs?			
• private venture capital companies?			
• suppliers? individuals?			
☐ How your taking a personal loan may be able to help your business with its financing requirements?			
☐ What are the general requirements of lending organizations that loan funds to a start-up situation?			
☐ What are some typical uses of funds in the operations of a business?			Chapter 11, "Guidelines for Financing a Going Concern," page: 148
☐ Why you need to match maturities of sources of funds and uses of funds?			
☐ What are the general types of credit arrangements available to small businesses and how the following are repaid: • short-term loans?			
• term or installment-type loans?			
• revolving loans?			
☐ What collateral is and why a lending organization demands it?			
☐ What are the various types of collateral: • real property?			
• "personal property" and fixtures?			

Do you know:	*Yes*	*No*	*If not, refer to:*
• "paper" collateral?			
☐ The four C's of credit analysis?			
☐ What are the following specific types of loans: • short-term unsecured loans?			
• short-term secured loans?			
• unsecured term loans?			
• secured term loans?			
• unsecured revolving loans?			
• secured revolving loans?			
☐ About special types of financing that may be available to small businesses, including: • floor plan financing?			
• commercial financing?			
☐ What types of data a commercial would require?			
☐ How to evaluate your assets as potential collateral?			
☐ What a bonded warehouse is?			
☐ What are the specific sources of financing for a going concern: • commercial banks			Chapter 12, "Financing a Going Concern—Sources of Funds," page: 161
• the Small Business Administration?			
• commercial finance companies?			
• factors?			
• equipment financing and leasing companies?			
• life insurance companies?			
• local development agencies for industrial revenue development funds?			
• other financial institutions (e.g., savings & loan associations)?			
☐ How to apply for an S.B.A. loan?			

Do you know:	*Yes*	*No*	*If not, refer to:*
☐ What funds may be available to you from governmental or quasi-governmental agencies for certain special situations, such as economic or natural disasters, minority loans, water and air pollution control, etc.?			
☐ What factors are important in choosing a commercial bank?			Chapter 13, "Banks, Creditworthiness, and You" page: 182
☐ What you can do to make yourself creditworthy?			
☐ How to analyze your situation from a banker's perspective?			
☐ What reasons bankers cite for rejections of loans to small businesses?			
☐ What specific attributes bankers and other lenders look for in making loans?			
☐ The basics about loan documentation, such as the difference between a guarantee and an endorsement, how a bank will secure a loan, and so on?			
☐ Why you should always have an attorney involved in your loan processing?			
☐ How to calculate your net worth?			

10

Financing A Start-Up Situation

BUT WHERE DO I GET THE MONEY?

That is the question most often asked in starting a business, and it is the question that will come up again and again throughout an entrepreneur's business career—money to start the business, money for buying assets and equipment, money for working capital, money for emergencies.

The sources of financing in a business are of two types: *equity financing* and *debt financing*. Equity financing is the money you and other investors put into your business; it gives you and them ownership or part ownership. Debt financing is the money you borrow and *must pay back* with interest, whether the business succeeds or not. Generally, before you can hope to qualify for debt financing, a significant part of the money to start your business must come from you—your assets or savings—or from investment by friends. In other words, it must come from equity financing. Once your business is up and running, there are other sources such as internal cash flow from operations, improved management of current assets, and increased supplier financing. There are full discussions of these techniques in Part III, "How to Manage Your Financial Resources."

WHERE DOES IT ALL COME FROM?

Surveys of small businesses indicate that by far the most common source of start-up capital comes from personal and family resources. The next most common source is banks and other institutional lenders. Friends constitute the third major source. Other sources—individual investors, venture capital firms, government agencies—represent an insignificant portion of start-up financing sources.

Therefore, in order to start a business, you should look to yourself, your family, a bank, and your friends to provide the initial capital. No lender will lend money to a start-up situation unless you as the entrepreneur can invest an adequate amount of capital in the business that you have obtained personally. There are two reasons for this:

1. Net worth, owners' equity, or capital invested in the business provides a cushion for creditors. It provides the margin by which assets can shrink in value or by which your company can sustain operating losses and still pay its creditors. This concept is discussed further in Chapter 23, which deals with ratio analysis.
2. The more personal funds you have invested in a business, the less likely you will be to throw in the towel if things get difficult. (As an aside, this is often the reason that banks require the personal guarantees or endorsements by the principal(s) in a business on a corporate note even if their personal net worth is not significant. The banks believe that having personal assets "on the line" will often make the difference in the entrepreneur's desire to stick it out.) If you are not willing to risk a substantial portion of your own funds, it suggests to the bank or other lender that you do not believe strongly enough in your concept.

Here are two brief examples, based on actual situations, of how business owners developed equity financing to start their businesses.

Case Example 1: John Reynolds Lawn Mower and Bicycle Repair Center

John Reynolds had worked for some years in a garage as a skilled mechanic when he decided to go into business for himself. He had savings of $11,000, but after careful calculation, with the aid of a knowledgeable friend, he figured he would need at least $30,000 to get started in the small vehicle repair shop that he contemplated. He thought he could also repair roller skates and skateboards. He went home and talked with his wife. They decided to increase the mortgage on their house. In this way he netted another $14,000. He now had $25,000, $5000 short of what he felt he needed, but he did not want to wait and he could not think of anywhere else to get more money.

He approached his brother-in-law to see if he might want to invest or help out at the beginning on repair work. His brother-in-law, a skilled mechanic with a good job, did not want to invest. However, for a small hourly rate, he agreed to help out in the beginning while keeping his regular job.

So John took his own capital, rented a store in the middle of town, invested in tools, parts, signs, and ads in the town paper, and made an agreement with his former garage to take on any small vehicle repair jobs that were generally unprofitable for the garage. Thus, with $25,000 from his savings and personal assets, John launched the Reynolds Lawn Mower and Bicycle Repair Center. Because of the rapid growth in bicycling, roller skating, and skateboarding, John's business was flourishing within six months. His brother-in-law quit his job and invested $10,000 of his own in this successful new business.

Case Example 2: Marketing Magazines, Inc.

Art Lane and Melissa Miles decided to start a publishing company to develop quarterly magazines for major corporations. These publications would be used as promotional tools in the marketing efforts of these firms. Art and Melissa decided that they would raise equity capital first from their savings and other assets and then from investments by their families. By these means, they managed to raise $25,000. They then consulted a number of publishing executives. One of them, a good friend, referred them to a business advisor, an individual with a record of success in starting up small businesses. This business advisor, through preparation of a business plan including financial statement forecasts, estimated that Art and Melissa would need at least $100,000 in capital. Thus, the two were faced with the need to raise another $75,000.

Art approached three friends who were knowledgeable in the industry. All three agreed to invest, and each contributed $10,000 of capital. Unexpectedly, the financial expert decided he would like to invest $10,000 and handle the financial aspects of the company without pay. So with $40,000 of capital added, the total equity capital was now $65,000. The financial expert suggested going to a bank for the rest. Melissa suggested a Connecticut bank that knew her well and with whom her family had an existing relationship as depositors. Moreover, the offices of the new company would be located in Connecticut near this bank.

Armed with their business plan, Art, Melissa, and the financial advisor discussed the matter with the bank officer. The banker felt that this was a somewhat risky enterprise because only one client was identified and the group was dealing in intangible and subjective materials. He decided, however, to offer the group $35,000 on a two-year loan with six-month renewal notes that each would personally guarantee. The banker agreed to do this because he felt that the bank would be protected by the personal guarantees. This would allow them to fund some start-up and initial developmental costs. In the first six months, Marketing Magazines, Inc. acquired two more large clients. The bank was repaid at the end of two years. Since then, during developmental phases, the company has borrowed several times on a short-term basis for working capital purposes.

What Do These Examples Show About Getting Money?

These examples show several approaches to equity financing. First, they indicate that if you want to go into business, you should *analyze your own assets carefully*. You may not be aware of the extent of your assets and the kinds of assets that may be converted into cash for seed money. Second, they show how, by *approaching friends and associates* who have knowledge of your talents and experience with a good business plan, you may *elicit offers to invest* in the business to help get it started. And finally, they show that by *approaching acquaintances* who might like to use their own talents in the kind of business proposed, you may induce such interested persons to come into the company with an investment of money as well as talent.

PROS AND CONS OF EQUITY FINANCING

There must be a certain minimum amount of equity in a business in order for it to be creditworthy and for you to approach a bank for additional (debt) financing for seed money. In addition, some start-up businesses have chosen to acquire all their seed money by using equity capital only. Equity financing has two principal advantages over debt in a start-up situation:

1. You do not have to pay back the money invested (in contrast to debt financing), assuming you maintain your status as the majority shareholder and thereby keep control of the business.
2. You have accepted money from people who have a personal interest in your success and who have bet on it.

However, certain potential difficulties are associated with equity financing. For example, you should consider the potential effect on personal relationships with your investors if the business venture is not as successful as anticipated. Furthermore, before investing your savings and other assets in your business, you must seriously consider the effect on you or your family during the period before the company begins to show a positive net income and cash flow. In other words, don't bet your house and life savings on your business if you can't afford to lose them (or a part of them).

BORROWING START-UP FUNDS

Although it is estimated that half of all business owners got the money to start their businesses from their savings or personal assets, most business owners sooner or later must obtain debt financing for additional seed money, for working capital, or for capital to expand their businesses.

Once you have accumulated some equity, you may want to attempt to borrow the rest of your seed money from an outside organization. Figure 10.1 summarizes the following major sources of such *start-up loans*.

1. Commercial banks.
2. The Small Business Administration (SBA), principally by guaranteeing loans from banks.
3. Small Business Investment Companies (SBICs) and Minority Enterprise SBICs (MESBICs).
4. Private venture capital companies (in special circumstances).
5. Prospective suppliers.
6. Individuals (relatives, friends, business acquaintances).

Money from Banks and Guarantees from the SBA

Banks are probably the most common source of borrowed start-up funds. Generally, a bank will advance start-up funds only if secured by a "hard" asset (for example, a new piece of general-purpose equipment). The term generally will not extend beyond three years (or 36 monthly payments). A bank might advance a short-term working capital loan, although this is less likely. The bank might also advance a loan secured by the business owner's whole life insurance. If the bank is not willing to extend the full amount of the loan itself, it may apply for an SBA guarantee whereby a portion (up to 90%) of the loan principal and interest is guaranteed to the bank by the SBA. This guarantee does not mean that the bank has no dollars at risk; it means only that the bank's risk is smaller in total

FIGURE 10.1
Borrowing Start-Up Funds

Source	*General Requirements*	*General Comments*
Banks	• Business plan • Adequate equity • Collateral available • Good personal credit history • Personal guarantees of the principals	• May require guarantee from spouse • "Market" interest rates (no ceiling) • Up to three-year repayment
Banks—SBA Guaranteed Loans	• Same as banks' • Unwillingness of a bank to lend on "normal" terms	• Equity and collateral requirements are usually less stringent than banks' • "Market" interest (with ceiling) • Up to three-year repayment
SBA Direct Loans	• Same as banks', but cannot have received another SBA loan within previous six months • Must have been refused credit by two banks	• Equity and collateral requirements are significantly less strict than banks' • Preference may be given to minorities, veterans, and disadvantaged persons • Low interest rate • Longer repayment • Funds are limited for such loans
Small Business Investment Companies (SBICs) and Minority Enterprise Small Business Investment Companies (MESBICs)	• Same as banks' but with longer terms • Prefer businesses with growth potential	• SBICs and MESBICs are privately owned • Usually require some equity participation by SBIC or MESBIC • MESBICs are limited to investments with businesses owned by minorities and disadvantaged persons • Cannot receive more than 49% equity participation in a company

FIGURE 10.1 (Cont.)
Borrowing Start-Up Funds

Source	*General Requirements*	*General Comments*
Venture Capital Companies	• Same as banks' but for businesses in high technology industries or companies with unusual growth potential	• Venture capital companies require equity participation by them May want 30% to 70% of the equity depending on the risk
Prospective Suppliers and/or Equipment Vendors	• Same as banks' but in less detail	• May offer generous extended terms on initial merchandise purchases • May offer a straight (short-term) loan, although this is unusual
Individuals	• Varies	• May receive straight "arm's-length" loans from individuals, friends and relatives

dollars. Therefore, the bank will still not lend money on an "unbankable" deal—that is, one not considered to have a reasonable prospect for success. (For a full discussion of bank lending and of SBA lending and guarantees, refer to Chapter 12).

Money from SBICs and MESBICs

SBICs and MESBICs generally require that the borrower issue some form of convertible debt. Convertible debt is a loan payable that, at the SBIC's option, would be converted to equity for a fixed number of shares in the company. This convertible debt is usually subordinated to other debt. Subordination means that it is paid off only after other (unsubordinated) debt. Both types of organization are required to deal only with organizations that are within the SBA's size criteria (discussed in Chapter 11). MESBICs must deal only with minorities and disadvantaged persons.

Money from Private Venture Capital Companies

Private venture capital organizations also deal in convertible subordinated debt, but they will generally limit their start-up participation to companies that have strong growth potential. Private venture capital is regaining popularity since the maximum rate of long-term capital gains tax was lowered from 49% to 20% (as of January 1, 1982). The Labor Department has started to allow pension funds to invest in new ventures. In both the SBIC and private venture capital cases, you may have to give up a substantial equity position, typically as much as 40% to 50% in the case of private venture capital.

Money from Suppliers

Prospective suppliers of inventory and equipment are also potential sources of start-up loans. The former may offer you extended payment terms, at least initially; the latter may actually offer a term loan secured by the equipment. (Equipment loans to purchase new equipment are discussed in more detail in Chapter 12.)

Money from Individuals

An additional source of a start-up loan might be those same people—friends, relatives, acquaintances—you approached regarding investment in your company. Some of them might very well be more interested in a businesslike, "arm's-length" loan transaction than they were in an equity participation. Under the right circumstances, this can be a situation where everyone wins. You can borrow funds at an attractive rate, and the individual can often earn more than he or she could earn otherwise. Of course, the individual must be aware that with increased return comes increased risk.

Personal Loans

There are also other forms of unsecured loans that you may convince a bank to make, as others starting a business have been able to do. These are *personal loans,* which depend solely on your net worth (after subtracting the value of your equity investment in your new venture) and your reputation. These loans are often unsecured and signed by the maker (you), often without other endorsement. (The calculation of your personal net worth is discussed in Chapter 13.) Personal loans may be in the form of:

- *Installment loans*, with level monthly payments.
- *Personal lines of credit*, which are agreements by the bank to allow credit automatically up to a certain limit, with monthly repayment. Usually, such an agreement extends for a year before being reassessed.

These other forms of unsecured loans would be made to an individual borrower regardless of the financial condition or prospects of the company. In other words, you would be borrowing totally on your own merit and your own creditworthiness and not on the credit history of your company.

Case Example 3: Borrowing Start-Up Funds for a Cosmetic and Drug Emporium

Look at the case of Martin Parker. Martin had been the regional manager of a large cosmetic company when he decided at the age of 40 to go into business for himself. During the year before he made his move, he had been thinking of what type of business he really wanted to run. He realized that he should go into the business he knew; it seemed to him he could make a success of a cosmetic and drug store in the thriving city where he lived.

Martin kept his job and began to look around for money to start the business. He found the exact location he wanted in one of the major shopping centers in town. And through sheer persistence, going back again and again, talking about his plans and building a relationship with the associated real estate company, he finally obtained a tentative agreement that he could obtain a lease on one of their stores within a few months.

Now his problem was to get the start-up funds. He figured, after developing his business plan, that he would need $150,000 to get started. First, he looked at his own assets. He had savings of $30,000. His other main asset was his house, which was currently worth $180,000. And his wife owned some land worth about $20,000. He decided to take a second mortgage on his house from his savings bank; the bank loaned him $80,000 on the house and his wife's land. He now needed to borrow $40,000.

He figured that he could go to a bank right next to where he would be locating the business, a bank that would be getting all his business. He had gone to one other bank and had been turned down. If he got one more rejection, he would go to the Small Business Administration (SBA). According to SBA requirements, a business is qualified to apply for a direct loan only after being rejected twice for conventional financing.

Martin went into the bank next to his site. He told the banker that he had a tentative agreement for a lease in the shopping center and that his store would be the bank's neighbor. He said he was thinking of using that bank for his business. The banker seemed to be very interested. So Martin showed him his business plan. He told him about the money he already had and what he needed, and suddenly he got a very sympathetic ear. The banker offered him $20,000 on a two-year term-loan basis, secured by inventory and leasehold improvements. He said that should be enough with normal trade credit.

Martin's business opened a year ago and is flourishing. His bank loan is half repaid now, and he has approached his bank with a proposal for a loan to open a prescription drug counter.

What does this example show? This example shows, first, that Martin needed persistence to get the loan. He had approached another bank before he found the right bank and the right way to present himself and his business. Martin also was planning on looking to his suppliers to provide some working capital (normal trade credit). In addition, he used some of the tips found in Chapter 13. For example, he appealed to the bank's own self-interest in making a loan, and by establishing a favorable credit history, he improved his chances of being approved for the second loan.

Case Example 4: Starting a New Software Company with Venture Capital

Paul Richards had worked for a number of years developing standard software programs for Major Software, Inc. (MSI). During that time, he realized that there was a good market for software that would greatly enhance the utility of smaller computers. He took this idea to his company, MSI. They considered it carefully but decided it was not for them. He then talked it over with two of his friends, also software developers at MSI, who agreed with the basic idea and could see how this would address a need in the marketplace. The three decided to invest some money to form a company that would develop this software. In addition, they all agreed to go without salary for the first few months.

With the help of a banker, Paul determined that they would need approximately $250,000, because the developmental period for their first software product would be approximately one year. Even if the three principals took drastically reduced salaries, operating expenses and computer time-sharing charges would be substantial.

Paul approached Venture Capital Associates (VCA) in Boston with his business plan, a description of the kind of software he hoped to develop for small computer manufacturers, some specifications, and the results of experiments he had made on the product. He talked with Harry Bains of VCA, who was a specialist in the electronic data processing (EDP) investment area. Harry was impressed with Paul's software product. He asked Paul to leave copies of his materials with him; Harry and his associates would look them over and get back to Paul with their thoughts. Harry planned to discuss the project with an expert in the field on a highly confidential basis.

When Paul returned for the later discussions, Harry had a proposal for him: "You're not quite ready yet for the whole commitment, though we do believe in your plan and will finance you on a percentage-of-completion basis. You and I will establish milestones in the development of your software, and VCA will disburse funds to your new company upon achievement of each milestone. Once your software is developed, we'll assist you in developing a marketing plan and assess your working capital needs. Our financing will be in the form of debt, subordinated to other creditors, and convertible at our option into 35% of the equity in your company." Paul accepted the offer.

What does this example show? A venture capital firm, like a bank, will require a business plan. Venture capital firms, however, will generally lend or invest only in those specialized industries where they have experience and where they believe they will achieve a rapid payback. In addition, they usually will demand (and get) a fairly large chunk of the equity of a start-up company.

CONCLUSION

Almost any start-up situation requires a substantial capital investment by the owner before anyone not directly involved will invest in the business. A substantial portion of the start-up capital in small businesses comes from family, friends, and business associates in the form of "cash equity" or "sweat equity" (i.e., investing time). Once you have invested your own capital, there are many places you can go to borrow additional start-up funds.

Figure 10.1 summarized the sources of start-up capital and described the probable requirements of lenders or investors. It also incorporated some general information regarding each source that may help you structure your approach to securing start-up funds.

11

Guidelines For Financing A Going Concern

As discussed in Chapter 10, there are two sources of funds for any new business: *equity* and *debt*. As your business grows, you may secure additional equity funds from either the existing owners or from new investors. One way of expanding the base of investors is by "going public"—selling a portion of your business's capital stock to the general public. A business that goes public is subject to a host of federal and state regulations. This topic is, however, beyond the scope of this chapter; it could fill an entire book by itself. Moreover, small businesses typically do not use this source of financing; private debt financing is used most frequently.

Therefore, this chapter focuses on the general principles of debt financing for a going concern. It discusses the various types of credit available and answers some questions regarding the use of collateral and the importance of matching sources and uses of funds.

HOW CAN YOU USE THE MONEY YOU BORROW?

Generally, you will use debt financing to *buy assets* (things of value) to run your business. These assets will be either current (converted into cash within the current fiscal year) or fixed (held as a permanent part of the company). Current assets will fluctuate with production and business cycles. However, there will always be a need for a base level. Therefore, there are "seasonal" and "permanent" current assets. This factor will influence your choice of financing alternatives. Working capital is equal to the difference between current assets and current liabilities. Working capital is discussed further in Part III, "How to Manage Your Financial Resources." Financing for current assets is often called "working capital financing."

MATCH THE SOURCE TO THE USES

Basically, you should use short-term credit (that with a maturity of one year) to finance seasonal current assets and long-term credit to finance permanent assets—current and fixed. *Match the maturities of sources and the maturities of uses of funds*. For example, you probably would not borrow on the basis of a 90-day note to buy a house. And you would not borrow on the basis of a four-year installment plan to anticipate by a month or so your tax refund check. You should apply the same sound judgment to your business and match the maturities of sources and uses.

As a further example, if you bought a truck (a fixed asset) using funds from a short-term note, you might be unable to repay the full amount of the note when it came due in 90 days. So you would have to refinance it. This presents two potential problems:

1. If the interest rates rose in the interim, you might find yourself in the unfavorable position of having to pay a higher rate of interest than the rate of return on your investment. (See Chapter 26 for a discussion of capital budgeting, which explains the concept of rate of return on your investment.)
2. You might conceivably be unable to refinance.

If, on the other hand, you financed a seasonal inventory expansion (a seasonal current asset) with a four-year term loan, you would be paying a lot of extra interest for the use of money that you needed for only a few months. In addition, bank long-term rates for unsecured working capital loans are generally higher than short-term rates, to compensate for the additional risk inherent in a longer period.

GENERAL TYPES OF CREDIT

Lending organizations make three general types of loan available to commercial borrowers for on-going operations:

- Short-term loans.
- Term (or installment) loans.
- Revolving loans.

Any of these loans may be secured—supported by specific collateral—or unsecured, guaranteed or not. The basic premise remains unchanged, however: Any financing arrangement is one or a combination of these basic types of loan. The types differ as to three basic characteristics—*maturity* of the loan, *purpose* of the loan, and *primary repayment source*.

Short-Term Loans

Generally a short-term loan matures within one year and takes the form of 30-, 60-, or 90-day notes or a "demand" note (technically, payable on demand). The usual requirement is that a borrower be out of debt (that is, have repaid a loan and remained out of debt) for some reasonable portion of the year, for example, two to three months. The traditional bank *line of credit* is simply a pre-authorized maximum borrowing limit under which a company borrows and repays its short-term loan(s).

The *purpose* of a short-term loan is to finance the purchase of current assets. It is useful especially for financing seasonal fluctuations in working capital.

The *primary repayment source* is the seasonal liquidation of these current assets—that is, the manufacturing and sale of inventories and the billing and collection of accounts receivable.

Term or Installment Loans

The *maturity* of a term or installment loan commonly ranges from one year up to as much as ten years. It is based, in part, on the estimated useful life of the asset to be financed (e.g., truck, machine, leasehold improvements, electronic data processing equipment). The *purpose* of a term loan is to finance the "permanent" level of working capital or noncurrent assets, such as equipment, furniture, and fixtures.

The *primary repayment source* is from the cash earnings from the business operations, which can be defined (roughly) as the after-tax profits plus depreciation and/or amortization. (It should be noted here that cash provided by operations should technically include permanent changes in the level of working capital. The usual repayment source for term debt, however, is viewed roughly as "cash throw-off," or net earnings plus non-cash expenses.)

Repayment of a term or installment loan is generally in one of two forms: (1) monthly or quarterly level principal payments, plus interest due (in this way the total payment decreases over time) or (2) monthly or quarterly level (in total) payments where the interest portion declines and the principal portion increases over time. The most familiar example of the second type is a home mortgage repayment schedule. (A mortgage is also an installment loan, although the term is longer than for other types of assets.)

Depending on the circumstances, other repayment schedules can be made in a term lending arrangement. Two examples are:

- Interest only for two years, followed by a four-year quarterly repayment schedule.
- Five-year maturity with regular payments, but based on 15-year amortization schedule. (Payments are made for five years, as if the loan were for 15 years. At the end of five years, the remaining principal must be refinanced or repaid as a "balloon"—in one lump sum.)

Revolving Loans

The *maturity* of a revolving loan can be finite or open-ended. Often a revolving loan is converted to a term loan or installment loan at the end of a specified period.

The *purpose* of a revolving loan is most often to finance the acquisition of non-temporary assets, especially when the outlay for the asset is not made in one lump sum. Two typical uses of revolving loans are:

1. To finance permanent growth in working capital when, for example, a company is experiencing substantial growth in sales that is expected to level off after a couple of years. At the end of the period, the loan is usually converted to a term loan.
2. To finance the revolving working capital requirements of a company that is undercapitalized. This is a typical commercial financing arrangement. (Commercial financing is discussed in detail later in this chapter.) Generally speaking, this would be a long-term, permanently revolving loan that gradually would be reduced as the company became increasingly well capitalized.

The *primary source of repayment* would in most cases be generated by converting the revolving loan into a term loan (with or without a balloon repayment). Another source would be the cash generated by the business.

WHY DOES A LENDING ORGANIZATION DEMAND COLLATERAL?

Collateral consists of those assets that a business agrees to pledge to a lender as a fallback repayment source. If the borrower defaults on the loan, the lender may take title to the assets, sell them, and apply the proceeds to repayment of the loan. This is what happens when a bank forecloses on a mortgage and sells the property to repay the loan.

A lender usually requires collateral on loans to small businesses for three reasons:

1 If the borrower experiences financial difficulties, the lender has a repayment source to the extent of the liquidation value of the collateral, with absolute preference over other general creditors.
2. By using the borrower's assets as collateral, the lender can be assured that no other creditor can take the collateral. The taking of collateral is a preventive measure.
3. As a secured creditor, which is a creditor who has specific assets identified as collateral for the loan, a lender often has a better day-to-day understanding of the borrower's situation since he or she presumably is monitoring the collateral closely.

A bank will not often consider a loan to a smaller business without collateral.

Types of Collateral

Any personal or business asset can be used as collateral on a loan. There are many special situations, but typical business loan collateral can usually be separated into three categories:

- Real property.
- Personal property and fixtures.
- Paper collateral.

Real property. Real property refers to land and buildings. These assets have traditionally been pledged and accepted as collateral because they generally have an intrinsic value. Your mortgage loan for your home purchase is an example of a transaction secured with real property.

Personal property and fixtures. Personal property and fixtures as a source of collateral applies to a wide range of businesses. Personal property is everything subject to ownership that is not real property. For example, the personal property belonging to your business may include accounts receivable, inventory, conditional sales contracts, equipment, farm products, and the like. Fixtures are things that have been affixed to real property but are considered separate assets. The specific properties of "good" receivables, inventory, and equipment collateral are discussed later in this chapter.

Paper collateral. This term generally refers to financial assets that the lender can take possession of (for example, savings passbooks, marketable securities, and capital stock certificates of the borrowing company). A bank may often (especially if it has a lien or security interest on all the assets of the business) also take the principal's capital stock in the business as collateral. The capital stock itself does not have any additional intrinsic value to the bank; however, it represents the net value of the assets after liquidation of the liabilities. Therefore, it generally gives the bank a lot more flexibility in dealing with a problem loan situation, because the bank can sell the company as a going concern instead of liquidating its assets.

WHAT ARE THE "FOUR C'S" OF CREDIT ANALYSIS?

In making a loan decision, a lender will focus on the "Four C's" of credit, which are:

- Character.
- Capital.
- Capacity.
- Collateral.

Collateral was discussed separately in the previous section. *Character* (individual creditworthiness) is discussed in Chapter 13. *Capital* and *capacity* refer to the capital structure of the company and its debt capacity and can be evaluated by studying the following factors and answering questions similar to the following:

- *Purpose, repayment source, and maturity*. Is this loan for a valid business purpose? Does it make sense for the company? How and when will the loan be repaid? Is the maturity of the loan consistent with the purpose of the financing, the repayment source, and the lender's policies?
- *Historical results*. Do the historical results engender confidence in the future of the company? Are the results reported consistently?
- *Ratio analysis*. What do the standard business ratios indicate regarding the following characteristics of financial condition: liquidity? leverage? turnover? profitability? trading?

- *How well has the company fared?* How does the company compare to its industry? What do the trends look like?
- *Financial statement forecasts*. Are the financial forecasts consistent with the analyst's or banker's knowledge of the economy and the industry?

WHAT ARE SOME SPECIFIC TYPES OF LOAN?

In the previous section, the basic types of lending arrangements available to a borrower were discussed. This section presents some specific types of loans and includes information about obtaining them. For each type of loan, a lender will usually require collateral from the less creditworthy borrowers. (Most smaller businesses will receive only secured loans.)

Characteristics of Specific Types of Loan

Short-term loan—unsecured. An unsecured short-term loan is the major component of a typical "seasonal" line of credit and is most commonly used to finance seasonal working capital needs. It often requires a two- or three-month annual payout period, during which the borrower is out of debt with the lender, although banks in very competitive situations may waive this requirement. This requirement ensures that the business has not paid off the bank by extending the business's accounts payable—"leaning on the trade." If a company normally paid its bills on 30-day terms, it could conserve its cash temporarily by paying on 60-day terms. It could then use the cash to repay the bank. If the company did this, the need for financing would be nonseasonal ("permanent"), rather than seasonal. The company would only be rotating short-term financing sources. The lender would want to know this was the intent because a short-term loan would be inappropriate.

An unsecured short-term loan can use 30-, 60-, or 90-day time notes or demand notes. (A demand note means that a company can pay back at will but that the bank can also demand payment at will in the event of default.)

Short-term loan—secured. This type of loan has the same general characteristics as an unsecured loan. However, it uses a "blanket" security interest, generally in receivables and inventory because that is what the loan is used to finance. A blanket security interest is one where the assets used as collateral are described in the financing documents as a "class" (e.g., all inventory) rather than as specific items, and the lender usually does not monitor the collateral closely.

Term loan—unsecured. An unsecured term loan has a typical term of two to ten years (although ten years is rare for a smaller business). It is typically used to finance equipment or permanent working capital, and its maturity is tied to the useful life of the asset being purchased. This type of loan is usually represented by a formal agreement between the borrower and the bank, in the form of a document that calls for performance of certain obligations by the borrower. The failure to perform any of these obligations is an incidence of default under the terms of the loan. Some of the common conditions (covenants) that apply under a term loan agreement are as follows:

- Periodic financial reporting requirements. Audited financial reports will often be required only if the loan is substantial (e.g., $100,000 or more).
- Restrictions on additional financing without the bank's permission. These restrictions may include lease obligations.
- Maintenance of a certain minimum dollar level of working capital and/or a certain current or quick ratio. (See Chapter 23 for a detailed discussion of common business ratios.)
- Limitation on the amount of inventory as a percentage of current assets.
- Restrictions on additional liens and/or encumbrances against other assets.
- Restriction on dividend payments and/or repayment of debt to owners or principals in the business.
- Limitations on officers' salaries and bonuses.
- Restrictions on mergers, consolidations, and acquisitions.
- Limitations on major capital expenditures.
- Limitations on total amount of debt and/or the debt-to-worth ratio.

Chapter 5 provides additional discussion of restrictive loan covenants.

Term loan—secured. A secured term loan has the same characteristics as an unsecured term loan except that it:

- Is usually secured by the asset that it was used to purchase (e.g., a commercial equipment loan).
- May have even more restrictive term loan covenants than an unsecured term loan since the lender ultimately looks at the creditworthiness of the borrower. (When the loan requires security, the lender is less confident of the borrower's creditworthiness; hence, the more restrictive covenants and the addition of security.)

The following are the important factors that a lender must consider in evaluating collateral in commercial equipment financing:

- What is the liquidation appraisal value of the equipment?
- Is the equipment specialized or general purpose?
- What is the normal life of this type of equipment?
- Does the relevant industry have a broad market for used equipment?
- Is the equipment (especially heavy, non-vehicular equipment) in a geographically remote location?
- How many pieces of equipment are being offered as collateral? In other words, if the borrower were in financial difficulty would the lender be selling so many pieces of the same type of equipment that this would depress the market price?
- What effect does inflation have on the resale price of the equipment?
- What is the current replacement cost?
- If the equipment is now being used in a fairly specialized application, could it be easily adapted to some other, more general-purpose application?

Revolving loan—unsecured. An unsecured revolving loan is usually available only to very creditworthy customers and usually has a maturity of two or three years. At that time it may be converted to a term loan or repaid in a balloon (i.e., one large payment). Such a loan is most often used to finance varying cash requirements—for example, a combination of seasonal cash requirements and growth in permanent working capital requirements.

Revolving loan—secured. Secured revolving loans take the form of floor plan financing or commercial financing.

Floor plan financing is used to finance a dealer's inventory of "big ticket" items. As an example, when an automobile dealer sells a car, he turns over to the bank all the proceeds of the sale, less the dealer's profit. The dealer can pay cash to the bank or can turn over the notes receivable from the purchaser to the bank for the bank to discount (this is called "discounting conditional sales contracts"). The bank reduces the inventory loan account by the amount of the remittance. When the dealer needs new inventory, he borrows from the bank, again pledging specific pieces of newly purchased equipment as collateral. Floor plan financing arrangements are subject to periodic surprise audits by bank staff.

Commercial financing relates to the lending of funds secured by (and with the amount of the loan dependent on) accounts receivable and inventory. Commercial financing is available from the commercial finance departments of banks and from commercial finance companies. (Both of these sources are discussed in the next chapter.)

The purpose of commercial financing is to obtain cash at the time of sale, rather than when the customer pays the bill. As the borrower invoices its customers, it creates additional collateral against which it can get immediate cash if needed. In this type of financing, the borrower is paying for only the funds that are immediately needed. The funds that are available to borrow are kept on separate records. In addition, there is no commitment fee or interest charged on funds available unless they are used.

The lender establishes a formula under which it lends to its borrower. For example, the lender may determine that it will advance 80% of the amount of accounts receivable less than 90 days old. Usually, this advance formula is accompanied with a maximum amount, or guideline, that is the total amount the lender will advance to the customer. The purpose of the guideline is to prevent an enormous borrower growth in sales. Because of the mechanics of a commercial finance loan, this could cause an "automatic" increase in the available collateral and, potentially, the loan. Even though the lender would theoretically be fully secured, the guideline performs the function of stopping automatic growth in the loan until the lender can re-evaluate the situation.

The mechanics of a commercial finance loan are as follows:

- The borrower makes a sale to its customer and creates an invoice (i.e., an account receivable).
- This invoice, along with others, is assigned to the lender (i.e., it is listed on an assignment sheet). The frequency with which the borrower reports this information to the lender is a function of transaction volume. It can be daily, every other day, or weekly.
- Assuming the invoice is not disallowed for some reason, such as a sale to an affiliated company, the total dollar amount of the invoice is added to a *collateral card*.
- To determine how much the borrower can borrow, the commercial finance lender takes the total collateral shown on the card, subtracts receivables that are outstanding for more than 90 days (the information is usually obtained from the monthly accounts receivable aging that the customer submits), and multiplies by the agreed-on percentage advance (e.g., 70%, 75%, 80%, 85%).
- In essence, when the borrower submits an invoice, it can borrow immediately 80 cents on the dollar under an 80% advance plan.
- The borrower requests advances (loans) that are deposited to its checking account.
- When it collects its receivables, the borrower remits the cash to the lender; this reduces the borrower's collateral account and directly reduces the loan by the amount of the remittance.
- The borrower's and lender's collateral and loan records are reconciled periodically.

- The larger of the agreed-on percentage advance against available collateral, or the guideline, is the maximum amount that is loaned.

The commercial finance customer also generally agrees to surprise visits every two or three months by a field examiner, who examines the company's books and records to assure the lender that all information was reported properly.

In a commercial finance field examination, the field examiner looks at certain characteristics and qualities of the borrower and its receivables, including the following:

- *Concentration of customers*. The lender does not want too many dollars' worth of receivables concentrated with any one customer of the borrower, unless that customer is very large and creditworthy. Generally, a bank looks at the concentration among the borrower's five largest customers to make sure that the concentration is not excessive.
- *Credit policies*. The borrower's credit policies are reviewed closely to ensure (a) that they are consistent with industry standards, and (b) that customers are remitting to the borrower in accordance with those credit policies.
- *Returns and allowances*. The field auditor ensures that returns and allowances are not excessive (i.e., not in excess of, perhaps, 0.5 to 1.5% of gross sales, depending on the industry).
- *Aged accounts receivable balance*. The field auditor checks to make sure that the latest aging received from the borrower is accurate.
- *Turnover*. The field auditor spotchecks totals on the borrower's accounts receivable subsidiary ledger cards to ensure that the detailed records agree with the trial balance, are accurate, and that there are no particularly slow payers (or, if there are, that they are being pursued vigorously).
- *Accounts payable*. The field auditor looks at the borrower's accounts payable trial balance to determine whether trade creditors are being paid promptly. This helps to ensure that the bank's working capital loan is being used to pay vendors rather than to finance an excessive inventory build-up, for example.
- *Payroll taxes*. The field auditor reviews receipted depository tickets to verify that the borrower has been depositing payroll taxes in a federal depository as required by law. This is important for two reasons. First, a bank that is lending money to a customer for its working capital needs can be construed to have made loans for payroll and may, therefore, be liable for payroll taxes not withheld. Second, if the federal government files a tax lien against the borrower, the tax lien can become senior to the other security interests filed against the borrower (i.e., those from banks or other lenders).

- *Checking account reconciliation*. The field auditor reviews the general ledger cash balance and the company's bank statement to ensure that cash balances reconcile and that all customer remittances are being deposited promptly.

What Type of Inventory is "Good" Collateral?

A commercial financing arrangement will often extend an additional loan amount secured by inventory, usually a flat amount or a small percentage advance against the inventory. This is generally done to increase credit availability to the borrower. The following characteristics increase the value of the inventory as collateral:

- Limited perishability.
- Interchangeability or homogeneity of goods.
- High value of the inventory in relationship to its bulk and weight.
- Price stability in the marketplace and a broad, organized market for the product.
- A clean, unencumbered security interest for the borrower.
- A nonspecialized, general-purpose type of product.
- A higher proportion of raw materials or (less so) finished goods, as opposed to work-in-process, which is harder to dispose of.

Although most accounts receivable qualify for an advance of somewhere between 70% to 85% of their total value, most inventory qualifies for an advance of between 30% and 60%. Many lenders may be even more conservative when accepting inventory as collateral.

Use of a Bonded Warehouse

Sometimes lenders will grant higher percentage loans against inventory, but when they do, they commonly require borrowers to use public or field warehouses. This puts the inventory in control of a bonded third party who will disburse it only on the basis of warehouse receipts, which are used to keep track of the exact level of inventory.

The fruit and vegetable canning industry in California makes wide use of the field warehouse. Fruits and vegetables are harvested at one time and processed quickly; therefore, the canning company needs to finance this finished goods inventory while it is sold gradually. Units of inventory are distributed throughout the year, warehouse receipts go to the bank, and the borrower's inventory collateral records are reduced. This warehousing method is considered to be an effective method of protecting the interests of the lenders and providing a higher percentage of advance against inventory.

CONCLUSION

This chapter has presented the general principles behind financing a going concern, including:

- The typical uses of funds in a business environment.
- The importance of matching the maturity of sources and uses of funds.
- The three general types of credit available.
- Certain specific types of loans.
- The "Four C's" of credit analysis.
- Collateral and how it is evaluated and monitored by the lender.

In the next chapter, the various institutional sources of these types of loans are described and compared with respect to interest rates and particular loan requirements.

12

Financing A Going Concern: Sources of Funds

The previous chapter presented the basic types of lending arrangements available to a borrower. It stressed the fact that any loan or lending arrangement is one or a combination of these basic types. This chapter focuses on the lending organizations which are the principal sources of external debt financing for small- and medium-sized businesses, including:

- Commercial banks.
- The Small Business Administration.
- Commercial finance companies.
- Factors.
- Equipment financing and leasing companies.
- Life insurance companies.
- Local development agencies (for industrial revenue bonds).
- Other financial institutions (e.g., savings and loan associations).

Figure 12.1 summarizes the types of loans offered and the requirements for each source. There is a priority sequence in the granting of

FIGURE 12.1

Summary of Sources and Requirements for Financing Small Businesses

Source	*Provides:* *Short-Term Loan*	*Term Loan*	*Revolving Loan*	*Requirements—General*	*Comments*
Commercial	X X	X X X X	X X X	• Proforma financial statements • Historical financial statements • Collateral valuation (if required) • Personal guarantee of principals (if required) • Permission for surprise audits of receivables, payables, and inventory records by lender's personnel	• Bank will generally lend for no more than seven years, although five is a bank's preferred maturity (see Life Insurance section) • Will generally lend 75% to 80% of book value of collateral • Seasonal borrowings require annual "clean-up" (i.e., for borrower to be out of debt for at least two months) • Generally advance funds on a formula basis (e.g., 80% of receivables less than 90 days old and 50% of inventory) • Market interest rates

FIGURE 12.1 (Cont.)
Summary of Sources and Requirements for Financing Small Businesses

Source	*Provides:* *Short-Term Loan*	*Term Loan*	*Revolving Loan*	*Requirements—General*	*Comments*
Commercial Banks—SBA Guaranteed	X	X		• Same as banks • SBA Form 4-1 (filled out by bank) to SBA (see Figure 12.6)	• Generally only lend on a secured term basis • Market interest rates (with a ceiling)
SBA—Direct	X	X		• Same as banks, and • SBA Forms 4 (see Figure 12.4) • Must have been declined credit by two banks	• Financial condition requirements are significantly less strict • Preference to minorities • Funds limited • Interest below market rates
Commercial Finance Companies			X	• Historical financial statements • Break-even (or better) operating record on average • Large (relatively speaking) investment in receivables and inventory of relatively good quality • Permission for surprise audits of receivables, payables, and inventory records by lender's personnel	• Can be of significant assistance in financing rapid growth situations • Relatively high interest rates • Generally advance funds on a formula basis (e.g., 80% of receivables less than 90 days old and 50% of inventory)

FIGURE 12.1 (Cont.)

Summary of Sources and Requirements for Financing Small Businesses

Source	*Provides:* Short-Term Loan	Term Loan	Revolving Loan	*Requirements—General*	*Comments*
Factors			X	• Relatively good quality accounts receivable • Break-even operating record on average • Thorough pre-screening of all a borrower's credit customers	• High financing charges • Frequently used by textile, garment, shoe, and clothing industry
Equipment Financing or Equipment-ment leasing Company	X	X		• Collateral valuation • Break-even (or better) operating record	
Life Insurance Companies	X	X		• Collateral valuation • General purpose land and building • At least five years of profitable operations • Same factors as bank	• Will lend up to 35–40 years on good commercial real estate • Will lend up to 15 years on large commercial equipment (will often participate with bank) • May offer unsecured term loan to very creditworthy borrower

FIGURE 12.1 (Cont.)

Summary of Sources and Requirements for Financing Small Businesses

Source	*Provides:* Short-Term Loan	Term Loan	Revolving Loan	*Requirements—General*	*Comments*
Local Development Companies/ Industrial Revenue Bonds	X	X		• Collateral valuation • Same factors as bank	• Will finance plant or heavy equipment investment • Loan decision takes into account the number of jobs created • Generally, investment should be at least $500,000 to make IRB issuance cost justifiable • Provides 100% financing
Other Financial Institutions		X		• Collateral valuation • General purpose land and building • Profitable operations	

credit to small- and medium-sized businesses. The more creditworthy the company, the more likely that it can obtain financing from more sources, including commercial banks. The most creditworthy businesses regularly use commercial banks for loans that are not for a special purpose, but they may use other types of loans in special situations. Some industries, however, have always borrowed from commercial finance companies or factors, regardless of the creditworthiness of the borrower. Among these industries are the shoe industry, the garment industry, and carpet and textile manufacturing. For any given type of loan, the sources are listed in Figure 12.1 in order of the creditworthiness of the borrower.

COMMERCIAL BANKS

Commercial banks are the supermarket of external financial services for the small- and medium-sized business. Banks offer all three types of loans—short-term, term, and revolving—on both a secured and an unsecured basis. In addition, banks offer other, more specialized services, such as commercial financing, equipment financing and leasing, floor planning, and commercial real estate financing, all of which were discussed in the previous chapter. They also offer special types of financing not discussed here, such as letter of credit financing and certain types of acceptance and export–import financing, which have limited applicability to smaller businesses.

Banks have the "'first pick" of borrowers in many nonspecial-purpose lending situations because a bank's credit requirements are more strict and the interest rates it charges tend to be lower than many alternative sources. And, because of the short-term nature of their funds' sources (i.e., demand deposits), a bank ordinarily will not lend on a term or installment loan basis for more than seven years so a borrower that needs a longer loan maturity will look elsewhere.

THE SMALL BUSINESS ADMINISTRATION (SBA)

The SBA makes two general types of loans: direct loans and participation loans. *Direct loans* are an arrangement between the SBA and the business enterprise; they do not go through a bank. These loans are very difficult to obtain, are probably soon to be abolished, and are not a meaningful source of funds for most small businesses.

The SBA makes two types of *participation loans*. They participate with banks in immediate loans, under which the SBA purchases an agreed-on percentage of the loan from the bank as soon as the bank has disbursed the funds to the borrower. By far the more frequent loan assistance by the SBA to small business is the *loan guarantee*. In this program, the lending institution applies to the SBA for a guarantee of the borrower's obligation. The SBA customarily will guarantee 90%, or up to $350,000, of the obligation, whichever is less. The stated limit on loans guaranteed by the SBA is $500,000, but this amount is used under only certain special circumstances: construction of medical facilities, creation or preservation of jobs, energy conservation, improvement of mass transit facilities, and so on. The SBA does not disburse funds to the bank. If the borrower defaults on the loan, the bank "calls" the SBA guarantee and the SBA buys back its 90% of the loan. The SBA then pursues collection.

The SBA guarantees loans for most valid business purposes. For example, it guarantees loans to:

- Finance the construction, conversion, or expansion of facilities and the purchase of land.
- Finance the purchase of machinery and equipment, supplies, materials, facilities, or other fixed assets.
- Finance permanent working capital.
- Assist in a change of ownership of the company (e.g., if one individual is buying the company from another individual).

The maturity of an SBA-guaranteed loan can run anywhere from one year to 20 years, depending on the intended use for the funds. A loan used to finance a new plant generally has a longer maturity, probably 20 years. A loan to finance permanent working capital probably has a maximum maturity of six years and may, in fact, have a much shorter maturity.

The interest rate that banks are allowed to charge on SBA-guaranteed loans is modified periodically. It is usually a "spread" above the prime rate. For example, the current allowable interest rate may be 2.25 points above prime for loans maturing in seven years or less and 2.75 points above prime for loans maturing in more than seven years. However, the SBA might set a "floor" and a "ceiling" on interest rates. For example, the interest rate on a five-year loan may be stated as 2.25 points above prime when that interest rate varies between 8% and 18%. In this example, by terms of the agreement with the SBA, a bank would not be allowed to charge more than 20.25% (18% plus 2.25%). This is helpful to the entrepreneur in determining the maximum repayment.

The SBA usually requires that the bank take as collateral any assets that are available to be pledged, as well as the assets that are being purchased with the loan proceeds. Because the SBA likes to lend only on a term-loan basis, it tends to be less likely to accept the working capital type of collateral; it is more likely to look to fixed assets and equipment as collateral. In addition, the SBA ordinarily requires the personal guarantee of the owners of the company.

SBA-guaranteed loans are most often repaid on a monthly basis. If you have borrowed money from a bank guaranteed by the SBA, you remit your loan payment directly to the bank; unless there is default by you on your loan, you never repay the SBA directly. These monthly payments are usually level payments of varying amounts of principal and interest and are calculated in much the same way that your home mortgage is, with reducing amounts of interest and increasing amounts of principal over the term of the loan.

SBA Eligibility Requirements

Qualification as a "small" business depends on the nature of the business and the type of loan being sought. Figure 12.2 lists eligibility requirements for SBA loans by type of business. In addition, the SBA has certain general requirements that a small business must fulfill in order to be considered for either direct SBA financing or SBA participation financing. Most of these requirements are addressed by a well-conceived business plan. The requirements are:

- The borrower must have been refused conventional financing on reasonable terms (direct SBA loans only).
- The borrower must be of good character and have sufficient experience and knowledge to operate the business successfully.
- The borrower usually must have a maximum debt-to-worth ratio of 4 to 1. (This rule is stretched and is, practically speaking, determined by the lending bank and the nature of the industry.)
- The borrower must have adequate collateral to secure the loan. (This does not necessarily mean that the SBA requires that the loan be secured 100%.)
- The historical financial record of the borrower must be such that repayment is likely.
- The borrower's principal(s) must have enough of his or her own personal resources at stake in order to have a continuing strong interest in the business.
- The borrower cannot use the loan to repay existing creditors, to pay dividends to owners, or to repay debt to a Small Business Investment Company (SBIC) (discussed later in this chapter).
- The borrower cannot be a not-for-profit or religious organization.
- The business cannot be in print media, gambling, lending or investments, or distribution sales ("home sales franchise" type of business, for example).
- The granting of the SBA aid cannot promote a monopolistic situation.

FIGURE 12.2
Loan Eligibility Requirements
Small Business Administration

Type of Business Concern	*Sales Not to Exceed ($ Millions)*	*Number of Employees Not to Exceed*	*Exceptions/Comments* [a]
Construction	$5.0 to 9.5	—	Depends on specific type of construction performed
Manufacturing	—	—	If number of employees exceeds 250, eligibility decision is on a case-by-case basis. If a firm has more than 1500 employees, it is automatically ineligible.
Retail			
Clothing, Shoes, Household Appliances	$2.5	—	—
Variety	3.0	—	—
Farm equipment	4.5	—	—
Motor vehicles	6.5	—	—
Department, grocery, meat, fish	7.5	—	—
All other	2.0	—	—
Services			
Hotel-Motel	$3.0	—	—
Laundry	3.0	—	—
Motion picture production	8.0	—	—
Engineering	3.5	—	—
Hospital	N/A	—	Not to exceed 150 beds.
All others	1.5	—	—
Shopping Centers	N/A	N/A	Assets cannot exceed $8 million. Net worth cannot exceed $4 million. Average net income cannot exceed $400,000. No more than 25% of gross leasable space leased to concerns exceeding SBA standards.
Transportation and Warehousing			
Air transportation	N/A	1000	
Grain Storage	$1.5	N/A	Stored grain cannot exceed 1 million bushels
Trucking, Warehousing, Packaging, Crating, Freight Forwarding			
Other	1.5	—	—
Wholesale	$9.5		There are exceptions that permit certain types of wholesale operations to have sales of between $14.5 and $22.0 Million.
Farming and Agriculture Related	$1.0	—	—

[a] For specific definitions and eligibility decisions, contact local SBA field office.

- A business cannot use the proceeds of the loan to relocate, except for a sound business purpose.
- Principals of the company cannot be government employees with a staff grade or designation of GS–13 or higher.

How to Get an SBA Loan

A small business does not apply for the SBA guarantee; a lender applies. Once the bank has determined that it would not be willing to lend money to the borrower under normal commercial circumstances, and at reasonable commercial rates, it may, along with the borrower, decide to file a "Lender's Application for Guarantee or Participation," SBA Form 4-I; this is filed with the local Small Business Administration field office. Most of the information required should already be included in your business plan; completing the application should be only a matter of putting the information into a different format.

The loan application asks for information from the lender about the proposed loan and about the borrower's available collateral, credit history, management skills, management structure, ratio analysis, and credit analysis. If the application is approved by the SBA, the bank can make the loan to the borrower with the assurance that 90% of the related principal and interest will be reimbursed to the bank by the SBA in the event of default.

Do not assume that just because the bank has an SBA guarantee on the loan that the bank is "home free." First, to apply for an SBA guarantee, the bank has to determine that it is not willing to lend to this business on a direct, non-guaranteed basis. This indicates that the bank feels the risk in the loan is too large. An SBA-guaranteed loan does not eliminate the risk, but it reduces the dollar amount of the bank's risk from 100% of the loan to, usually, 10% of the loan. Also, the bank has less freedom in terms of its relationship with the borrower than it might otherwise have if the loan were not guaranteed by the SBA. For example, if you were to request that the bank allow you to make your normal monthly payment a week late, the bank might be concerned about granting the credit because the SBA could construe the extension as an effective renegotiation of loan terms. Potentially, the guarantee could be made void.

In addition to commercial banks, other financial organizations are getting into the business of making SBA-guaranteed loans. For example, a large insurance company and a large brokerage firm have recently been given permission to make 90% SBA-guaranteed loans.

COMMERCIAL FINANCE COMPANIES

Commercial finance companies provide exactly the same service as the commercial finance departments of banks. (Commercial financing is discussed in detail in Chapter 11.) This type of financing is often referred to as *asset-based lending* and is provided by such companies as Commercial Credit Corporation, Walter Heller, and others. (A list of commercial finance companies can be obtained from the National Commercial Finance Conference, One Penn Plaza, New York, New York 10001.)

The commercial finance department of a bank and a commercial finance company have different philosophies regarding the repayment of loans. The bank still regards the customer as being a reasonably good credit risk, despite the fact that the bank has taken collateral. The bank regards the collateral as only a secondary repayment source. Often, a commercial finance company is more concerned with the quality of the underlying collateral than with the creditworthiness of the borrower. Commercial finance companies, because of their expertise with receivables and inventory-based loans, can frequently advance to the borrower a higher percentage against the collateral. Because of its contacts and experience, it will generally receive more for the assets in liquidation than a commercial bank will. As a result of higher risks and greater handling costs, however, *interest rates are generally significantly higher at a commercial finance company than they are with a commercial finance department of a bank*. (The difference can be 1% to 3%.)

FACTORS

Factoring is similar to the financing arranged by a commercial finance company, except that the factor buys, and therefore legally owns, the receivable rather than taking it as collateral. The factor buys on either a recourse basis (i.e., if the account debtor does not pay, the factor can go back to the borrower for collection) or nonrecourse (just the opposite) basis. In a factoring arrangement, therefore, the accounts receivable credit risk is shifted from the borrower to the factor. Most factoring is done on a notification basis. The factor notifies the account debtor to remit directly to the factor.

Factoring is generally considered to be the next alternative for a borrower once it can no longer qualify for a commercial finance company loan. The factor is remunerated for the potentially higher risk with a higher return. For years, however, certain industries have tended to use factors, regardless of whether the borrower is creditworthy. These industries are the garment industry, the shoe industry, and the carpet and textile manufacturing industries. Some commercial bank holding companies and many commercial finance companies even own factoring subsidiaries.

SOURCES OF COMMERCIAL EQUIPMENT FINANCING

Commercial equipment financing can take any of the following forms:

1. New equipment purchase financing (loans).
2. Lease financing.
3. Sale-and-leaseback financing of owned equipment.
4. Owned equipment as collateral for a new loan.

Of these four types of equipment financing, the first two relate principally to acquiring a new piece of equipment. The second two relate principally to using existing fixed assets to release working capital for other uses.

Commercial equipment loans and leases can be obtained through three principal sources:

- Commercial banks and their leasing departments (previously discussed).
- Equipment vendors.
- Independent (not affiliated with banks) equipment financing or leasing companies.

Characteristics of Commercial Equipment Lending Companies

Commercial equipment lending companies supply the first and fourth types of financing—new or existing equipment loans—listed earlier. The two types of equipment loan have very similar requirements, as follows:

- The *type* of loan used for equipment is often an installment-type loan.
- The *maturity* of the loan is generally tied to the useful life of the equipment. The "normal" term would be between three and seven years.
- The *down payment* required will range between 10 and 30 percent.
- The *rate* is a function of collateral, maturity of the loan, and creditworthiness of the borrower. It may be slightly higher from a vendor financer or from an independent commercial equipment company than from a bank, especially if you purchase several pieces of equipment and include them all in one term or installment loan.

Characteristics of Commercial Equipment Leasing Companies

Commercial equipment leasing companies provide the second and third listed types of financing—leases and sale-and-leaseback loans.

The requirements for *leases* are:

- The *payment schedule* on an equipment lease is generally on a monthly basis.
- The *term* of the lease is somewhat less than the useful life of the equipment, most often three to ten years.
- A *down payment* is usually not required; however, the leasing company often will require a few (sometimes six) months' prepayment of the lease.
- The *effective rate* is a function of the equipment financed and the creditworthiness of the lessee and is generally higher than a straight equipment loan.

The requirements for *sale-and-leaseback* are:

- Sale-and-leaseback is offered by the same organizations that would offer direct leasing arrangements.
- The prospective borrower sells assets which it presently owns to the leasing company and leases them back.
- This arrangement converts an investment in a fixed asset to working capital (cash).
- The ownership rests with the lessor (leasing company).
- Lease payments generally are tax deductible to the lessee and the lessor can deduct depreciation.
- Major emphasis is placed on the lessee's general financial position and ability to pay the lease. In addition, the quality, location, and the designated purpose of the asset are of importance. The lessee generally continues to assume all costs of operating the asset (i.e., insurance, maintenance, taxes, etc.). You should confer with your accountant or attorney before consummating a sale-and-leaseback.
- IRS rules could require capitalization of certain assets.

There are two *types of lease financing*. A lease can be written as an *operating lease* or as a *financial lease*. Confer with your tax advisor regarding the substantial tax differences between the two. Some of the nontax characteristics of a *financial lease*, as opposed to an operating lease are:

- The financial lease is a fixed, noncancellable obligation.

- The total of all payments under a financial lease exceeds 90% of the purchase price.
- The financial lease is a "net" lease, which means that the lessee pays all property taxes, maintenance costs, and utilities.
- The financial lease can be viewed as debt, except that under bankruptcy laws for a broken lease the allowed lessor claim is usually only one year's lease payments.

LIFE INSURANCE COMPANIES

Life insurance companies make only term or installment loans and are an important source of intermediate- and long-term debt financing for businesses. Ordinarily, they make commercial mortgages secured by real property; many insurance companies make 35- and 40-year commercial mortgages. And often, they are the source of permanent financing that pays off a bank's construction loan.

Today, life insurance companies make many other long-term loans, generally secured by equipment. And they are participating (sharing) more frequently in long-term loans with commercial banks. The two entities jointly make a long-term loan (e.g., 15 years) with the understanding that interest to both parties will be paid as due, but that the bank's principal will be repaid first. Often a bank's participation will extend no more than seven years. This practice has allowed the commercial banking industry to meet its customers' increasing demands for longer-term credit.

Insurance companies are often willing to lend at a fixed rate because, in keeping with the philosophy of matching the maturity of sources and uses of funds, the insurance company's sources of funds (actuarial reserves) are also relatively long-term and fixed in cost to the insurance company.

LOCAL DEVELOPMENT AGENCIES (LDAs)

Industrial revenue bonds (IRBs) allow private companies to issue debt at tax-free low interest rates comparable to those typically paid by tax-exempt public agencies and municipalities. In the case of IRBs, a local government development agency serves as an intermediary between the borrower and lender. The funds are used for plant construction and expansion usually.

The bonds are issued, although not usually guaranteed, by the development agency (which usually sells them as a block to a bank(s), an insurance company, or other lender). The proceeds of the sale are loaned directly to the borrower (after the development agency deducts underwriting costs).

Because the bonds are issued by a government agency, the interest income is tax-free to the lender. Therefore, the interest rate on the debt is 2.0% to 4.5% lower than if the interest was taxable. The ultimate borrower benefits from the low interest rate and is charged a small administrative fee.

Most costs associated with the acquisition or construction of an industrial site can be financed. The bonds are also exempt from SEC filing requirements. Because of fairly heavy issuance costs, $500,000 is considered the IRB break-even point, below which a business would be better off with another form of financing. Above this level, IRBs result in significant savings to the company. Below it, other forms of conventional financing are probably more cost-effective, depending on the interest rate differential.

OTHER FINANCIAL INSTITUTIONS

The only other principal source of credit for small- and medium-sized businesses is the savings institution, which usually provides commercial mortgage financing for general-purpose commercial property. A savings bank considers the borrower's creditworthiness and the underlying value of the collateral in making the loan.

SPECIAL SITUATIONS

There is loan money available for minority businesses headed by women, blacks, and other minorities, for farmers, and for businesses that are in certain unusual or difficult situations. There are loans to assist in air and water pollution control. There are disaster loans, economic injury loans, and the like. Unfortunately, securing these loans usually requires heavy paperwork, which is extremely time-consuming. In addition, the decision-making process by the leader is often lengthy. Figures 12.3 and 12.4 summarize assistance offered by Federal Government Agencies to small business loans available for special situations.

There are many other types of loans available to small business in special situations—as those with handicapped owners, native American owners, minority owners, a particular proportion of handicapped or minority employees, and so on. An excellent book is available from the Northeast–Midwest Institute. It is *Guide to Federal Resources for Economic Development* (3589 House Annex #2, Washington, D.C. 20515, (202) 225-1082). The book, funded through a grant by the U.S. Department of

Commerce, provides an inventory of the large number of loan programs that are available.

Another useful source book is published by the U.S. Department of Commerce, Task Force on Women's Business Enterprise. The report is entitled *The Guide to the U.S. Department of Commerce for Women Business Owners*. It is for sale by the Superintendent of Documents, U.S. Government Printing Office, Washington, D.C. 20402, stock number 003-000-00556-9.

At this date some programs listed in Figures 12.3 and 12.4 are under budgetary scrutiny and may be cut. If you are interested in any of these programs, check with the responsible agency to obtain an update.

CONCLUSION

This chapter has described the various institutions that are practical sources of credit to small businesses. These sources have been presented in a rough priority sequence on the basis of the availability of funds and the required degree of creditworthiness of the borrower. The types of services available from each source have been summarized. Heading the list are commercial banks, which often have the broadest range of financing alternatives and have the funds available. Also discussed are loans available from federal government agencies for special situations. Remember, though, that dealing with the government can result in tremendous red tape.

The next chapter presents various practical details of "getting the money," including how to choose your bank and how to make yourself creditworthy.

FIGURE 12.3

Types of Loan Assistance Offered By Federal Government Agencies To Small Businesses[a]

Type of Loan	*Objective of Program*	*Eligible Activities*	*Range*	*Where to Apply*	*Who May Apply*	*Comments*
Regular Business Loans—Section 7 a	To assist small business unable to obtain financing in the private credit market	Construction, conversion, expansion, purchase of machinery, equipment, acquisition of working capital, change of ownership	Up to $500,000	SBA field offices or bank (for guaranteed loans)	Small businesses which meet the various size eligibility requirement	Loans can either be directly from SBA or from bank, guaranteed by SBA (See Chapters 11 and 12.)
Economic Opportunity Loans	To make funds available on a reasonable basis to business concerns located in economically disadvantaged areas or to low income individuals	Purchase of real estate, machinery, and equipment; acquisition of working capital	Up to $100,000	SBA field offices	Low income, economically disadvantaged individuals who own businesses	
Displaced Business Loans Economic Injury Loans Physical Disaster Loans	To assist firms suffering economic injury due to: 1. displacement from federally aided construction (highway, urban renewal) 2. a major natural disaster 3. inability to market a product because of toxicity due to natural causes	Replacement cost of realty, equipment, re-establishment of business, interim operating expenses	Up to $200,000	SBA field offices	Businesses that have been displaced or injured by federal government action or natural disaster	
State and Local Development Company Loans (SDC and LDC)	To provide long-term financing to small businesses through state and local development companies	Plant and equipment acquisition, conversion, construction, modernization	Up to $1 million	State or local development companies	Small businesses	Funds not available for working capital or refinancing

FIGURE 12.3 (Cont.)
Types of Loan Assistance Offered By Federal Government Agencies To Small Businesses

Type of Loan	Objective of Program	Eligible Activities	Range	Where to Apply	Who May Apply	Comments
Occupational Safety and Health Loans	To provide aid to small businesses that (either voluntarily or under order) wish to comply with the Occupational Safety and Health Act of 1970	Additions, alterations in facilities, equipment or procedures that are needed for compliance with the Occupational Safety and Health Act of 1970	Up to $750,000	SBA field offices	Small businesses with OSHA requirements	
Air and Water Pollution Control Loans	To assist small companies in meeting federal air and water pollution control requirements	Additions, alterations in facilities, equipment, or procedures to comply with the Federal Water Pollution Control Act or the Clean Air Act	Up to $850,000	SBA field offices	Small businesses that, because of discharge of waste, come under the jurisdiction of one of the acts	
Strategic Arms Economic Injury Loans	To assist small businesses that are suffering injury caused by loss of federal contracts due to an international agreement to limit arms spending	Provision of working capital while the firm is recovering from economic dislocation	Up to $250,000	SBA field offices	Small businesses	
Emergency Energy Shortage Loans	To assist small businesses that have been or are likely to be seriously affected by shortages of energy, fuel, or raw or processed materials	Purchase of equipment to use an alternative energy source, provision of interim working capital during changes in equipment or procedures	Up to $250,000	SBA field offices	Small businesses	

FIGURE 12.3 (Cont.)
Types of Loan Assistance Offered By Federal Government Agencies To Small Businesses

Type of Loan	*Objective of Program*	*Eligible Activities*	*Range*	*Where to Apply*	*Who May Apply*	*Comments*
Seasonal Line of Credit Program	To assist highly seasonal small business (e.g., toy manufacturers, ice skating rinks)	Provision of seasonal working capital	Up to $500,000	SBA field offices	Small businesses	Annual payout required
Contract Loan Program	To provide small businesses with financial assistance on specific contracts (up to the cost of labor and materials)	To finance a specific contract(s)	Up to the amount of the specific contract	SBA field offices	Small businesses	Contract proceeds must be legally assignable to SBA (as collateral)
Small Business Investment Company (SBIC) and Minority Enterprise Small Business Investment Company (MESBIC)	To funnel loan and equity funds to small businesses and to economically and socially disadvantaged entities	To provide 5- to 20-year loans and/or purchase of convertible securities	Up to 20% of SBIC's capital (usually no more than $1 million)	Private SBIC or MESBIC	Small businesses	SBICs are privately owned. They are licensed and loaned to by SBA. They, in turn, loan/invest in companies that meet SBA size requirements
Export-Import Bank of the U.S. ("Eximbank")	To assist in the financing of U.S. foreign trade	To provide insurance covering commercial and political risks, guaranteeing payment of short- and medium-term export transactions	N/A	Eximbank Washington, DC 20571	Exporters (businesses), Banks	

[a] Many of these programs are being re-evaluated and could be discontinued.

FIGURE 12.4
Additional Sources of Financing For Small Businesses in Special Situations

Type of Loan	*Agency*	*Purpose in Brief*
Energy Loans	Department of Energy	To assist firms and companies that wish to manufacture, distribute, or service certain energy equipment, such as solar energy equipment, wood-burning devices, hydroelectric devices, wind energy equipment, etc.
Electric and Hybrid Vehicle Loans	Department of Energy	To arrange for financing for small businesses engaged in the development of electric or other non-combustion engine motor vehicles.
Bureau of Commercial Fisheries	U.S. Department of the Interior, Bureau of Commercial Fisheries	To assist members of the domestic fishing industry in the cost of purchasing, constructing, equipping, or maintaining new or used commercial fishing vessels and fishing gear.
Bureau of Reclamation	Bureau of Reclamation Regional offices	To provide loans and grants for small reclamation and irrigation programs, primarily in the western states and Hawaii.
Ship building	Maritime Administration, Washington, D.C.	To assist small shipowners in obtaining construction loans and ship mortgages for the construction, conversion, or reconditioning of ocean-going vessels.
Bureau of Indian Affairs	Bureau of Indian Affairs	To finance commercial enterprises of and education of native Americans.

FIGURE 12.4 (Cont.)
Additional Sources of Financing For Small Businesses in Special Situations

Type of Loan	*Agency*	*Purpose in Brief*
Geological Survey	Office of Minerals Exploration Geological Survey, Washington, D.C.	To encourage exploration and discovery of domestic mineral deposits by providing financial assistance.
Agricultural Loans	The Agricultural Stabilization and Conservation Service	To provide loans to farmers in commodities that are stored awaiting shipment to market, to facilitate crop support programs, and to expand or build physical farm storage facilities.
Rural Business and Industry Loans	The Farmers Home Administration	To start or expand family farming businesses in rural areas in the United States and to provide financing for land improvement, equipment, labor, and working capital.
Banks for Cooperatives	Local Bank for Cooperatives/ Farm Credit Administration	To provide loan services to farmer cooperatives.
Federal Land Banks	Local Federal Land Bank Association	To provide long-term mortgage financing for the purpose of enlargement or improvement of farms.

13

Banks, Creditworthiness, and You

This chapter discusses some additional factors that you should be aware of in order to "get the money," including:

- How to choose a commercial bank.
- How to improve your odds of getting the money by improving your creditworthiness.
- What the basic facts are regarding loan documentation and why you should retain an attorney.
- How to figure out your personal net worth.

You should not underestimate the importance of these factors. They are valuable tips that will improve your chances of getting the money and understanding the related terms and conditions.

HOW TO CHOOSE A COMMERCIAL BANK

Willie Sutton, the late notorious bank robber, visited banks because, as he said, "That's where the money is." You should establish a relationship with a bank for exactly that reason, but the selection criteria are considerably different for you!

What are the important attributes to look for in a commercial bank? Some of the more significant ones are discussed in this section.

Financial Counseling and Advice

One of the most valuable services that a commercial loan officer can perform for you is the function of external financial expert. It is your banker's job to stay abreast of financial developments. You and your banker's self-interest also coincide. Both you and your banker are interested in your having a strong, viable company. So you should look for a bank where the loan officers specialize in businesses of your size and type. The relationship with the person handling the loan should be strong, and the commercial loan officer should be well versed in financial management for businesses in your industry.

Loyalty

The loyalty of a commercial bank to its customers is extremely important. Certain banks, when times get a little rough, may quickly shut the window on applications for credit line increases (especially for smaller customers). Others will work with you as much as possible to help solve your problems.

Degree of Loan Specialization

It is important to you as the owner of a smaller business that your lending arrangement be serviced by the department in the bank that specializes in your particular kind of loan. For example, you would not want a national accounts officer handling your loan, nor do you want your commercial finance loan handled by an officer who specializes in personal and automobile loans.

Understanding of Your Industry

A banker who has adequate knowledge of your industry and its particular financing requirements can be an invaluable resource. The banker will not have to familiarize himself with your business—taking your time to do so—and will be in a better position to provide the financial counseling service you need. If you actively request your banker's advice on certain matters, he or she may be more responsive to you as an interested customer. Most professionals, including bankers, accountants, lawyers, and consultants, like to give advice, and your banker generally will not send you an invoice for the cost of that advice because it is also in his or her best interests to keep you financially strong.

Full Range of Services

Choose a bank that offers you a full range of banking services. These services include not only commercial loans but also commercial financing, leasing, international services (even if you do not do any international business in the normal course of events, there may be a time when you will need a letter of credit or banker's acceptance financing), commercial equipment financing, investment in money market instruments, wire transfers, and the like.

The Bank's Overall Reputation

Some banks have a reputation for being aggressive in making loans to small and developing companies. A bank's size and stance relative to competing banks in the market, its geographical proximity, and your access to its key officials are other types of the more general and subjective factors that you must evaluate.

MAKING YOURSELF CREDITWORTHY

Why may a lender refuse to grant you credit? The potential reasons are numerous, ranging from the objective to the very subjective. Figure 13.1 shows the results of a survey: "Reasons Cited by Banks for Loan Rejections Involving Small Business." This information is important because it shows *from the lender's perspective* why credit was refused.

You should try to analyze your situation from the bank's perspective. Listen to a banker: "Before applying for credit, a prospective borrower should attempt to analyze his or her own situation from the perspective and viewpoint of the banker or lender who will be lending the company money. The entrepreneur should anticipate the banker's questions and give careful consideration to the answers." Although specific and detailed questions will vary according to the particular situation, the following are some questions to which the entrepreneur should be sure to have the answers before making a trip to the bank. (Almost all these questions are answered by your business plan.)

FIGURE 13.1
Reasons Cited by Banks for Loan Rejections Involving Small Businesses

Reasons for Loan Rejections Involving Small Businesses	*Percentage of All Banks Citing Each Reason as "Relatively Important"*
Reasons involving creditworthiness of borrower:	
1. Not enough owner's equity in the business.	93%
2. Poor earnings record.	85%
3. Questionable management ability.	84%
4. Collateral of insufficient quality or quantity.	73%
5. Slow and past due in trade or loan payments.	69%
6. Inadequacy of borrower's accounting system.	51%
7. New firm with no established earnings record.	48%
8. Poor moral risk (i.e., "character" questions).	48%
9. Other reasons.	6%
Reasons involving bank's overall policies:	
1. Requested maturity of the loan too long.	71%
2. Applicant has no established deposit relationship with the bank.	49%
3. Applicant will not establish a deposit relationship with bank.	36%
4. Type of loan not handled by the bank.	33%
5. Line of business not handled by the bank.	21%
6. Loan portfolio for that type of loan already full.	19%
7. Other reasons.	4%
Reasons involving federal or state banking laws or regulations:	
1. Loan too large for bank's legal loan limit.	23%
2. Other reasons.	9%

Source: *Report of Federal Reserve System to Committees on Banking and Currency and Select Committees on Small Business:* U.S. Congress: Government Printing Office: Part II, Volume III, p. 415: Financing Small Business.

- What is the purpose of the proposed loan?
- How much is needed and how is this need documented (i.e., with a business plan, cash flow projections, etc.)?
- How and when will the loan be repaid? One of the most important questions a banker will ask in making a credit evaluation is the source of repayment. Any banker wants a primary and secondary source of repayment and wants the terms of repayment carefully spelled out.

- What is the probability that the plan, as outlined, will deviate significantly from what is stated?
- If the plan does backfire, what will be the situation of the company and how will it meet its commitment to the bank? In other words, if the primary source of repayment fails, how good is the secondary source of repayment?
- What is the background, character, and experience of the principal executives or owners of the business? This is critical information in the case of a very small business, where typically the success or failure of the business can truly depend on only one or two individuals.
- What is the record of profitability and earnings of the company?
- What is the current financial position of the company?
- What is the quality of collateral available in the event that the bank loan officer wishes to secure the loan?
- And, finally, if this is not a start-up situation, why is the entrepreneur no longer banking with his or her former bank?

As has been mentioned several times before, development of a business plan is the first step in making a financing presentation to a bank. Preparing a business plan in accordance with Part II of this book provides you with the answers to the questions the banker will ask and assures him or her of your management ability. Figure 13.2 "Guide to Creditworthiness," asks a series of questions regarding what banker and lender organizations look for in making loans.

Now follow the seven elements of creditworthiness given in Figure 13.2, and ask yourself these questions in more detail.

Do You Have Enough Equity in the Business?

Have you put enough into the business or induced investors to put enough into the business? You must have enough equity in your business so that the loan does not raise your debt-to-worth ratio too high. "Enough" is different for different situations, but it generally ranges from 20% to 50% of total assets. The bank does not want to "own" your business; it wants you to own it. The bank wants the loan to be simply an adjunct source, usually for some specific aspect of your operations. Also, the bank wants you to have enough invested so that, in time of financial difficulty, you will stick it out and not walk away. The major reason cited by banks for loan rejection involving small businesses was, as you can see in Figure 13.1, "not enough owner's equity in the business."

FIGURE 13.2
Guide to Creditworthiness

What Do Banks and Lending Organizations Look for in Making Loans?	
Capital	Do you have enough equity in the business?
Management capability	Have you shown evidence that you are a good manager and understand how to run the business?
Collateral	Do you have any personal assets that can be used as collateral? What business assets will be available as collateral?
Business plan	Do you have a convincing business plan?
Background and experience	Do your background and experience indicate that you are knowledgeable in your business?
Appearance, personality, and character	Do you show, by your appearance and character, that you believe in yourself and your business and that you are trustworthy?
Community	Have you tried a bank or lending agency in the community where you live and are known or the community in which your business is located? Banks favor their own communities.

Have You Shown Evidence That You Are a Good Manager And Understand How to Run a Business?

It is somewhat more difficult for bank or lending agency to assess whether you understand management techniques and have the ability to manage a business. Because many businesses fail largely because of poor management, this is an important element in judging whether to make the loan.

If you have been in business before in any executive capacity, it is important that this be brought out. You should give any concrete examples of your managerial ability. Your success in running any type of organization, outside activities that show your organizing ability, voluntary efforts in the community where you headed a community charity drive or blood donors' drive or the like—all indicate your ability to manage. A demonstrated ability to plan, organize, administer, and control reassure a creditor that you will be able to use these talents in your own enterprise.

Do You Have Any Assets That Can Be Used As Collateral?

Particularly with loans that involve start-up situations, the bank will ask for collateral. The bank may ask for personal collateral—that is, a lien on your assets outside the business. Second mortgages on property or savings accounts can be used as collateral. If you do pledge your personal assets, the bank may be willing to give you a "purchase money" loan to finance the acquisition of business assets.

Do You Have a Convincing Business Plan?

We have shown you how to put together a business plan, which is the basic tool for convincing a bank or any lending agency to give you a loan. It indicates what type of loan you may need and other essential information. It also helps to convince the banker that you have invested time, have given your business a lot of thought, and most important, that you are in command of the necessary financial and management skills.

Do Your Background and Experience Indicate That You Are Knowledgeable in Your Business?

You will be asked many questions by a banker or lending institution to assess your knowledge of the business you are in or are proposing. Any demonstration of this knowledge will help in your presentation and in building creditworthiness.

One entrepreneur had a remarkable record in his former job and could show his familiarity with the market his proposed company would be attempting to penetrate. Another could demonstrate, by his many years of manufacturing experience, his skill in making the product that his company was to market. A third was starting a construction business similar to one his father had been in years before. He had worked in his father's business and could call upon his father, now retired, for guidance in his new company.

Do You Show, By Your Appearance and Character, That You Believe in Yourself and Your Business and That You Are Trustworthy?

Many people seem to think, and many treatises on getting credit seem to imply, that only objective measurements—such as the business plan, your net worth, your collateral, and so on—have any weight in securing credit. Such objective measurements are necessary, but there are several subjective elements—for example, your appearance, personality, and reputation—that are usually given weight, even if only in a negative fashion.

Therefore, dress conservatively. Appeal to the bank's interest in its own profitability and its own future by convincing the bank that you will become a valued customer. Remember, any banking relationship is a two-way street; the bank needs to be convinced that it is going to benefit as much from its association with you as you will.

An additional technique is to be introduced to your prospective banker by a third party whom he or she trusts. This technique helps enormously in increasing your credibility and your viability as a prospective bank borrower.

And remember, in the "care and feeding" of your bank relationship, that *bankers do not like unhappy surprises*. When you talk to the officer about your loan application, do not try to hide the risks or the bad news. Chances are, if the individual is relatively experienced, he or she already knows a lot of the problems in your industry or with your type of company; your failure to acknowledge these problems does an enormous amount of damage to your credibility. In addition, all through your bank relationship, always be the first to let your banker know about bad news. If your explanations are reasonable and if you let the banker know in enough time to act, he or she will respect the fact that your business is well managed and will stick by you.

Have You Tried a Bank or Lending Organization In the Community Where You Live and Are Known or the Community in Which Your Business Is to Be Located?

In most cases it is best to approach your local banks first. This is especially important in a community where you have built a reputation and have family or friends. If you are a depositor in one of the commercial banks, that is a plus.

LOAN DOCUMENTATION—THE BASICS

There are some important legal ramifications of the loan documentation that you will sign with any lender. Therefore, it is important to *retain an attorney*. These documents can have a significant legal impact on your company. It is *imperative* that you understand exactly what you are signing. Get copies from your banker of all documents before the loan closing. Require that any blank spaces be filled in so that you will see everything you will be called upon to sign at the loan closing. Read the documents carefully. A few illuminating points are in order here:

- Unless you intend to personally back the repayment of the note for the monies that your company has borrowed, make sure you sign the note in your corporate capacity, rather than as an individual. For example, sign the note "John Smith, President, ABC Company" not "John Smith." Signing the note in your personal capacity technically makes you an endorser on the note; the bank could legally look to you personally for repayment if your company defaults on the obligation.
- A personal guarantee is a separate document and in most cases says that you personally back all obligations to the bank from your company, rather than just a particular note. In other words, endorsing a note is a narrower obligation in some cases than is a personal guarantee.
- If you have agreed to pledge collateral, either personal or company assets, ensure that those and only those assets are being used as collateral on the loan. Generally speaking, for a lending agency to take a lien on an asset (to have an asset pledged to it), two things have to happen. First, you and the lender must enter into a security agreement of some type that indicates that you in fact agree to pledge these assets. Second, either the bank will take physical possession of the asset (e.g., of marketable securities or a passbook to a savings account) or it will have to file a public notice, indicating that it is a secured creditor and has an interest in the asset. Depending on the asset in question, the filing can take place at any one of a number of different locations.

Have your attorney read and approve all the documents before you sign them. Sometimes in the haste of the closing, it is easy to overlook an important point.

Do not rely on the verbal assurances of a banker, just as you would not rely on verbal assurances of any person with whom you are entering into a legal business arrangement. For example, assume that you are giving the bank a personal guarantee for its loan to your company. The banker may say to you, "Well, yes, in fact, we could get a lien on your house if your company defaulted on its obligation, if, after the company was liquidated, there was still an obligation to the bank. We do not, however, as a matter of bank policy, foreclose on primary residences." Although bankers as a group are honorable people and it may be that the bank would prefer not to have to foreclose on a personal residence, if push comes to shove, the bank might in fact foreclose. It has the legal obligation to its stockholders to pursue whatever legal means are available to it to secure full repayment of the loan. Moreover, if you have personally guaranteed repayment, your equity in your family silver and your stamp collection are probably at stake.

Remember, this is a business relationship and the bank has had its lawyers draw up standard forms that you will be signing. There is no reason why you should not have your lawyer look at the forms to make sure that they are acceptable from your perspective. This is not to say that you should not guarantee or endorse your company's loan. Nor does it imply that you should not give collateral to the bank. Very possibly the bank may not grant the loan otherwise. The point is that you must be aware of the legal recourse the bank has to you and your personal assets. And you must consider, before you close on the loan, what your risks are and whether they are worth the potential reward.

In Chapter 12, there is a listing of some typical restrictive loan covenants in a term loan agreement. Before you sign *any* loan agreement, you should be aware that these covenants *are exactly what the name implies*—restrictive and confining. From the lender's viewpoint, the purpose of the covenants is to prevent any deterioration in the bank's position. Usually, violation of any covenant without the prior written approval of the lender is grounds for the lender to declare the loan in default and, possibly, payable on demand. Do not agree to any covenant that you believe is impossible to live with—you'll only get your business into trouble and give up much of your management prerogative.

A number of legal complications can evolve from the lending and borrowing relationship. For example, a few states protect a guarantor's primary residence by a homestead act. Also, in some states, the type of ownership that you have of your primary residence along with your spouse can determine whether your residence is "attachable." These are some of the reasons why you must retain an attorney. Because cash may be tight and they want to cut expenses, many small businesses decide to "go it alone." However, for a commitment of this magnitude, an attorney is a must for both corporate and personal reasons.

YOUR PERSONAL NET WORTH

Do you know how much you are worth personally? Oddly enough, most people, even entrepreneurs, do not. Yet your net worth is one of the major qualifications for creditworthiness if you are to be personally liable on a loan. You will almost invariably have to make out a personal financial statement when you approach a bank or a lending agency for money if you are to be personally liable.

Figure 13.3 is a reproduction of a personal financial statement form used by a number of banks. You may review it item by item and determine how the fictitious Jack Sprat made out his financial statement when he applied for a loan at his neighborhood bank:

Assets

- *Annual salary or net income*. Annual salary is easy; Jack can show his W-2 Form. But if his income fluctuates (e.g., if he is on commission),

FIGURE 13.3
Personal Financial Statement

PERSONAL FINANCIAL STATEMENT

Name	Social Security No.	Date of Birth	How long at Current Address
Jack Sprat	XXX-XX-XXXX	XXXXX	

Address	City	State	Zip Code
XXXXXXXXXX	XXXXXXXXXX	XXXXXXXXXX	XXXXX

Occupation	How long at Current Occupation?	Position
Telephone Engineer	10 years	Supervisor

Business Address	City	State	Zip Code
Telephone Company	XXXXXXXXXX	XXXXXXXXXX	XXXXX

Important: Income from alimony, child support or separate maintenance payments need not to be revealed if you do not choose to disclose such income and do not wish the Bank to consider it in its credit decision.

Salary or Net Income (after Taxes)	Number of Dependents	Date of Statement
$56,000 Annual Salary	4	

DO NOT LEAVE ANY QUESTIONS UNANSWERED; WRITE "NO" OR "NONE" WHERE APPROPRIATE

ASSETS		LIABILITIES	
Cash In Banks & On Hand (Sch. No. 1)	$ 8,000	Notes Payable To Banks - Unsecured, Secured Direct borrowings only (Sch. No. 1)	$ 6,900
Notes Receivable/Accounts Receivable (Sch. No. 2)	none	Notes Payable To Others - Unsecured, Secured (Sch. No. 3)	none
Loans Receivable (Sch. No. 2)	none	Accounts Payable Due Affiliates, Companies & Individuals (Sch. No. 3)	none
Securities - Readily Marketable U.S. Govt. & listed on Stock Exchanges (Sch. No. 4)	$ 10,000	Loans Against Life Insurance (Sch. No. 5)	$ 5,000
Securities - Not Readily Marketable Unlisted stocks bonds & Investments (Sch. No. 4)	none	Real Estate Taxes & Assessments Payable (Sch. No. 6)	$ 3,000
Life Insurance - Cash Surrender Value (Do not deduct loans) (Sch. No. 5)	$ 11,000	Real Estate Mortgages Payable (Sch. No. 8)	$ 30,000
Mortgages Owned (Sch. No. 6)	none	Federal and State Income Taxes	$ 6,800
Real Estate (Sch. No. 7)	$ 200,000	Charge Accounts Payable	$ 3,000
Automobile(s) Registered in own name (two cars)	$ 20,000	Brokers' Margin Accounts (Sch. No. 9)	none
Other Assets (Itemize) Furnishing of home	$ 30,000	Other Liabilities	
Silver	$ 9,000	Total liabilities	$ 54,000
Paintings	$ 4,000		
Collectibles antiques, stamp collection, etc.	$ 20,000	Net Worth Assets less Liabilities	257,300
TOTAL ASSETS	$ 312,000	TOTAL LIABILITIES AND NET WORTH	$ 312,000

SUPPLEMENTARY SCHEDULES

NOTE: The following data should be furnished as of the same date as this Financial Statement. Fill in all spaces, insert "NONE" where appropriate.

NO. 1 - BANKING RELATIONS List all bank accounts, including savings accounts:

Name and Location of Bank	Cash Balance	Amount of Loan	Indicate How Loan is Endorsed, Guaranteed or Secured
Suburban Bank	$ 2,000	$ 4,000	Personal Loan
Savings Bank	6,000	2,900	Secured by savings balance

NO. 2 NOTES, LOANS, AND ACCOUNTS RECEIVABLE List the largest amounts owed to you:

Name and Address of Debtor	Amount of Debt	Age of Debt	Nature of Debt	If Secured, Describe Security	Date Payment Expected
none	$				

NO. 3 - NOTES, LOANS, AND ACCOUNTS PAYABLE: List the largest amounts owed to you:

Name and Address of Creditor	Amount of Loan	Indicate How Loan is Endorsed, Guaranteed or Secured
See Bank Relations		

NO. 4 - SECURITIES: List all stocks, bonds, etc.:

No. of Shares (Stocks) Face Value (Bonds)	Description of Security	Registered Owner(s)	Cost	Market Value	Book Value	If Pledged, Indicate to Whom
IBM	100 shares	self	$7,000	$ 10,000	$	(not pledged)

03 4486* (5/78)

FIGURE 13.3 (cont'd.)

SUPPLEMENTARY SCHEDULES (Continued)

NO. 5 - LIFE INSURANCE: List all policies in which you are named as the insured.

Beneficiary	Insurance Company	Type of Policy	Face Amount of Policy	Total Cash Surrender Value	Total Loans Against Policy	If Assigned Indicate To Whom
Wife and children	Life Co.	Life	$ 100,000	$ 11,000	$ 5,000	(not assigned)

NO. 6 - MORTGAGES OWNED

Location and Description of Mortgaged Properties	Assessed Value	Market Value	Amount of Owned Mortgage	Mortg. Interest Due & Unpaid	Indicate if 1st or 2nd Mortgage	Amount of Prior Mortgage
none	$	$	$	$		$

MORTGAGE INCOME - During the 12 months period ended ______ 19___. I received interest payments of $______ and ______ principal payments totaling $______ on the above described mortgages.

NO. 7 - REAL ESTATE

Location and Description of Owned Properties	Cost with Improvements	Assessed Value	Market Value	Book Value	Annual Gross Rental Income	Ann. Net Rental Income (Before Depreciation)
11 Maplewood Ave.	$ 80,000	$ 100,000	$ 120,000	$	$ none	$ none

TITLE TO REAL ESTATE - The title to all of the above described properties is in my name solely, except as follows (give details). ______

NO. 8 - REAL ESTATE MORTGAGES PAYABLE - List all mortgages on the above properties: follow the same sequence

FIRST MORTGAGES		SECOND MORTGAGES		Mortgage Payments Due Within One Year	MORTGAGEE
Amount	Maturity	Amount	Maturity		
$60,000	20 yrs.	none		$7,200	Savings & Loan

NO. 9 - BROKERS' MARGIN ACCOUNTS - List the names and addresses of the brokers and indicate the net Amount due to each:

GENERAL

1. ARE YOU CONTINGENTLY LIABLE AS ENDORSER, CO-MAKER, OR GUARANTOR ON ANY DEBT OF CORPORATIONS OR OF OTHERS?
   ☐ YES ☒ NO IF YES, GIVE DETAILS: ______
2. DO YOU MAINTAIN ADEQUATE AMOUNTS OF FIRE, EXTENDED COVERAGE, AND LIABILITY INSURANCE? ☐ YES ☐ NO
3. ARE ANY ASSETS PLEDGED? ☐ YES ☒ NO SEE SCHEDULE(S) ______
4. ARE YOU DEFENDANT IN ANY SUITS OR LEGAL ACTIONS? ☐ YES ☒ NO

   IF YES, GIVE DETAILS: ______
5. HAVE YOU MADE A WILL? ☒ YES ☐ NO IF YES, NAME EXECUTOR Suburban Bank
6. HAVE YOU EVER BEEN DECLARED BANKRUPT? ☐ YES ☒ NO

   IF YES, EXPLAIN: ______

In the following statement the words *I*, *me* and *my* mean anyone signing below. *You* and *your* refer to

PURPOSE: I have given you this financial statement in order to obtain credit or some other benefit from you. I know that you will rely on it and I represent to you that it is correct and truthfully sets forth all of my assets and liabilities, including all indirect liabilities as of this date.

CONTINUING NATURE: I understand that until I give you another written financial statement you will assume and rely on the fact that my financial condition is at least as good as shown on this statement.

ADDITIONAL INFORMATION: If you ask me for any other information about my financial condition, I agree to give it to you.

EXCHANGING CREDIT INFORMATION: You may request credit information about me from others and may furnish credit information about me to others.

OBTAINING CONSUMER REPORTS: I understand that you may request a consumer report about me in connection with my application to you for credit. If I ask, you will tell me whether or not a consumer report was requested and will also tell me the name and address of the consumer reporting agency that furnished it. If you update, renew or extend my loan you may obtain subsequent reports without telling me.

OFFICER'S SIGNATURE ______ SIGNATURE ______ DATE ______

SIGNATURE ______ DATE ______

03 4486* (5/78)

or if his income comes from several sources (e.g., if he receives royalties), the bank might like to see his tax returns for one or two previous years.

- *Cash in banks or on hand*. This item includes savings and checking accounts. Jack has $6,000 savings and $2,000 in his checking account (on average).
- *Notes receivable/accounts receivable*. No business or person owes Jack any money for anything he has sold or done.
- *Loans receivable*. No one owes Jack for any loan he has made.
- *Securities—readily marketable*. Jack has some stock worth about $10,000.
- *Securities—not readily marketable*. Jack is about to receive shares in his new company, but they have no market value as yet. And, in any case, he has not yet incorporated. So he enters, "None."
- *Life insurance—cash surrender value*. Jack has $11,000 cash surrender value on his $100,000 life insurance policy. He has taken a couple of loans against this but notes the instruction: "Do not deduct loans."
- *Mortgages owned*. Jack has none.
- *Real Estate*. Jack's house in the residential area where he lives has a conservative market value of $22,000. He has not deducted what he owes on his mortgage. The bank will ask about that on the liabilities side of the form. Jack made a notation on the form to let the bank know that the value he showed was assessed value, not cost.
- *Automobile(s)*. Jack lists the estimated market value of his new Buick ($16,000) and his wife's Ford ($4,000). Both cars are registered in his name.
- *Other assets*. Jack has the contents of his house insured for $70,000; he divides these assets into furnishings, silver, paintings, and some valuable collectibles.

Liabilities

- *Notes payable to banks*. Jack has a personal loan of $4,000 from Suburban Bank and a line of credit loan of $2,900 from his savings bank.
- *Notes payable to others*. Jack does not have notes payable to anyone other than the banks.
- *Accounts payable*. Jack has no accounts payable except department stores and credit card charges.
- *Real estate taxes and assessments payable*. Jack's real estate and school taxes come to $3,000.
- *Federal and state income taxes*. Jack pays a total of $16,800 a year in taxes, mostly withheld from his salary each month.

- *Real estate mortgages payable*. Jack has a $60,000 mortgage, of which $30,000 has been paid off.
- *Charge accounts payable*. Here Jack includes what he owes on his charge accounts, credit cards, and gas cards—about $3,000.
- *Brokers' margin accounts*. Jack has none. Jack's investment in IBM stock is long-term; otherwise, he does not play the market.
- *Other liabilities*. Jack has none. This entry should include any major outstanding medical and legal fees, legal claims, and the like.

Net Worth

The supplementary schedules request particulars, which Jack has included. He has also answered all the general questions. Because his home is also in his wife's name, the bank requests that she also sign a loan guarantee form when the loan is offered, so that the bank will have a clear access to the equity in the house if the loan must go into default.

These net worth forms are simple to fill out. After completing one, you will probably discover that you are worth more than you realized.

CONCLUSION

We have discussed some important factors in getting the money. Your success can be influenced significantly by your smart choice of a bank and the care and feeding of a banking relationship. The chapter has told you how you can make your business as creditworthy as possible, thereby minimizing the number of possible reasons why a bank would turn down your request for a loan. In addition, some of the basics of loan documentation have been discussed, and the importance of retaining an attorney to represent you has been stressed. Finally, the chapter has told you how to calculate your net worth and find out what you are really worth.

As an entrepreneur, you need to raise capital for your business. We have discussed raising that capital, or getting the money. This capital can come in the form of:

- *Debt*, which is money you borrow from others and must pay back.
- *Equity*, which is the money you and other investors put into the business and doesn't usually have to be paid back.

In summary, the steps you must take in order to get the money for your business are as follows:

- Develop a business plan.
- Evaluate your business creditworthiness using ratio analysis.
- Based on your business plan, decide on the type of financing you need.
- Based on your creditworthiness and the type of financing, decide on the source of financing to try first.
- Present the prospective lender with your business plan and put your best foot forward in terms of creditworthiness factors.
- Be ready to answer all questions honestly and intelligently.
- Calculate your net worth in case you need to obligate yourself personally to get the loan.
- Retain an attorney to review any documentation that you may be required to sign.
- After the loan is made, keep your lender apprised of all material events—favorable and unfavorable. This will raise your credibility and improve your chances next time you request financing.

III
HOW TO MANAGE YOUR FINANCIAL RESOURCES

Chapters 14 through 20 of Part III focus on managing individual balance sheet and income statement items. They cover the management of cash, accounts receivable, inventories, fixed assets, accounts payable, sales, and the cost of goods sold.

In Chapters 22 through 25 Part III looks at the broad picture of how these individual items interact in the overall operation of your business. Several techniques that will help you to guide and measure the overall performance of your business are discussed. There is also a self-assessment checklist that will help you to identify the techniques on which you need to focus.

Chapter 14 focuses on effective money or cash management. It will help you to determine how much money you need to operate your business and when this money will be needed. In addition, it discusses how to borrow money, how to "stretch" it, and how to protect it from unauthorized disposition.

Chapter 15 deals with accounts receivable management. It discusses ratios that can be used to determine the length of your collection period and the anticipated percentage of bad debts. It discusses what these measures mean to you in dollars and cents and shows you how you can improve your results.

Chapter 16 covers the management of inventories. It will help you to address the conflicting objectives of trying to minimize inventory cost and trying to maintain adequate production supplies. It discusses several management techniques, including the preparation of an ABC analysis of inventory usage, the use of a sales forecast and production schedule to anticipate material requirements, and the determination of inventory reorder points.

Chapter 17 deals with managing the acquisition of fixed assets. It will show you how to control related construction and financing costs through good project management. It provides helpful hints on using accelerated depreciation for tax benefits.

Chapter 18 addresses the development of an effective purchasing and accounts payable function that will prevent you from paying your bills too fast but will protect your relationships with suppliers. The system requirements discussed include a good sales forecast, use of formal purchase orders, and an authorized vendor list.

Chapter 19 discusses the elements of a good sales management program. It covers the importance of a sales forecast, the tracking and analysis of sales trends and sales-force performance, and the quick processing of orders. It describes the benefits of a computerized order entry system in minimizing associated clerical tasks and in preparing analyses for management.

Chapter 20 describes an approach to developing a standard cost accounting system. Such a system will help you to estimate the costs of manufacturing or assembling your products, and it will help you to establish competitive prices.

Chapter 22 deals with the technique of ratio analysis, which will help you monitor the vital signs of your business. Five types of ratio are discussed—liquidity, leverage, turnover, profitability, and trading ratios. In addition, the chapter tells you where to find published ratios for your industry to help you determine how your company measures up to the competition.

Chapter 23 discusses the technique of break-even analysis. This technique will help you to calculate the sales level that you must attain to begin operating at a profit. The chapter reexamines the case of Empire Accessories, Inc., introduced in Chapter 20, to demonstrate how break-even analysis can be used to make fundamental business decisions.

Chapter 24 discusses effective working capital management—the overall management of the current assets and current liabilities. It shows you how to determine whether you have enough working capital, how to obtain additional working capital for specific purposes, and how to invest excess working capital on a short-term basis.

Capital budgeting is the subject of Chapter 25. It is a process that will help you to evaluate long-term investments and projects whose returns are expected to extend beyond one year. This chapter, together with Chapter 24, will guide you in the overall smart use and management of your capital or financial resources, both long- and short-term.

14

Managing Your Money

This chapter shows you how to manage your most liquid financial resource—cash—more effectively. It helps you to determine how much cash you will need and when you will need it. It identifies some basics that you need to consider if you want to borrow money. And finally, it shows you how to stretch your cash and how to protect it from misappropriation. You can determine how you measure up in the cash management of your business by filling out the self-assessment checklist at the end of the chapter.

CASE STUDY: PETER O'HENRY FACES A CASH CRISIS

Let us look at the experiences of Peter O'Henry, a case based on a successful entrepreneur's actual experiences in building his business. Peter O'Henry, president of Lucky Fuel Oil introduced in Part I, had $6.9 million in sales. In September he received a letter containing two pieces of bad news from a major oil company that was his main supplier.

First, he learned that the price of his major raw product had been increased to $1.10 a gallon. This meant he would have to charge his customers $1.23 a gallon to maintain a gross margin of 13¢ a gallon and to provide an acceptable return on his net worth in the business. Second, he learned that the supplier was tightening his credit terms to net 10 days from net 30 days, which meant that Peter would have to pay for the oil before he could expect payment from his customers.

Peter knew that because of the price increase his customers might find it difficult to pay for the full amount of each delivery. He saw that by January he would have no cash to pay his supplier and that he would have to do something fast. What could he do?

Luckily, Peter had developed a plan of action. First, he had estimated how many gallons he would be likely to sell. He had based this estimate on a long-range weather forecast for a moderate winter and on the fact that his customers had been conserving fuel because of rising prices, thereby reducing his gallon sales.

Then he had estimated the prices he would have to charge on the basis of his estimate that the prices he would probably have to pay throughout the winter season could rise to well over $1.23. Since he had a good idea of when he would have to pay his supplier and could estimate when he would be paid by his customers, he had a rough idea of how much cash he would need. Next, he had estimated the amount of his payroll and his other operating expenses. He wanted to be sure of meeting every payday and of maintaining a good credit rating with his vendors. He decided that the new service truck he had hoped to purchase might have to wait until next season.

Once he had completed this analysis, he had recognized that because of the rapid increase in his supply cost and, therefore, the price he would have to charge his customers and the fact that they might take longer to pay, he would probably have to increase his line of credit substantially over what it had been at the peak of the season the past year when there was the greatest lag between incoming and outgoing cash. This had startled him, and he was sure that it would also startle his banker. Therefore, he set out to demonstrate to his banker that he was a good manager and a good credit risk.

He first developed financial statement forecasts and a cash flow forecast, reasoning that this would prove he was aware of his predicament. He then wrote a letter to his customers explaining the situation and encouraging them to adopt a budget payment plan to start in September. A budget payment plan would smooth out the impact of heating costs on his customers by extending their payments over ten months rather than the three or four months at the height of the heating season. He also indicated in the letter that he was forced to charge an interest penalty for accounts receivable balances that were outstanding for more than 30 days. Finally, he reviewed the credit limits and credit positions of his customers, tightened those limits where applicable, and suggested that chronically "slow" or "no" payers mend their ways or seek fuel elsewhere.

Peter went to his banker and presented his case. The banker asked him how many people had adopted his budget plan, how he was going to meet his cash forecast, and what he would do if his cash forecast did not materialize. Peter was prepared to give reasonable answers. He was granted an extended line of credit.

This is one example of managing your money so you will have some when you need it.

ARE YOU MANAGING YOUR MONEY EFFECTIVELY?

There are six primary ways you can evaluate whether you are managing cash effectively. Consider the following questions first:

1. Do you know how much money you need?
2. Do you know when you will need it?
3. Do you know how to borrow it?
4. Do you know how to stretch it?
5. Do you know how to protect it?

Clearly, Peter O'Henry was a good cash manager. The following discussion will show you what Peter did right, and it will help you to do the same.

How Much Money Do You Need?

Your business plan provided you with a method to figure out how much money you need to run your business and when those needs would take place. The tools described were financial statement forecasts and cash flow forecasts.

O'Henry knew how to use these cash management tools. He developed a cash flow forecast by carefully estimating his expected inflows and outflows of cash. He estimated the number of gallons of fuel oil he would sell, and he knew from past experience when those gallons would be sold. He knew from his supplier's letter how much he would have to pay to acquire fuel oil and calculated how much he would have to charge his customers to cover his costs and make a profit. Finally, he knew that, because he would deliver the bulk of the fuel oil in the heavy winter months, his customers who were not on the budget plan would have difficulty paying their bills completely. Therefore, he realized that he would probably have to borrow money from the bank on a short-term

FIGURE 14.1

Lucky Fuel Oil Company

Cash Flow Forecast: April 30, 19X1 Through March 31, 19X2 [a]

Sources of Cash	*April 19X1*	*May 19X1*	*June 19X1*	*July 19X1*	*August 19X1*	*September 19X1*	*October 19X1*	*November 19X1*	*December 19X1*	*January 19X2*	*February 19X2*	*March 19X2*
NET INCOME	($ 3,235)	($ 3,133)	($ 12,661)	(24,860)	($ 33,524)	($ 9,314)	$ 5,008	$ 26,553	$ 53,428	$ 44,398	$ 27,786	$ 10,266
DEPRECIATION	6,473	6,483	6,666	6,667	6,746	7,147	7,147	7,146	7,147	8,040	8,040	8,039
INCREASE IN LIABILITIES:												
Accounts Payable Trade					38,233	19,063	87,003	84,477	158,521	50,077		
Accrued Income Taxes	6,750									17,472	11,380	
Accrued Expenses			2,564		2,262				2,790		604	1,885
Long-Term Debt						28,110						
DECREASE IN ASSETS:												
Cash	65,411											
Accounts Receivable	171,768	154,442	145,891	80,604								143,440
Allowance for Doubtful Accounts	1,228	2,506	591	2,629	851	1,101	2,080	477	563	313	535	299
Inventory		24,404		3,745			31,266	1,770			26,611	6,382
Fixed Assets (net of change in depreciation)	344											
TOTAL SOURCES	248,939	184,702	143,051	68,785	14,568	46,107	132,504	120,423	222,449	120,300	74,956	170,311
INCREASE IN ASSETS:												
Accounts Receivable					22,572	62,550	239,734	271,897	391,907	322,927	91,286	
Inventory	8,272		2,092		14,242	11,958			62,450	3,764		
Fixed Assets		1,200	23,000		10,000	50,000						
DECREASE IN LIABILITIES:												
Accounts Payable Trade	160,409	38,194	33,908	18,880							20,018	64,898
Accrued Income Taxes				29,525								22,205
Accrued Expenses		377		679		2,262		1,206		2,489		
Long-Term Debt	11,890	11,890	11,890	11,890	11,890		11,890	11,890	11,890	11,890	11,890	11,890
TOTAL USES	180,571	51,661	70,890	64,405	58,704	126,770	251,624	284,993	446,247	341,070	123,194	98,993
NET CASH FLOW	$ 68,168	$133,041	$ 72,161	$ 4,380	($ 44,136)	($ 80,663)	($119,120)	($164,570)	($243,798)	$220,770)	($ 48,238)	($ 71,318)
CUMULATIVE CASH FLOW	$ 68,168	$201,209	$273,370	$277,750	$233,614	$152,951	$ 33,831	($130,739)	($374,537)	($595,307)	($643,545)	($572,227)
BEGINNING BALANCE SHORT-TERM DEBT (March 31, 19X1)	($226,000)											
CUMULATIVE SHORT-TERM DEBT (1)	($157,832)	($ 24,791)				($ 73,049)	($192,164)	($356,739)	($600,537)	($821,307)	($869,545)	($798,227)
CUMULATIVE SHORT-TERM INVESTMENTS			$ 47,370	$ 51,750	$ 7,614							

[a] May be off $1 due to rounding.

basis in order to have cash to meet his payroll and operating expenses and to pay his supplier. Peter summarized these facts in a cash flow forecast for his business. Figure 14.1 shows his forecast and that his need for credit would reach a peak of $869,545 in February.

How to Leverage Your Equity

Borrowing money from the bank to finance expanded operations is referred to as *leveraging*. Anyone who has moved a boulder with a crowbar knows that a lever is something used to accomplish a great deal of work with a minimum amount of effort. This concept is true in financial management as well. O'Henry borrowed money to finance those portions of his business that he couldn't finance from his own resources or equity in the business. Thus, Peter leveraged his equity—that is, he used his equity as a base on which to borrow money to run a bigger business.

Although leverage has this positive side, it also has a negative side. When you have a great deal of leverage in the form of bank debt, the bank can wind up having a much bigger stake in your business than you do. Your banker will closely watch the ratio of your debt financing to your equity financing to make certain that the bank doesn't have an inordinate share of your business. Bankers are concerned that if their share is much larger than yours you may not dedicate yourself to the growth and proper management of the business. If this is the case, there is the possibility that you may walk away from the business, and the bank will have to try to recover its investment by selling your assets. Clearly, bankers are not anxious to take this risk.

And you should generally be aware that the greater the bank's stake in your business, the greater the bank's influence on your management. Thus, although it is wise to use leverage to help your business to grow, you must monitor the ratio of debt to equity, both to keep the banker happy and to preserve some autonomy in your management of the business.

Finally, if you have substantial bank borrowings, they carry an interest cost that is fixed and is an expense of the business. If the business slows down, this high fixed cost can adversely affect or even kill a small business, whereas the same business with little or no debt might continue to prosper.

In our example, Peter was able to estimate the amount he needed to borrow in order to supplement his equity. In addition, he recognized the need to show the banker what his cash inflows and outflows would be, how he would retire the debt, and what his debt-to-equity ratio would be at any time.

He also recognized that when all his customers finally paid their oil bills he would have the cash to pay his debt to the bank in full. The bank required such a payment at least once a year to justify extending the credit. Peter realized that he did not need permanent financing—simply a temporary, or short-term, loan. Thus, Peter properly matched the assets to be funded (the current assets of accounts receivable and inventories) and the source of the funding (short-term debt). He was borrowing to help himself over a tight cash period in the normal business cycle of his industry.

Borrowing Long Term

O'Henry had a certain amount of long-term debt that he owed the bank in addition to his temporary loan. He had borrowed this money in the past to finance the construction of fuel storage tanks. He had anticipated that the tanks would provide him with a good return on his investment that he could use to retire the long-term debt owed the bank. He anticipated the useful life of the storage tanks to be at least 15 years. He believed he would derive benefits from having this storage facility because it would allow him to take advantage of favorable prices in the marketplace and protect him if shipments from suppliers were delayed for any reason. Again, Peter properly matched the assets to be funded (storage tanks or long-term assets) with the source of the funding (long-term debt).

Avoid Being "Whipsawed"

The preceding paragraph stressed that Peter properly matched the assets to be funded with the source of the funding. This is important because borrowing short-term to finance a long-term investment has the danger that the cost of short-term funds, always volatile, may rise so that it exceeds the return on the long-term investment. This reveals another fact about leveraging—it is helpful only if the borrowed funds can be invested at a return *greater than* the cost of the funds. Chapter 25 provides a more detailed discussion of return on investment.

Borrowing long-term to finance short-term assets is dangerous, even if possible at all. The danger is that when the need for funding disappears, you may be reluctant to pay back the loan.

Make Sure You Borrow Enough

Peter recognized his need for funding was due to the credit gap, or the lag, between his cash inflows and his cash outflows. This lag was revealed in his cash flow analysis (see Chapter 7). Because of his awareness of the lag, Peter built into his analysis a cash reserve, and he monitored actual cash flow against the plan. The cash reserve allowed for potential differences between his actual cash inflows and outflows and his estimates.

Monitoring actual cash flows with the help of daily, cumulative reports made it possible for him to detect decreases in collections quickly and to postpone making purchases that were not absolutely necessary. He could, therefore, make sure that he had enough money to meet his obligations to the bank. Thus, even though his cash flow analysis was on a monthly basis, with his *cumulative daily reports* he was able to tell during the month whether he was ahead of or behind his month's goal. He could then make appropriate adjustments.

Stretch the Money That You Have

You have already seen how Peter began to stretch his cash even before he went to see his banker. Basically, he did this by:

1. Changing his billing policies by starting a budget plan and finance charges to speed up cash collections.
2. Reviewing his credit policy by identifying slow payers and then tightening the reins on them.
3. Making certain that his customers were paying on a timely basis. He produced a report on all customer balances to which finance charges had been added and used this report to identify early those customers who might be turning sour.
4. Delaying making purchases that were not essential.

Two other cash management techniques were employed by Peter to get the most out of the cash he had on hand: zero balance accounts and repurchase agreements.

Zero balance accounts. Peter recognized the difference between a checking account and a savings account. He knew that the former did not bear interest (unless it was a negotiable order of withdrawal, a "Now" account, generally not available to commercial enterprises). Furthermore, he knew that his bank required compensating balances—funds that had to be left in his demand deposit (checking) account to compensate the bank for servicing his account. He knew that he should leave no more than the required compensating balance in an account that did not earn interest. The remaining funds should be put to work. Either they should be used to reduce short-term debt, thereby saving the interest cost, or they should be invested in short-term securities to earn interest. The latter alternative might be preferable because if he paid back his loan too early, during a period of particularly high collections, he might have to turn around and borrow the funds back again if collections fell off in the future.

Peter discovered that the bank could help in this part of his cash management program. He could arrange for the bank to pay checks presented for payment on his account even though the balance in his account was zero, and then the bank would automatically transfer funds from his interest-bearing account and remove the deficit in his checking account. Not surprisingly, this is called a "zero balance account." A bank charges a fee for this service.

Repurchase agreements. Peter also discovered that he could negotiate a repurchase agreement with the bank, under which the bank would sell Peter government securities and agree to repurchase them at any time in the future. Peter could invest excess cash in this manner and receive the cash back again simply by means of a telephone call. This and other investment opportunities are discussed in greater detail later in Part III.

The important consideration for Peter was the ability to convert any temporary investments in securities to cash as soon as possible, a concept knows as *liquidity*. U.S. Treasury bills, federal agency issues, and several other instruments require an investment of more than a few days. Although they are liquid in the sense that they can be converted to cash quickly, to convert them before they reach maturity means a loss in expected income. Unlike these investments, the repurchase agreement is essentially an overnight investment. Its only drawback is the relatively large denominations that are required to be purchased at one time.

MANAGING THE FLOAT

Peter came to realize that a portion of the lag between the time he delivered his oil and the time he received payment for it was attributable to the time it took for the customer to write and mail the check and for the bank to deposit it in Peter's account. During this time, the check came through the mail, was received in Peter's office, recorded, and deposited. His bank then sent the check back to the customer's bank through a clearing bank in the Federal Reserve System. On presentation of the check to the customer's bank, funds were transferred to Peter's bank and into his account. This whole process might take as much as five to six days. This is called *float*. It represented unusable dollars to Peter (see Figure 14.2).

The float works to the advantage of the buyer and to the disadvantage of the seller. The buyer recognizes that there will be five to six days before the funds represented by his check are removed from his account. The seller recognizes the fact that it will be several days before the funds represented by the buyer's check will be available for payment of bills. The secret is to try to minimize the float.

It is also important to keep in mind that you, as an entrepreneur, are both a buyer and a seller. (Peter was reminded of this when he

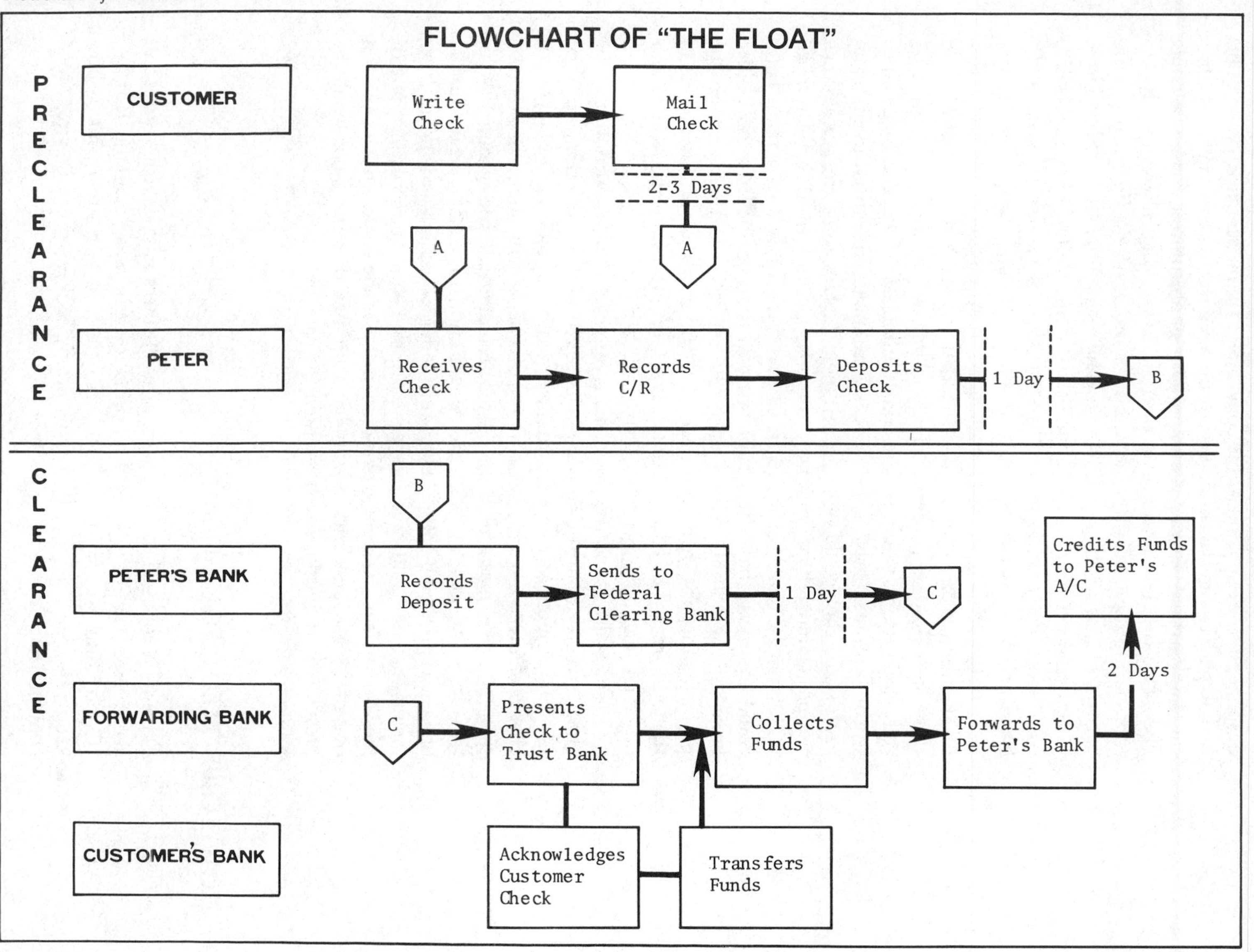
FLOWCHART OF "THE FLOAT"
PRECLEARANCE
CUSTOMER
Write Check
Mail Check
2-3 Days
A
PETER
A
Receives Check
Records C/R
Deposits Check
1 Day
B
CLEARANCE
PETER'S BANK
B
Records Deposit
Sends to Federal Clearing Bank
1 Day
C
Credits Funds to Peter's A/C
2 Days
FORWARDING BANK
C
Presents Check to Trust Bank
Collects Funds
Forwards to Peter's Bank
CUSTOMER'S BANK
Acknowledges Customer Check
Transfers Funds

received the letter from his supplier.) He found that he could do something about the time lag between his delivery of the oil and when the customer wrote out a check. He could affect the *preclearance float* with his budget plan by having customers pay on a regular basis regardless of when oil was delivered, and by the imposition of an interest charge he could encourage his customers not on the plan to pay their bills promptly. (In fact, during the late fall, some of his customers on the budget plan were actually prepaying their oil bills.) Now he needed to speed up the process of getting the money into his bank (his *clearance float*). When speaking to his banker, Peter found that he had two choices—*a lockbox system* and a *balance reporting system.*

In the ensuing years, Peter planned to acquire several small heating oil distributors and to expand his market so that it served customers in three states—Massachusetts, Rhode Island, and Connecticut. As a result, cash receipts would be sent from fairly remote locations to his office in the Boston suburbs, but if checks were mailed to central locations in each state, they could be deposited more rapidly and thereby cut down the preclearance float by a day or two. In speaking to his banker, Peter found that he could set up a *lockbox plan*. According to this plan, Peter could arrange to have his customers send their payments to post office boxes in their local areas. Designated banks could then pick up the payments, deposit them in his account, and start the clearing process in the local areas. The banks would then send copies of the checks to Peter's office for recording in Peter's cash receipts book.

Peter also found that he could have the banks report not only the checks received but the account balances as well. In addition, he could use those remote accounts for disbursements. The banks would report all checks received into the accounts and all checks written on the accounts that had cleared, as well as the balance remaining in the accounts. With this *balance reporting system,* Peter would know his exact cash position at any time and, being both a buyer and a seller, could "play the float." This meant that he could invest excess cash on a short-term basis for one or more extra days and receive extra income. And he could write a check on one of his accounts with reasonable assurance that the funds would be present when checks were presented for payment.

HOW TO PROTECT YOUR CASH

O'Henry recognized that the cash in his business was a valuable asset and yet an asset that others could make use of if he wasn't careful. Part IV, "Controlling Your Business," will tell you how to control your cash to keep this from happening. Let us briefly look at the following broad controls that Peter used to protect his cash:

1. He made certain that *the people who handled cash* in the business did not also *have responsibility for recording cash transactions* in the general ledger, thereby making sure that no one would have the opportunity to cover up misappropriations of cash.
2. He made certain that a *bank reconciliation was prepared* every month and that he personally reviewed it. He could make certain that it reconciled to his general ledger cash account for that bank and that it contained no unusual reconciling items.
3. *He signed all checks* for his business. In doing so, he reviewed the support for the checks and made certain that *support was cancelled after payment so that it could not be resubmitted.*
4. He made certain that all checks were either delivered personally to their intended recipients (in the case of payroll checks) or were *mailed by someone independent of the person who drew the checks.*
5. He *reviewed his cash flow analysis* comparing actual cash flow to what he had estimated *and then tracked down the major differences.*

CONCLUSION

This chapter has followed the moves of a smart cash manager in a small business environment. Here are some of the things that can be learned from this example:

You as a good cash manager should know:

- How much cash you will need.
- When that cash will be needed.
- How much cash you will receive or can obtain from which sources.
- How to adjust your spending plans according to positive and negative fluctuations from cash forecasts.
- Cash is an asset that must be protected from theft.

If you want to borrow funds, you should:

- Prepare a detailed cash flow forecast.
- Be certain to match the maturity of the assets to be funded with the source of the funding (i.e., avoid financing long-term investments with short-term debt).
- Provide an adequate cash reserve in the cash flow analysis to make room for fluctuations in cash inflows and outflows.
- Receive frequent, preferably daily, reports on actual cash inflows and outflows.

- Understand the concept of leverage.
- Recognize that the lender will want to evaluate your management skills as well as your cash flow statement.

You can stretch your cash flow by:

- Setting credit policy and individual credit limits.
- Monitoring receivables and payables.
- Deferring nonessential purchases if need be.
- Minimizing your balance in demand deposit (checking) accounts.
- Investing excess cash in short-term investments (repurchase agreements, federal funds).
- Managing the float with a lockbox or balance reporting system.

You can protect your cash resources by:

- Separating the functions of cash reporting from cash handling.
- Making certain that all cash payments are adequately supported.
- Insisting on the preparation of a bank reconciliation every month for each active bank account.
- Carefully reviewing disbursements, perhaps by signing the checks yourself.

SELF-ASSESSMENT CHECKLIST
CASH MANAGEMENT

	YES	NO	N/A	COMMENTS
(1) Do you have a cash flow forecast?				
(2) Is this forecast a result of, or tied to, your operating budget?				
(3) Do you have adequate lines of credit?				
(4) Do you know how long it takes to receive cash from your customers?				
(5) Do you know how long it takes for checks to clear your bank and be credited to your account?				

SELF-ASSESSMENT CHECKLIST
CASH MANAGEMENT

	YES	NO	N/A	COMMENTS
(6) Do you measure actual cash flow against your plan?				
(7) Do you modify your cash flow forecast for changes in your operations?				
(8) Are your operations (sales, distribution centers) dispersed across the country?				
(9) Do you take advantage of: —Concentration banks? —Lock boxes? —Wire transfers to put cash into your accounts as quickly as possible?				
(10) Do you put excess cash (all cash in excess of basic operating needs and any compensating balances) to work by investing them in short-term investments?				
(11) What % of your total assets is cash?				

15
Managing Accounts Receivable

If you sell on credit, you postpone receiving cash for your goods or services for the purpose of stimulating sales and providing your customers with the convenience of paying by check based on an invoice. Often this is simply a matter of custom in certain types of business. But you do not want to wait too long to get your money. Accounts receivable are not cash, so they cannot be used to pay your payroll or to buy materials. Therefore, you want to convert these receivables into cash as quickly as possible. This chapter shows you several techniques to help accomplish this. At the end of the chapter is a self-assessment checklist to test your accounts receivable management ability.

HOW FAST ARE YOU BRINGING IN THE CASH?

You can estimate how fast your receivables are being collected by calculating your average collection period (the average number of days of credit sales represented by your receivable balances). The following formulas can be used to compute this ratio:

$$\text{Average collection period} = \frac{\text{Accounts receivable balance}}{\text{Average daily credit sales}} = \text{The number of days' sales tied up in accounts receivable}$$

$$= \frac{\text{Annual credit sales}}{360}$$

or

$$\text{Average daily credit sales} = \frac{\text{Semiannual credit sales}}{180}$$

or

$$= \frac{\text{Credit sales to date}}{\text{Days in year to date}}$$

Assume the following facts:

Accounts receivable	= \$431,505	
Credit sales to date	= \$1,447,945	
Days in year to date	= 151	
Average daily sales	= \$1,447,945 / 151	= \$9,589.04
Average collection period	= \$431,505	÷ \$9,589 or 45 days

As a practical matter, sales probably do not flow into your company in the same amounts every day. In many companies, sales and accounts receivable balances fluctuate over a broad range during the year in response to seasonal trends. Therefore, the ratio—credit sales to date ÷ days in year to date—gives the best approximation of average daily credit sales because this ratio incorporates any seasonal fluctuations that have occurred to date.

The ratio refers to sales on credit only. If your business also has sales for cash and they are significant to the total, they should not be included in the calculation. Also, one or two large, slow-paying customers can distort the ratios. As is discussed later, it is important to review the components of your receivable balance periodically to identify slow payers.

The average collection period, or the average day's sales in receivables, is a good ratio to include in your financial reports, perhaps at the bottom of your balance sheet (see Part IV "Controlling Your Business," Chapter 26 for a sample presentation). In addition, this ratio can be used to compare your company to others in your industry and to other industries. Finally, you can make use of this statistic to estimate when sales on credit will be paid as you develop a cash flow forecast for your company.

HOW FAST ARE YOU GETTING OUT YOUR BILLS?

Another factor that you should consider when calculating your average collection period is the average time it takes to bill a customer *after* goods have been shipped. Most goods are shipped f.o.b. (free on board) at the shipping point, which means that they become the customer's goods as soon as they are loaded on a truck (or other transportation vehicle) at your premises. If it takes two or more days to fill out an invoice, send it to the customer, and record it in your accounts receivable ledger, this adds to the time lag between the sale and the receipt of cash. Therefore, you should be concerned with getting bills out as fast as possible in order to reduce the collection period.

One way to speed up the billing process is to make sure that all shipping documents are sent to your billing department as soon after shipping as possible. It can be worthwhile to send someone to the shipping area several times a day in order to collect all the shipping documents processed up to that time.

You can also minimize the time required to process and mail the invoice itself. Here, minicomputers and systems for billing can help by handling the routine calculations involved in processing invoices. And a minicomputer can allow for quick recording of shipping notices as soon as the goods are shipped. It can automatically match these notices with the record of a customer's purchase order and produce a bill automatically. Computers can also provide ready access to customer purchase, credit, and payment records. This can alert you to chronically slow payers, so that you can take steps to restrict further purchases by such customers and to minimize the collection time.

WHAT ABOUT THE CUSTOMERS WHO NEVER PAY?

In managing your accounts receivable, you must figure out the percentage of receivables that you will probably have to write off as bad debts. You may calculate these bad debts as a percentage of average accounts receivable or as a percentage of sales. Assume that you have had to write off $33,000 as bad debts over the year. The ratio is simply:

$$\text{Bad debt \%} = \frac{\text{\$ written of as uncollectible}}{\text{\$ sales}} = \frac{\$33{,}000}{\$3{,}500{,}000} = 0.94\%$$

or

$$= \frac{\text{\$ written off as uncollectible}}{\text{\$ credit sales}} = \frac{\$33{,}000}{\$3{,}000{,}000} = 1.1\%$$

or

$$= \frac{\text{\$ written off as uncollectible}}{\text{\$ average accounts receivable balance}} = \frac{\$33{,}000}{\$291{,}666} = 11.3\%$$

$$(\$3{,}500{,}000 \div 12)$$

This ratio is a useful piece of information because it can point out a trend toward better or worse receivables management. And, like the average collection period, it can be used to compare your company to others in the industry and to other industries.

WHAT DO THESE RATIOS MEAN IN DOLLARS AND CENTS?

It is important to understand the monetary value of good receivables management. For example, assume that your average collection period is 45 days and that your average daily credit sales is $9,589 (to the nearest dollar). If you can improve your collection period by 15 days, you will have a one-time additional cash flow of $143,835, which is the average daily sales multiplied by the number of days of improvement ($9,589 × 15 = $143,835). Furthermore, if you had to borrow to finance this balance in accounts receivable, and you have to pay 16% for this working capital loan, the extra 15 days is costing you approximately $23,000 ($143,835 × 0.16) in interest annually.

On the other hand, a deterioration of 15 days in the average collection period, from 45 to 60 days, has exactly the opposite impact. You will have an additional $143,835 in accounts receivable. If you borrow to finance these receivables, it will cost you an additional $23,000 in interest over the course of the year.

Changes in the bad debt ratio have similar effects. A 10% improvement can mean a positive impact on earnings of $3,300 ($33,000 × 0.10) in the example, whereas a deterioration of the same magnitude can have the opposite effect.

DO YOU SELL TO ONLY CREDITWORTHY CUSTOMERS?

This is an important question that must be answered before you ship goods or provide services to customers who purchase on credit. Your ability to judge the creditworthiness of customers will be reflected in your level of bad debt expense.

If your business is large enough to support it, you can establish a formal credit department to monitor customer credit limits. Set credit limits on the basis of a review of Dun & Bradstreet or other credit bureau reports on large commercial customers, information from commercial finance companies, or direct knowledge of the customer's paying history. Approve all credit limits and any subsequent changes in them yourself. Review the financial position of your major customers periodically (perhaps quarterly) thereafter.

A credit department can assess the impact of the general economy on groups of customers. For example, if there is a sharp downturn in a major industry, suppliers to that industry will also be affected. Companies providing goods or services to these suppliers should prepare for a decline in related receivable payments. You can take the anticipated decline into account in developing cash flow forecasts and take steps to encourage faster payment.

You will have to decide whether the cost of establishing a formal credit department (which could be only one person part-time) is justified by the savings in interest and bad debt expense. Companies too small to afford a formal credit department may have to take alternative steps. Small companies generally take one of two approaches to accounting for bad debts. Frequently, the company will operate as though there will be no bad debts. As bad debts arise, they are simply written off. Although this is a commonly used procedure, it has an important drawback. If either a single large receivable or many receivable balances are written off in a single month, it will have a sudden negative impact on profits.

Alternatively, you may wish to avoid this volatility by setting up an allowance for doubtful accounts, or a reserve for bad debts. Each month you can set aside an allowance in anticipation of bad debts. This amount is a reduction of your income. Then, as bad debts arise, you write them off against the allowance. This serves to smooth out the impact on profits over the year and means there is no *further* impact on profits unless the write-offs exceed the allowance.

The Internal Revenue Service has rules for the establishment of a bad debt reserve that take into consideration historical bad debt experience. The intent of the IRS is to be certain that actual bad debts are reasonably close to the amounts provided for in the allowance. Check with your accountant to be certain that your bad debt allowance will be deductible for taxes.

WHO ARE THE SLOW PAYERS?

The average collection period and the bad debt ratio can tell you how effectively you are managing your receivables. And they can give you insight into the monetary impact that an improvement or deterioration in receivables management would have on your company. But these broad measures do not tell you which specific customers are slow payers or potential bad debts.

You can get this information from an aged trial balance of accounts receivable. See Figure 15.1, which shows that each customer is listed on a single line in customer number sequence. Alternatively, customers may be listed in alphabetical order. In an automated system, it is easier to refer to a customer by number to avoid confusion when customer names are similar. The following information is provided for each customer:

FIGURE 15.1
Summary Aged Trial Balance of Accounts Receivable
Date: May 31, 19X1

Customer Number	Customer Name	Contact Phone Number	Date of Last Payment	Credit Limit	Total	Current	Over 30 Days	Over 60 Days	Over 90 Days	120 + Over	Comments
12476	Intersport	R. Ziegler 746-1155	5/12/X1	$10,000	$ 9,76C.85	$ 6,610.85	$ 2,758.50			$ 391.50	Called 6/2. Will pay by 6/7/X1 JRL
12479	High Speed Power Equipment	D. Watson 561-8360	5/16/X1	22,000	23,590.00	16,519.20	7,070.80				
12492	Aurora 2000	H. Kieffer 944-1234	5/23/X1	12,000	2,057.00	2,057.00					
12497	Berg & Brown Inc.	L. Kesk 369-5803	5/5/X1	54,000	36,895.00	21,795.00	9,100.00	$ 4,500.00	$ 1,500.00		Defective mdse returned 5/15/X1. Awaiting debit memo; will pay balance. JRL
					$431,505.00	$287,671.20	$101,530.00	$28,923.00	$12,129.80	$1,257.30	

FIGURE 15.2
Detailed Aged Trial Balance of Accounts Receivable
May 31, 19X1

Customer Number	Customer Name	Transaction Date	Transaction Type	Transaction Reference	Transaction Amount	Applicable Period: Current	30	60	90	120	Comments
12476	Intersport	1/29/X1	INV.	M12973	$ 691.50					$ 691.50	
		4/14/X1	INV.	M01596	1,352.80		$1,352.80				
		4/28/X1	INV.	M01621	3,405.70		3,405.70				
		5/ 4/X1	INV.	M01717	4,665.00	$4,665.00					
		5/12/X1	C/R	M01621	(2,000.00)		(2,000.00)				
		5/18/X1	INV.	M01844	1,945.85	1,945.85					
		5/25/X1	DM	M12973	(300.00)					(300.00)	
					$ 9,760.85	$ 6,610.85	$ 2,758.50			391.50	
					$431,505.00	$287,671.20	$101,530.00	$28,923.00	$12,129.50	$1,257.30	

- A contact and a telephone number for the customer, easy things to maintain if the report is automated. In a non-automated environment this information can be maintained separately in a simple Rolodex card file.
- The customer's credit limit. Note that High Speed Power Equipment, customer no. 12479, has exceeded its credit limit. This would warrant a telephone call.
- The total outstanding receivable balance, as of the date of the report, which is usually the end of the month. To be accurate, the total of all customer outstanding balances must equal the balance of accounts receivable appearing in the general ledger and on the company's financial statements for the month.
- The amount of time outstanding, or the "age," of each portion of the outstanding balance. Derive aging by subtracting the invoice date from the effective date of the report (May 31, 1981, in this example). If the invoice was issued in the month (period) just closed, the balance appears in the "current" column. If it was issued in the previous month, it falls into the 30-day-old column, and so forth. The last column is marked 120 days and over on this report. You could extend your schedule to 180 days or more, depending on the nature of your company.

Receivables that fall in the 90-day or older columns have a high likelihood of becoming bad debts. Therefore, you should follow up on them and keep a close watch on those in the 60-day column. Sometimes, failure to pay is a signal that the goods or services were inferior in some way. Close follow-up will uncover these problems and allow for steps to be taken to resolve them.

Another report that can help you to monitor individual accounts is the detailed aged accounts receivable trial balance (Figure 15.2). This report is similar to the summary report, but it shows all outstanding items, invoices, debit and credit memos, and cash receipts. It can be helpful when discussing outstanding balances with a customer if the customer is withholding payment of the entire balance because of problems with a single invoice or one credit memo. Availability of this information is also important when it is necessary to recreate a balance for a customer.

Speed up the Collection Process

You can use several practical methods to minimize your receivables collection period:

- *Offer incentives or disincentives*. Incentives can be both positive and negative. You can offer a discount for prompt payment—for example, if an invoice is paid within 10 days of billing. Or you can assess a finance charge for payment after a reasonable period, for example—30 days after billing. In the latter case, the assessment should be accompanied by an announcement that all payments will be applied to the finance charge before being applied to the outstanding bill. As a practical matter, the latter approach may be preferred because experience has shown that customers may take discounts even if they do not generally pay on time. The important thing to remember about an incentive is that it should accomplish the purpose. If it does not, it should be discontinued.

- *Carefully determine the creditworthiness of your customers and monitor credit limits.* Set credit limits based on an assessment of customer creditworthiness, and monitor sales to be certain credit limits are not exceeded.
- *Monitor accounts receivable balances by customer, and follow up on slow payers.*

Finance Your Accounts Receivable

You can turn your receivables into cash quickly by either selling or pledging them to a finance company. There are organizations that will buy your accounts receivable at a discount for cash and offer the service of collecting those receivables at a fee. Such organizations are referred to as *factors*. Factors relieve you of the effort of collecting your receivables, freeing you to concentrate on sales and production. Such companies may be able to help you to assess the creditworthiness of your customers and to set your credit limits.

Other organizations will lend you money, using your receivables as security, and will monitor the collections, but will leave the ultimate responsibility for the collection of the receivables with you. Typically, such commercial finance companies will accept only current receivables as collateral. If this is the case, customer balances that become delinquent and, of course, those that are paid will reduce your security for the loan. You may be required to make periodic payments to reduce your loan balance by the amount of the delinquent accounts.

Both factors and finance companies charge a fee for their services. Often, the factor discounts a receivable to allow for the possible bad debt experience and for the finance charge. In addition, the factor receives a service charge for managing the receivable balances. These service charges may be deducted from the proceeds from collecting your receivable balances, and the net proceeds are used to repay the factor's initial advance to you. Commercial finance companies charge for financing the receivables and for servicing the business and deduct both of these from the proceeds before they use the balance to reduce your outstanding loan balance.

Typically, finance charges run 2% to 3% above prime rates, and service charges are 1% to 1.5% of the financed amount. In determining whether to factor or to pledge your receivables, you should equate the costs with the benefits. The costs have just been described. The benefits equal the value of the time that you and members of your staff would ordinarily spend to monitor the receivables and follow up on collections.

Many distributors and some manufacturers have large numbers of customers—500 to 1,000 or more. Managing customer balances can require a great deal of time and effort. For these companies, it may be wise to hire a professional accounts receivable management company, such as a factor, or to hire someone to join the organization to provide this function. However, this may not be true for companies with a small number of customers. An analysis of the costs and benefits can help you to determine which approach is best for you.

CONCLUSION

This chapter has described two broad measures to determine the quality and status of your accounts receivable balances:

- Average collection period.
- Bad debt percentage.

By analyzing these ratios and comparing them over time, you can tell if management is improving or deteriorating, and you can figure out the impact in dollars and cents of this trend.

The chapter has also explained that to take action with regard to individual customers, you must develop an aged trial balance of accounts receivable and, possibly, a detailed aged accounts receivable trial balance. In addition, several suggestions have been provided for speeding up collections.

Finally, you must remember the importance of assessing the cost of implementing a new collection procedure versus the benefit of doing so. Frequently, the costs are easy to compute, but benefits such as increased management time for other activities are more difficult to quantify and evaluate. Only you know how valuable your time is.

SELF-ASSESSMENT CHECKLIST
ACCOUNTS RECEIVABLE MANAGEMENT

	YES	*NO*	*N/A*	*COMMENTS*
(1) Do you have a formal credit policy?				
(2) Do you have procedures to check customer credit before authorizing shipment of goods or before providing services?				
(3) Do you receive a Summary Aged Trial Balance of Accounts Receivable on a regular basis (monthly)?				
(4) Do you receive a Detailed Aged Trial Balance of Accounts Receivable on a regular basis?				
(5) Do you agree the total accounts receivable balance from each trial balance to your general ledger control account for Accounts Receivable—Trade?				
(6) Have you established incentives (discounts) to encourage prompt payment?				
(7) Have you established disincentives (interest on delinquent balances, dunning notices, etc.) to encourage prompt payment?				
(8) Do you take firm action against chronically slow payers?				
(9) Do you know the average collection period for your receivables (days sales in receivables)?				
(10) Do you know the percentage of your receivables that you have to write off?				
(11) Do you know how much write-offs and slow payers are presently costing your company?				

SELF-ASSESSMENT CHECKLIST
ACCOUNTS RECEIVABLE MANAGEMENT

	YES	*NO*	*N/A*	*COMMENTS*
(12) Do you have to borrow to finance your receivables?				
(13) Have you considered using a factor or finance company?				
(14) What percentage of your total assets are your trade accounts receivable?				

16

Managing Inventories

There are three basic objectives of inventory management:

- To have enough raw materials inventory on hand to maintain continuous production.
- To meet customer order delivery dates on time.
- To minimize the carrying costs of and capital tied up in inventories.

Meeting these objectives is generally a complex and time-consuming process, and you will immediately recognize the conflict between minimizing inventories and maintaining adequate production supplies. This chapter describes some techniques that can help you to do a better job of inventory management, using the example of the Wright Brothers' Bicycle Company to define the components of inventories in a small fabrication and assembly business and to illustrate the following techniques:

- Deciding on and measuring customer satisfaction, calculated as a percentage of orders delivered on time.

- Preparing an ABC analysis of inventory usage, in order to concentrate limited management resources on those areas of inventory management that will do the most good.
- Using a sales forecast and production schedule to anticipate material requirements.
- Calculating inventory reorder points, based on ordering and production lead time and expected usage.
- Maintaining accurate perpetual inventory records to signal the need for reordering.
- Maintaining a stock status report in order to monitor inventory status.
- Maintaining an order status report as a way of verifying or adjusting the sales and production forecasts.
- Determining the appropriate order quantities when placing an order for materials.

Because the subject is complex, it is important to note that the chapter is intended to be illustrative, to highlight important concepts and not to be all-inclusive. Seek advice and counsel from your accountant in employing the techniques described. The self-assessment checklist at the end of the chapter will enable you to test your inventory management skills.

CASE STUDY: ROGER WRIGHT WORKS OUT A MONEY-SAVING INVENTORY SYSTEM

Roger Wright mused as he wrote out a check to an air freight company. This payment was about the only mistake he had made in the last year, since he had made a conscious effort to control his inventory better. But then, he thought, this was not a mistake, it was a calculated risk. As he pondered this cost against the savings he had achieved in reducing his inventory, he felt that he was way ahead.

He had incurred the air freight cost in order to have several sets of derailleurs (a mechanism for shifting gears on a bicycle) flown to his plant in Ohio from his supplier in New York who, in turn, imported them from Germany. He needed the derailleurs to finish an order of bicycles that he had promised to a large retail bicycle and moped distributor in Chicago. If he had not obtained the gears overnight, he would have had to call some of his work force in over the weekend and he would have incurred an overtime charge.

Although his bicycle manufacturing business had been growing for several years, Roger knew he would remain in business and continue to grow only if he continued to follow the principles that had enabled him to get the business started:

- Produce a quality product.
- Sell it at a competitive price.
- Meet delivery schedules.
- Back up the product with prompt and efficient service.

He knew that if he could stick to these principles, the sales would be there and his volume would continue to grow. Beyond that, making a profit would be largely a result of how skillful he could become in managing the business. For the most part, this would involve managing the assets of the business and keeping a tight rein on production costs.

Roger was fortunate that his brother Ted had decided to join him in the business. Ted was also a retired bicycle racer of some renown. But, unlike Roger, Ted was also a skillful mechanic. When the two were racing, Ted maintained their bicycles. He designed stronger, lighter frames and adapted the gear action to aid their competitive endeavors. This original design was largely responsible for the fact that their bicycles are now highly regarded and well spoken of in sports journals and bicycle racing publications. Ted, therefore, naturally filled the role of chief product designer and production scheduler.

Roger's son Jonathan and Ted's son Dennis also worked in the business. Jonathan, taking after his father, seemed naturally inclined toward the marketing arm of the business. Dennis, following in his father's footsteps, supervised the production shop. Together, the four made up the management team and conferred on all decisions that related to the business.

SHOULD YOU PRODUCE TO ORDER OR TO STOCK?

One of the first questions the group had to answer was whether to produce for stock or only to orders from customers. They recognized that it was important to fill their customers' orders promptly. There were many bicycle afficionados who could wait to have a bicycle manufactured for them, but the vast majority of bicycle purchasers would more than likely pick one from the stock on hand at the bicycle shop. But the Wrights also realized that although it would be nice to build a lot of bicycles and to keep them in stock to fill orders, it would be expensive. Theirs was a small business with many competing demands for funds. And figuring out how much stock to keep required an ability to predict the future with some precision: What sizes, styles, and colors should they produce to satisfy future orders? Therefore, they decided to produce to customer orders rather than to stock. Jon and Roger would generate the orders, and Ted and Dennis would make sure they were filled promptly.

WHAT GOES INTO YOUR INVENTORY?

To make a set of rational decisions relating to their inventory, the Wrights first looked at the nature of their inventory. It consisted of the following categories:

- Raw materials.
- Purchased parts—components and subassemblies.
- Work in process.
- Finished goods.
- Supplies.

Each group was slightly different. The raw materials consisted of tubular aluminum, magnesium, and steel of various gauges and lengths, and paint and sealers. These materials were essential because production could not begin without them. The purchased parts consisted of derailleurs, hand brake assemblies, wheels, sprockets, pedals, seats, tires, tubes, handlebars, and forks. They too were important because if they were not on hand to insert into the production process at the proper time, production would bog down and workers would be idle. The Wrights knew that idle time cost money both because the workers in the plant were being paid even though they were not producing and because the lost production would have to be made up, perhaps at an overtime premium. They knew that with 55 employees, any amount of idle time would rapidly offset the cost of carrying some additional inventory, often referred to as *safety stock*. In fact, Roger adjusted the safety stock on derailleurs after he paid the bill to the air freight company in the hope of avoiding a similar bill in the future.

As it is in most businesses, work-in-process inventory—the value of goods in the process of being produced—was a fact of life in the bicycle manufacturing business. It took approximately five man-days to build a bicycle, including time to cut, paint, and finish the frame, add component parts, and pack the bike for shipment. In part, the Wrights were spared the full assembly cost because it was easier to ship the bikes partially dismantled. They were later assembled and prepared for the consumer by the distributor.

Although the Wrights produced to customer order, they had to maintain a certain amount of finished goods—bicycles that had passed through the production cycle and were waiting to be shipped. And they recognized that certain supplies, such as bolts, washers, nuts, reflectors, handlebar tape, decals, oil, grease, and so on, were sufficiently inexpensive to maintain in large volumes at a minimal cost.

MEASURING CUSTOMER SATISFACTION

The company had a delivery schedule that called for shipment within three weeks of the receipt of the order and that they were usually able to meet. Roger kept track of every order—when it was due to be shipped and when it actactually was shipped (see Figure 16.1). By simply dividing the on-time shipments by the total shipments, he was able to calculate a customer satisfaction percentage. In his case it was 91.8%.

Because the Wright Brothers' bicycles had a good reputation and deliveries were almost always on time, the company received several standing orders from large distributors. These orders allowed them to smooth out production, because they could be scheduled during gaps in the production cycle. Roger calculated that it was cheaper to carry the finished goods than to try to balance production with part-time help or with overtime. He quickly came to realize that a steady stream of orders or a backlog of standing orders would allow Ted to develop a level

FIGURE 16.1
Wright Brothers
Customer Service Level
January 19X1[a]

Wright Order No.	*Order Date*	*Customer*	*Order Due Date*	*Date Shipped*	*√—On Time o Late*
F01763	1/2/X1	Westside Bicycle	1/28	1/27	o
F01764	1/2/X1	All Sport Center	1/23	1/23	√
F01765	1/2/X1	Stuyvesant Bicycle House	1/23	1/23	√
F01766	1/5/X1	Metio Bikes	1/26	1/26	√
F01767	1/6/X1	Gene's Bicycles	1/27	1/27	√
F01768	1/6/X1	Different Spokes	1/27	1/27	√
F01769	1/7/X1	Bicycles Plus	1/28	1/27	√
F01770	1/8/X1	Bicycle Habitat	1/29	1/27	√
F01903	1/30	Morris Toyland	2/20	—*	
F01904	1/30	Angelo's Bicycles	2/20	—*	
F01905	1/30	Sid's Bike Shop	2/20	—*	
		TOTAL ORDERS	135	110	
		TOTAL ON TIME			101
		TOTAL LATE			9
		CUSTOMER SATISFACTION %		91.8%	

$$\frac{\text{Total on time}}{\text{Total orders shipped}} = \frac{101}{110}$$

[a] In calculating percentage of customer satisfaction, only orders that should have been shipped are included. Since these orders are not due until the month following the date of the report, they are not included in the calculation.

production schedule that would be most efficient. It would also help to minimize inventory levels. He knew that good inventory management could also help to achieve level production.

HOW MUCH INVENTORY SHOULD YOU KEEP?

One of the first questions Roger had to deal with was how much inventory of each type to keep on hand. Because he attempted to ship as soon after production as possible and started production only on receipt of a firm customer order, he could keep his work in process and finished goods at the lowest possible level and still meet his production and delivery schedules. Therefore, he could concentrate his efforts on managing raw materials and purchased parts.

In coming to a decision as to how much of each raw material or purchased part to maintain, Roger first reviewed his bills of materials for each style of bicycle offered in the catalog. Each bill of materials listed all the components necessary to build and finish that particular bicycle. Roger used these bills to put together a list of all the raw materials and component parts he needed. In completing the list, he noticed that, although the company offered several sizes of frame and certain frames required distinct parts, there were many common parts (pedals, handlebars, reflectors, nuts and bolts, etc.) that were transferable or interchangeable. This fact helped Roger to minimize his list to three categories of inventory items (see Figure 16.2).

Once he had a complete list, Roger listed the average or standard unit cost beside each item and then estimated the average annual unit volume by looking at the past sales and adjusting them for his estimate of growth. He obtained a growth estimate from his sales forecast, which Jonathan put together by talking to their major customers. Next, Roger multiplied the average unit cost by the estimated annual usage in units to arrive at the average annual dollar usage.

Looking down the column of average annual dollar usage, Roger was able to pick out those items that represented a major portion of his overall annual usage of raw materials and purchased parts. Next, he looked at the nature of the high-volume items. He decided to designate all high-volume items that were critical to the production process as "A" items. High-volume items that were not as critical to production, or those that were interchangeable, he designated as "B" items. The rest he labeled "C" items, which tended to be low-volume items that often were interchangeable. At the bottom of his schedule, he summarized the A, B, and C items.

When he finished, he found that the A items, roughly 20% of his inventory by number of items or 26 items out of 136, accounted for 70% of the value of his raw materials and purchased parts. He found that the B

FIGURE 16.2

Wright Brothers 19X0 Annual Usage of Inventory By Value

Item No.	*Description*	*Unit of Measure*	*Estimated Annual Usage Units*	*Average Unit Cost*	*Average Annual $ Usage*	*% of Total Value*	*Class*	*Comments*
R 1154	Tubular Aluminum 1/2"	lbs	180,000	$ 1.27/lb	228,600	11.5	A	
R 1155	Tubular Magnesium 1/2"	lbs	20,000	2.97/lb	59,400	2.9	B	
R 1156	Tubular Steel 1/2"	lbs	120,000	1.15/lb	138,000	6.9	A	
PP1167	Derailleurs	each	32,000	7.89/ea	252,480	12.6	A	
PP1783	Pedals	pair	3,200	$ 4.87	155,840	7.8	A	
PP1795	Sprockets	gross	230	534.24/gross	122,875	6.3	A	
PP1827	Wheels 25"	dozen	5,400	27.70/doz	149,580	7.5	A	
PP1831	Tires 25"	dozen	5,400	53.96/doz	291,384	14.6	A	
PP1847	Seats	dozen	5,400	63.12/doz	170,424	8.5	B	
PP1852	Handlebars	dozen	5,400	76.44/doz	206,388	10.4	A	
PP1856	Hand Brakes	sets of 2	3,200	2.18/set	69,760	3.5	B	
PP1859	Chains	each	3,200	.87/ea	27,840	1.4	C[a]	
R 1007	Primer	50 gal drum	640	56.00	35,840	1.8	C	
R 1021	Paint—Maroon	50 gal drum	60	83.50	5,010	0.3	C	
R 1022	Paint—Black	50 gal drum	90	83.50	7,515	0.4	C	
R 1023	Paint—Silver	50 gal drum	80	97.20	17,496	0.9	C	
R 1025	Paint—White	50 gal drum	90	77.70	6,993	0.3	C	

[a] Slow production by manufacturer; consider for "A" item status in 19X1.

FIGURE 16.2 (Cont.)

Wright Brothers 19X0 Annual Usage of Inventory By Value

Item No.	*Description*	*Unit of Measure*	*Estimated Annual Usage Units*	*Average Unit Cost*	*Average Annual $ Usage*	*% of Total Value*	*Class*	*Comments*
R 1027	Paint—Yellow	50 gal drum	120	83.50	10,020	0.6	C	
PP1517	Reflectors—Fender	gross	240	36.00	8,640	0.5	C	
PP1518	Reflectors—Wheel	gross	480	33.50	16,080	0.8	C	
PP1519	Lock washers	lbs	1,200	1.65/lb	1,980	0.1	C	
PP1527	Butterfly nuts	lbs	1,200	1.83/lb	2,196	0.1	C	
PP1417	Decals	dozen	5,400	1.20/doz	6,480	0.3	C	
					$1,990,821	100.0		
		A Items		19%	26	70.1%		
		B Items		17%	23	22.4%		
		C Items		64%	87	7.5%		
				100%	136	100.0%		

	Number of Items	*% of Total*	*Dollar Value*	*% of Total*
A	26	19%	$1,395,565	70.1%
B	23	17%	445,944	22.4%
C	87	64%	149,312	7.5%
	136	100%	$1,990,821	100.0%

items amounted to another 22% of the value of his total raw materials and purchased parts inventory. Finally, he found that C items—nuts, bolts, reflectors, and the other miscellaneous supplies—accounted for only 8% of the value of his inventory, even though they represented by far the largest number of inventory items.

This type of analysis is referred to as an ABC analysis. Many manufacturers who have followed the procedure have arrived at results similar to Roger's. They have found that:

- 10% of the number of items = 70% of the $ usage
- Another 10% of the number of items = 20% of the $ usage
- The remaining 80% of the items = 10% of the $ usage

Therefore, a manager should concentrate inventory management resources on the A and B items, where the greatest benefit to the com-

FIGURE 16.3
ABC Inventory Classification

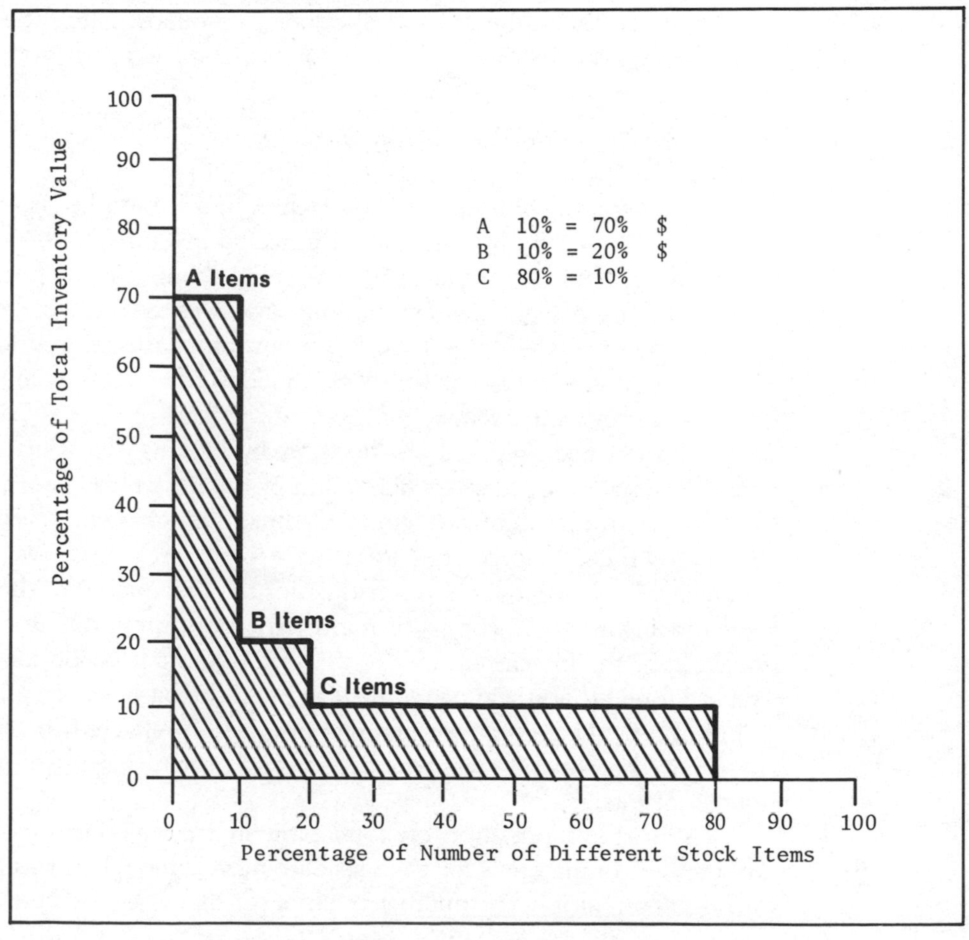

pany can be derived. This was especially true in the Wrights' small business, where the time that management could devote to inventories was at a premium. See Figure 16.3 for a graphic representation of this concept.

HOW TO CONTROL YOUR INVENTORY

Roger recognized that in attempting to control the A and B items in his inventory, he would have to answer the following questions:

1. How much of each A and B item was he going to use over the course of the year?
2. When should he place an order for additional material? (What was his reorder point?)
3. How much should be maintained on hand to cover the lead time for ordering and receiving the additional inventory?
4. How would he know when his reorder point was reached?
5. How much should he order at one time to properly match the cost of processing the order with the cost of carrying the inventory?

How Much Inventory Would Be Used?

Although Roger knew how much of each A and B item he had used in the past (from his analysis of annual usage of inventory), this did not necessarily tell him how much he was going to use in the future. He decided that his best source of this information was the sales forecast that Jonathan had prepared. Figure 16.4 is a portion of this overall forecast, which shows expected orders for specific models of bicycles by month for the first quarter of the year.

Jonathan had prepared this forecast by looking at historical sales figures, by analyzing orders on hand, and by talking to his major customers to ascertain their tentative commitments to purchase bicycles for the year. Using the sales forecast, Ted was able to prepare a tentative production schedule. The production schedule for the first quarter of the year is shown in Figure 16.5. For each month, the beginning inventory is deducted from the forecasted sales to arrive at required production. Since Ted had found that it was convenient to build the bicycles at a minimum in lots of ten, the column for planned production reflected the fact that the required production was rounded up (or down) to arrive at an even number of lots.

Using the information on total estimated production for the year and the bills of materials for each specific bicycle model, it was possible for Roger to multiply the number of units per model by the components

FIGURE 16.4
Wright Brothers Sales Forecast for the Quarter Ending March 31, 19X1

No.	Style Description	Aluminum	Units	Jan. Selling Price	Sales	Units	Feb. Selling Price	Sales	Units	Mar. Selling Price	Sales	Total Quarterly Forecast Units	Selling Price	Sales
A123	25″ Men's	Silver	350	$149.50	$ 52,325	300	$149.50	$ 44,850	275	$149.50	$ 41,113	925	$149.50	$138,288
A124	25″ Men's	Yellow	200	149.50	29,500	200	149.50	29,900	175	149.50	26,162	575	149.50	85,562
A125	25″ Men's	Black	150	149.50	22,425	125	149.50	18,688	125	149.50	18,688	400	149.50	59,800
M091	27″ Men's	Silver	100	178.80	17,880	100	178.80	17,880	100	178.80	17,880	300	178.80	53.640
Total			2,258		$350,000	1,780		$276,000	1,465		$227,000	5,503		$853,000

FIGURE 16.5
Wright Brothers Production Forecast for the Quarter Ending March 31, 19X1

Style		Units—Month 1					Units—Month 2				Units—Month 3				Total Units—Quarter				
No.	Description	Beginning Inventory	Forecasted Sales	Required Production	Planned Production	Ending Inventory	Forecasted Sales	Required Production	Planned Production	Ending Inventory	Forecasted Sales	Required Production	Planned Production	Ending Inventory	Beginning Inventory	Forecasted Sales	Required Production	Planned Production	Ending Inventory
A123	25″ Men Al. Sil.	25	350	325	330	5	300	295	120	25	275	250	300	50	25	925	900	950	50
A124	25″ Men Al. Yel.	19	200	181	200	19	200	181	200	19	175	156	160	4	19	575	556	560	4
A125	25″ Men Al. Bl.	23	150	127	150	23	125	102	110	8	125	117	120	3	23	400	377	380	3
M091	27″ Men Mag. Sil.	10	100	90	100	10	100	90	100	10	100	90	90	—	10	300	290	290	—
		322	2,258	1,936	7,200	264	1,780	1,516	1,750	134	1,465	1,131	1,500	369	322	5,503	5,181	5,550	369

of each model in order to calculate how much of each item of inventory in the A and B categories the company expected to use over the course of the year. The resulting analysis looked very much like Figure 16.2, but it was based on the anticipated activity for the coming year.

When Should You Place an Order?

Once he knew how much material he would use and when he would use it and had compared this to what he already had on hand, Roger believed he could calculate when to order more. Roger recognized that his suppliers were located in many parts of the country and overseas. It would take time for his order to reach the supplier, and it would take time for the materials shipped by the supplier to reach him. Furthermore, if the supplier had a small business like Roger's, he might have to produce Roger's materials after he received the order. Therefore, in some cases, the necessary lead time for placing an order and receiving the goods could be a week for some items and three months for others. Roger knew he could not afford to wait until he was completely out of an item before he placed an order for more, so he had to figure how much he was going to use each day (his expected usage) and multiply this by the number of days he believed it would take to receive the new goods (the purchase lead time). More specifically:

Expected usage = Number of units (bikes) per day × number of items per unit of a particular item to be used per day. Roger added a small amount of *safety stock* (several days' to one week's production) to the expected usage to cover any variations in the expected usage or any delays in receiving the goods, so that:

Expected usage = Number of items to be used per day + *safety stock;*

Purchase lead time = Number of days to order and receive the item.

Thus, if Roger built 125 bicycles per workday, and each bicycle had one derailleur, then he would need 125 × 1, or 125, derailleurs per day (his expected usage rate). Next, if he figured he had a purchase lead time of 20 working days, or one calendar month, he should place an order when he had:

$$125 \times 20 = 2{,}500 \text{ derailleurs left in stock}$$

or, if he wished to provide two days' safety stock (125 × 2) = 250 when he had 2,500 + 250 or 2,750 derailleurs left in stock.

In other words:

$$\text{Expected usage} \times \text{purchase lead time} = \text{reorder point}$$

Thus, his reorder point was the product of the expected usage multiplied by the purchase lead time. This was the point at which the items he had on hand (derailleurs, in this example) would allow for continued production during the time needed to place the order and receive the materials.

To help him keep this lead time concept in mind, Roger drew the diagram shown in Figure 16.6. The vertical axis represents the level of stock or inventory, and the horizontal axis represents time. The expected rate of usage of inventory is represented by the slanting line going through Q to R. The shape of the line assumes that inventory is used *at the same rate each day*. This is a reasonable assumption even though production might be more or less than average on a given day. The triangular space under the line going from Q to R represents the amount of material to be used during the lead time (i.e., the time necessary to reorder); this is called the reserve stock. As mentioned earlier, this reserve stock may be increased by a small percentage to account for possible variations in either the daily production usage or in the purchase lead time. Such an adjustment is referred to as the *safety stock*.

The line extending to the right from point S is the *minimum stock level* or *the reorder point*. If Roger waited until after this point to reorder, he would probably run out of stock and have to make special costly arrangements to replace it, just as he had in his most recent order of derailleurs. T is the amount of the order. So, over time, the inventory

FIGURE 16.6
Using Inventory Levels to Determine Reorder Point

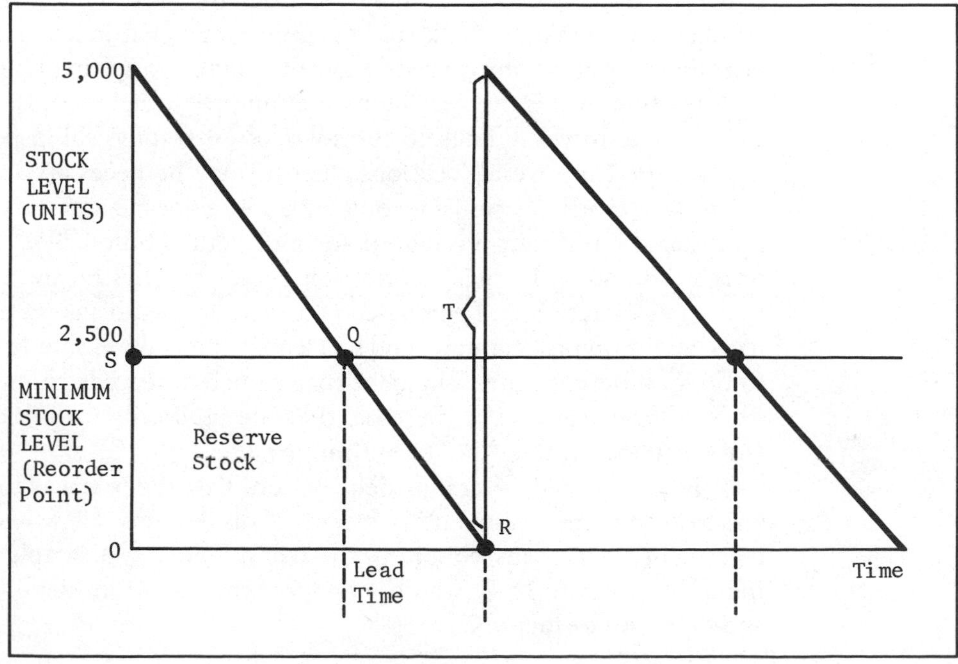

level would be worked down to the minimum stock level or reorder point, an order would be placed, the reserve stock would keep production going until the order was received, and the cycle would start again. Therefore, calculation of the reorder point tells you when to reorder and how much reserve stock to maintain to cover the purchase lead time.

How Do You Know When Your Reorder Point Is Reached?

Now that Roger had decided to reorder when his stock level for derailleurs reached 2,500, he needed a way to clearly signal when this level was reached. He realized that he had two alternatives: a periodic physical inspection of the inventory items, or to maintain perpetual records that would record transactions into and out of raw materials and purchased parts inventories and reflect remaining balances by part number.

As a practical matter, in any matter of procedure, the simplest method that is also reliable is the best method to use. Therefore, Roger should use the method of physical inspection if he is certain that he will place a reorder at the appropriate time. One way to do this is to place a specific inventory item consistently in a single location or bin. Then, by measuring the amount of space required in the bin bv the reserve stock and painting that portion of the bin in a distinctive color, you can tell if you need to reorder by looking at the bin to see if any of that color is showing. If it is, it is time to reorder. Another method is to mark on the boxes or on the bin the amount remaining in the bin and adjusting that figure for units added to or removed from the bin. This method can produce acceptable results if space permits storing all items of the same type together and if appropriate thought is given to setting up the bins. This method avoids the cost of maintaining perpetual records.

If inventory is difficult to control or assess by physical inspection or if it is stored in several locations, then it may be necessary to prepare perpetual records. Perpetual records are a waste of time and the money to maintain them if they are inaccurate and, hence, unreliable. Such records are simply a financial representation of the physical units relating to the raw materials and purchased parts inventories. It takes some effort to maintain them accurately, and so adequate procedures should be set up to do so. There is no requirement that perpetual records be used for all items. Often, because of the cost, they are used only for critical items (i.e., A items in the ABC classification).

Roger decided, after long deliberation, that the best way to proceed was to keep perpetual inventory records of his A items. He would use the method of physical inspection for the B and C items. A sample record is included as Figure 16.7, which represents the record for derailleurs and shows the following:

- The item description.
- Vendor names and their average lead times.
- The reorder point.
- The order quantity (calculated in the next section).
- The standard unit cost and measuring unit.
- All receipts, uses, and adjustments.
- The balance on hand.

Each transaction into and out of the record has a date, a reference number (either a purchase order or work order number), and an amount.

Because the balance at the top of the record shows only 2,500 remaining, it signals that a reorder point has been reached. The record shows issues to production on work orders while the purchase order was

FIGURE 16.7
Raw Material/Purchased Parts Perpetual Inventory Record

RAW MATERIALS/PURCHASED PARTS PERPETUAL INVENTORY RECORD

RM/PP Description ______ RM Code ______ Location ______

Vendor Names	Lead Times

Rcorder Point ______
Order Quantity ______ Std. Cost/Unit ______
Standard Measuring Unit ______

Date	Reference No.	Quantities			
		Received	Issued	Adjustments	Balance

being filled. Finally, the record shows the new order being received at about the time the reserve stock is depleted.

Roger knew that it was not practical for him to look at each individual inventory record every day in order to tell when the reorder point for an item had been reached. So he devised a weekly stock status report (see Figure 16.8) which is simply an abstract of the inventory records for the A items and a count of the stock on the floor for the B and C items. It shows for each item the balance at the end of the prior week, the transactions for the current week, the balance at the end of the current week, the normal reorder point for the item, the lead time, the order quantity, the orders outstanding, and the quantity available for production, the latter being simply the balance on hand plus the amount on order.

The Importance of Accurate Records

Roger realized that for his information to be useful, it had to be both timely and reliable. Therefore, he established a system whereby the perpetual records would be posted with work orders and purchase orders on a daily basis to keep them up to date. At the end of the week, after the posting, the stock status report would be prepared. Roger knew that if the posting was delayed, it would mean a delay in his finding out about the need for placing orders, which could cause the company to run out of the reserve stock before a new shipment could arrive. Therefore, he took care to adjust his safety stock to allow for some slippage, and he kept a watchful eye on the inventory record-keeping system.

What Quantity Should You Order?

Roger knew that his reserve stock for derailleurs was 2,500 units (20 days × 125/day). This would carry him during the time from placing the order until receiving it, but he now wondered what quantity he should order. If he ordered only 2,500 units, he would have to place another order as soon as the first was received. If he ordered all 31,250 units, the expected annual usage (125 per day x 250 production days), it would cost him $246,563 when the order arrived ($7.89 per derailleur × 31,250 units). This was more than Roger wanted to commit to this piece of inventory at any particular time. And it was much more than he needed to cover his current orders.

Thus, Roger had to decide on an order quantity that would allow him to minimize his investment in inventory, his ordering costs, and his risk of being out of stock, while allowing him to take advantage of available purchase discounts. Individually, derailleurs cost $8.76 wholesale, but the supplier offered quantity discounts of up to 10% for orders of 5,000 units and 12.5% on orders of 10,000 units. Roger believed that an

FIGURE 16.8

Wright Brothers Stock Status Report for the Week Ending March 27, 19X1

Item Number	Description	Balance 3/20/X1	Receipts	Issues	Adjustments	(1) Balance 3/27/X1	Normal Reorder Point	Normal Lead Time Weeks	Normal Order Quantity	(2) Quantity on Order	(1) + (2) = (3) Total on Hand Plus Ordered
A Items											
PP1167	Derailleurs	2,493	—	2,217	—	256	2,500	4	5,500	5,500	5,756
PP1831	Tires	4,783	6,035	4,765	—	6,053	2,500	2	6,035	—	6,053
R 1154	1/2″ Aluminum Tubular	30,080	16,904	24,120	—	22,864	20,592	6	8,452	8,452	31,316
C Items											
PP 1527	Butterfly Nuts	600	—	93	—	507	200	1	523	—	507

order of 10,000 would be too large an investment in this particular inventory item, since he would have to borrow to carry the inventory and his short-term interest rates were 16%. On the other hand, an order of 5,000 would earn most of the possible discount and would not be as substantial an investment. It would mean reordering only five times in the year and would allow for about a month between orders.

Therefore, Roger considered the following:

- The length of time it would take to place an order and receive the materials.
- The number of orders he would have to place and the cost to place those orders.
- The cost to carry the inventory, including interest, insurance, storage space, and handling.
- The discounts offered by his suppliers.
- The cost of being out of stock and either flying in a part (as he had already done) or halting production.

Using these considerations, he established order quantities for each of his A and B items. Then he established broad inventory levels for his C items, fixing on a half year's supply in each case. Thus, he significantly reduced the purchasing and management time for 65% of the total items, the C items, and that gave him time to focus on the large dollar volume A and B items.

WHAT IF THINGS CHANGE?

Roger recognizes that many factors come into play in his calculations. If any of these factors change over time, the results of his initial calculations will no longer be valid. Therefore, he knows that he must monitor the process to assure himself that he is in control of his inventories. For example, he realizes that if he receives more orders and increases his production schedule, he will have to reorder sooner. So he needs good feedback on his order status and his inventory status. He also knows that if his productivity increases, he will need to order sooner and even increase his order quantities, because he will use up his reserve stock faster. If production falls off, he will not need to order as quickly or as much.

Furthermore, if his suppliers' discounts change or if their ability to meet delivery schedules increases or decreases, this will have an impact on his order quantity, as would a scarcity in raw materials. And he knows that if the interest rates on working capital loans go up, it would have an unfortunate impact on his profits and he might have to reduce his order quantities. But Roger consoles himself with the fact that most of his inventory is not bulky; if he has to order greater quantities, he will have sufficient storage space.

He realizes that he can keep track of his inventory status by using the perpetual records and stock status report. To keep track of orders, he has developed an order status report.

Keeping Track of Orders

Roger's order status report, shown in Figure 16.9, lists items by finished product number. It shows Jonathan's sales forecast versus the current customer order status for the year to date. If the current order status is close to or more than the sales forecast, this tells Roger whether the sales forecast is apt to be achieved. In addition, it shows him the status of customer orders in-house to be scheduled for production. He can compare these outstanding orders to his finished goods and work-in-process inventories and to the anticipated production schedule to see if these items will be produced within an appropriate time. If not, he can take action to put more orders into production, or if the scheduled production is unnecessary, he can cut back.

Roger recognizes that any good report should be brief, to the point, and serve a specific management need. If there is a way to obtain the information in a simpler way, he would be wise to do so. Yet he knows that his board of directors is vitally interested in this information, so he has decided to continue with this report.

Production Reporting

The order status report shows Roger that there are enough orders to meet the sales forecast. He needs to be certain that production scheduled for the next month is actually achieved, because the sales do not materialize until the bikes are produced, shipped, and billed to the customer.

To monitor this part of the business, he has developed a production report (Figure 16.10), which shows scheduled production, completed production, finished goods on hand, shipments, and the balance of finished goods at the end of the month. Roger receives this report monthly to be certain that the orders are not only being produced on schedule but that they are being shipped promptly.

CONCLUSION

What are the essential elements of the inventory control system developed by Roger? Consider the following points:

1. Roger, like many small manufacturers, decided to produce to customer order rather than to stock. This reduced some of the guesswork

FIGURE 16.9

Wright Brothers Order Status Report March 31, 19X1

Item	Description	Sales Forecast Y-T-D Qty.	Sales Forecast Y-T-D $	Order Status Y-T-D Qty.	Order Status Y-T-D $	Variance Forecast Over (Under) Qty.	Variance Forecast Over (Under) $	Finished Goods + Work In Process	Unshipped Orders On Hand	Required Production 4/X1	Scheduled Production 4/X1	Action Step
A 123	25″ Men's Al-Silver	925	138,288	1,025	153,238	100	14,950	53	181	128	150	
A 124	25″ Men's Al-Yellow		575	85,562	600	89,700	25	4,138	26	130	104	120
A 125	25″ Men's Al-Black	400	59,800	370	55,315	(30)	(4,485)	24	123	99	120	Reduce to 100
M091	27″ Men's Mag-Silver	300	53,640	315	56,322	15	2,682	19	79	60	60	
		5,503	$853,000	5,610	$869,550	107	$16,550	354	2,827	2,473	2,500	

FIGURE 16.10

Wright Brothers Production Report for the Month Ended April 30, 19X1

				Finished Goods			
Item	*Description*	*Scheduled Production*	*Actual Production*	*Opening Balance*	*Qty. Produced*	*Qty. Shipped*	*Ending Balance*
A123	25″ Men's Al-Silver	150	130	53	130	150	33
A124	25″ Men's Al-Yellow	120	130	26	130	140	16
A125	25″ Men's Al-Black	100	90	24	90	110	4
M091	27″ Men's Mag-Silver	60	60	19	60	70	9
		2,480	2,390	354	2,390	2,470	274

necessary in estimating appropriate inventory levels and reduced his overall investment in inventories, but it meant he had to closely monitor his order, production, and inventory status.

2. Roger realized that his inventory was really comprised of several inventory groups, namely:

- Raw materials.
- Purchased parts and subassemblies.
- Work in process.
- Finished goods.
- Supplies.

And he recognized that each group had different characteristics that required different control techniques.

3. Roger knew that he could obtain a complete list of his inventory items by consulting his bills of materials for the various styles, colors, and sizes of bicycles the company produced. By reviewing these bills, he was able to determine where a single inventory item could be used on several different bicycles, thereby minimizing the overall number of inventory items.

4. Roger took the list of items and calculated an *average annual dollar* usage ranking—often referred to as an ABC analysis. With this information obtained from the ABC analysis, Roger reasoned that he should concentrate his management efforts on the A and B items and any C items that were critical to smooth production flow.

5. Roger realized that he would have to estimate his expected inventory usage and that he could do this by constructing a sales forecast integrated with, and adjusted by, his order backlog and a production schedule, initially based on the sales forecast and adjusted for changes in the order status.

6. He decided that he would track his inventory status for A items by using a set of perpetual records that would be updated on a continuing basis for purchase receipts, issues to production, and other adjustments. Other items he would monitor by physical inspection.

7. Roger reasoned that he would have to allow enough *reserve stock* to cover the purchase lead time between when he placed the order and when the order was received. This he adjusted for a factor to allow for unexpected events. He referred to the adjustment as his *safety stock*.

8. Roger weighed all the economic and subjective criteria regarding the amount of each item to be ordered, including the following, in order to select an economic order quantity:

- *Cost of a stock-out*—in terms of lost sales, an idle production force, incurrence of overtime to catch up, and the like.

- *Carrying costs of excessive inventory.*
- *Supplier reliability.*
- *Quantity price discounts.*
- *Goods availability.*
- *Seasonality.*
- *Cost to reorder.*

9. Roger devised an order status report and a production report—the first to compare actual customer orders to the sales forecast, and the second to keep track of his production and shipments to customers.

All in all, Roger believed that over the past year he, together with his brother and their sons, had developed an inventory management system that would carry them through several years of continued growth.

SELF-ASSESSMENT CHECKLIST
INVENTORY MANAGEMENT

	Yes	*No*	*N/A*	*Comments*
(1) Does your company produce: —to order? —to stock?				
(2) Based on your production lead times, do you firmly establish customer delivery dates?				
(3) Do you monitor customer delivery dates and calculate a customer satisfaction level or percentage?				
(4) Have you prepared an A, B, C analysis of the items in your inventory?				
(5) Do you use the A, B, C analysis to focus your management efforts?				
(6) Do you prepare a detailed sales forecast?				
(7) Do you schedule production based on your sales forecast?				
(8) Do you know the length of your production cycle (i.e., the time from the cutting of a work order to the completion of the lot or unit)?				

SELF-ASSESSMENT CHECKLIST
INVENTORY MANAGEMENT

	Yes	*No*	*N/A*	*Comments*
(9) Do you know purchase order lead times for your A and B inventory items?				
(10) Do you have several reliable suppliers and/or alternate supplier for your A and B items?				
(11) Have you calculated reorder points for your A and B items?				
(12) Do you maintain perpetual records for your A and B items?				
(13) Do you receive a stock status report periodically that shows the status of your A and B items?				
(14) Do you know your costs of: —a stock-out of a major item? —carrying excessive inventory? —preparing a purchase order?				
(15) Have you calculated order quantities for your A and B items?				
(16) Do you receive an order status report periodically?				
(17) Do you adjust your sales forecast for changes in customer ordering patterns?				
(18) Do you receive a production report that shows actual as compared to scheduled production?				

17

Managing Fixed Assets

This chapter shows you how to analyze whether the acquisition of additional plant or equipment can help your business to grow. And it shows you how to manage that acquisition process by controlling your construction and financing costs through good project management. It provides information on tax benefits of the new accelerated cost recovery system. This chapter also helps you to figure out how your fixed assets measure up in terms of profitability. A self-assessment checklist is included at the end of the chapter.

CASE STUDY: RAPHAEL HERNANDEZ LEARNS HOW TO ACQUIRE AND FUND NEW EQUIPMENT AND LARGER PREMISES

Raphael Hernandez has reached a decision. If he is going to build his business, he is going to have to expand his plant and acquire more machines. He got into business by developing a machine that enabled him to produce wrought iron nails for use by "do-it-yourselfers" in finishing their playrooms or for use in commercial establishments (bars, restaurants) to provide that rustic, colonial look. He has been able to produce a good product using modern metals that do not shatter, as the original wrought iron did. And he has been able to meet customer deliveries with sufficient regularity. This has earned him a reputation as a reliable supplier with a quality product. As a result, his order books are always full.

IS GROWTH WORTH THE COST?

He has determined that if he is going to grow, he must branch out into new products because the market for his specialty product is limited. To do this, he will have to acquire new equipment and expand his shop. He has considered moving to a different building, but an interest rate of 17% for mortgage financing has discouraged him. So he has decided to expand his current quarters, in which case he will have to pay the current financing rate on only his new equipment and a portion of his facility, rather than on a whole new building. In addition, he will save the brokerage costs of selling his property as well as the expense of moving.

Raphael has made several computations of the costs and benefits of his various alternatives. He knows within reason what the expansion would cost and what it would cost to fund the project and to provide for operations until the new equipment could begin to generate revenues. And he knows that he can arrange to borrow the necessary funds. He has used capital budgeting techniques to figure out if he should go ahead with this project. He has computed that with even modest success, he will be able to pay back the loan and achieve the growth he hopes for.

WHERE CAN YOU GET THE MONEY?

Even though Hernandez could have gone to his local bank for a long-term loan, he has submitted a request to the Industrial Development Authority in his county to obtain financing through the proceeds of an industrial development revenue bond. The department is favorably disposed toward his application because of his careful analysis and ability to repay the loan and because he would be providing employment to minorities within the county. Therefore, they have granted him a loan.

TELL YOUR CONTRACTOR EXACTLY WHAT YOU WANT AND PUT IT IN WRITING

Thus assured of his funding, Raphael contacted the equipment supplier to place an order for the machinery. He stated the required specifications and requested in return specifications regarding wiring, footing requirements, and other conditions necessary to install and operate the equipment.

He then requested bids from several contractors. He provided information regarding the nature of the project, the appropriate specifications and zoning restrictions, and other covenants of which the contractors should be aware. The contractors were to prepare a detailed bid, showing detailed components of the construction costs, an anticipated construction timetable, and an estimate of when the construction draws or payments might have to be made. Raphael analyzed all bids received and made a selection. He signed the appropriate contracts, arranged for construction financing, and then settled back to monitor the implementation.

GOOD PROJECT CONTROL CAN SAVE YOU MONEY

Raphael figured that, in order to monitor his construction costs effectively, he would have to accumulate those costs and compare them both to the estimate or budget of costs *and* to his estimate of the state of completion of the various components of the project. To do this, he developed a form (see Figure 17.1) that enabled him to accumulate costs by the various components of the project. Fortunately, he had hired a general contractor who would be responsible for employing the proper building subcontractors to work on the project. In addition, the general contractor would accumulate the invoices from these subcontractors and provide Raphael with a summary bill classified by project component. Raphael could then review the information from the summary bill and use it to update the form illustrated in Figure 17-1. In this way, he could

FIGURE 17.1
Project Control Record

PROJECT CONTROL RECORD

Date ______________________

Request No. ______________________

Const Cost	Original	Budg Ch Order		Total	Expended Before Current Request	Current Request	Expended to Date	Balance	% Expended	% Completed
		Ref	Amt							
Excavation										
Concrete										
Iron Work										
Framing										
Insulation										
Siding										
Roofing										
HVAC										
Electrical										
Plumbing										
Finish Carpentry										
Retainage										
Total										

keep track of the progress of the construction as it related to each of the components.

To monitor these costs, he first calculated the expenditures to date by adding the current request for payment to the year-to-date totals from prior requests. Then he divided the amount expended by the amount budgeted to calculate the percentage of the budget expended to date. Finally, he made his own estimate of the state of completion of the project. If the percentage expended and percentage completed, according to his observations, were roughly equivalent, then he could be reasonably sure that the project would be completed within the budget. He tested this by looking at the remaining balance in the budget for each component to see if what remained to be done could reasonably be accomplished with what remained in the budget. This served as a double check.

In addition, when Raphael initially completed the form, he included an estimated date when each component should be finished. As the construction proceeded, he entered the date on which each component was *actually* finished. By comparing the actual completion date with the estimate, he was able to assess whether the overall project would be completed on schedule and, if not, how far behind it was. It was important to know whether the project was behind schedule because this could have an impact on the cost of the construction loan he would have to carry. Normally, in capital improvement projects such as Raphael's, there is a short-term (construction) loan to finance the construction period, which may extend over a year or more. Once the construction is complete, the entrepreneur obtains permanent financing (a long-term loan) which, because it is secured by the property, bears a lower rate of interest than the construction financing. Therefore, if Raphael's project were held up for two or three additional months, it would cost him the difference between the interest rate on the construction loan and the interest rate on the permanent financing for the period of the delay. The following example illustrates this cost:

> *Assume that the rate on the construction loan is 17% and that the rate on the permanent financing is 14%. Therefore, the difference in the two rates is 3% per year. If Raphael's construction balance is estimated to be $128,000, the additional 3% would cost him $3,750. If he assumed that the project was going to be three months late, it would cost him one quarter of this amount, or $937.50. In addition, he would be delaying the start of his expanded facilities, which might mean losing customer orders or even missing a particularly critical part of his business cycle.*

Raphael attached a copy of the project control form (Figure 17.1) to each invoice from the general contractor. He filed this packet, after the invoice had been paid, in a separate file for fixed assets, so that he would have it available to fill out his fixed asset ledger sheet when the project was completed.

FIGURE 17.2
Fixed Asset Record

Asset Number ____________

Location ____________

FIXED ASSET RECORD

Last Inventory Date ____/____/____

Description ____________

Acquired Date __/__/__

Acquired From ____________

New ☐ Used ☐

Depreciation Method ____________ Rate ______

Estimated Useful Life ____________

Inventory Tag # ____________

Original Cost ____________

Gain or Loss on
Sale or Trade-In ____________

Salvage Value ____________

Basis for Depreciation ____________

Disposal Date ____/____/____ Proceeds $ ______

Gain or Loss on Disposition ____________

Components of Cost

Base Cost:

____________ $ ______

____________ ______

____________ ______

____________ ______

Financing Cost
Other

____________ ______

____________ ______

Total Cost $ ______

Accumulated Depreciation

Date	Depn. Amt.	Accum. Depn.	Date	Depn. Amt.	Accum. Depn.

MAINTAIN GOOD FIXED ASSET RECORDS

His fixed asset records, illustrated in Figure 17.2, enabled Raphael to keep track of each asset he owned. It also enabled him to calculate the cost recovery allowance, (i.e., depreciation) on his buildings and equipment for the purpose of preparing his tax returns. Finally, the record contained all the information he would need to calculate whether he had a gain or a loss if he sold the asset. (The terms *cost recovery* and *depreciation* are used interchangeably in this discussion.)

In addition, Raphael knew that his accountant periodically would take an inventory of his fixed assets to support the figures in the company's financial statements. He therefore tagged each item and noted its location on the form so that he could find it easily when it was time to take an inventory. Because his shop was small, this procedure was not absolutely necessary to keep track of his major pieces of equipment, but it was particularly helpful where furniture, fixtures, and office machines were concerned.

A closer look at the form reveals another feature. It has a space in which to enter the date the asset was acquired. This helps when it is time to calculate the amount of allowable depreciation.

Raphael was aware that the tax rules for depreciation were completely revised in 1981. He asked his accountant to explain the new rules to him.

HOW PROFITABLE ARE YOUR FIXED ASSETS?

As a final measure of effectiveness, Raphael calculated some simple ratios. First, he equated dollars of sales with dollars in his fixed assets.

Assuming that the cost of the new machinery is \$67,000, that the full 10% investment tax credit was taken, and that it is placed in service

$$\frac{\$\ \text{sales}}{\$\ \text{fixed assets}} = \frac{\$1{,}787{,}000}{\$167{,}000} = \$10.70$$

In this way, he discovered that every \$1 of his fixed assets could be thought of as generating \$10.70 in sales. With the plant expansion and the addition of new machines, his productive fixed assets would now cost

$362,000 ($167,000 + $195,000 = $362,000). Therefore, he would have to generate sales of $3,873,400 to maintain the $10.70 sales to $1 of assets ratio he had previously achieved. This was his goal and he intended to monitor his progress to determine if he was achieving it.

Raphael also used another set of measures to test the productivity of each machine. By keeping records of how long each machine operated each month and how many pounds of nails each produced, he was able to calculate the following for each machine:

$$\frac{\text{Hours of production per machine}}{\text{Available hours for production}} = \_\_\text{\% of capacity}$$

$$\frac{\text{Units of production per machine}}{\text{Standard units expected}} = \_\_\text{\% of standard}$$

$$\frac{\text{Sales value of production per machine}}{\text{Dollar value of standard production}} = \_\_\text{\% of profitability}$$

These ratios showed him how much each machine contributed to his growth and to his financial results.

CONCLUSION

Raphael Hernandez is a good manager who gets the most out of his fixed assets. His success is attributable to the following factors:

1. He analyzes the productivity of his assets on a continuing basis.

2. He thoroughly analyzed the financial aspects of acquiring his new plant addition and equipment by using capital budgeting techniques.

3. He established a system to monitor the project during the construction phase, using a sound project control system that also served to accumulate all his costs to facilitate his calculation of his yearly cost recovery allowance (depreciation).

4. He maintains good records of his fixed assets to provide a single consistent source for analyzing their productivity, to calculate their cost recovery, to provide a record for Internal Revenue Service audits, and to show their unrecovered cost (in order to calculate gain or loss on their disposition). These records also serve as subledgers for his general ledger balance and are a handy source for an inventory of fixed assets.

5. Finally, because of the advantage of using ACRS, Raphael was able to minimize his tax liability and retain additional working capital in his business.

SELF-ASSESSMENT CHECKLIST
FIXED ASSET MANAGEMENT

	Yes	*No*	*N/A*	*Comments*
(1) Do you have a formal plan for acquiring plant and equipment to expand your business?				
(2) When you decide to acquire plant and/or equipment do you analyze the costs and benefits employing capital budgeting techniques?				
(3) Do you have a capital expenditure project control system to monitor the acquisition cost of your fixed assets?				
(4) Do you review your capital expenditures after the fact to determine if the expected results were attained?				
(5) Do you maintain complete fixed asset records to: —support your cost recovery allowance (depreciation) calculations? —enable you to take a periodic physical inventory? —support calculations of gain or loss on the sale or disposition of those assets?				
(6) Do you know the dollars of sales generated by your fixed assets: —in total? —by each asset?				
(7) Do you know which of your machines is most productive?				
(8) Do you know why?				
(9) Are you taking advantage of the accelerated cost recovery system (ACRS) for tax purposes, where applicable?				

18

Managing Purchasing And Accounts Payable

Raw materials and supplies are fundamentals without which you cannot run your business. You are, therefore, dependent on your suppliers for these essentials. And your relationship with them, particularly your credit standing, is critical to the life of your business. But you can also go too far in trying to guarantee a good credit standing; it can cost you money if you pay too quickly or lose purchase discounts. This chapter shows you how to strike an effective balance in your relationships with suppliers by illustrating a model for a purchase ordering and accounts payable function. You can test your purchasing and accounts payable management techniques by completing the self-assessment checklist at the end of the chapter.

CASE STUDY: GRANT AND MARY RICHARDS LEARN HOW TO WORK EFFECTIVELY WITH THEIR SUPPLIERS

Mary Richards and her husband Grant have been operating their cosmetic manufacturing business for six years. The business has grown to a reasonable level of $4 million in sales. When they started the business,

Mary had a graduate degree in chemistry. She not only knew what went into the cosmetics, but over the last several years, she had developed her own formulas. Her background and her desire to be independent were what motivated her to strike out on her own.

Grant had a degree in marketing, which was helpful in the sales and distribution end of the business. Neither of them had any extensive training in business management, although they had taken some courses in preparing to start the business and after it had begun operations. However, the product was a good one, and Grant's effective promotional efforts allowed them to survive the first few years. And they learned a lot by trial and error.

Early in the process, they came to realize that they were more dependent on their suppliers, in terms of the availability and quality of the ingredients for their products and their prompt delivery, than the suppliers were dependent on the Richards for orders. Therefore, after learning a number of lessons the hard way, Mary and Grant developed an effective purchase ordering and accounts payable function for the business.

HOW TO DEVELOP A PURCHASING AND ACCOUNTS PAYABLE FUNCTION

Start with a Good Sales Forecast

First, Mary and Grant developed a sales forecast similar to the one shown in Figure 16.5. They used this to estimate their required ingredients for the whole year. Furthermore, because they knew that there was something of a seasonal nature to the cosmetics business, they estimated when the peaks and valleys would occur and adjusted their requirements for ingredients accordingly.

Establish Perpetual Inventory Records

The Richards then developed a series of perpetual inventory records (see Figure 16.8) to keep track of their ingredients, so that they would know if any items were being depleted faster than anticipated. They found they could use these records to check the current stock status of ingredients when issuing new orders.

Use Formal Purchase Orders

Grant instituted a procedure whereby all major purchases of raw materials, equipment, and the like were made by using a formal carbonized purchase order that had four copies. One copy was to be matched with the vendor's invoice. One went to the receiving area to put them on notice to receive the goods. The remaining two copies went into a purchase order filing system—one alphabetically by vendor, the other numerically by purchase order number. The original went to the vendor.

Prepare an Authorized Vendor List

From their alphabetical purchase order file, they made a list of the vendors with whom they had done business (see Figure 18.1). They worked this list down to a manageable number of reliable vendors over several years. It provided them with the ability to identify those vendors who represented the *sole source* of certain ingredients and those ingredients that were available from several reliable suppliers. They noted the annual dollar volume of ingredients they purchased from these suppliers, the payment terms offered, the vendors' quality level, and their reliability (number of back orders or stock-outs).

Because they were relatively unsophisticated in financial management and because they had the resources and felt a dependency on their suppliers, Mary and Grant tended to pay their bills almost as soon as they were received. This gave them a good credit rating. However, their own customers were taking a full 30 days or more to pay them. As a result, the Richards had to go to the bank to borrow funds to finance their receivables and their inventory purchases. Furthermore, the time was rapidly approaching when they would have to borrow additional funds to support the growth of their business and the corresponding need for more working capital.

At about this time, due to general economic circumstances, interest rates were being pushed up, and the prime rate (the rate offered by banks to their preferred, usually large, customers) had reached 14%. The Richards knew that as a small business, even with a good credit rating, they might have to pay 16% or more to borrow additional short-term funds. They decided to analyze their situation to see if they could avoid taking an additional loan by managing their working capital a little better.

ARE YOU PAYING YOUR BILLS TOO FAST?

Grant recalled two ratios that he understood were used to evaluate businesses. He began to ponder them and to calculate them on a sheet of paper. (A complete discussion of ratio analysis is contained in Chapter 22.) The first was the current ratio, which is a company's current assets (including cash, receivables, short-term investments, and inventories) divided by its current liabilities (including the current portion of notes payable, accounts payable, payroll taxes withheld, and other accrued

FIGURE 18.1
Richard's Cosmetics Authorized Vendors List

Item #	*Name*	*Vendors*	*Annual Dollar Volume*	*Lead Time*	*Terms*	*High, Medium, or Low Quality*	*Availability of Product*	*Average A/P Turnover*
415	Talc	Davis Chemical	$127,000	2 weeks	N/30	H	—	6 days
		Lanza, Inc.	53,290	2 weeks	N/30	H	—	5 days
		Fanning Chemical	22,170	1 week	N/30	H	3	15 days
			$202,460					
417	Zinc Stearate	Baker Chemical	$ 12,153	4 weeks	N/30	H	—	5 days
		N.J. Industries	6,545	2 weeks	N/30	H	—	8 days
			$ 18,698					
421	PVP	Heterene Chemical	$ 16,175	5 weeks	N/30	H	—	3 days [a]
425	Propylene Glycol	Ashland Chemical	$ 4,583	3 weeks	N/30	M	—	7 days
		Emery Industries	7,156	5 weeks	2/10 N/30	H	—	5 days
			$ 11,739					
593	Kaolin	Tobey Chemical	$ 18,453	4 weeks	N/30	H	—	5 days [a]
597	Emollient-A150	Sylva Chemical	$ 17,650	3 weeks	N/30	H	1	7 days
		Union Industries	6,853	2 weeks	N/30	H	—	5 days
			$ 34,503					
		TOTAL R.M. PURCHASES	$953,127					
		AVERAGE TURNOVER A/P						12 days
		# SOLE SOURCE SUPPLIERS	5					

[a] Sole source.

liabilities—those items expected to be paid off in the current business cycle or fiscal year).

$$\text{Current ratio} = \text{current assets} - \text{current liabilities}$$

This ratio should be close to 2 to 1 in a highly creditworthy business. In the Richards' business, it was nearly 3 to 1, which was very high and left room for the ratio to fall before it would signal a problem to creditors.

The second ratio was the rate of turnover in accounts payable, expressed in terms of days. This calculation is made by dividing the average payables balance by the total estimated annual purchases and multiplying the result by 365 days. Grant calculated his company's turnover rate as follows:

$$\frac{\text{Average payables balance}}{\text{Estimated annual purchases}} = \frac{\$\ 36{,}059 \text{ (Figure 18.3)}}{953{,}127 \text{ (Figure 18.1)}}$$

$$= 0.038 \times 365 = \underline{\underline{14 \text{ days}}}$$

This meant that a typical supplier's bill would be outstanding for only 14 days. He tested this ratio on a few specific accounts and found that, for his sole source suppliers, some bills were only outstanding four or five days. These two calculations suggested to Grant that he was not taking full advantage of the available credit extended from suppliers.

Next, Grant calculated the impact of increasing or decreasing this turnover rate by one day. He divided estimated annual purchases by 365, which worked out to be approximately $2,611. Therefore, if he postponed payment by one day, he would free up $2,611 of working capital. And if he wished to contract his payment schedule and pay sooner, he would have to raise an additional $2,611.

With this information in hand, he went back to his list of suppliers (Figure 18.1) and calculated and recorded the average A/P turnover by supplier. He reviewed the list and noted that not all suppliers gave discounts, yet he paid the bills to these suppliers nearly as rapidly as he did to those who gave discounts for prompt payment.

WHAT SHOULD YOUR PAYABLES STRATEGY BE?

Grant thought he should take advantage of the full 30 days of credit offered by many of his suppliers, provided their terms of credit were "n/30"—which means that net payment is due 30 days after receipt of the goods. Next, he wondered if it was economically sound to borrow money to take advantage of the discounts offered by other suppliers. He did the following calculations to arrive at an answer:

1. Grant considered a recent invoice for $6,000 from a major supplier of talc, which formed the base for many of the company's cosmetics. The terms were 1.5/10, n/30, meaning that the Richards could take a 1½% discount if they paid the bill in 10 days; the bill under any circumstances was due in 30 days. The amount of the discount was therefore $90, or $6,000 × 0.015.
2. He then considered borrowing the $6,000 at 14% for 25 days. This was the time he figured it would take to collect sufficient receivables to pay off the loan. (He had calculated a receivables turnover of 35 days and reasoned that he would pay his bill on the last available day, or the tenth day, so 35 − 10 = 25). Therefore, the loan would cost him $57.53, or $6,000 × 0.14 × 25/365.
3. Thus, he would save $32.47 ($90 − $57.53) if he borrowed the money to pay on the discount date. He also reasoned that if the discount were 2% instead of 1.5%, paying within the discount date would be even more favorable and if he was paying bills with terms of net 30 before the end of the 30 days, this practice was costing him money.

So the strategy seemed clear:

1. *Take advantage of discounts* and, if necessary, borrow the money to pay them. But Grant knew he would have to keep an eye on short-term interest rates and refigure the break-even point—the point where the interest cost equaled the discount—if the rates went above 14%.
2. *Defer payment on bills with terms of 30 days* or with no specific terms until the end of the credit period or until the payment date agreed to by the supplier.
3. *Try to collect receivables within the normal credit terms*, 30 days in the Richards' case.

However, Grant understood that management of payables is something of a double-edged sword. His company was both a vendor and a customer; this was also the case for his vendors and customers. Thus, if the Richards were becoming better at managing their payables, they faced the prospect that *their vendors might be seeking to tighten up on their management of receivables* and would thereby resist Mary's and Grant's efforts to extend their payables.

Tell Your Suppliers What You Plan to Do

Furthermore, Grant understood that unless they were very careful and made their actions known, their suppliers might misinterpret these actions as signs of a business in trouble. And the Richards might hurt their credit rating, have their supplies shut off, or be placed on a COD (cash on delivery) basis with their suppliers. A deterioration in their credit rating would increase the difficulty of future borrowing and would, in any case, lead to higher interest costs and, therefore, lower profits.

Mary and Grant decided to proceed with caution. Going back to their list of suppliers, they first scanned to see which were sole source suppliers, which represented one of a few sources, and which had lots of competition. They also noted how much business they had done with each supplier. They then phoned each supplier and explained that now they were an established business, they wished to extend their payables from the current 14-day average to closer to a 30-day average, where the terms so permitted. They also stated that they would continue to pay on the discount date, where this was an option.

Many of the suppliers understood the Richards' request and, in fact, indicated that they had been a bit surprised at the overly prompt payment in the past. They would find the extension acceptable. Others acknowledged the Richards' problem but remained adamant about the prompt payment schedule. In some of these cases, Mary and Grant had alternative sources of supply. They decided to take a chance and implement their new strategy where there were alternative sources and to retreat where there were no alternatives. In any event, the process did result in freeing up approximately $75,000 in working capital.

DO YOU HAVE AN EARLY WARNING SYSTEM?

But Mary and Grant were not finished. They decided that since they now had less room to maneuver, they had better make certain that they were paying their bills on time. Therefore, they decided to prepare a weekly cash requirements report (see Figure 18.2). This showed them when invoices were due and when they would have to pay particular vendors to take advantage of discounts. The report also indicated those vendors that had to be paid immediately because they were either sole source suppliers or they were particularly adamant about prompt payment.

Mary and Grant also reviewed an accounts payable trial balance (Figure 18.3) each month that listed the balance to each supplier and indicated how long it had been outstanding. This was a precaution to assure that no outstanding items remained unpaid for too long. The trial balance tied into the general ledger balance for accounts payable and was an abstract of their accounts payable subledger.

Although they could have reviewed a stack of open invoices from suppliers just as easily, the report assured them that all items were represented; it grouped the items by vendor and provided a total to tie into the general ledger.

FIGURE 18.2

Richard's Cosmetics Cash Requirements Report Week Ending June 5, 19X1

Vendor	*Vendor Name*	*Invoice Number*	*Invoice Amount*	*Invoice Date*	*Terms*	*Sole Source T/N*	*Pay By*
R12486	Davison Chemical	0823	$ 685.00	5/25	N/30	N	6/25
R12489	Fanning Chemical	19596	$ 1,853.11	5/19	N/30	N	Hold
R12551	GAP Chemical	1754	$ 2,229.50	5/19	1.5/10 N/30	N	6/1
R12573	Heterene	12263	$ 896.00	5/26	N/30	Yes	6/5
		12751	716.00	5/27	N/30		6/5
			$ 1,612.00				
R13615	Tobey Chemical	K1675	$ 421.00	5/27	N/30	Yes	6/5
TOTAL MENTS	CASH REQUIRE- FOR THE WEEK	$14,480.76					
	TOTAL DEFERRED	(3,571.17)					
	NET CASH REQUIREMENTS FOR THE WEEK	$10,909.59					

FIGURE 18.3
Richard's Cosmetics Aged Accounts Payable Trial Balance
As of June 30, 19X1

Vendor No.	*Vendor Name*	*Total Outstanding*	*30 Days*	*60 Days*	*90 Days Total*	*Comments*
R1105	Ashland Chemical	$ 1,256.17	$ 1,256.17			
R1152	Baker Chemical	$ 592.00		$ 592.00		Goods returned—poor quality, awaiting debit memo from Baker
R1219	Emery Industries	$ 2,561.71	$ 2,561.71			
R1417	Union Industries	$ 419.23	$ 419.23			
	TOTAL A/P	$36,059.85	$34,284.12	$1,592.23	$183.50	

CONCLUSION

Mary and Grant Richards learned a number of important techniques in purchasing and payables management in the process of running their business. They learned the following:

1. A *sales forecast* was a good basis for estimating their purchases for the year and that such an estimate would be important in negotiating with suppliers.
2. *Perpetual inventory records could help them keep track of raw material purchases and would be a source to consult when considering future purchases compared to usage.*
3. It would be wise to maintain a *list of suppliers* and to note on the list the quantity purchased from the supplier, the supplier's price and credit terms, the quality of the product, the reliability of service, and whether or not the supplier was a sole source.
4. It was important to develop a *sound purchasing and accounts payable system,* consisting of a purchase journal, voucher register, accounts payable subledger, and cash disbursement journal. With this system, they were reasonably certain that they would not lose track of any vendor invoices. And they could determine the dollar volume of business done with their various suppliers by reviewing the accounts payable subledger.
5. Three sets of calculations were important indicators in the management of payables. First, the *current ratio* told them whether they had sufficient short-term assets that could be converted into cash to pay their current liabilities as they came due. Second, the accounts payable *turnover rate* confirmed whether the current ratio was too high by indicating how quickly (or slowly) bills were being paid. The third calculation showed *whether it was wise to borrow to take advantage of discounts on purchases.*
6. It was important to develop a *strategy* to take advantage of discounts and credit terms offered by suppliers. During the development of their strategy they came to realize that payables management is a double-edged sword. Although they were customers of certain vendors, they were also vendors to some of their customers. They also realized that to implement their strategy without first notifying their suppliers could result in a lower credit rating, restricted credit, higher interest rates, reduced borrowing capacity, and lower profits. Therefore, they decided to proceed with caution and to notify their suppliers of their intended strategy.
7. When their strategy was fully implemented, they would have less room to maneuver with their unpaid bills, so they developed two

reports—a weekly cash requirements report and an aged accounts payable trial balance—to help them *to keep track of vendor invoices*. These reports would ensure that individual vendors would be paid on appropriate predesignated bases.

SELF-ASSESSMENT CHECKLIST
MANAGING PURCHASING AND ACCOUNTS PAYABLE

	Yes	*No*	*N/A*	*Comments*
(1) Do you use a sales forecast to estimate raw materials and purchased parts needed during the year?				
(2) Do your inventory records signal when to place an order?				
(3) Do you have a formal purchase order form and a policy for using it?				
(4) Have you compiled an authorized vendors list?				
(5) Do you know which suppliers: —are most reliable? —are sole sources? —give trade discounts?				
(6) Do you know your payables turnover ratio: —in total? —by vendor?				
(7) Have you calculated the dollar impact of changing your payables payment habits (pay faster, pay slower)?				
(8) Do you have a formal strategy for paying vendors?				
(9) Do you receive a cash requirements listing periodically?				
(10) Do you receive an aged A/P trial balance periodically?				

19 Managing Sales

Sales give life to your business. Unless your sales meet your expectations, your business may not be able to survive without severe cost reductions. Because sales are so important, this chapter shows you how one entrepreneur developed an effective sales management program. You can test the effectiveness of your sales management program by completing the self-assessment checklist at the end of the chapter.

CASE STUDY: HERB BALDWIN FINDS SALES MANAGEMENT A KEY TO STEADY GROWTH

Veritas Electronics Corporation had just passed the $15 million sales level, and Herbert Baldwin, its president, was reflecting on how he had been able to accomplish this goal.

- He had a quality line of products and had been able to keep pace with changes in the industry.

- He had adopted a formal planning approach and had used his operating budgets to manage the company.
- He had hired good people and given them the authority and responsibility to help the company grow.
- He had received comprehensive financial statements on a monthly basis.
- He had analyzed these statements and taken action when it was necessary.

As he thought it over, he decided that his system of managing his sales was as important as any other factor contributing to the company's growth. His system consisted of three basic elements:

- Developing a formal sales forecast.
- Tracking and analyzing sales performance.
- Processing orders quickly.

Developing a Sales Forecast

In the early years of Veritas Electronics, Herb had tried to estimate what products he would sell. As he grew and began to use his own salespeople as well as manufacturers' representatives, he found that he had to develop a sales forecast for each of his own salespersons. He used the forecasts to establish sales quotas on which to calculate each person's commissions. He then extended his forecast to include what he considered to be reasonable quotas for these manufacturers' sales reps.

Tracking and Analyzing Sales Performance

Baldwin had developed what he considered to be realistic sales quotas and had convinced his sales force and the sales reps that the quotas were realistic. The convincing was made easier by his having his historical results to back him up, and he recognized that he would have to monitor each salesperson's progress against those quotas. Tracking sales made by the sales force was necessary to calculate commissions and to know early whether individuals were going to meet their quotas and, thereby, enable Veritas to achieve its overall sales forecast. In addition, Herb would have the information in sufficient time to investigate why certain individuals had failed to meet their quotas and to take corrective action.

In order to track sales it was necessary that every order processed by the company indicate the salesperson's or sales rep's identification number, as well as the customer number, product identification number, and customer location code. With this information, Herb could not only prepare reports to show him how his sales force was doing in comparison to their quotas (Figure 19.1) but he could also construct reports to present various combinations of these data, such as:

- Sales by product type (Figure 19.2).
- Sales by customer.
- Sales by geographic location.
- Sales by customer, by item (Figure 19.3).
  Sales by location, by item (Figure 19.4).

In this way he could also determine:

- Which products were doing well.
- Who his major customers were.
- What customers purchased what products and in what amounts.

Baldwin was also able to determine whether there were any sales patterns that seemed to depend on the location, the particular salesperson, or the time of the year. By analyzing these sales figures, he was able to assess whether a particular rep seemed to be skillful at selling any particular product, whether a product seemed to sell well in a certain area of the country, and if certain customers ordered only at specific times during the year. With this information, he could begin to be selective in his sales strategy and incentive compensation plans, to encourage his sales force to emphasize a particular product with a certain customer or in a certain location.

Sales information can help you guide the business. Herb realized that his sales analysis and tracking system not only served a monitoring function; it actually helped him to plan for the growth of his business. For example, when he coupled the information he learned from his sales analysis with the information he learned from his cost accounting system, concerning which products had the greatest contribution margins (see Chapter 23, "Break-Even Analysis," for a detailed discussion of contribution margin), he could then focus the sales force's commissions and quotas on emphasizing those products with the highest margins.

If his sales analysis indicated that a particular item was very popular, he could rework his production process to see if he could produce the product at a slightly lower cost in order to increase his margin. He could also assess the impact of switching his manufacturing resources from producing less popular products or products with lower margins to producing the more popular products or the products with higher margins.

Another analysis that he could perform with this information on sales was whether to set up distribution points around the country for products that seemed to sell well in particular geographic locations. He

FIGURE 19.1
Veritas Electronics Corporation
Sales (Orders) by Members of Sales Force (Six Months Ended June 30, 19X1)

I.D.	*Name*	*Month*		*Year to Date*		*Over*
No.	*Inside Salesperson*	*Actual*	*Quota*	*Actual*	*Quota*	*(Under)* [a]
15163	J. Aiderman	$4,894.15	$3,500.00	$28,951.80	$24,500.00	$4,451.80
12481	T. Alizzi	5,127.85	5,200.00	33,896.70	$31,200.00	2,696.70
	Mfrs. Reps					
451	D. Halton	$8,417.92	$9,000.00	$50,507.52	$54,000.00	($3,492.48)

[a] Printed in descending order by size of variance with favorable variances listed first.

FIGURE 19.2
Veritas Electronics Corporation
Sales (Orders) by Product Type (Six Months Ended June 30, 19X1)

Product		*Month*		*Year to Date*			*Gross Margin*			
Code No.	*Description*	*Actual*	*Budget*	*Actual*	*Budget*	*Prior Year*	*Month*		*Y-T-D*	
400XXX Transistors							$	%	$	%
400049	A-21 Transistor	$ 5,421.60	$ 5,800.00	$ 36,529.60	$34,800.00	$33,117.22	$1,030.11	19.0	$ 7,305.92	20.0
400056	H-73 International Circuit	17,152.30	14,400.00	112,159.80	86,700.00	57,124.25	4,459.60	26.0	28,039.95	25.0
400059	H-89 International Circuit	7,164.70	8,900.00	42,960.50	53,400.00	51,176.60	716.47	10.0	4,725.65	11.0

FIGURE 19.3

Veritas Electronics Corporation Sales (Orders) by Customer by Item (Six Months Ended June 30, 19X1)

Customer No.	Item No.	Description	Month		Year to Date		Gross Margin			
			This Year	Last Year	This Year	Last Year	Month $	Month %	Y-T-D $	Y-T-D %
11857		MCF Corp.—Total	$12,156.80	$10,178.04	$24,192.97	$22,095.17	$3,039.20	25.0	$5,564.38	23.0
	600051	Tantalum Elect. Capac.	4,117.16	7,059.16	6,208.74	11,153.18				
	600065	Alum. Elect. Capac.	5,829.17	3,118.88	5,829.17	3,895.22				
	400056	N-73 Integ. Circuit	2,210.47	—	12,155.09	7,046.77				

FIGURE 19.4

Veritas Electronics Corporation Sales (Orders) by Location by Item (Six Months Ended June 30, 19X1)

Location Code	Item No.	Description	Month		Year to Date	
			This Year	Last Year	This Year	Last Year
0128		Atlanta SMSA—Total	$8,215.61	$7,811.72	$82,156.17	$75,117.16
	40049	A-21 Transistor	3,083.33	5,001.19	22,013.80	$31,182.08
	40059	H-89 Int. Circuit	1,115.15	959.17	7,575.75	5,401.11

reasoned that if he were able to ship carloads of a product to a main distribution center, close to some of his major customers, he might benefit in two ways. First, he might be able to save on the transportation costs. Second, he might be able to fill an order more quickly and thereby increase his customer satisfaction percentage.

Processing Orders Quickly

Herb knew that tracking and analyzing sales trends and sales force performance were only part of the job of managing his sales. It was also important to make sure that orders were being processed quickly. So, a year and a half ago, Herb bought a minicomputer and automated his order entry system. The system enabled the order entry clerks to process orders more quickly, and, thereby, to process more orders in total.

Having acquired the minicomputer and "debugged" the order entry system, Herb recently decided to acquire a billing system and an accounts receivable system for the minicomputer. The billing system would enable him to use the information on orders filled from the order entry process to automatically create a bill for the customer. And the information from the billing system, in turn, would send information from the customer invoice to the accounts receivable system.

A minicomputer does a "maxi" job. Herb purchased only an order entry system initially because, although he was aware of the potential benefits of computerization, he was cautious. He started with an order entry system because that was the area of his greatest amount of paperwork, but he did not invest in many input terminals. He preferred to wait to see how the system operated in his business. (He did have the forethought to make certain he could add to the system when the need arose.)

Salespersons and sales reps either mailed or phoned in orders. As the orders were received, an order entry clerk reviewed them for completeness, making certain that the proper codes (sales rep, customer, product, location) were filled in. If the order was delivered over the phone, the clerk immediately went to the computer if it was free and entered the information directly. Otherwise, the information was recorded on an order form and entered later. As the codes were entered, the computer compared them to internal lists of acceptable codes and showed the description of each code on the input screen. In this way, the clerk could verify that the order was being processed to the right customer and for the right sales rep and location.

Next, the clerk entered the product code and the quantity ordered. Because the computer was linked to a finished goods inventory file, it showed the balance on hand; this made it possible for the clerk to determine whether the order could be filled. If it could be, it was processed and the finished goods inventory was reduced. If not, the clerk had three alternative courses of action:

1. The clerk could check to see how recently the finished goods inventory had been updated. A major advantage of the computer, Herb had found, was that it made it easier to maintain his finished goods inventory records. As the product was finished, the inventory records were updated immediately so that the order entry clerks would have a current balance and could fill orders more quickly.
2. The clerk could back order the goods. The back order would signal a need for the product, which in turn would trigger a work order in the plant to schedule the goods for production. The clerk, by checking with the production scheduler, could tell the customer when the goods would be produced and delivered.
3. If there was some question as to when the item would be produced, the clerk could tell the customer it was out of stock and should be reordered at a later date.

Clearly, Herb hoped that his order entry clerks would have to back order infrequently and rarely resort to a stock-out. Nevertheless, he was realistic and knew that both actions would have to be taken on occasion. Therefore, he instructed the order entry clerks to record all orders with a clear indication of their status (filled order, back order, or stock-out). In some cases, when the goods were back ordered, the customer would simply find the lead time unacceptable and would cancel the order. Stock-outs typically resulted in a lost sale. Herb had the computer summarize these items to produce a lost order analysis (Figure 19.5).

The best thing about the computerized order entry system was that it allowed Herb to produce his sales analysis reports from the processed orders. He had seized the opportunity with the order entry system to computerize what in the past had been a fairly laborious manual effort. Now he received the sales order analysis on a more timely basis.

FIGURE 19.5

Veritas Electronics Corporation Lost Order Analysis (Six Months Ended June 30, 19X1)

Product Code	*Description/Reason*	*No. Orders Lost*		*$ Sales Lost*	
		This Year	*Last Year*	*This Year*	*Last Year*
400XXX	Transistors	5	5	$3,183.17	$4,451.85
	—Back order	2	—	1,710.93	—
	—Stock out	3	5	1,472.24	4,451.85
600XXX	Capacitors	6	7	5,126.81	4,111.17
	—Back order	1	4	893.10	3,001.15
	—Stock out	5	3	4,233.71	1,110.02

FIGURE 19.6
Veritas Electronics Corporation Individual Sales Report

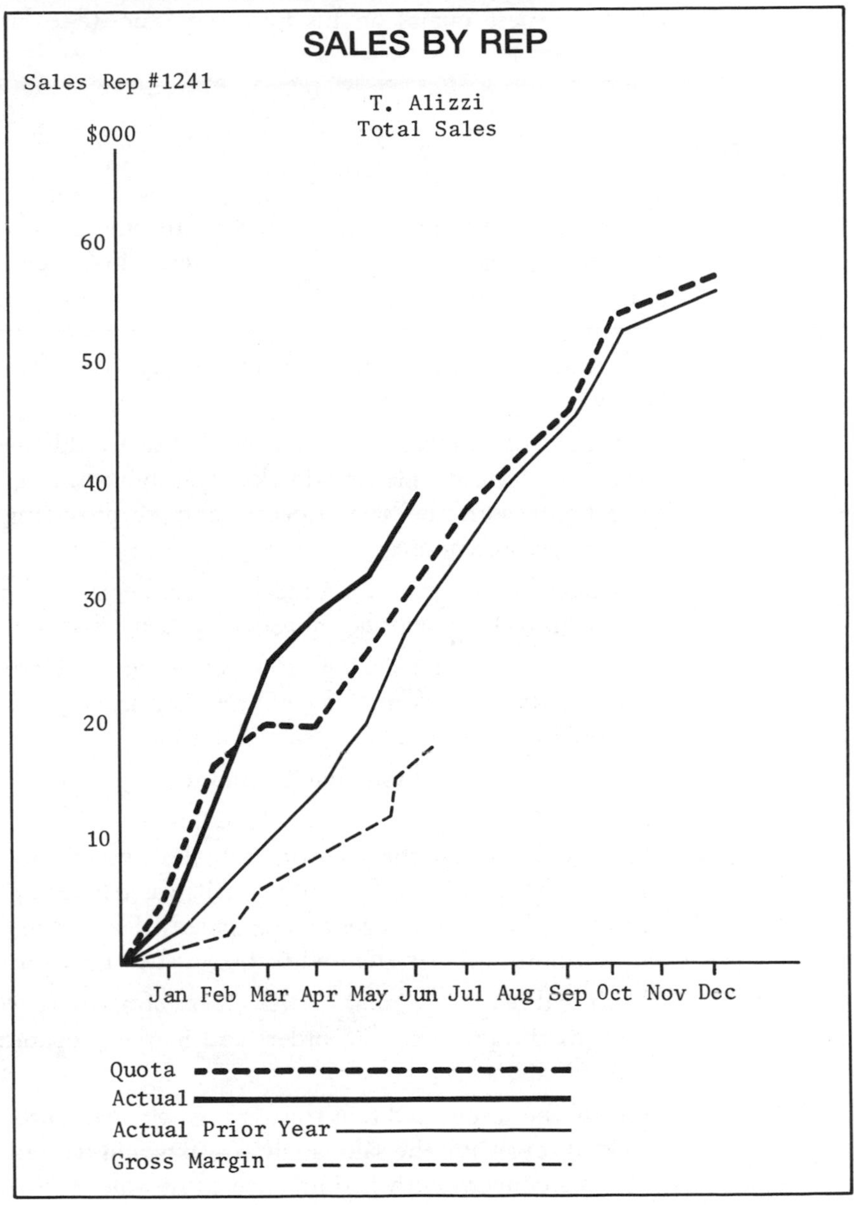

LOOK AT THE "TOTAL PICTURE"

The computerization of the sales order reporting process freed up enough staff time to develop charts showing the activity of each member of the sales force over the year. Herb found that it was easier to see what was going on by looking at a picture (chart) of the results than it was to review the detailed lists of numbers. Herb was so enthusiastic about the charting process that he was exploring the possibility of buying a system to prepare these charts on his minicomputer. (See Figure 19.6 for a sample chart.)

CONCLUSION

Baldwin believed that his sales management program had helped him to reach his latest goal of $15 million in sales. This success was a result of the following factors:

1. He recognized that he would need a formal sales forecast in order to grow.
2. To achieve this forecast, he realized that he would have to *motivate his sales force*. He decided to do this by establishing quotas that were consistent with the sales forecast and by providing incentives for reaching those quotas.
3. To make certain that the forecast would be achieved, he realized he would have to *monitor actual performance* against the quotas.
4. In the process of tracking sales performance, Herb recognized an opportunity to perform a *detailed sales order analysis* by product, customer, location, and various combinations of these categories.
5. This sales order analysis enabled him to *reinforce or redirect his strategy for growth.*
6. Herb realized that the sales order analysis was only part of the sales management process. The other half was delivering the goods. He recognized the advantages of a *computerized order entry system* and the integration of that system with the finished goods inventory.
7. Herb realized that a *computerized order entry system* would be helpful both in the processing of orders and in the preparation of his sales order analysis.
8. Finally, he recognized that the *use of graphs and charts* could save him time in reviewing the sales analysis and would help him to communicate his concern with performance to his sales force.

SELF-ASSESSMENT CHECKLIST
SALES MANAGEMENT

	Yes	*No*	*N/A*	*Comments*
(1) Do you prepare a sales forecast?				

SELF-ASSESSMENT CHECKLIST
SALES MANAGEMENT

	Yes	No	N/A	Comments
(2) Do you develop sales quotas: —by salesperson? —by sales representative (distributor)?				
(3) Do you use incentives to encourage the meeting of sales quotas?				
(4) Do you track sales performance by: —Salesperson/sales rep? —Customer? —Location? —Product (type or item)? —Salesperson, by item? —Customer, by item? —Location, by item? —Other combinations?				
(5) Do you analyze these sales data in order to modify your sales forecast?				
(6) Do you use your sales analysis in developing or changing your sales strategy?				
(7) Do you have a good order entry system?				
(8) Do you know what your order backlog is?				
(9) Do you generate a lost order report from your order processing activities?				

20

Managing Cost Of Goods Sold

One of the most challenging and essential tasks you face in running your business is estimating the costs of manufacturing your products. Your ability to develop good estimates helps you to compete profitably in your industry. These estimates help you to price your products competitively, value your inventory, control your manufacturing costs, and develop better management reports. This chapter provides you with a wide range of tools to use in accomplishing this important task by showing you how one entrepreneur developed an effective standard cost accounting system for his business. As with the preceding chapters, there is a self-assessment checklist at the end of this chapter to allow you to test your approach to cost accounting.

CASE STUDY: BARRY ROSEN OF EMPIRE ACCESSORIES CONSIDERS THE COST OF ADDING PRODUCT LINES

Barry Rosen has been in the business of manufacturing ladies' handbags for 20 years. He joined his father's company—Empire Accessories,

Inc.—after finishing college and putting in four years in the Navy. His father started the business in 1935 and operated it until his retirement. Then Barry took the reins and set about making changes.

Empire Accessories had a good reputation in the marketplace for producing high quality, stylish leather handbags. Major department stores in New York, Boston, Chicago, Dallas, Miami, and Los Angeles had been steady customers over the years, providing the company with the basis on which to build a $4 million business.

Barry believed he could expand the business by adding lines in high quality vinyl and designer fabrics. He thought that this would be a critical move for the following reasons:

1. He knew that the drought in the southwest and the increasing cost of grain would push up the price of leather and have an impact on the market for leather bags.
2. He also recognized that the industry as a whole had been hurt by competition from Brazil, Argentina, Italy, and other countries that had access to raw materials and large pools of relatively inexpensive labor.
3. He believed that he had some excess production capacity at certain seasons of the year. Therefore, the expansion of his line would enable him to produce for the holiday and cruise markets, which he had not been able to address in the past. This would enable him to level out his production and produce more for roughly the same amount of overhead.

Barry recognized that he had to consider this move carefully. His leather bags were selling at a price point of $65 to $85. The fabric and vinyl bags would sell at price points of $10 to $20 and $25 to $35, respectively. Aside from raw material cost, the cost to manufacture the handbags was approximately the same, so that the profit margins on the new lines would tend to be lower and there would be less margin for error.

DO YOU KNOW HOW MUCH YOUR PRODUCT COSTS?

With the foregoing points in mind, Barry pondered whether a more formal approach to estimating production costs would be of any benefit. In the past, his father had prided himself on being able to estimate the cost to produce a handbag simply by looking at it. In addition, the manufacturing costs were controlled in large part by the production supervisor, who had been with the company since its inception. The supervisor knew how each bag was produced, how to move goods through the factory, and how to cajole the workers into giving their best. These skills had been acquired over 40 years and were not documented anywhere, so that if the supervisor left the company, it would have a serious impact on production schedules and, thereby, on production costs.

Also, Barry knew that many of the workers on the floor had been with the company a long time. For that reason, they were quite efficient. They were comfortable with their tasks and the level of production they were asked to achieve. Barry recognized that if some of them left or retired, efficiency was likely to go down and consequently costs were likely to go up or quality might suffer.

Barry realized that in the past the company had been able to set a selling price that would yield a profit margin sufficient to cover all costs and to provide room for error. And in the past an informal cost estimating approach had been satisfactory. Now, however, he depended on many things that he could not control; he had less room for error. For this reason, he believed that it was necessary to be more precise in estimating costs. With greater precision, he would be better able to estimate the impact on profits from a change in prices or the acceptance of orders at a discount.

Good Cost Estimates Will Help You Plan for Profits

Barry figured that if he did a good job of estimating costs, he could use the resulting information to:

1. *Estimate inventory values* for financial reporting and thereby avoid a physical inventory whenever he wished to produce reasonably accurate financial statements.
2. *Control costs* because the estimates could be used as benchmarks against which actual costs could be compared. This process would highlight which costs varied substantially from the estimates. By analyzing these variances, he could determine which areas of the factory, or even which individuals, were contributing to cost overruns. With this knowledge he could focus on cost control problems, take corrective actions, and anticipate the results of such actions.
3. *Build an overall profit plan* for the company. Barry's bankers were increasingly interested in more formal profit plans. With reasonably accurate cost estimates, Barry knew that he would be able to cost out his sales forecast and combine the results with his estimates of selling, general, and administrative overhead to arrive at a more representative profit plan.

But Barry also knew that he would have to learn to walk before he could run. So he started by laying out a plan for good estimates of his standard costs.

WHAT GOES INTO A STANDARD COST ACCOUNTING SYSTEM?

Standard Cost Sheet

Barry knew that in the manufacture of his handbags, raw materials represented 27% to 35% of the total cost and labor was roughly 30%. Manufacturing overhead (both fixed and variable) was the balance, or 43% to 35%. Since each component (material, labor, and overhead) was roughly equivalent, it would be necessary to estimate *each* component with some precision. Therefore, he constructed a standard cost sheet that he planned to use to capture the estimates of all of the relevant costs (see Figure 20.1). Barry included space in the heading to enter a style number, description, and picture. The form also includes a place to indicate a standard lot size. Barry decided to calculate the costs for a single bag of a particular style and then to multiply the costs by the various lot sizes in which each style was produced. The form heading shows both who prepared the form and who reviewed and approved it.

The body of the form is divided into four areas—raw materials, direct labor, manufacturing overhead, and a summary section. The following discussion shows you how Barry developed a system to build the information necessary to complete the first three parts. Then there follows a discussion of how to summarize and analyze them.

Raw materials. The form provides Barry with the space to indicate the nature of his prime materials—the leather, vinyl, fabric, lining material, and the material added to give the bag body. Other materials such as zippers, clasps, and decorative ornaments are included in the "trim and findings" category. Tissue and packaging materials can be added as well to complete the cost.

For each item, specify a unit measure as well as the cost per measuring unit (e.g., square yard, dozen, pair) and the quantity per unit. Then multiply the cost per unit by the number of units to find the unit cost of each component of the bag. Sum these individual component costs to arrive at the total raw material cost. Then enter the total in the summary section of the form.

Figures 20.2, 20.3, and 20.4 support the raw material section of the form. Figure 20.2 is a bill of materials for the style. It includes all the components, both prime materials and trim and findings. It provides space to show the standard measuring unit and the quantity per unit for this style. If the components are too voluminous to enter on the standard cost sheet, the form shown in Figure 20.2 can be used as a supplement. Figure 20.3 can be used to develop the quantity of prime materials by estimating the material, by type, underneath each of the dies used to cut out the style. Anyone who has cut out cookies knows that there is some

FIGURE 20.1

EMPIRE ACCESSORIES
STANDARD COST SHEET

STYLE NO. ________ STYLE DESCRIPTION ________

COLOR ________ SEASON ________

PREPARED BY ________ DATE ________

APPROVED BY ________ DATE ________

(PICTURE)

RAW MATERIALS

CATEGORY/ITEM	MEAS. UNIT (STANDARD)	COST/ M.U. (STANDARD)	QUANT./ UNIT (STANDARD)	UNIT COST (STANDARD)
		$		$
PRIME MATERIALS:				
OUTSIDE MATERIALS:				
				___
				___
INSIDE MATERIALS:				
				___
				___
TOTAL PRIME MATERIALS:				___
TRIM AND FINDINGS:				
TOTAL TRIM AND FINDINGS:				___
				___
TOTAL RAW MATERIALS:				$ ___

DIRECT LABOR

COST CENTER/OPERATION	RATE/ HR. (STANDARD)	HRS./ UNIT (STANDARD)	UNIT COST (STANDARD)
	$		$
CUTTING:			
		___	___
		___	___
CEMENTING:			
		___	___
		___	___
SEWING:			
		___	___
		___	___
ASSEMBLY:			
		___	___
		___	___
PACKING:			
		___	___
		___	___
TOTAL DIRECT LABOR:		___	$ ___

SUMMARY

COST/UNIT	$	%
RAW MATERIAL		
DIRECT LABOR		
CONTRACT LABOR		
FIXED MFG. OH		
VAR. MFG. OH	___	___
TOTAL	$ ___	___

GROSS MARGIN/UNIT	$	%
SELLING PRICE	___	___
LESS DIRECT COSTS:		
RAW MATERIAL		
DIRECT LABOR		
CONTRACT LABOR		
VAR. M. OH	___	___
CONTR. MARGIN	___	___
FIXED M. OH	___	___
GROSS MARGIN	___	___

MANUFACTURING OVERHEAD

COST CENTER	DL HRS. (STANDARD)	VAR. M. OH RATE (STANDARD)	FIXED M. OH RATE (STANDARD)	VAR. M. OH (STANDARD)	FIXED M. OH (STANDARD)	UNIT COST (STANDARD)
		$	$	$	$	$
CUTTING						
CEMENTING						
SEWING						
ASSEMBLY						
PACKING				___	___	___
TOTAL MANUFACTURING OVERHEAD				$ ___	$ ___	$ ___

FIGURE 20.2

EMPIRE ACCESSORIES
BILL OF MATERIALS

STYLE NO. __________ STYLE DESCRIPTION ____________________

COLOR ______________ SEASON ______________

PREPARED BY ______________________________ DATE ____________

APPROVED BY ______________________________ DATE ____________

(PICTURE)

RAW MATERIAL CATEGORY/ITEM	STANDARD MEAS. UNIT	STANDARD QTY./UNIT
PRIME MATERIALS:		
OUTSIDE MATERIALS:		
INSIDE MATERIALS:		
TRIM AND FINDINGS:		

FIGURE 20.3

EMPIRE ACCESSORIES STANDARD PRIME MATERIALS OUTPUTS AND REQUIREMENTS LISTING

(PICTURE)

STYLE NO. ____________ STYLE DESCRIPTION ________________

COLOR ____________________ SEASON ____________________

PREPARED BY ____________________________ DATE ________

APPROVED BY ____________________________ DATE ________

STANDARD OUTPUTS

DIE NO.	OUTPUT DESCRIPTION	QUANTITY/UNIT – PRIME MATERIALS			
		OUTSIDE MATERIALS		INSIDE MATERIALS	

STANDARD REQUIREMENTS

PRIME MATERIAL CATEGORY/ITEM	MEAS. UNIT	NET QTY./ UNIT	WASTE FACTOR	WASTE	GROSS QTY./ UNIT
OUTSIDE MATERIAL:					
INSIDE MATERIAL:					

FIGURE 20.4

EMPIRE ACCESSORIES
RAW MATERIAL
STANDARD PRICE LIST

RAW MATERIAL CATEGORY/ITEM	STANDARD	
	MEAS. UNIT	PRICE/ M.U.

excess dough after the cookie cutter has been used. However, unlike cookie dough, leather, vinyl, or fabric cannot be balled up and rolled out to cut more cookies. Even with careful die placement, there is always some scrap, and this should be estimated when calculating the quantity of material used. Barry can do this by adding a waste factor at the bottom of the form in order to arrive at a gross quantity per unit.

Figure 20.4 is simply a price list for raw material. This form can be used to list the various types of raw material, both prime materials and trim and findings, and their measuring units and prices per unit. Take care to ensure that the measuring units on this form and on the forms discussed are consistent. Barry recognized that he should use the costs that he *anticipated* paying for these materials, when preparing the form shown in Figure 20.4. He would use only *historical costs* as a gauge in estimating what material costs would be in the future. He wanted to make sure that he did not price his product too low and wind up with an unfavorable variance in the purchase price of his raw materials.

Direct labor. In support of the second major section on the standard cost sheet—direct labor—Barry decided he would need to document the operations required to manufacture each handbag. And he would need to know who performed the various operations. For this purpose, he designed the forms shown in Figures 20.5 and 20.6. Regarding the first form, he divided the body into five major production cost centers—die cutting, cementing, sewing, assembly, and packing. For each of these functions, for each style, he planned to list the specific operations performed, the job class of the employee who performed each task, and the standard hours or fractions thereof (expressed as a decimal; for example, 0.0571 hours) required.

Barry knew that there would be times when the employees would be waiting for work, taking a break, making samples, or switching from one style to another (set-up time). Yet he refrained from including an efficiency factor on each style at this point. When these efficiency factors were aggregated, he feared that they might well account for more production time than was realistic and he would have built in more cost to the style than was necessary. Instead, Barry decided to apply an efficiency factor to the overall results when he anticipated how much labor was required to meet his total sales forecast. Therefore, he decided he would estimate the time required to perform the various operations listed and calculate the labor cost by using the total estimated elapsed time. He realized that he could develop these estimates with a great deal of precision by calculating "engineered" standards. But he decided to simply time some of his average production workers while they were performing specific functions and to use those estimates as the standards for the rest of his work force. In this way, he could complete the cost estimating process and not get bogged down in more detail. Later, he could refine

FIGURE 20.5

EMPIRE ACCESSORIES STANDARD OPERATIONS ROUTING AND LABOR ESTIMATING LIST

(PICTURE)

STYLE NO. __________ STYLE DESCRIPTION ____________________

COLOR ________________ SEASON ________________

PREPARED BY ________________________ DATE __________

APPROVED BY ________________________ DATE __________

COST CENTER / OPERATION	JOB CLASS	STANDARD HOURS ALLOWED	REMARKS
CUTTING:			
CEMENTING:			
SEWING:			
ASSEMBLY:			
PACKING:			

FIGURE 20.6

EMPIRE ACCESSORIES
STANDARD WAGE RATE LISTING

COST CENTER/OPERATION	POSITION	JOB CLASS	STANDARD WAGE RATE/ HOUR

the process. Ultimately, the standard hours allowed for each operation by cost center would be transferred to the standard cost sheet.

Barry planned to use Figure 20.6 to compile a list of employees by cost center, position, and job class. He planned to use this list to develop standard wage rates for each job class. With this list, and the estimates of time to perform each operation, he would be able to enter a rate per hour on the standard cost sheet for each operation. He could multiply this rate by the standard hours to arrive at the unit labor cost for the style. Then he could add all the labor costs for the cost centers through which the style had been processed and enter the total in the summary at the bottom of the form.

Manufacturing overhead. Now Barry was ready to consider the difficult task of calculating and allocating manufacturing overhead. The tricky part about this was not in calculating the dollar value of the overhead but in allocating it to the styles. Barry decided that he would use the direct labor hours required to produce each style as a basis for the allocations. He decided on this measure for a number of reasons. First, direct labor hours were a significant component of producing the style and were easily measured. Also, direct labor hours were a reasonable measure of the time it took to move the style through the plant. The longer it took, the more it cost in terms of overhead. In addition, the hours spent in producing the style tended to increase with the complexity of the style and the nature of the raw material. For example, in Barry's case, vinyl and fabric were being cut 6 or 12 high, but leather was cut only 1 high because hides are not uniform in shape or in quality. Sewing, however, did not vary by the nature of the material because it was only slightly easier to sew fabric and vinyl than leather. Therefore, if one style involved more labor than another because it was larger or more complex, Barry reasoned it should absorb more overhead. If two styles, regardless of the raw material used, required the same amount of labor, then they should absorb the same amount of overhead.

As another way of looking at it, the longer it took to produce one style, the less time there would be available to produce another style. Therefore, each style that was produced should absorb or contribute to overhead in some proportion. Barry reasoned that the relative proportion was best determined by how long it took to produce the style, because if another style absorbed or contributed the same amount to overhead but took less time to produce, then Barry should produce that style rather than the more complex one.

Barry realized that he might have used machine hours instead of man hours, but he reasoned that, although machines were used extensively in the cutting and sewing operations, machine hours were not as easily measured as man hours in his plant. Furthermore, his plant was constrained more by available manpower than by machine time so that man hours really seemed a better gauge of the complexity of a style.

Barry planned to divide his estimate of total manufacturing overhead by his estimate for direct labor hours to arrive at an *overhead rate per hour*. He could apply that rate to the direct labor hours for each style and, in this way, allocate overhead to each style. So he needed to estimate total direct labor hours and his total manufacturing overhead.

Estimating Total Direct Labor Hours

Barry decided that in order to determine his estimate of total direct labor hours, he would have to start with his sales forecast (see Figure 20.7). He would use this form to list the styles he expected to sell for the next season, which roughly corresponded to a three-month period. He would simply enter the units and leave space to enter the selling price and sales dollars, which he would fill in later if he decided to use this information to build a profit plan.

He would then complete Figure 20.8, again listing the styles he expected to sell but also including the inventory of finished goods on hand for that style. The difference between these two figures would show him the *required production* to meet his sales forecast. Barry would then complete the column for planned production. He recognized that this figure might be more than the previously calculated required production. This would be the case if, in arriving at his planned production, he allowed for building extra inventory. It might also result if Barry did not arrive at an even number when dividing the required production by the average lot size for the style. Then he would have to increase the planned production to equal a round number of lots. Adding across, he could estimate the planned production for the season.

With the forecast of production by style, Barry could estimate direct labor hours, using Figure 20.9. By multiplying the forecasted production units by standard direct labor hours per unit for each cost center for each style, which he obtained from the standard cost sheet, the product would be the total budgeted direct labor hours for each style for each cost center. These he could add across to obtain the total budgeted direct labor hours.

Next, using Figure 20.10, Barry planned to list the individuals in his current work force and to multiply the number of possible work days for the season by the hours per day to reach the gross capacity hours. He could then enter any holidays or vacation days anticipated and an estimate for sick days. By deducting these from the gross capacity hours, he would arrive at the net available hours for production. These he could split into three groups—supervisory, indirect, and direct labor. Supervisory labor is just what the name implies. Indirect labor is labor not

FIGURE 20.7

EMPIRE ACCESSORIES
SALES FORECAST
FOR THE SEASON

STYLE		TOTAL SEASON FORECAST		
NO.	DESCRIPTION	UNITS	SELLING PRICE $	SALES $
TOTAL				$

FIGURE 20.8

EMPIRE ACCESSORIES
PRODUCTION FORECAST
FOR THE SEASON

STYLE		UNITS				
NO.	DESCRIPTION	INVENTORY	FORECASTED SALES	REQUIRED PRODUCTION	PLANNED PRODUCTION	ENDING INVENTORY
TOTAL						

FIGURE 20.9

EMPIRE ACCESSORIES
FORECAST OF DIRECT LABOR HOURS
FOR THE SEASON

STYLE			PRODUCTION COST CENTERS										
			CUTTING		CEMENTING		SEWING		ASSEMBLY		PACKING		
NO.	DESCRIPTION	FORECASTED PRODUCTION UNITS	STD. D.L. HRS/UNIT	BUDGETED D.L. HOURS	STD. D.L. HRS/UNIT	BUDGETED D.L. HOURS	STD. D.L. HRS/UNIT	BUDGETED D.L. HOURS	STD. D.L. HRS/UNIT	BUDGETED D.L. HOURS	STD. D.L. HRS/UNIT	BUDGETED D.L. HOURS	TOTAL BUDGETED D.L. HOURS
	TOTAL												

FIGURE 20.10

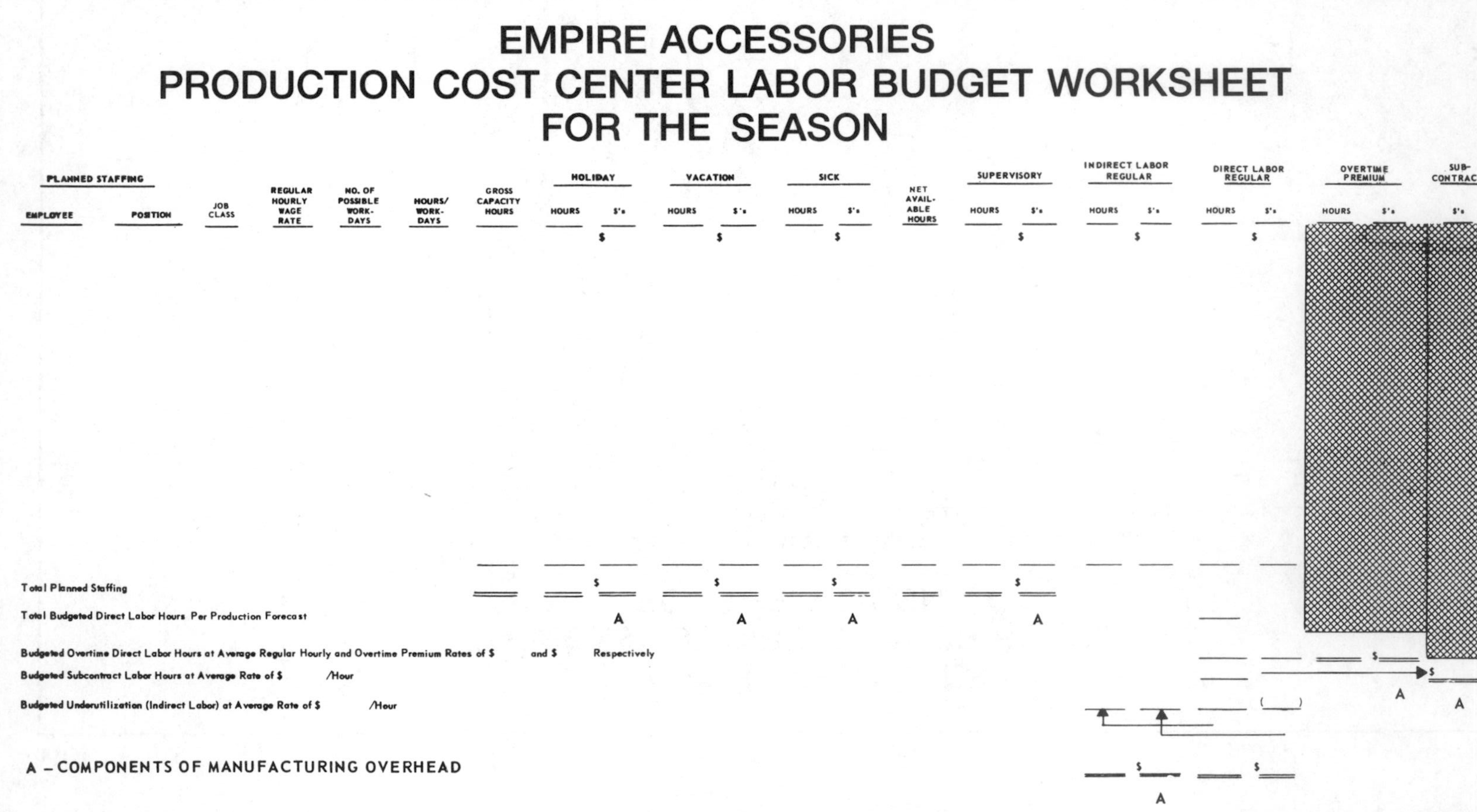

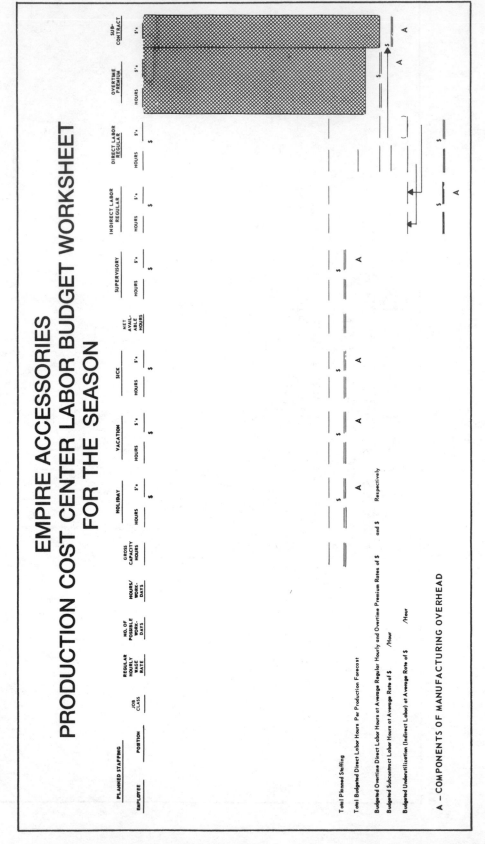

EMPIRE ACCESSORIES
PRODUCTION COST CENTER LABOR BUDGET WORKSHEET
FOR THE SEASON

Planned Staffing							Holiday		Vacation		Sick			Supervisory		Indirect Labor Regular		Direct Labor Regular		Overtime Premium		Sub-contract
Employee	Position	Job Class	Regular Hourly Wage Rate	No. of Possible Work-Days	Hours/Work-Days	Gross Capacity Hours	Hours	$'s	Hours	$'s	Hours	$'s	Net Avail-able Hours	Hours	$'s	Hours	$'s	Hours	$'s	Hours	$'s	$'s

Total Planned Staffing

Total Budgeted Direct Labor Hours Per Production Forecast

Budgeted Overtime Direct Labor Hours at Average Regular Hourly and Overtime Premium Rates of $ and $ Respectively

Budgeted Subcontract Labor Hours at Average Rate of $ /Hour

Budgeted Underutilization (Indirect Labor) at Average Rate of $ /Hour

A – COMPONENTS OF MANUFACTURING OVERHEAD

directly involved in production, such as the work of maintenance people, die makers, stockkeepers, and others. This category on the form can also be used to record an estimate of the time during which members of the direct labor force would not be productively employed. He referred to this as an *inefficiency factor*. Barry figured that if employees worked 160 hours per month, or 420 hours per season, and if they were directly employed in production from 85% to 90% of the time, this was all he could expect. The remainder of the time they might be waiting for work, using the "facilities," making samples, or performing other types of activities not directly related to production. Therefore, he would enter the hours they were directly employed in production in the direct labor column; the remainder he planned to include in the indirect labor column.

He planned to compare the total of the direct labor hours column to the total budgeted direct labor hours from the production forecast (Figure 20.9). If the required labor was more than he had available, he knew that he would incur some overtime and that he should consider the overtime *premium* as an overhead item. If he had excess capacity—more direct labor than required to meet his production goals—he would have to consider the excess as indirect labor or overhead. Or he could sell some of it by subcontracting production for other manufacturers and thereby reduce his overhead. His last alternative would be to let some people go.

If the required labor was more than he had available in his work force, rather than incurring overtime, he could hire subcontractors to handle some of his production and add the associated cost that was in excess of his average direct labor cost to his overhead. Notice that, by including the pay rates for each individual listed on the form, he would be able to calculate hours and costs and then divide them between direct labor and all other items that are part of manufacturing overhead.

Calculating Other Overhead Items

Barry decided he would estimate his labor budget for his service cost centers—including his shipping and receiving, order entry, and accounting and inventory control functions—just as he would estimate his direct labor. He planned to use Figure 20.11 for this purpose. As with the direct labor hour worksheet, Figure 20.10, Barry planned to complete Figure 20.11 by listing all the employees engaged in service cost centers such as shipping, receiving, die making, production control, and design. He would estimate the standard number of days and hours per day that he would expect them to work for the season. The product of the two would yield the capacity hours. He could deduct anticipated holiday, vacation, and sick pay and spread the available hours into the categories of managerial, supervisory, regular indirect labor, clerical labor, and temporary

FIGURE 20.11

EMPIRE ACCESSORIES
SERVICE COST CENTER
LABOR BUDGET WORK SHEET

FOR THE MONTH (QUARTER) ENDING __________________,19XX

PLANNED STAFFING							HOLIDAY		VACATION		SICK			MANAGERIAL		SUPERVISORY		REGULAR INDIRECT LABOR		CLERICAL		TEMPORARY LABOR	
EMPLOYEE	POSITION	EMPLOYEE TYPE	REGULAR HOURLY WAGE RATE	NO. OF POSSIBLE WORK-DAYS	HOURS/WORK-DAYS	CAPACITY HOURS	HOURS	$'s	HOURS	$'s	HOURS	$'s	AVAIL-ABLE HOURS	HOURS	$'s	HOURS	$'s	HOURS	$'s	HOURS	$'s	HOURS	$'s
								$		$		$			$		$		$		$		$
TOTAL PLANNED STAFFING								$		$		$			$		$		$		$		$

DEVELOPED BY PRICE WATERHOUSE FOR THE NATIONAL HANDBAG ASSOCIATION — INDUSTRY — WIDE RECOVERY PROGRAM labor. By using Figures 20.10 and 20.11, he believed he would be able to get a good handle on payroll dollars throughout the company.

Next, he decided he would estimate payroll-related expenses by using Figure 20.12. These expenses included state and federal taxes, workmen's compensation insurance, and payments to the unions for dues and retirement plans. Barry planned to note which of these costs were fixed and which were variable. Fixed costs are those that stay about the same regardless of the level of production. Variable costs change with or in response to the level of production. (Chapter 23, "Break-Even Analysis," discusses the impact of volume on fixed and variable costs.)

Barry then planned to estimate his common overhead expenses, such as light, heat, rent, insurance, taxes, telephone, and so forth. He planned to list these expenses and to indicate whether they were fixed or variable and the basis used to estimate them on the form provided in Figure 20.13. After completing this form, Barry planned to allocate each item to manufacturing, selling, and general and administrative overhead, using Figure 20.14. He planned to employ an appropriate basis of distribution for each item, such as the square feet of floor space occupied by the manufacturing, selling, and administrative areas, in order to allocate the rent and utilities expense. The number of employees employed in each function would be the basis on which he would allocate insurance expense. Barry would then summarize the nonpayroll-related manufacturing overhead on Figure 20.15, showing the fixed and variable portions and the total.

Furthermore, Barry planned to use Figure 20.16 to estimate a factory overhead rate by dividing the budgeted manufacturing overhead by the forecasted direct labor hours. If he separated the costs into their fixed and variable portions, he would be able to calculate both a fixed and a variable manufacturing overhead rate. Using the factory overhead rates, he would be able to complete the manufacturing overhead portion of the standard cost sheet (Figure 20.1) by multiplying the fixed and variable overhead rates by the direct labor hours for each cost center.

SUMMARIZING THE STANDARD COST SHEET

By adding the raw material costs, the direct labor costs, and the overhead allocated to the style in the summary section at the bottom of Figure 20.1, Barry would know with some precision what it would cost him to produce a particular style. Using the sum of these three cost components, he could determine whether he could set a selling price that would be both competitive in the marketplace and high enough to earn him a profit after covering his selling, general, and administrative expenses.

He could determine this fact by assigning a selling price to the style, pricing out his sales forecast, subtracting the standard production cost of

FIGURE 20.12

EMPIRE ACCESSORIES
SERVICE COST CENTER LABOR BUDGET WORKSHEET
FOR THE MONTH (QUARTER) ENDING ,19

PLANNED STAFFING							HOLIDAY		VACATION		SICK			MANAGERIAL		SUPERVISORY		REGULAR INDIRECT LABOR		CLERICAL		TEMPORARY LABOR	
EMPLOYEE	POSITION	EMPLOYEE TYPE	REGULAR HOURLY WAGE RATE	NO. OF POSSIBLE WORK-DAYS	HOURS/ WORK-DAYS	CAPACITY HOURS	HOURS	$'s	HOURS	$'s	HOURS	$'s	AVAIL-ABLE HOURS	HOURS	$'s	HOURS	$'s	HOURS	$'s	HOURS	$'s	HOURS	$'s
								$		$		$			$		$		$		$		$
TOTAL PLANNED STAFFING								$		$		$			$		$		$		$		$

DEVELOPED BY PRICE WATERHOUSE FOR THE NATIONAL HANDBAG ASSOCIATION — INDUSTRY — WIDE RECOVERY PROGRAM

FIGURE 20.13

EMPIRE ACCESSORIES
COMMON OVERHEAD EXPENSES BUDGET WORKSHEET
FOR THE SEASON

COMMON OVERHEAD EXPENSE ITEM	BUDGET BASIS	FIXED (F) OR VARIABLE (V)	BUDGET AMOUNT		
			FIXED	VARIABLE	TOTAL
			$	$	$
TOTAL			$	$	$

FIGURE 20.14

EMPIRE ACCESSORIES
DISTRIBUTION OF BUDGETED COMMON OVERHEAD EXPENSES TO MANUFACTURING, SELLING, AND GENERAL AND ADMINISTATIVE OVERHEAD ACCOUNTS FOR THE SEASON

COMMON OVERHEAD EXPENSE					MANUFACTURING OVERHEAD				SELLING OVERHEAD		G & A OVERHEAD	
	BUDGET AMOUNT					BUDGET AMOUNT						
ITEM	FIXED	VARIABLE	TOTAL	DISTRIBUTION BASIS	A/C NO.	FIXED	VARIABLE	TOTAL	A/C NO.	BUDGET AMOUNT	A/C NO.	BUDGET AMOUNT
	$	$	$				$	$		$		$
TOTAL	$	$	$			$	$	$		$		$

FIGURE 20.15

EMPIRE ACCESSORIES
NONPAYROLL–RELATED MANUFACTURING OVERHEAD BUDGET WORKSHEET
FOR THE QUARTER

ACCOUNT				BUDGET AMOUNT		
NO.	DESCRIPTION	BUDGET BASIS	FIXED (F) OR VARIABLE (V)	FIXED	VARIABLE	TOTAL
				$	$	$
DISTRIBUTED COMMON OVERHEAD:						
OTHER OVERHEAD:						
TOTAL				$	$	$

FIGURE 20.16

EMPIRE ACCESSORIES
MANUFACTURING OVERHEAD
RATE CALCULATION
FOR THE SEASON

EMPIRE ACCESSORIES
MANUFACTURING OVERHEAD RATE CALCULATION
FOR THE ____________ SEASON

	FIXED	VARIABLE	TOTAL
BUDGETED MANUFACTURING OVERHEAD			
PAYROLL (SUPERVISION INDIRECT)	______	______	______
PAYROLL RELATED	______	______	______
COMMON OVERHEAD	______	______	______
OTHER	______	______	______
TOTAL MANUFACTURING OVERHEAD	======	======	======
FORECASTED DIRECT LABOR HOURS		======	
FACTORY OVERHEAD RATE	====== (1)	====== (2)	======

(1) $\frac{\text{FIXED MANUFACTURING OVERHEAD}}{\text{FORECASTED DIRECT LABOR HOURS}}$

(2) $\frac{\text{VARIABLE MANUFACTURING OVERHEAD}}{\text{FORECASTED DIRECT LABOR HOURS}}$

the goods sold, and comparing the result to his selling, general, and administrative expenses (S, G, & A). The excess of sales over cost of sales and S, G, & A expenses would be his expected profit for the year. If the excess of sales over cost of sales did not equal his S, G, & A expense, he would incur a loss for the year. Barry did not plan to allocate S, G, & A expenses to each style because those costs bore little relation to the nature or quantity of the particular styles produced, and they were easier to control by budgeting for them separately and comparing actual cost to budget.

With his new system, Barry believed he would have more control over both his pricing process and over his manufacturing operation. Chapter 23 shows you how Barry used his standard cost information and the fact that certain of his costs were fixed while others varied with production levels to calculate a break-even level of sales for his company. The break-even level is the level of sales at which his revenues from sales just cover his cost of sales and his S, G, & A expenses.

CONCLUSION

Let us review what Barry did and why it was necessary.

1. He decided he needed more precise cost estimates for his styles so that he could do a more competitive job of pricing without adversely affecting profits.
2. He knew that he would have to estimate the material, labor, and overhead components of his costs because each represented roughly a third of the total cost.
3. He designed a *standard cost sheet* to capture the three components of the cost and included a summary section to use in calculating his selling price.
4. He developed a *bill of materials, standard prime material outputs and requirements listing*, and a *raw material standard price list* to help him calculate the cost of raw materials for each style.
5. He developed a *standard operations routing and labor estimating list* and a *standard wage rate listing* to enable him to calculate the direct labor content of each style.
6. He developed a *sales forecast*, and from that a *production forecast*, and used the latter as a way to determine a *forecast of the direct labor hours* required to complete the estimated production.
7. He designed *labor budget work sheets* for the production cost centers and the service cost centers as a way of calculating the payroll dollars in manufacturing overhead.

8. He developed additional budget work sheets for:
   - Other payroll-related overhead expenses.
   - Common overhead expenses.
   - Non-payroll-related manufacturing overhead expenses.
9. He designed a form to distribute the common overhead expenses to manufacturing, selling, and general and administrative expenses.
10. He developed a *factory overhead rate calculation* form, which he used to complete the *standard cost sheet*.
11. Finally, Barry realized that although he could develop cost estimates for the purpose of better pricing his styles, he could also use this information, provided he kept it up to date, to help him do the following:
    - Value his inventory.
    - Control his costs.
    - Build his profit plan.
    - Develop more informative management reports.

SELF-ASSESSMENT CHECKLIST
MANAGING COST OF GOODS SOLD

	Yes	*No*	*N/A*	*Comments*
(1) Do you know the portion of total cost of goods sold represented by: —raw materials? —direct labor? —manufacturing overhead?				
(2) Do you know how those costs vary with changes in: —your sources of supply? —the economy?				
(3) Do you know which of your costs are relatively fixed?				
(4) Do you know which of your costs tend to vary with your production load?				
(5) Are you certain you have considered all relevant costs in pricing each of your products?				

SELF-ASSESSMENT CHECKLIST
MANAGING COST OF GOODS SOLD

	Yes	No	N/A	Comments
(6) Do you use standards to estimate the costs of each component of your products: —raw material? —direct labor? —manufacturing overhead?				
(7) Do you use your standard cost estimates to value your perpetual inventory rather than take a physical inventory periodically?				
(8) Do you use your standard cost estimates to develop an overall profit plan?				
(9) Do you use your standard cost estimates to control manufacturing costs, by calculating manufacturing variances (e.g., purchase price, material usage, direct labor rate and efficiency, overhead volume, and spending variances)?				
(10) Do you use your standard cost estimates and variance analyses for financial reporting purposes?				
(11) Do you know which products contribute the most to company profits (i.e., do you know your "contribution margins" by product)?				
(12) If you could estimate your costs with greater precision would you be able to price your products more competitively?				

21

Self-Assessment Checklist

Before getting into Chapter 22-25, fill out the following checklist. In the case of any question in which your response is "no," refer to page numbers listed to the right of the question.

Do you know:	*Yes*	*No*	*If Not, refer to:*
			Chapter 22, "Ratio Analysis," page: 313
Why a small business manager would bother to calculate the ratios?			
What tools and information you need in order to calculate the ratios?			
What a spread is?			
What a ratio trends chart is and how to fill one out?			

Do you know:	*Yes*	*No*	*If Not, refer to:*
Where you can get comparative industry ratio information?			
What the following ratios are, how to calculate them, and what they measure: • Current ratio?			
• Quick ratio?			
• Debt-to-net worth?			
• Growth ratio?			
• Accounts receivable turnover?			
• Days sales outstanding?			
• Inventory turnover?			
• Days stock in inventory?			
• Payables turnover?			
• Days payables outstanding?			
• Pretax return on assets?			
• Pretax return on net worth?			
• Pretax profitability?			
• Gross margin percentage?			
• Net working capital turnover?			
• Total assets turnover?			
What the telltale ratio is and why it is a good predictor of bankruptcy?			
How well you measure up to the competition?			
What an evaluation of trends tells you about how you got where you are?			
When you should calculate the ratios?			
How you can use ratio analysis as a way of analyzing your business?			
			Chapter 23, "Break-Even Analysis," page: 343
How you can use break-even analysis to answer the following difficult question:			
• Whether or not to sell a large order to a customer at a reduced price?			

Do you know:	*Yes*	*No*	*If Not, refer to:*
What the following types of expenses are and how they should be classified:			
• Fixed costs?			
• Variable costs?			
• Semivariable costs?			
How to calculate semivariable costs?			
How to calculate a contribution margin?			
What the relevant range is?			
How to calculate break-even volume?			
How to answer questions such as the following:			
• Is your company operating at capacity?			
• Will additional units produced still keep your company within its relevant range of production?			
• Is your variable cost per unit covered by the selling price?			
How to estimate the level of sales necessary to achieve a given level of profit?			
How to construct a break-even chart?			
Why and how a break-even analysis can be important to the small business?			
What net working capital is?			Chapter 24, "Managing Working Capital," page: 359
Why working capital is important to the small business?			
What a cash contingency plan is and how you can develop one?			
That the following important aspects of your company can help you decide what level of working capital to keep:			
• Cash-to-cash cycle?			

Do you know:	*Yes*	*No*	*If Not, refer to:*
• Seasonal and permanent working capital needs?			
• Trade-off between liquidity and risk?			
What your "seasonal" and "permanent" working capital needs are?			
How to measure the trade-off between risk and return in deciding on the level of working capital to keep in your company?			
What specific factors determine your company's working capital requirements?			
How a company should finance its current assets?			
Where to invest surplus cash and what are the principal characteristics of the following alternatives: • Security?			
• Maturity?			
• Liquidity?			
• Yield?			
About the following specific investment vehicles for surplus cash: • U.S. Treasury bills?			
• Federal agency issues?			
• Money market funds?			
• Bankers' acceptances?			
• Commercial paper?			
• Negotiable certificates of deposit?			
• Repurchase agreements?			
• Tax-exempt obligations?			
Where you can buy money market securities?			
What capital budgeting is?			Chapter 25, "Your Long-Term Use of Capital," page: 376
How to determine cash flows?			

Do you know:	*Yes*	*No*	*If Not, refer to:*
How to calculate an investment's payback?			
What bail-out payback is?			
What the advantages and disadvantages of the payback method are?			
Why $1.00 today is worth more than $1.00 a year from now; why money has a time value?			
What a hurdle rate is and how to select one?			
What the net present value method is and how to calculate it?			
What the internal rate of return is and how to calculate it?			
That there is a handy estimating method for the internal rate of return?			
How you can monitor and evaluate your capital budgeting analysis program?			
About other important considerations in performing your capital budgeting analysis?			

22

Ratio Analysis

This chapter presents a technique for quickly assessing your company's financial health and indentifying areas that require improvement. The technique is called *ratio analysis.* It involves calculating certain relationships among various aspects of your business. These relationships or ratios are grouped into five major categories as follows:

- Liquidity ratios.
- Leverage ratios.
- Turnover ratios.
- Profitability ratios.
- Trading ratios.

The chapter uses a case study to illustrate the calculation of a number of ratios in each of these groups.

CASE STUDY: HOW THE PRESIDENT OF AMBROSIA FRAGRANCES USED RATIO ANALYSIS TO CHECK ON HER COMPANY'S FINANCIAL HEALTH

Ambrosia Fragrances Company, Inc., established in 1903, is a manufacturer of fine fragrances for perfumes, high quality soaps, and other toiletries. Helen Spencer, the current president, is of the third generation of Spencers to own and operate Ambrosia. Under Helen's leadership, Ambrosia has grown from a small regional manufacturer to a $16 million fragrance manufacturer.

Over the years, Ambrosia has arranged for borrowing with its bank, First Merchants National, with very little difficulty. During the past two or three years, however, Helen has noticed an increasing reluctance on the part of the bank to extend the increased amounts of credit that Ambrosia needs to finance its growth. Helen has figured that this reluctance might relate to the fact that Ambrosia had not, at any time during the past two years, "cleaned up," or repaid, its short-term bank loans. Her bank had a policy of requiring its customers to be free of short-term debt for at least two months each year. If a firm was unable to do this, then it was in effect using these loans for permanent or long-term financing. Helen made an appointment with John Carlton, a vice president at First Merchants who handled the Ambrosia account, to discuss Ambrosia's future borrowing requirements.

Because Helen was concerned about the banking relations, she took a seminar in ratio analysis. She knew that her banker used ratio analysis in analyzing the creditworthiness of her business. Therefore, she wanted to be familiar with the techniques in order to anticipate and be able to answer any questions her banker might ask at their upcoming meeting. The course was a half-day seminar sponsored by the bank for its corporate borrowers.

Armed with seminar handouts and notes, Helen was determined to apply the tools and techniques of ratio analysis that she had learned to her company's financial statements. She intended to perform all the calculations herself the first few times in order to completely understand how the ratios were calculated. In addition, she planned to ask her accountant to perform the same calculations and to meet with her to discuss the results.

How Can You Calculate the Ratios?

Helen knew that she had to carve some time out of her busy schedule in order to calculate Ambrosia's ratios. She closed her office door and gathered the materials she needed, including:

1. The past three years of financial reports for Ambrosia.

2. A blank ratio trends chart, which was provided to her at the seminar (see Figure 22.3).
3. The Robert Morris Associates' *Annual Statement Studies*, a source of industry statistics (see Figure 22.4).
4. Some columnar paper, pencils, an eraser, and a calculator.
5. The ratio definition matrix (see Figure 22.5).

FIGURE 22.1
Ambrosia Fragrance Company, Inc.
Comparative Balance Sheet

Account Name	12/31/X9	12/31/X8	12/31/X7
1 Cash	170,814	$ 230,380	$ 208,510
2 Accounts receivable	1,143,611	1,252,009	1,167,144
3 Merchandise inventory	2,505,627	2,061,881	2,088,016
4 Prepaid expenses	202,026	199,084	193,853
5 Other current assets	107,936	99,611	88,221
6 Total current	4,130,014	3,842,965	3,745,744
7 Notes receivable	111,250	86,250	125,000
8 Gross property, plant, and equipment	4,560,000	4,560,000	1,960,000
9 (Accumulated depreciation)	(1,000,000)	(775,000)	(675,000)
10 Net property, plant, and equipment	3,560,000	3,785,000	1,285,000
11 Other noncurrent assets	32,809	71,320	73,642
12 Goodwill	50,000	50,000	50,000
13 Total assets	$7,884,073	$7,835,535	$5,279,386
14 Accounts payable	$1,630,875	$1,230,883	$1,609,934
15 Accrued expenses	698,513	599,311	545,614
16 Bank notes payable	500,000	1,218,663	1,488,521
17 Current maturities, L.T.D.	200,000	200,000	—
18 Total current	3,029,388	3,248,857	3,644,069
19 Note payable	2,200,000	2,400,000	—
20 Deferred income	108,790	152,068	150,809
21 Total liabilities	5,338,178	5,800,925	3,794,878
21 Capital	5,000	5,000	5,000
23 Capital in excess of par	45,000	45,000	45,000
24 Retained earnings	2,495,895	1,984,610	1,434,508
25 Owners' equity	2,545,895	2,034,610	1,484,508
26 Total liabilities and owners' equity	$7,884,073	$7,835,535	$5,279,386

The seminar instructors had suggested that it would be a worthwhile investment of time to summarize the company's financial results on columnar paper. This format would ensure that items were classified consistently from period to period. It would also save time to have the numbers needed for the ratios all on one or two pages, and it would assist in the analysis of the ratios, because trends would become more obvious when financial results were lined up side-by-side.

Helen prepared the columnar comparative balance sheet and income statement—which bankers call spreads—that are illustrated in Figures 22.1 and 22.2. She summarized the financial results for three years, which is considered to be the minimum basis for comparison. You may want to compare the results of your business for four or five years if these earlier years provide a legitimate basis for comparison. Use a worksheet with extra columns so that you can simply add to it in future years.

Once Helen developed her spreads, she consulted her ratio definition matrix and began to compute ratios. Because she had never calculated ratios before, she decided to write down every step used in calculating each ratio for the first year. Her work sheet is shown as Figure 22.6. You should also write down every step the first time you calculate your ratios, because you are less likely to make mistakes and more likely to remember the significance of individual ratios. Furthermore, you should

FIGURE 22.2
Ambrosia Fragrance Company, Inc.
Comparative Income Statement

Account Name	*12/31/X9*	*12/31/X8*	*12/31/X7*
27 Net sales	$16,359,008	$13,784,736	$12,516,499
28 Cost of sales [a]	9,074,631	7,443,513	6,802,244
29 Gross margin	7,284,377	6,341,223	5,714,225
30 Other income	155,383	50,135	333,538
31 S,G,&A expenses [b]	5,640,138	4,534,840	4,678,764
32 Research & development	354,780	518,977	430,035
33 Interest expense	400,036	294,336	288,136
34 Total other expenses	6,394,954	5,348,153	5,396,935
35 Profit before taxes	1,044,806	1,043,205	650,858
36 Taxes	533,521	493,106	325,000
37 Net profit	$ 511,285	$ 550,099	$ 325,858

[a]Invoiced purchases of raw materials used in production, and office materials total $7,848,615, $8,929,010, and $11,088,064 for the years 19X7, 19X8, and 19X9, respaatively.

[b]Depreciation expense of $100,000, $100,000, and $225,000 is included in S,G,&A (Selling, General and Administrative expenses) for years 19X7, 19X8, and 19X9, respectively. Net working capital for 19X8 is $594,108 ($3,842,965 − $3,248,857); net working capital for 19X9 is $1,100,626 ($4,130,014 − $3,029,388).

FIGURE 22.3
Ratio Trends Chart

RATIO TRENDS CHART

	Ratio Date						Ind	Goal	Comments
LIQ	Current								
	Quick								
LEV	Debt-to-Worth								
	Cash Earnings-to Current Maturity								
TURNOVER	AR Turnover								
	Days Sales O/S								
	Inventory T/O								
	Days Stock								
	Payables T/O								
	Days Payables								
PROFITABILITY	Pretax Return on Assets								
	Pretax Return on Net Worth								
	Pretax Profitability								
	Gross Margin								
	Operating Expenses								
	Interest Expenses								
	Depreciation Expense								
TRAD	Sales/Working Capital								
	Sales/Total Assets								

FIGURE 22.4
Industry Ratios

MANUFACTURERS - PERFUMES, COSMETICS & OTHER TOILET PREPARATIONS
SIC# 2844

Current Data						Comparative Historical Data			
22(6/30-9/30/79)		24(10/1/79-3/31/80)				6/30/76-3/31/77	6/30/77-3/31/78	6/30/78-3/31/79	6/30/79-3/31/80
0-250M	250M-1MM	1-10MM	10-50MM	ALL	ASSET SIZE	ALL	ALL	ALL	ALL
5	8	13	20	46	NUMBER OF STATEMENTS	29	24	39	46
%	%	%	%	%	**ASSETS**	%	%	%	%
		7.2	7.1	6.9	Cash & Equivalents	8.6	9.5	9 1	6 9
		26.4	29.9	30.8	Accts. & Notes Rec. - Trade(net)	27.9	26.2	30.5	30 8
		35.7	24.8	30.0	Inventory	31.1	32.9	30.2	30 0
		1.0	2.0	1.3	All Other Current	3.7	2.2	2.0	1 3
		70.2	63.8	69.1	Total Current	71.3	70.8	71.8	69 1
		19.0	24.6	20.7	Fixed Assets (net)	19.3	19.3	21.4	20 7
		.8	2.9	1.5	Intangibles (net)	2.6	1.3	1.5	1 5
		10.0	8.8	8.7	All Other Non-Current	6.9	8.7	5.3	8 7
		100.0	100.0	100.0	Total	100.0	100.0	100.0	100 0
					LIABILITIES				
		14.5	6.8	9.1	Notes Payable-Short Term	5.3	11.6	8.2	9 1
		1.7	.8	1.6	Cur. Mat.-L/T/D	2.1	1.0	2 1	1 6
		21.8	13.8	19.3	Accts. & Notes Payable - Trade	13.6	13.0	15.9	19 3
		7.5	8.3	9.1	Accrued Expenses	8.0	7.2	8.5	9 1
		4.3	2.7	4.5	All Other Current	4.4	6.6	4.0	4 5
		49.9	32.4	43.7	Total Current	33.4	39.3	38 7	43 7
		8.5	10.9	11.8	Long Term Debt	5.3	10.8	8 8	11 8
		5.5	2.5	3.3	All Other Non-Current	1.2	.7	1.1	3 3
		36.2	54.2	41.2	Net Worth	60.2	49.2	51 3	41 2
		100.0	100.0	100.0	Total Liabilities & Net Worth	100.0	100.0	100.0	100 0
					INCOME DATA				
		100.0	100.0	100.0	Net Sales	100.0	100.0	100.0	100 0
		57.4	49.7	53.8	Cost Of Sales	55.9	51.1	54 3	53 8
		42.6	50.3	46.2	Gross Profit	44.1	48.9	45 7	46 2
		34.9	42.7	39.7	Operating Expenses	37.3	42.9	38.0	39 7
		7.7	7.6	6.5	Operating Profit	6.7	6.0	7.8	6 5
		1.0	1.1	1.2	All Other Expenses (net)	–.1	.3	.3	1 2
		6.7	6.5	5.3	Profit Before Taxes	6.9	5.7	7.5	5.3
					RATIOS				
		1.9	3.1	2.6		3.1	3.3	3.4	2 6
		1.3	2.1	1.8	Current	2.3	2.2	1.9	1 8
		1.1	1.5	1.3		1.5	1.6	1.5	1.3
		1.2	1.9	1.6		1.7	1.8	1.9	1 6
		.6	1.1	.9	Quick	1.3	1.0	1 1	.9
		.4	.8	.6		.8	.7	6	6
		27 13.6	56 6.5	40 9.2		38 9.6	32 11.5	36 10.2	40 9 2
		58 6.3	66 5.5	60 6.1	Sales/Receivables	50 7.3	52 7.0	59 6.2	60 6 1
		63 5.8	83 4.4	68 5.4		68 5.4	76 4.8	79 4.6	68 5.4
		78 4.7	69 5.3	70 5.2		68 5.4	83 4.4	87 4.2	70 5.2
		118 3.1	140 2.6	122 3.0	Cost of Sales/Inventory	91 4.0	122 3.0	114 3 2	122 3.0
		166 2.2	166 2.2	166 2.2		146 2.5	174 2.1	166 2 2	166 2.2
		4.3	3.6	4.1		3.5	2.8	3.5	4 1
		8.8	4.6	5.4	Sales/Working Capital	5.9	5.3	5 9	5 4
		44.4	9.4	21.9		10.4	11.0	8 8	21.9
		13.3	15.7	10.7		346.9	38.0	40.7	10.7
		(10) 5.8	(15) 7.0	(34) 6.0	EBIT/Interest	(20) 36.9	(17) 5.8	(28) 10 6	(34) 6 0
		1.5	3.0	2.0		2.6	1.6	2.6	2.0
		14.9	42.7	14.6		67.4		17 1	14.6
		(11) 5.7	(13) 8.8	(30) 6.5	Cash Flow/Cur. Mat. L/T/D	(13) 7.8		(23) 5.6	(30) 6.5
		1.7	3.2	2.0		1.8		1 2	2.0
		.1	.3	.3		.2	.2	.2	.3
		.5	.5	.5	Fixed/Worth	.3	.3	.4	.5
		.7	.6	.7		.5	.6	.6	.7
		1.5	.5	.7		.4	.4	.4	.7
		1.9	.8	1.5	Debt/Worth	.6	.8	.8	1.5
		3.5	1.5	3.4		1.1	1.8	1.7	3.4
		68.6	40.2	44.1	% Profit Before Taxes/Tangible	44.8	43.3	38.1	44.1
		35.6	19.6	(44) 21.4	Net Worth	22.4	(22) 20.9	(38) 22 3	(44) 21 4
		6.8	8.9	8.9		6.2	8.4	9 7	8 9
		25.9	19.1	17.5	% Profit Before Taxes/Total	24.2	23.3	19 8	17 5
		14.9	9.2	9.3	Assets	14.3	10.1	12 7	9.3
		2.1	4.2	2.7		3.5	2.3	4.1	2.7
		50.4	9.3	20.2		25.5	24.7	25.6	20.2
		11.3	6.0	10.3	Sales/Net Fixed Assets	12.8	11.4	10 1	10.3
		5.4	4.7	5.3		6.5	6.0	5 8	5.3
		2.5	2.1	2.4		2.6	2.3	2 4	2.4
		2.1	1.5	2.0	Sales/Total Assets	2.0	1.9	1.9	2.0
		1.4	1.3	1.4		1.7	1.4	1.5	1.4
		.6	1.3	1.1		.9	.8	.9	1 1
		1.2	(19) 1.6	(43) 1.5	% Depr., Dep., Amort./Sales	(27) 1.2	(21) 1.4	(37) 1.3	(43) 1.5
		2.9	2.1	2.1		1.9	2.1	1.8	2.1
				.4		1.1	.9	1.1	.4
				(14) 1.2	% Lease & Rental Exp/Sales	(16) 1.3	(12) 1.7	(17) 1.5	(14) 1.2
				1.9		1.6	3.1	2.4	1.9
				1.9					1 9
				(13) 2.6	% Officers' Comp/Sales				(13) 2 6
				7.1					7.1
3192M	9309M	86006M	833527M	932034M	Net Sales ($)	672407M	317000M	616018M	932034M
673M	3802M	42340M	521977M	568792M	Total Assets ($)	331376M	219978M	399093M	568792M

M = $thousand MM = $million

See Pages 1 through 10 for Explanation of Ratios and Data

Reproduced by permission of Robert Morris Associates. Page from *RMA Annual Statement Studies*, Copyright © 1980. (See the following publisher's statement).

FIGURE 22.4 (Cont.)
Interpretation of Statement Studies Figures

RMA recommends that Statement Studies data be regarded only as general guidelines and not as absolute industry norms. There are several reasons why the data may not be fully representative of a given industry:

(1) The financial statements used in the *Statement Studies* are not selected by any random or statistically reliable method. RMA member banks voluntarily submit the raw data they have available each year, with these being the only constraints: (a) The fiscal year-ends of the companies reported may not be from April 1 through June 29, and (b) their total assets must be less than $50 million.

(2) Many companies have varied product lines; however, the *Statement Studies* categorize them by their primary product Standard Industrial Classification (SIC) number only.

(3) Some of our industry samples are rather small in relation to the total number of firms in a given industry. A relatively small sample can increase the chances that some of our composites do not fully represent an industry.

(4) There is the chance that an extreme statement can be present in a sample, causing a disproportionate influence on the industry composite. This is particularly true in a relatively small sample.

(5) Companies within the same industry may differ in their method of operations which in turn can directly influence their financial statements. Since they are included in our sample, too, these statements can significantly affect our composite calculations.

(6) Other considerations that can result in variations among different companies engaged in the same general line of business are different labor markets; geographical location; different accounting methods; quality of products handled; sources and methods of financing; and terms of sale.

For these reasons, RMA does not recommend the Statement Studies *figures be considered as absolute norms for a given industry. Rather the figures should be used only as general guidelines and in addition to the other methods of financial analysis. RMA makes no claim as to the representativeness of the figures printed in this book.*

Robert Morris Associates
Philadelphia National Bank Building
Philadelphia, PA 19107

calculate "vertically"—do all the ratios for one year first—rather than "horizontally." With this approach, you will be less likely to confuse the data from different years. In addition, it will cause you to focus on the relationships among ratios for a given year.

Helen calculated each ratio on her work sheet and entered the results in the appropriate box on the blank ratio trends chart; Figure 22.7 shows her entries for the three years. The results are calculated to hundredths and rounded to the nearest tenth; calculating the ratio to any more places than tenths conveys a false sense of precision. As Helen did, always show the most recent year to the right. This makes it easier for you to compare your current results with those of the industry. It also simplifies the process of updating next year.

Comments on Figure 22.4. The assets and liabilities sections of Figure 22.4 show each balance sheet line item as a percentage of total assets. The section on income data shows the income statement line items as a percentage of net sales.

The ratios are listed after these three categories. Notice that the three values are shown for each ratio. For example, the current ratio values are 2.6 to 1, 1.8 to 1, 1.3 to 1 in the column for all companies in the current data section. The Robert Morris Associates derives these numbers by listing the current ratios of all respondents (46 respondents in this case) from the best ratio to the worst. The list of ratios is then divided evenly into four parts, or quartiles. The three values represent, respectively, the boundary point between the first ("best") and second quartiles, the boundary point between the second and third quartiles (the middle or median value), and the boundary between the third and fourth ("worst") quartiles.

The additional columns to the left of "sales/receivables" and "cost of sales/inventory" correspond to the days sales outstanding and days stock in inventory, respectively.

Pretax profits are used to compute the profitability ratios. This is done because tax rates among respondents and, therefore, their net profit, can vary significantly for reasons unrelated to their current operations (e.g., tax loss carry-forwards and investment tax credits).

What Are the Key Ratios?

Analysts look at certain key ratios that measure the vital signs of your business. These key ratios can be classified by the financial characteristics they measure, namely, liquidity, leverage, turnover or activity, profitability, and trading. The following discussion provides you with workable formulas for calculating these ratios, and it shows you how Helen Spencer computed them for Ambrosia Fragrances. Figures 22.5 and 22.6 summarize these definitions and computations.

FIGURE 22.5
Ambrosia Fragrance Company, Inc.
Ratio Definition Matrix

TYPE	*RATIO*	*FORMULA*	*PRINCIPLE*
LIQUIDITY	Current ratio	(Cash + Marketable securities + Accounts receivable + Inventory) / Current liabilities	This ratio is one of the measures of the ability to repay short-term debt. In theory, it measures the cushion of current assets over current liabilities. It measures how quickly a current creditor can be paid and by how much current assets could shrink before current creditors would not be paid.
	Quick ratio	(Cash + Marketable securities + Accounts receivable) / Current liabilities	This ratio is a more conservative measure of the ability to repay short-term debt. In theory, it assumes that inventory is much less liquid than other current assets and indicates what portion of current liabilities could be retired very quickly by liquidating quick assets.
LEVERAGE	Debt to net worth	Total liabilities / (Net worth—intangible assets)	The ratio expresses the relationship of capital contributed by creditors to capital contributed by owners. It records the leverage or potential risk to creditors—the lower the ratio, the greater the protection for creditors.
	Cash earnings to current maturities of long-term debt (LTD)	(Net profit + Noncash charges) / Current maturities of LTD Depreciation, amortization, etc.	This ratio measures a company's ability to repay its existing borrowings. It also measures the amount by which net earnings can decrease before a company is unable to meet its principal and interest payments.

FIGURE 22.5 (Cont.)

TYPE	*RATIO*	*FORMULA*	*PRINCIPLE*
TURNOVER	Accounts receivable turnover	$\frac{\text{Net credit sales (annual)}}{\text{Average accounts receivable balance}}$	The ratio measures the relationship of the volume of business to the outstanding receivables. The higher the turnover ratio (the lower the days sales outstanding), the more rapidly receivables are being collected and, therefore, the more liquid they are.
	Days sales outstanding	$\frac{\text{360 days}}{\text{Accounts receivable turnover}}$	
	Inventory turnover	$\frac{\text{Cost of sales (annual)}}{\text{Average inventory balance}}$	This ratio measures the relationship of the cost of sales to inventory. It indicates, relatively, how liquid inventory is and whether there appears to be a problem with obsolete or damaged inventory. The inventory turnover will vary depending on the type of company and length of its manufacturing process.
	Days stock in inventory	$\frac{\text{360 days}}{\text{Inventory turnover}}$	
	Accounts payable turnover	$\frac{\text{Purchases (annual)}}{\text{Average accounts payable balance}}$	This ratio discloses the average amount of time a company takes to repay creditors. It can be compared to the days sales outstanding to compute the credit gap between payables and receivables.
	Days payables outstanding	$\frac{\text{360 days}}{\text{Accounts payable turnover}}$	

FIGURE 22.5 (Cont.)

TYPE	RATIO	FORMULA	PRINCIPLE
PROFITABILITY	Pretax return on assets	$\frac{\text{Pretax profit}}{\text{Total assets}}$	This ratio relates the results of the year's operations before taxes to the total assets used in operations. It shows the profitability of the use of all resources of the firm and can be used to examine trends in the firm's efficiency.
	Pretax return on Net Worth	$\frac{\text{Pretax profit}}{\text{Net Worth}}$	This ratio relates the results of operations before taxes to the owner's investment in the business. It could be compared with alternative uses of the owner's funds on a pretax basis.
	Pretax profitability	$\frac{\text{Pretax profit}}{\text{Net Sales}}$	This ratio relates the pretax results of a company's operations to its sales. It measures how much of each dollar of sales is left to pay taxes and to either pay dividends or reinvest in the company.
	Gross margin percentage	$\frac{\text{Gross margin}}{\text{Net sales}}$	This ratio measures how much of each dollar of sales is left to pay operating expenses after direct costs of goods sold are deducted.
	Other expense ratios	$\frac{\text{Expense item}}{\text{Net sales}}$	Each expense ratio measures how much of each dollar of sales is used for each expense category.
TRADING	Net working capital turnover	$\frac{\text{Net Sales}}{\text{Average net working capital}}$	This ratio measures the turnover of net working capital. It expresses the number of dollars of annual sales generated by each dollar of net working capital. A low ratio could indicate an unprofitable overinvestment in net working capital. A high ratio indicates overtrading, which is a dangerous practice.
	Total assets turnover	$\frac{\text{Net sales}}{\text{Total assets}}$	This ratio measures the turnover of total assets and expresses the number of dollars of annual sales that are generated by each dollar of assets.

FIGURE 22.6

Ambrosia Fragrance Company, Inc. Calcuation of 19X9 Ratios Work Sheet

	Ratio	Formula		Computation		Result		Value
LIQUIDITY	Current ratio:	Cash(1)+Accounts receivable(2)+Inventory(3)+Marketable securities	=	$170,814+1,143,611+2,505,627+0	=	$3,820,052	=	1.26
		Current liabilities(18)		$3,029,388		$3,029,388		
	Quick ratio:	Cash(1)+Accounts receivable(2)+Marketable securities	=	$170,814+1,143,611+0	=	$1,314,425	=	.43
		Current liabilities(18)		$3,029,388		$3,029,388		
LEVERAGE	Debt to net worth:	Total liabilities(21)	=	$5,338,178	=	$5,338,178	=	2.14
		Net worth(25) – Intangibles(12)		$2,545,895-50,000		$2,495,895		
	Cash earnings to current maturities of long-term debt:	Net profit(37)+Noncash charges(depreciation)(39)	=	$511,285+225,000	=	$736,285	=	3.68
		Current maturities of LTD(17)		$200,000		$200,000		
TURNOVER	Accounts receivable turnover:	Net credit sales (annual) (27)	=	$16,359,008	=	$16,359,008	=	13.66 times per year
		Average accounts receivable balance(2)		$1,143,611+1,252,009)÷2		$1,197,810		
	Days sales outstanding:	Number of days in the year (360)*	=	360	=	26.35 days	=	26 days
		Accounts receivable turnover (above)		13.66				

*Note: Most sources of comparative data use 360 days, rather than 365 or 366 in a year.

Ratio	Formula		Computation		Result		Value
Inventory turnover:	Cost of sales (annual) (28)	=	$9,074,631	=	$9,074,631	=	3.97 times per year
	Average inventory balance(3)		($2,505,627+2,061,881)÷2		$2,283,754		
Days stock in inventory:	360 days	=	360 days	=	90.68 days	=	91 days
	Inventory turnover (above)		3.97				

FIGURE 22.6 (Cont.)

Category	Ratio	Formula		Computation		Result		Value
TURNOVER (CONTINUED)	Accounts payable turnover:	Purchases (annual)(38) / Average accounts payable balance (14)	=	\$11,088,064 / (\$1,630,875+1,230,883)÷2	=	\$11,088,064 / \$ 1,430,879	=	7.75 times per year = 7.8
	Days payables outstanding:	360 days / Accounts payable turnover (above)	=	360 days / 7.75	=	46.45 days	=	46 days
PROFITABILITY	Pretax return on assets:	Pretax profit(35) / Total assets(13)	=	\$1,044,806 / \$7,884,073			=	13.25%
	Pretax return on net worth:	Pretax profit(35) / Net Worth (owners' equity(25))	=	\$1,044,806 / \$2,545,895	=	\$1,044,806 / \$2,495,895	=	41.0%
	Pretax profitability:	Pretax profit(35) / Net sales(27)	=	\$1,044,806 / \$16,359,008			=	6.39%
	Gross margin percentage:	Gross margin(29) / Net sales(27)	=	\$7,284,377 / \$16,359,008			=	44.53%
	Other expenses ratios:	Operating expense(34) / Net sales(27)	=	\$6,394,954 / \$16,359,008			=	39.09%
		Interest expense(33) / Net sales(27)	=	\$400,036 / \$16,359,008			=	2.45%
		Depreciation expense(39) / Net sales(27)	=	\$225,000 / \$16,359,008			=	1.38%
TRADING	Net working capital turnover:	Net sales(27) / Average net working capital(40)	=	\$16,359,008 / (\$1,100,626+\$594,108)÷2	=	\$16,359,008 / \$847,367	=	\$19.31 of sales per dollar of net working capital
	Total assets turnover:	Net sales(27) / Average total assets(13)	=	\$16,359,008 / (\$7,884,073+\$7,835,535)÷2	=	\$16,359,008 / \$7,859,804	=	2.08 of sales per dollar of assets

FIGURE 22.7
Ambrosia Fragrances Company, Inc.
Ratio Trends Chart

AMBROSIA FRAGRANCES COMPANY, INC.
RATIO TRENDS CHART

	Ratio / Date	12/31/87	12/13/88	12/31/89			Ind	Goal	Comments
LIQ	Current	1.0	1.1	1.3			1.9 1.3 1.1	1.8	
	Quick	.4	.5	.4			1.2 .6 .4	.6	
LEV	Debt-to-Worth	2.6	2.9	2.1			1.5 1.9 2.5	2.0	
	Cash Earnings-to Current Maturity	N/A	3.3	3.7			14.9 5.7 1.7	5.0	
TURNOVER	AR Turnover	10.7	11.4	13.7			13.6 6.3 5.8	13.0	
	Days Sales O/S	34 da	32 da	26 da			27 58 63	27	
	Inventory T/O	3.3	3.6	4.0			4.7 3.1 2.2	4.5	
	Days Stock	109 da	100 da	91 da			78 118 166	80	
	Payables T/O	4.9	6.3	7.8			N/A	9.0	
	Days Payables	74 da	57 da	46 da			N/A	40 da	
PROFITABILITY	Pretax Return on Assets	12.5%	13.3%	13.3%			25.9 14.9 2.1	15%	
	Pretax Return on Net Worth	43.8%	51.3%	41.0%			68.6 35.6 6.8	42%	
	Pretax Profitability	5.2%	7.6%	6.4%			6.7%	10%	
	Gross Margin	45.7%	46.0%	44.5%			42.6%	46%	
	Operating Expenses	43.1%	38.8%	39.1%			34.9%	36%	
	Interest Expenses	2.3%	2.1%	2.5%			N/A	2.0%	
	Depreciation Expense	.8%	.7%	1.4%			.6% 1.2% 2.9%	2.0%	
TRAD	Sales/Working Capital	123.1%	39.6%	19.3%			4.3 8.9 44.4	9.0	
	Sales/Total Assets	2.4	2.1	2.1			2.5 2.1 1.4	2.1	

In each calculation, reference numbers are i… These numbers refer to the line items in Helen's s… and 22.2.

Liquidity Ratios

Liquidity ratios measure your firm's ability to repay its short-ter… tions as they come due. However, they are only a quick measure … …ur liquidity. A thorough analysis requires the development of a cash flow forecast for the year, such as the one illustrated in Part I. Two of the most commonly used liquidity ratios are the *current ratio* and the *quick ratio*.

Current ratio. The current ratio measures the "cushion" of current assets over current liabilities. It measures by how much current assets could shrink before current creditors would not be paid and is calculated by using the following formula:

$$\text{Current ratio} = \frac{\text{Current assets}}{\text{Current liabilities}}$$

or

$$\text{Current ratio} = \frac{\text{Cash} + \text{Accounts receivable} + \text{Inventory} + \text{Marketable securities}}{\text{Current liabilities}}$$

When Ambrosia's figures were plugged into the formula, Helen got the following:

$$\begin{aligned}\text{Current ratio} &= \frac{\$170{,}814 + 1{,}143{,}611 + 2{,}505{,}627 + 0}{\$3{,}029{,}388} \\ &= \frac{\$3{,}820{,}052}{\$3{,}029{,}388} \\ &= 1.26 \text{ to } 1\end{aligned}$$

Note that Helen excluded prepaid expenses and other current assets in the numerator of her ratio because she knew that for liquidity purposes bankers generally do not consider these to be current assets.

Quick ratio. The quick ratio is a more conservative measure of the ability to repay short-term debt. It recognizes that inventory is much less liquid than other current assets. Therefore, it measures the portion of current liabilities that can be retired quickly by liquidating quick assets—that is, assets that can be converted into cash quickly. The formula for this ratio is as follows:

$$\text{Quick ratio} = \frac{\text{Current assets} - \text{Inventory}}{\text{Current liabilities}}$$

or

$$\text{Quick ratio} = \frac{\text{Cash} + \text{Accounts receivable} + \text{Marketable securities}}{\text{Current liabilities}}$$

For Ambrosia, the formulas worked out as follows:

$$\text{Quick ratio} = \frac{\$170{,}814 + 1{,}143{,}611 + 10}{\$3{,}029{,}388}$$

$$= \frac{\$1{,}314{,}425}{\$3{,}029{,}388}$$

$$= 0.43 \text{ to } 1$$

Leverage Ratios

Leverage ratios, also known as *solvency* or *financial condition* ratios, measure the relative investments of creditors versus the owners of your business. They show you the cushion, or safety margin, of ownership in your business by measuring the percentage of debt to net worth, or equity. Basically, your net worth is equal to the capital that you and other owners have invested in the business plus the retained earnings that you have put back into the business. You can view your net worth as the money you would have left if you liquidated all your assets and repaid all your creditors. Or you can view it as the proportion of your assets that you own.

The assets of a business will shrink upon liquidation, but they will also shrink in the normal course of business—for example, as a result of operating losses, asset write-offs, uninsured casualties, and the like. Therefore, the greater your net worth or cushion, the lower the proportion of your assets that others have claims on and the easier it will be for you to repay your debt during periods of financial difficulty. Your creditors, therefore, will be concerned with the leverage ratios for your company. If these ratios indicate that your proportion of debt to net worth is high, creditors will view your company as a higher risk candidate for a loan than another company with a lower ratio of debt to net worth. Your company would be said to be "too highly leveraged."

Leverage can be a distinct advantage, however, if your company can earn more on the assets in which it invests than it has to pay in interest charges for a loan to finance those assets. However, if you are earning a smaller rate of return on the assets than you are paying for the loan that is financing those assets, leverage is disadvantageous because it reduces your profitability.

Debt to net worth. You can use the following formula to measure your company's financial leverage:

$$\text{Debt to net worth} = \frac{\text{Total liabilities}}{\text{Total net worth} - \text{Intangible assets}}$$

In Ambrosia's case, the following figures were used to arrive at the ratio of debt to net worth:

$$\text{Debt to net worth} = \frac{\$5{,}338{,}178}{\$2{,}545{,}895 - 50{,}000}$$

$$= \frac{\$5{,}338{,}178}{\$2{,}495{,}895}$$

$$= 2.14 \text{ to } 1$$

Your intangible, or nonphysical, assets may include goodwill, patent rights, trademarks, organization costs, and the like. Theoretically, a number of these assets can be converted into cash or other assets if they are sold or if the business is disposed of. However, for the purpose of calculating this ratio, subtract those intangibles that you believe cannot be sold for amounts equivalent to their carrying value in your financial records. A variation of this ratio, which measures the proportion of long-term debt to net worth, is often calculated by large companies that rely more heavily on long-term financing than do most small businesses.

The Growth Ratio. In addition to reviewing your ratio of debt to net worth, your banker may look at the relationship between your company's cash earnings, or cash flow from operations, and the current maturities of your long-term debt. This ratio measures your firm's ability to meet its payments of principal on existing debt. It is also a rough measure of your company's ability to grow. In other words, if the ratio for your company is approximately 1 to 1, you are using virtually all of your internally generated funds to repay existing debt, leaving no additional internal funds for asset expansion. The following formula can be used to find the growth ratio:

$$\text{Cash earnings to current maturities of long-term debt} = \frac{\text{Net earnings + Noncash charges*}}{\text{Current maturities of long-term debt}}$$

Ambrosia's growth ratio was determined as follows:

$$\text{Cash earnings to current maturities of long-term debt} = \frac{\$511{,}285 + 225{,}000}{\$200{,}000}$$

$$= \frac{\$736{,}285}{\$200{,}000}$$

$$= 3.68 \text{ to } 1$$

*Depreciation, amortization, and so on.

You can use other ratios to measure your ability to meet your fixed obligations. Two commonly used ratios are the times-interest-earned ratio and the fixed-charges-coverage ratio. Their formulas follow:

$$\text{Times-interest-earned ratio} = \frac{\text{Pretax profit} + \text{Interest charges}}{\text{Interest charges}}$$

$$\text{Fixed-charges-coverage ratio} = \frac{\text{Pretax profit} + \text{Interest charges} + \text{Other fixed charges}}{\text{Interest charges} + \text{Other fixed charges}}$$

A conservative approach to the fixed-charges-coverage ratio is to include all payments that you are required to make at fixed, regular intervals, including lease payments, interest, payments of principal on outstanding debt, and the like. Industry data for these two ratios are not readily available. However, in the event that you locate such data be aware that they may not include the same charges and therefore may not be comparable.

Turnover Ratios

Turnover ratios, often referred to as *activity ratios*, tell you how many times your company turns over its receivables, inventory, or payables during a year. Expressed in days, they indicate how quickly, on the average, your assets are being converted into cash (in the case of receivables) or into receivables (in the case of inventory). The following turnover ratios are among the more commonly used.

Accounts receivable turnover and days sales outstanding. These ratios measure the relationship of the volume of your business to your outstanding receivables. The higher the turnover ratio (the lower the days sales outstanding), the more rapidly receivables are being collected and, therefore, the more liquid they are. Generally, the days sales outstanding should be consistent with your company's credit policy. The formulas used are the following:

$$\text{Accounts receivable}^{*}\ \text{turnover} = \frac{\text{Net credit sales (annual)}}{\text{Average accounts receivable balance}}$$

$$\text{Days sales outstanding} = \frac{\text{Number of days in the year (360)}}{\text{Accounts receivable turnover}}$$

*Net sales, or net credit sales, is equal to sales less related returns and allowances. The average accounts receivable balance (or any other balance sheet item) is equal to the sum of the balances at the beginning and the end of the year divided by 2.

Ambrosia's results were:

$$\text{Accounts receivable turnover} = \frac{\$16,359,008}{(\$1,143,611 + 1,252,009) \div 2^{*}}$$

$$= \frac{\$16,359,008}{\$1,197,810}$$

$$= 13.66 \text{ times per year}$$

$$\text{Days sales outstanding} = \frac{360}{13.66}$$

$$= 26.35 \text{ days}$$

$$= 26 \text{ days}$$

Inventory turnover and days stock in inventory. These ratios measure the relationship of your cost of sales to your inventory. They can help you to determine how liquid your inventory is and whether you have a problem with obsolete or damaged inventory. Your inventory turnover will vary depending on the nature of your company and the length of its manufacturing process. Use the following formulas:

$$\text{Inventory turnover} = \frac{\text{Cost of sales (annual)}}{\text{Average inventory balance}}$$

$$\text{Days of stock in inventory} = \frac{360 \text{ days}}{\text{Inventory turnover}}$$

These formulas applied to Ambrosia gave the following results:

$$\text{Inventory turnover} = \frac{\$9,074,631}{(\$2,505,627 + 2,061,881) \div 2^{**}}$$

$$= \frac{\$9,074,631}{\$2,283,754}$$

$$= 3.97 \text{ times per year}$$

$$\text{Days stock in inventory} = \frac{360 \text{ days}}{3.97}$$

$$= 90.68 \text{ days}$$

$$= 91 \text{ days}$$

*Average of December 19X9 and December 19X8

**Average of December 19X9 and December 19X8 inventories.

Payables turnover and days payables outstanding. These ratios disclose the average amount of time your company takes to repay creditors. They can be compared to the industry averages and to the days sales outstanding ratio so that you can compute the "credit gap" between your payables and receivables. The formulas are:

$$\text{Payables turnover} = \frac{\text{Purchases (annual)}}{\text{Average accounts payable balance}}$$

$$\text{Days payables outstanding} = \frac{\text{360 days}}{\text{Payables turnover}}$$

Ambrosia's results were:

$$\text{Inventory turnover} = \frac{\$11{,}088{,}064}{(\$1{,}630{,}875 + 1{,}230{,}883) \div 2^{*}}$$

$$= \frac{\$11{,}088{,}064}{\$1{,}430{,}879}$$

$$= 7.75 \text{ times per year}$$

$$\text{Days payables outstanding} = \frac{\text{360 days}}{7.75}$$

$$= 46.45 \text{ days}$$

$$= 46 \text{ days}$$

A common practice is to use 360 days in the formulas to represent one year rather than 365 or 366 days because most sources of comparative data use 360 days.

Profitability Ratios

A key question that these ratios will help you to answer is: "How profitable is my firm?" There are profitability ratios related to the investment in assets and profitability ratios related to sales. Ratios that fall into the former group include the pretax return on assets and the pretax return on net worth.

Pretax return on assets. The pretax return on assets ratio expresses the results of your operations for the year, before taxes, compared with the total assets used in operations. The ratio, therefore, shows the profitability of the use of all the resources of your firm. It can be used to

*Average of 12/X9 and 12/X8 payables.

examine trends in your firm's efficiency. You can calculate this important ratio by using the following formula:

$$\text{Pretax return on assets} = \frac{\text{Pretax profits}}{\text{Total assets}}$$

Ambrosia's pretax return was derived as follows:

$$\text{Pretax return on assets} = \frac{\$1{,}044{,}806}{\$7{,}884{,}073}$$

$$= 13.25\%$$

Pretax return on net worth. The pretax return on net worth ratio expresses the results of your operations before taxes compared with *your* investment in the business (your net worth). This ratio could be compared with alternative uses of your funds on a pretax basis. Use the following formula:

$$\text{Pretax return on net worth} = \frac{\text{Pretax profits}}{\text{Net worth}}$$

Ambrosia found the following results:

$$\text{Pretax return on net worth} = \frac{\$1{,}044{,}806}{\$2{,}545{,}895}$$

$$= 41.0\%$$

Pretax profitability. The profitability ratios that relate to sales include the pretax profitability and gross margin percentage ratios and various expense item ratios. The pretax profitability ratio measures the pretax results of your company's operations compared with sales. It measures how much of each dollar of sales is left to pay taxes and dividends or to reinvest in the company. To calculate this ratio, use the following formula:

$$\text{Pretax profitability} = \frac{\text{Pretax profits}}{\text{Net sales}}$$

For Ambrosia, this formula translated into:

$$\text{Pretax profitability} = \frac{\$1{,}044{,}806}{\$16{,}359{,}008}$$

$$= 6.39\%$$

Gross margin percentage. The gross margin percentage ratio measures how much of each dollar of sales is left to pay operating expenses (selling, general, and administrative expenses) after the cost of goods sold is deducted. Your gross margin is equal to the difference between your sales and your cost of goods sold. Your cost of goods sold includes all items of expense directly related to the production of goods for sale. Often, companies also deduct selling expenses directly associated with products (e.g., commissions) to arrive at their gross margins. For purposes of comparability with industry ratios, however, you would be wise not to deduct these selling expenses. To find your gross margin percentage, use the following formula:

$$\text{Gross margin percentage} = \frac{\text{Gross margin}}{\text{Net sales}}$$

For Ambrosia this worked out as follows:

$$\text{Gross margin percentage} = \frac{\$7,284,377}{\$16,359,008}$$

$$= 44.53\%$$

Expense ratio. An expense ratio measures how much of each dollar of sales is used for each category of expense. A general formula that can be used to calculate these ratios is as follows:

$$\text{Expense ratio} = \frac{\text{Expense item}}{\text{Net sales}}$$

When this formula was applied by Ambrosia, the following results were obtained:

$$\text{Operating expense ratio} = \frac{\$\ 6,394,954}{\$16,359,008}$$

$$= 39.09\%$$

$$\text{Interest expense ratio} = \frac{\$400,036}{\$16,359,008}$$

$$= 2.45\%$$

$$\text{Depreciation expense ratio} = \frac{\$225,000}{\$16,359,008}$$

$$= 1.38\%$$

Trading Ratios

Trading ratios, unlike the turnover ratios, measure the percentage of use of productive assets—net working capital and total assets—in producing a given level of sales. (Your net working capital is equal to the difference between your current assets and your current liabilities.) In essence, they measure how many dollars of sales are produced by a given level of assets. Like the leverage ratios, a high trading ratio is a double-edged sword. Overtrading—that is, when too many dollars of sales are supported by too few dollars of net working capital or total assets—is quite common among small- and medium-sized businesses. This situation can be dangerous because there may be no room for error; one slow receivable or one delayed lot of raw materials can send you running to the bank for more credit, which your banker may be reluctant to grant.

Net working capital turnover. An important ratio to calculate is your net working capital turnover ratio, which measures the dollars of annual sales generated by each dollar of net working capital. A low ratio may indicate an unprofitable overinvestment in net working capital. A high ratio indicates overtrading, which, as discussed earlier, is a dangerous practice. The formula to obtain this ratio follows:

$$\text{Net working capital turnover} = \frac{\text{Net sales}}{\text{Average net working capital}}$$

This formula applied to Ambrosia's case gives the following results:

$$\text{Net working capital turnover} = \frac{\$16{,}359{,}008}{(\$1{,}100{,}626 + \$594{,}108) \div 2^{*}}$$

$$\frac{\$16{,}359{,}008}{\$847{,}367} = \$19.31 \text{ of sales per dollar of net working capital}$$

Total assets turnover. Another important ratio is your total assets turnover, which measures the number of dollars of annual sales generated by each dollar of assets and which may be obtained by using the following formula:

$$\text{Total assets turnover} = \frac{\text{Net sales}}{\text{Average total assets}}$$

*Average of December 19X9 and December 19X8 net working capital.

Ambrosia's results when using this formula were:

$$\text{Total assets turnover} = \frac{\$16{,}359{,}008}{(\$7{,}884{,}073 + \$7{,}835{,}535) \div 2^{*}}$$

$$= \frac{\$16{,}359{,}008}{\$7{,}859{,}804}$$

$$= \$2.08 \text{ per dollar of assets}$$

The ratios may be somewhat misleading for a small business for various reasons, including the facts that profits are taken by owners as compensation and financial statement line items are sometimes categorized in different ways. In addition, your results may be distorted by inflation, since its impact on your income statement is not synchronized with its effect on your balance sheet. This is because your income statement items are stated in today's dollars, and your balance sheet items are based on historical costs. Therefore, use these ratios only for internal comparative purposes. If you use the profitability ratios, remember to use pretax profits for comparison with industry sources because effective tax rates, especially in the small business area, can vary a great deal for reasons that are not related to the current year's operations.

The Telltale Signs of Bankruptcy

The liquidity, leverage, turnover, profitability, and trading ratios will give you useful information about these individual measures of your company's financial health. A value known as your Z *factor* will give you a relative measure of your company's overall financial position. The Z factor is an indicator of the potential for bankruptcy. Are you approaching bankruptcy, or are you managing your financial resources in a way that will steer your company away from it? You can compute your Z factor on a regular basis to make sure that your company is moving in the right direction. The Z factor formula, developed by Edward I. Altman, is a weighted composite of the following ratios:

$$a = \frac{\text{Net working capital}}{\text{Total assets}}$$

$$b = \frac{\text{Retained earnings}}{\text{Total assets}}$$

$$c = \frac{\text{Pretax profit + Interest charges}}{\text{Total assets}}$$

*Average of December 19X9 and December 19X8 total assets.

$$d = \frac{\text{Net worth*}}{\text{Total debt}}$$

$$e = \frac{\text{Net sales}}{\text{Total assets}}$$

The weighted average of these ratios is calculated as follows:

$$Z \text{ (factor)} = 1.2a + 1.4b + 3.3c + 0.6d + 1.0e$$

If your Z factor score is above 2.99 to 1, your company is considered to be in a strong financial position. If your score is below 1.81 to 1, you have serious problems. You should act quickly to identify these problems and to take corrective action in order to avoid bankruptcy. If your score is between 1.81 to 1 and 2.99 to 1, you should figure out how you can improve the ratios that are holding your Z factor, and therefore your margin of safety, down.

Notice how important the quality and the management of your assets are to your Z factor; the dollar value of your total assets is included in the denominators of four of the five ratios used in the calculations.

Helen calculated *Ambrosia's Z factor* for 19X9 as follows:

$$a = \frac{\$1,100,626}{\$7,884,073} = 0.14 \text{ to } 1$$

$$b = \frac{\$2,495,895}{\$7,884,073} = 0.32 \text{ to } 1$$

$$c = \frac{\$1,044,806 + \$400,036}{\$7,884,073}$$

$$= \frac{\$1,444,842}{\$7,884,073} = 0.18 \text{ to } 1$$

$$d = \frac{\$2,545,895}{\$5,338,178} = 0.48 \text{ to } 1$$

$$e = \frac{\$16,359,008}{\$7,884,073} = 2.07 \text{ to } 1$$

$$Z = 1.2\ (0.14) + 1.4\ (0.32) + 3.3\ (0.18) + 0.6\ (0.48) + 1.0\ (2.07)$$
$$= 0.168 + 0.448 + 0.594 + 0.288 + 2.07$$
$$= 3.568 \text{ to } 1$$

*A publicly held company would use the market value of equity in computing the ratio, in place of net worth.

Since Ambrosia's Z factor was above the 2.99-to-1 zone, Helen felt that her company was in relatively good financial health. However, she figured that if she could improve the company's pretax return on assets, which was currently not as good as the industry average, she could raise its Z factor to an even safer level.

Do You Measure Up to the Competition?

At the seminar, Helen learned that there are a number of sources of comparative industry data, which are available at your public library. They include:

- Robert Morris Associates, *Annual Statement Studies*.
- Dun & Bradstreet, *Key Financial Ratios.*
- *Troy's Almanac.*
- Trade association publications.

The most extensive source of those listed is the Robert Morris Associates (RMA) *Annual Statement Studies*. RMA is an association of bank credit and loan officers that attempts to codify the exchange of credit information among banks in order to improve the quality of credit decisions. *Annual Statement Studies* is an anonymous compilation of financial statement information provided to the RMA by banks. The information is classified by the Standard Industrial Classification (SIC) Code. A sample page relating to Ambrosia's industry is reproduced as Figure 22.4. The page is explained in more detail in Comments on Figure 22.4 on page 318. Helen Spencer wrote these RMA ratios in the industry column on her ratio trends chart to simplify her comparative analysis (see Figure 22.7).

How did Ambrosia score? After Helen calculated the ratios for Ambrosia, she posted them to her ratio trends chart. Ambrosia's general financial position in 19X9, in comparison with its industry, was as follows:

1. *Liquidity*. Ambrosia's current and quick ratios, and therefore its liquidity, were somewhat lower than the median ratios for its industry. For example, Ambrosia's current ratio in 19X9 was 1.26 to 1 versus the industry mean of 1.3 to 1. However, Ambrosia's current ratio is improving; it was 0.95 to 1 in 19X7 and 1.09 to 1 in 19X8.

In addition, Ambrosia was turning over its inventory and receivables more quickly than the average firm in its industry. This indicates, respectively, that Ambrosia probably has a lesser problem with obsolete or damaged inventory and with overdue receivables (potential bad debts). Ambrosia could rely on its ability to turn these current assets into cash and to do this more quickly than its average competitor.

2. *Leverage*. Ambrosia was more heavily leveraged than its average competitor. Its debt to net worth ratio was 2.14 to 1 versus an industry mean of 1.9 to 1. Consistent with this is the fact that Ambrosia's cash earnings to current maturities ratio was lower than the median, 3.68 to 1 versus 5.7 to 1. Ambrosia's current maturities, like its total debt, were proportionately higher than the industry average in 19X9.

3. *Turnover*. As discussed, Ambrosia's receivables and inventory were turning over more quickly than the industry averages. However, payables were not turning over as quickly as generally in the industry. Helen estimated the industry figure to be an average of 40 days, whereas Ambrosia's turnover was 47 days.

4. *Profitability*. Ambrosia's gross margin percentage ratio was *higher* than the industry average, 44.53% versus 42.6%, indicating that its cost of goods sold was somewhat lower than average. However, the company's operating expenses were higher than average; its ratio of operating expenses to net sales was 39.09% versus 34.9% for the industry. These two ratios netted out to a pretax profitability that was approximately equal to the industry mean. These ratios suggested that Helen should concentrate her efforts on controlling her operating expenses.

The company's pretax return on assets was not as good as the average, 13.3% versus 14.9%. But its pretax return on net worth was better, 41.9% versus 35.6%. These results are to be expected from a company that is heavily leveraged.

5. *Trading*. Ambrosia's working capital turnover ratio indicates that the company is overtrading—meaning that too many dollars of sales are supported by too few dollars of net working capital. Ambrosia's ratio in 19X9 was 14.86% versus 8.8% for the industry. This ratio reinforces the information gained from an analysis of the company's liquidity ratios, which were lower than the industry average. The company's total assets turnover ratio was, however, more in line with the industry average, 2.08 to 1 versus 2.1 to 1.

How Did She Get Where She Is?

Helen knew that the ratios presented her with a consistent story. Over the past three years, Ambrosia had made a significant investment in assets—in new plant and equipment and in increased levels of current assets. This investment was financed principally with long-term debt, thereby increasing the company's leverage or proportion of debt to net worth (as measured by the leverage ratios). The remainder of the funds came from the company's earnings.

Helen considered her present situation and developed an action plan to improve Ambrosia's financial condition. She thought that if she could convince her banker to increase her long-term loan by about $1 million, she could improve her ratios and, therefore, Ambrosia's financial position. First, the proceeds from this loan could be used in part to finance the needed permanent growth in net working capital—a long-term investment—that she had been financing incorrectly with short-term loans. In the past, she had not been properly matching the maturity of her working capital investments with the maturity of her financing. In addition, she could use the remainder of the proceeds of the long-term loan to improve her current and quick ratios by reducing the short-term loans and the additional accounts payable that were no longer required to finance the permanent addition to net working capital. This action would also improve her payables turnover ratio and, therefore, her credit standing with her suppliers.

Helen calculated that her pro forma, or newly estimated, current ratio would be 1.6 to 1, her quick ratio would be 0.5 to 1, and her debt to worth ratio would remain unchanged because she was only exchanging long-term for short-term debt. She figured, however, that if she maintained her present asset level, she could reduce her leverage over the next few years by using her anticipated earnings to repay the debt.

The next week, Helen discussed Ambrosia's situation with her banker John Carlton. John agreed with her strategy and was willing to increase the long-term loan and to extend a short-term line of credit for seasonal needs. In return, the bank required that Ambrosia slow its growth until it repaid its term loan and improved its debt to net worth ratio. The bank also required that Ambrosia be free of short-term loans for at least two months in every year that this kind of debt was incurred.

To ensure that these requirements would be met, restrictive covenants would be written into the loan agreement. These covenants would require Ambrosia to maintain a certain current ratio and to decrease gradually its debt to net worth ratio. Now that Helen knew how to calculate and analyze Ambrosia's ratios, she could monitor the company's performance against her own goals and could monitor compliance with loan covenants.

When Should You Calculate the Ratios?

The seminar instructors had recommended that Helen analyze her ratios at least every quarter. In addition, they had recommended calculating certain critical ratios more frequently. You should develop a similar plan for your business, based on your individual management needs. In carrying out your plan, remember the following factors.

1. For any ratio that consists of an income statement item and a balance sheet item (e.g., the accounts receivable turnover ratio), you must annualize or estimate the level of the income statement item for the

year in order to do an interim period (e.g., monthly or quarterly) analysis. This is required because your company's balance sheet items will generally remain level except for seasonal fluctuations because these accounts are always a "snapshot" of a balance at a period of time.

Your income statement items, on the other hand, represent the accumulation of transactions over time (one year, for example). Therefore, these items will start at $0 on day 1 of the year and will rise to their total annual level only by day 365.

Example. Assume that a company sells a product that has no seasonal peaks and has a sales volume of $30 million annually. On June 30, its sixth month, its sales are $15 million and its receivables are $2.5 million. If the receivables turnover ratio and the days sales outstanding are calculated without annualizing, the results are as follows:

Accounts receivable turnover = $15,000,000 ÷ $2,500,000 = 6 times

Days sales outstanding = 360 ÷ 6 = 60 days

If the company's terms are net 30 days, 60 days of receivables outstanding would be cause for concern. However, if the sales are annualized, the results are as follows:

Accounts receivable turnover = $30,000,000 ÷ $2,500,000
= 12 times

Days sales outstanding = 360 ÷ 12 = 30 days

The latter results are more in line with the company's credit terms. (For an additional example of annualizing, see Chapter 15, "Managing Accounts Receivable.")

2. Even balance sheet to balance sheet ratios will be skewed by seasonal factors. Therefore, unless your business is extremely level, never compare your interim balances with fiscal year-end balances or with the balances of different interim periods without first taking the seasonality into effect. You may, however, compare a period this year with the same period in the last year or another prior year.

3. Many companies estimate the cost of goods sold on monthly statements by *assuming* a certain gross margin percentage and "*backing into*" the cost of goods sold. If you make these assumptions, then your gross margin and the inventory turnover calculations will be meaningless on an interim basis because they only give back your initial assumptions, which you already know.

CONCLUSION

Helen Spencer saw ratio analysis as an excellent way of assessing the financial health of her business for the following reasons:

1. She knew that her banker used ratio analysis in analyzing the creditworthiness of her business. Therefore, she wanted to be familiar with the technique in order to anticipate and answer any questions. She thought that she would have to explain why her company had deviated from the standard ratios defined for her industry. In addition, she was anxious to determine whether her company was meeting the relevant ratio requirements established in her loan agreements.
2. Helen also realized she could use ratio analysis to compare her company with its own past performance. She figured that this would allow her to focus quickly on those areas where improvements were required.
3. She recognized that certain ratios could be used to form a set of goals for the business and to develop underlying assumptions for her financial forecasts.
4. She recognized that the tools and techniques of ratio analysis would enable her to make her own credit decisions regarding Ambrosia's customers.

No one ratio should be analyzed independently of the other possible ratios for your company. They should be taken as a whole. If your company's ratios do not compare with those of your industry, it could mean that you have some financial problems brewing. If you can identify such a trend when you still have time to do something about it, it will be well worth the time required to calculate the ratios.

23

Break-Even Analysis

In Chapter 20, "Managing Cost of Goods Sold," Barry Rosen realized that in order to compete in the marketplace, he would require more precise estimates of his manufacturing costs by style. These better estimates would enable him to establish selling prices that would be competitive in the marketplace and yet high enough to assure him of the level of profitability that he wanted. This chapter shows how Barry used the information that he developed in his cost accounting analysis to prepare a break-even analysis that helped him to make some decisions about a particular customer's order.

CASE STUDY: HOW BARRY ROSEN MADE A DIFFICULT OPERATING DECISION USING BREAK-EVEN ANALYSIS

An inquiry from the Kenney Company in New York, which was planning a handbag and leather goods sale, precipitated Barry's analysis of the break-even point for his company. Kenney asked if Barry would be willing to sell them 5,000 handbags of various styles at substantially *reduced prices*. As it turned out, Kenney was interested in obtaining an average unit purchase price on this batch of handbags of $30, rather than $35, which would be Barry's normal average selling price.

The Kenney Company needed to receive an answer to their inquiry as soon as possible so that they could arrange for alternative sources if Empire was not interested in the order. Barry's main concern was that the $30 average selling price would not cover his total standard costs to manufacture the handbags, based on his analysis of the styles to be sold. Barry wondered if there was any reason to consider the order further. He promised that he would get back to the Kenney Company the next day.

Solving the Problem with Break-Even Analysis

Barry decided that he might be able to answer this question with break-even analysis, a technique used to determine the level of sales that will generate the revenues required to exactly cover the costs of producing and selling the goods and of managing the company. Break-even analysis requires knowledge of the following:

- The *fixed* and *variable costs* of making and selling the goods.
- The *contribution margin,* or excess of selling value over variable costs, for each piece sold and for the company as a whole.
- The *relevant range* over which the fixed and variable cost relationships hold.

What are your fixed and variable costs? Having performed his detailed analysis of the standard costs of each style, Barry recognized that the costs of producing his handbags could be divided into fixed and variable costs. In basic terms, the fixed costs were those that he incurred just to open the door of his factory, without manufacturing a single piece of goods. These costs included depreciation of plant and equipment, rental of the office and warehouse space, real estate taxes, officers' salaries, insurance, taxes, and the like. Variable costs, on the other hand, were the specific costs that he incurred to manufacture and to sell his handbags and that varied with the level of production. If he did not manufacture anything, he would not incur these variable costs. Barry knew the following:

1. Fixed costs remain constant and are unaffected by changes in volume over a broad range of production. That range of production was the *capacity* of his plant. Therefore, so long as he did not have to add machinery and equipment or increase the size of his plant in order to increase production, he could lower the fixed costs *per unit* by producing more goods. When fixed costs remain constant, the fixed cost per unit decreases as volume increases, as illustrated in Figure 23.1. Notice that the first column reflects $100,000 of fixed costs. The second column

FIGURE 23.1
Empire Accessories, Inc.
Fixed and Variable Costs—An Illustration

Fixed Costs: [a]

Total Fixed Costs	*Unit Volume*	*Fixed Costs/Unit*
$100,000	40,000	$2.50
100,000	50,000	2.00
100,000	75,000	1.33
100,000	90,000	1.11

[a] As unit volume increases, total fixed costs remain constant whereas fixed costs per unit are reduced.

Variable Costs: [b]

Total Variable Costs	*Unit Volume*	*Variable Costs/Unit*
$ 80,000	40,000	$2.00
100,000	50,000	2.00
150,000	75,000	2.00
180,000	90,000	2.00

[b] As unit volume increases, total variable costs increase whereas variable costs per unit remain constant.

shows the unit volume increasing from 40,000 units to 90,000 units. The third column shows the fixed costs per unit. Barry divided the total fixed costs by the number of units produced and saw that the fixed costs per unit decreased from $2.50 at a volume of 40,000 units to $1.11 at a volume of 90,000 units.

2. *Variable costs* are incurred specifically to make and sell the product. They include direct material, direct labor, and manufacturing overhead. Barry knew that variable costs change in direct proportion to the level of production. Increases or decreases in the unit volume produced result in proportionate increases or decreases in the total level of variable costs. Figure 23.1 shows how this relationship is established. Notice that the first column shows total variable costs, the second column shows unit volume, and the third column shows the variable cost per unit, which remains at $2 per unit whether Barry's unit volume is 40,000 or 90,000 units. Therefore, as unit volume increases, total variable costs increase, but the variable costs per unit remains constant.

3. Some costs have both a variable and a fixed component and are, therefore, neither perfectly variable nor absolutely fixed with respect to volume changes. Many of these *semivariable* or *mixed* costs arise because there is a minimum level of expense that is incurred even if the company is operating at an extremely low volume. However, as volume rises, the costs tend to rise as well. Although these semivariable or mixed costs change in the same direction as production volume, they do not change

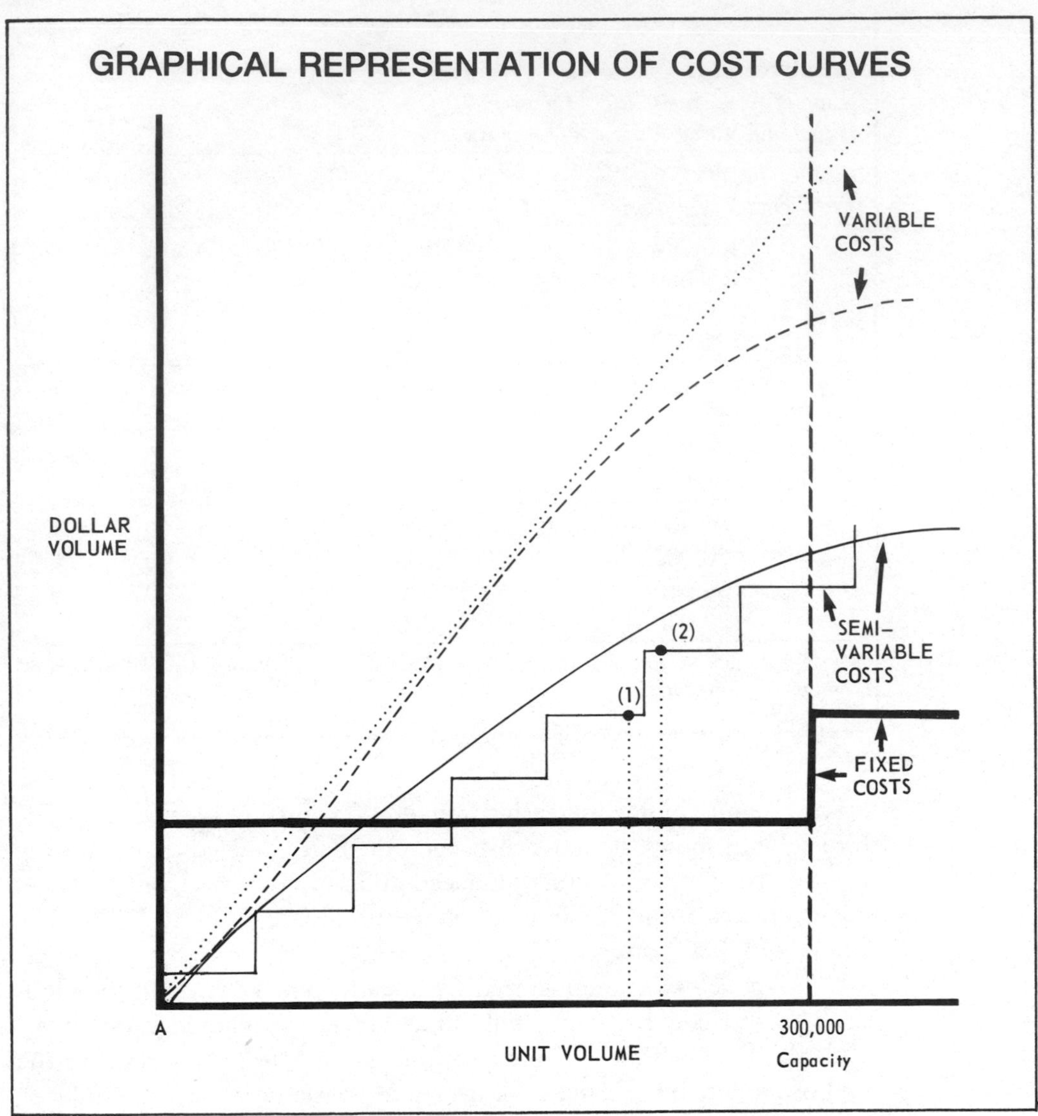

FIGURE 23.2
Graphical Representation of Cost Curves

in *direct proportion* to that volume. Therefore, all semivariable costs can be divided into an estimated fixed and a variable component. Often, semivariable expenses increase in what is referred to as a "step" function—that is, they remain constant for certain increases in volume, but at specific points they increase to a new plateau.

Figure 23.2 illustrates the three types of costs. You will see that *variable costs* are represented by a straight diagonal dotted line extending up from the origin (A). This line illustrates the fact that the dollar volume of costs increases in direct proportion as the unit volume increases. *Fixed costs,* on the other hand, are reflected as a straight horizontal line, which represents the fact that the dollar volume of fixed costs remains the same at any unit volume. *Semivariable costs* are reflected as a series of steps. As unit volume increases, these costs increase in jumps or increments.

None of the lines have to be straight. The variable cost line, for example, could be curved, which would simply reflect the fact that with discounts for bulk purchases of raw materials or other economies of scale, as unit volume increases, the dollar volume of cost increases, but not in direct proportion. Similarly, semivariable costs might also be represented as a curved line rather than a step function. The line is not as steep as the variable cost line because of the fixed cost portion of the semivariable costs. Notice that if the semivariable costs increase in a stepwise fashion, it is always better to produce at a unit volume that corresponds to point (1) rather than to point (2). The reason is that point (1) minimizes the semivariable costs for approximately the same unit volume.

Remember, Figure 23.2 is only an illustration of how costs often rise in relation to increases in volume. No costs fit the illustration exactly. If you understand the differences among fixed, variable, and semivariable costs, you will have a better chance of maximizing your volume and minimizing your costs.

Calculating semivariable costs. Barry had a good idea which costs were wholly variable and which were fixed in his company. Therefore, he was interested in dividing his semivariable or mixed costs into their fixed and variable cost components. He decided to use the "high/low" method to estimate their variable component as follows.

The high/low method simply calculates the change in a semivariable cost item and the change in the volume of sales from one year to the next. The change in the cost is then divided by the change in the volume of sales to arrive at the variable cost per item sold. This result is then used to estimate the variable component of the semivariable cost item. Here is an illustration.

Assume Barry sold 255,000 bags in 19X0 and 231,000 bags in 19X9. The difference is 24,000 bags.

Now assume his cost of electricity was $20,800 in 19X0 and $20,348 in 19X9. The difference is $452.

Divide the change in cost ($452) by the change in sales (24,000) and arrive at the variable cost per handbag (assuming the price of the electricity did not increase):

$$\frac{\$452}{24{,}000} = \$0.01883 \text{ variable cost per bag}$$

Multiply the variable cost per bag by the total bags sold in 19X0 to arrive at the total variable portion of the cost of electricity for the year.

$$\$0.01883 \times 255{,}000 = \text{total variable cost in 19X0}$$
$$= \$4{,}800 \text{ variable cost}$$

Then the total cost of electricity less the variable cost should equal the fixed portion of the cost of electricity:

$$\$20{,}800 - \$4{,}800 = \$16{,}000 \text{ fixed cost}$$

After applying this technique to all the semivariable costs, Barry was able to divide all of his costs into two groups—fixed and variable. He summarized these costs as shown in Figure 23.3. He totalled the two columns and found that his fixed costs were $1,647,600 and his variable costs were $6,869,360.

FIGURE 23.3
Empire Accessories, Inc.
Summary of Fixed and Variable Costs

	Per Income Statement July 31, 19X0		*Fixed*	*Variable*
Sales:				
255,000 units @ $35.00		$8,925,000		
Costs (cost of sales):				
Direct material	$3,272,320			$3,272,320
Direct labor—Dept. A	2,713,920			2,713,920
Direct labor—Dept. B	73,600			73,600
Direct labor—Dept. C	67,200			67,200
Group insurance	136,000			136,000
Buying expense	19,200			19,200
Total cost of sales		$6,282,240		
Factory overhead				
Auto expenses	12,800		10,000	2,800
Computer service	9,600		9,600	
Depreciation	30,400		30,400	
Dies and patterns	67,200		67,200	
Electricity	20,800		16,000	4,800
Heat	16,000		12,000	
Insurance	51,200		51,200	
Miscellaneous factory expense	56,000		54,000	2,000
Rent, equipment	22,400		22,400	
Repairs and parts	24,000		20,000	4,000

Sample bags	32,000		32,000	
Taxes, payroll	208,000			208,000
Taxes, other	12,800		12,800	
Telephone	19,200		15,000	4,200
Total factory overhead		582,400		
Selling, General, and Administrative				
Advertising	160,000		160,000	
Association dues and contributions	20,800		20,800	
Bad debts	14,400		14,400	
Computer service	19,200		19,200	
Commissions	7,200			7,200
Delivery	136,000			136,000
Electricity	5,600		5,600	
Interest expense	129,920		65,000	64,920
Legal and accounting	27,200		20,000	7,200
Miscellaneous	26,400		26,400	
Rent, New York office	28,800		28,800	
Salaries—office	80,000		80,000	
Salaries—sales	136,000		136,000	
Sales discounts and allowances	69,200			69,200
Stationery and supplies	20,800		20,800	
Payroll taxes	28,800		28,800	
Other taxes	3,200		3,200	
Telephone—N.Y.	48,000		36,000	12,000
Travel and entertainment	160,000		60,000	
Branch office expenses	530,800		470,000	60,800
Total S, G, & A		1,652,320		
Total Costs		$8,516,960	$1,647,600	$6,869,360
Profit before taxes		$ 408,040		

Analysis of contribution margin

$8,925,000	Sales
(6,869,360)	Variable costs
2,055,640	Contribution margin
1,647,600	Fixed costs
$ 408,040	Profit before taxes

Contribution margin %

$$\frac{\text{Contribution margin}}{\text{Sales}} = \frac{\$2,055,640}{\$8,925,000} = 23\%$$

Calculating a contribution margin. Barry knew that each style that he produced had a "contribution margin" equal to its selling price less the total variable costs incurred to produce it. Therefore, the contribution margin was the amount that each product "contributed" to the fixed costs of the company and to its profits, after deducting the variable costs. Figure 23.3 shows the contribution margin for the company as a whole. The total variable costs of $6,869,360 are subtracted from total sales of $8,925,000 to yield the contribution margin of $2,055,640. It is this contribution margin that is intended to bear all the fixed costs and provide a profit to Barry from his operations. Subtracting the fixed costs of $1,647,600 from the contribution margin yields a profit of $408,040. The contribution margin may be expressed in total dollars, in dollars per unit, or as a percentage. In the case of Empire Accessories, the company's contribution margin is 23%.

The relevant range. Barry knew that there was a limit to the sales volume level over which the fixed cost relationships would remain valid. This limit is the relevant range over which fixed costs remain constant. Above the relevant range, the cost relationships are no longer valid. For example, if Barry's sales volume doubled, he would have to rent more floor space, hire more people, and acquire more machinery and equipment. Therefore, if the relevant range for Empire Accessories is zero to 300,000 handbags (the current capacity of his plant), once Barry tried to produce more than 300,000 handbags, he would have to increase his fixed costs through the addition of people, property, plant, and equipment.

Barry realized two other factors about the break-even analysis for the company:

1. Break-even analysis is intended to be used as a general guideline or yardstick. There is always a degree of imprecision inherent in the analysis because of the difficulty of accurately categorizing the costs as fixed or variable and of calculating the relevant range.
2. It is not necessary to analyze the fixed and variable components of every item of cost. It is wise to focus on the top 20% of the costs, which represent 80% to 90% of the dollar total. These may be separated into their fixed and variable components. You can be less concerned with the proper categorization of the remaining items.

When do you just break even? So far, Barry had tried to establish the relationships among costs, volumes of production, and profit to the business. Break-even analysis is the device for determining the volume of sales that will generate those revenues required to just cover total costs, yielding a zero profit. Sales in excess of the break-even point will yield a profit because the contribution margin more than covers fixed costs. The excess is profit. Sales below the break-even point will generate a loss for the company because the contribution margin does not cover all the fixed costs.

In Barry's case, *as long as he had reached the break-even point, or could be certain of doing so within the year,* that is, as long as his contribution margin in Figure 23.3 was greater than his fixed costs of $1,647,600, he could sell additional handbags at a price *just above his variable cost of producing the style and still contribute to his profits.* If he had not reached the break-even point, *or could not be certain of doing so within the year,* he would be unwise to sell at a price that did not recover both his fixed *and* variable expenses.

Before Barry called the Kenney Company and accepted their order, he decided to find out about how many units (handbags) he had to sell to break even. To do this he used the following formula:

$$\text{Break-even point in units} = \frac{\text{Total fixed costs}}{\text{Average contribution margin per unit}}$$

Barry went back to his standard cost analysis and added up the contribution margins for all his styles. He divided the total by the number of styles and arrived at an average contribution margin per unit. (He could have taken more time and used his sales forecast to calculate a weighted average of the contribution margins by giving emphasis to the styles in which he expected to do the most volume.)

His estimate was as follows. If the average bag sold for $35 and the average variable costs were $26.94, then the average contribution margin per unit was $8.06 ($35 − $26.94). This meant that every unit sold contributed $8.06 toward the overall pool of fixed costs. Therefore, dividing *total fixed costs* by this *average contribution margin* should yield the break-even point in units. His break-even point was 204,417 units ($1,647,600 ÷ $8.06). Once Barry had calculated this, he multiplied the break-even point in units by $35 per unit to estimate his break-even point in dollars—$7,154,595. These calculations are summarized in Figure 23.4.

Break-Even Analysis Will Help You to Make Management Decisions

Now that Barry had completed his break-even analysis, he was prepared to determine whether he should sell 5,000 handbags to the Kenney Company at a reduced price. Barry believed he could take the order, but he did not want to make a mistake. So he considered three more factors:

1. Is Empire operating at full capacity?
2. Will the additional 5,000 units still keep Empire within its relevant range; that is, can these units be produced with no increase in fixed costs?

FIGURE 23.4
Empire Accessories, Inc.
Calculation of the Break-Even Point

$$\text{Break-even point in units} = \frac{\text{Total fixed costs}}{\text{Average contribution margin per unit}}$$

- Total fixed costs = $1,647,600
- Average contribution margin per unit = average selling price per unit minus average variable cost per unit (from Figure 23.3)
  = $35 − ($6,869,360 ÷ 255,000 units sold)
  = $35 − $26.94
  = $8.06

Therefore:

Break-even point in units = $1,647,600 ÷ $8.06
= 204,417 units

Break-even point in dollars = break-even point in units times the average selling price of the units
= 204,417 × $35
= $7,154,595

3. Is the variable cost per unit covered by the selling price that Kenney is offering?

With regard to the *capacity* of Empire Accessories, Barry had determined that he could produce as many as 300,000 handbags without having to add additional machines or expand his plant. Up to this limit, he could increase his production from its current level at 255,000 units without incurring additional fixed costs; he would incur only additional variable costs—that is, additional direct labor, direct materials, and variable manufacturing overhead. If his overall capacity was 300,000 bags and he was presently producing 255,000, an additional 5,000 could be produced without incurring any additional fixed costs. Therefore, Empire would be well within its *relevant range*.

As Barry had calculated, the average variable cost per unit to be sold was $26.94. Therefore, since Kenney was offering $30 per unit, the sale would be beneficial to Empire, because it would result in a contribution margin of $3.06 per unit ($30.00—$26.94). Since Barry was already above the break-even point, this would mean additional profit of $15,300 (5,000 × $3.06). Barry recognized that his actual profits might be lower because he would probably have to incur overtime to produce

FIGURE 23.5
Empire Accessories, Inc.
Additional Profit Calculation

$$\text{Pretax profit} = \text{sales} - (\text{fixed costs} + \text{variable costs})$$

$$\frac{\text{Fixed costs} + \text{desired pretax profit}}{\text{Average contribution margin}} = \text{Break-even units to achieve desired profit}$$

Desired pretax profit = $550,000

Fixed costs + desired pretax profit = $1,647,600 + $550,000 = $2,197,600

Average contribution margin = $8.06

Therefore;

$$\text{Break-even units to achieve desired profit} = \frac{\$2{,}197{,}600}{\$8.06} = 272{,}655$$

the goods on schedule. Nevertheless, he figured that producing the extra 5,000 handbags would be to his benefit, not only because he would increase his profits but because he would demonstrate to Kenney that he was capable of handling a large order and producing it on time. In the future, they might do more business with him.

When will you reach your goal in profits? Barry also realized that he could use break-even analysis to determine the level of sales necessary to reach his targeted goal of $550,000 in net income. He did this using the following formula:

$$\frac{\text{Fixed costs} + \text{desired profit}}{\text{Average contribution margin per unit}} = \text{Units of sales to achieve the desired profit}$$

Barry knew that he could divide his fixed costs by his contribution margin to achieve his break-even level of sales. So, if he simply added his desired profit to his fixed costs and divided that sum by the contribution margin, it should yield the number of units required to cover fixed costs and generate the desired profit.

$$\frac{\$1{,}647{,}600 + \$550{,}000}{\$8.06} = 272{,}655 \text{ units}$$

The calculation is summarized in Figure 23.5. This indicated that Barry would have to sell 272,655 units at full price in order to reach a pretax profit of $550,000. Once again, Barry had to ask himself the following questions:

- Is this within the company's capacity? *Yes.*

- Is this within the company's relevant range; that is, can these units be produced without an increase in fixed costs? *Yes.*

It is important to note that once Empire was beyond its break-even point profits could be increased very quickly by increasing the volume. In Empire's case, with an average contribution margin of $8.06 per handbag, an additional 5,000 handbags sold at the normal selling price would increase profits by $40,300 (5,000 × $8.06).

The impact of reducing costs. Once Barry had completed the foregoing analyses, he began to reason that if he could better control his costs, this would have substantial impact on his profitability. The more he reduced his variable cost per unit, the higher his contribution margin would be. Furthermore, the more he reduced his fixed costs, the sooner he would reach the break-even point and show profits on the bottom line. Barry made the following calculations.

Barry estimated what the impact would be if he *reduced his average variable costs* per unit from $26.94 to $25.94, representing only a 4% reduction in variable costs. First, it would increase his contribution margin by $1.00 and reduce the number of units necessary to break even. And if he sold the same number of units, it would dramatically increase his profitability. This can be seen in the following example:

$26.94 − $25.94 = $1.00 added to the contribution margin
$8.06 + $1.00 = $9.06

$$\frac{\$1{,}647{,}600}{\$9.06} = 181{,}854 \text{ units to break even}$$
versus 204,417, previously

(204,417 − 181,854) = 22,563 × $9.06 = $204,420 additional profit.

Barry made another calculation. He calculated what would happen to his profitability if he were able to *reduce fixed costs* by 10%. His fixed costs were presently $1,647,600; reducing these by 10% would yield fixed costs of $1,482,940. The difference of $164,760 would fall to his bottom line.

Barry realized that small reductions in variable and fixed costs could have a substantial impact on his overall profitability once he had reached the break-even point. The reduction in this break-even point meant he could take on more orders like the one from the Kenney Company and still contribute to profits. Now, he could begin to evaluate ways of increasing his profits by reducing costs, by increasing his sales price, or by increasing the sale of more profitable items in order to get a better sales mix and a higher average contribution margin.

Constructing a Break-Even Chart

Barry constructed a break-even chart to demonstrate the relationships that he had just discovered. The components of the chart are illustrated in Figure 23.6. Drawing A represents fixed costs; Drawing B represents variable costs. Drawing C combines Drawings A and B to illustrate the fact that variable costs have to be considered *in addition* to fixed costs. Therefore, the variable costs line begins not at the origin but where the fixed costs line reaches the vertical axis. Finally, Drawing D shows that sales revenues generally increase in direct proportion to the number of units sold. As a practical matter, the line representing sales is apt to be curved, representing the fact that some sales may be made at a discount like those made to the Kenney Company. In such a case, sales dollars would not increase in direct proportion to the units sold.

Figure 23.7 shows all these components combined. To the right of the break-even point, the difference between sales and total cost is profit.

FIGURE 23.6
Break-Even Chart Components and Steps

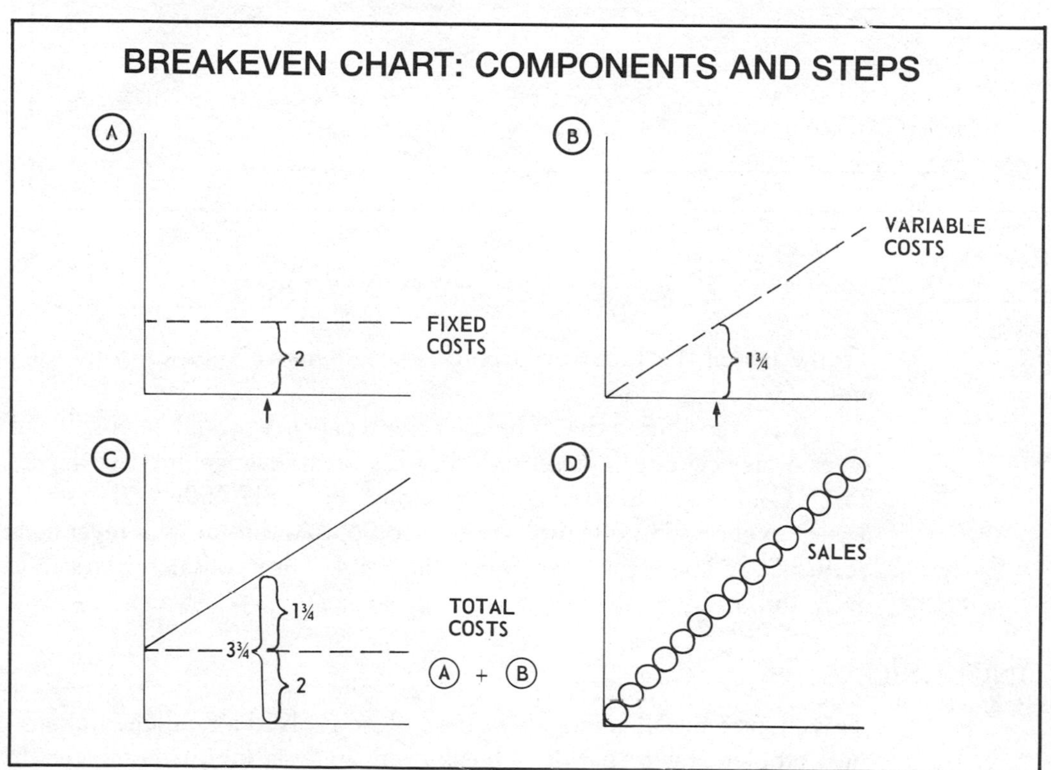

FIGURE 23.7
Break-Even Analysis Break-Even Point

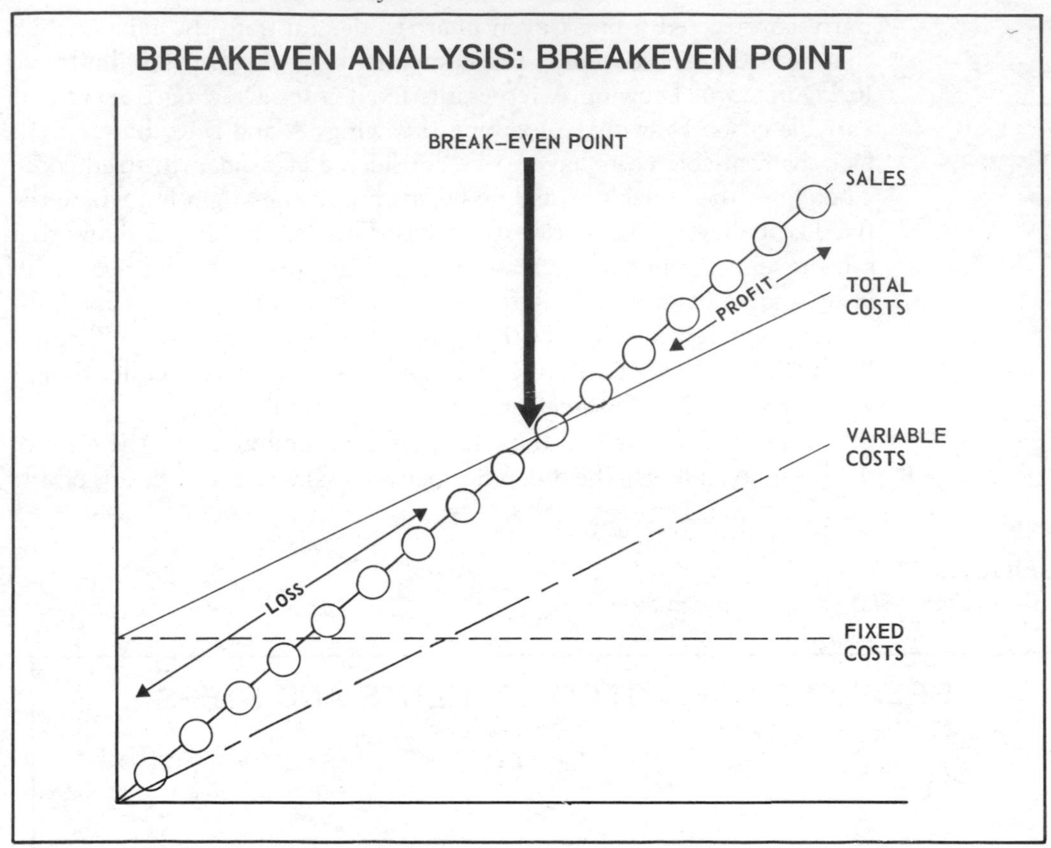

To the left of the break-even point, the difference between total sales and total cost is a loss.

Barry recognized that if he used graph paper, it would be possible to prepare an accurate representation of his break-even point (see Figure 23.8). On the graph, fixed costs are shown at $1,647,600; total costs, at a sales level of 255,000 units, are $8,516,960. And total sales revenue is $8,925,000. The break-even point is at 204,417 units of sales, or revenue of $7,154,595.

CONCLUSION

This chapter has illustrated how Barry Rosen solved a fundamental business problem by preparing a break-even analysis for his company. In order to do this Barry did the following:

1. Classified costs as fixed and variable. Semivariable or mixed costs he separated into their fixed and variable components.

FIGURE 23.8
Break-Even Chart Empire Accessories, Inc.

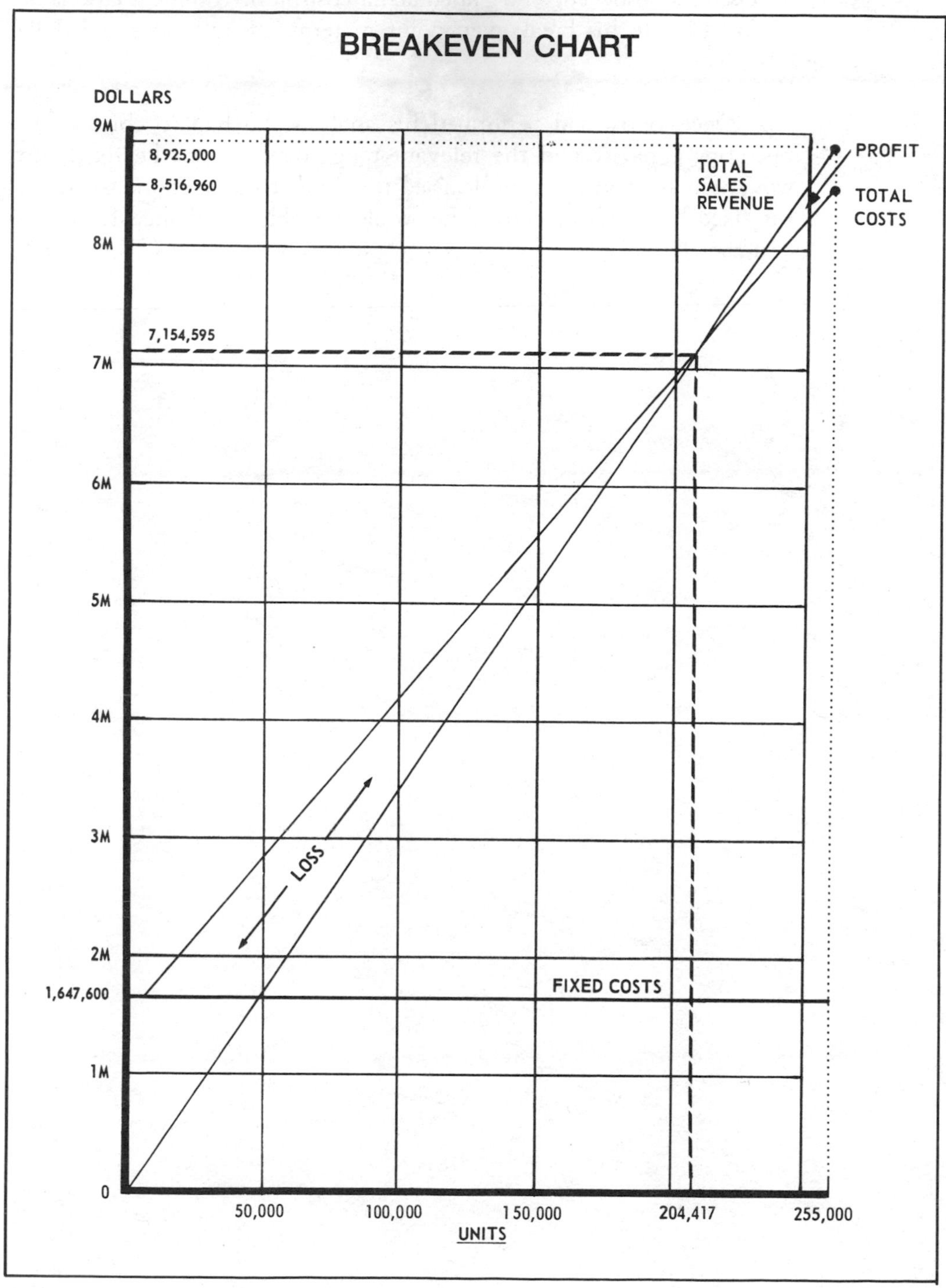

2. Calculated a contribution margin for the company.
3. Used the knowledge he gained about cost/profit/volume relationships to calculate his break-even point in terms of unit sales and dollar volume.

Once Barry had performed his analysis, he had to consider the operating capacity and the relevant range over which the fixed costs would remain constant. He learned that with modest efforts to control his fixed and variable costs, he would be able to change his profits dramatically.

24

Managing Working Capital

The working capital of any business is the capital required to fund its current assets. Current assets are defined as either cash or those assets that can be converted into cash within the current fiscal year, including marketable securities, accounts receivable, and inventories. *Working capital*, therefore, is the capital that allows the business to operate on a day-to-day basis.

Net working capital is the difference between the current assets of the business and its current liabilities. Current liabilities are those liabilities that must be paid in the current fiscal year, including accounts payable, accrued liabilities, short-term debt, and the current portion of long-term debt. Net working capital is the portion of current assets that are funded by sources other than current liabilities.

Management of working capital, therefore, is the management of the current assets and the current liabilities of the company. We have already discussed the management of cash, receivables, inventory, and accounts payable. This chapter extends the discussion to consider the following:

- How to decide how much money should be invested in current assets.
- How that money should be spread among the categories of current assets.
- How the current assets should be financed.

Figure 24.1 illustrates the composition of net working capital and shows

FIGURE 24.1
Financing Relationships in a Typical Small Business

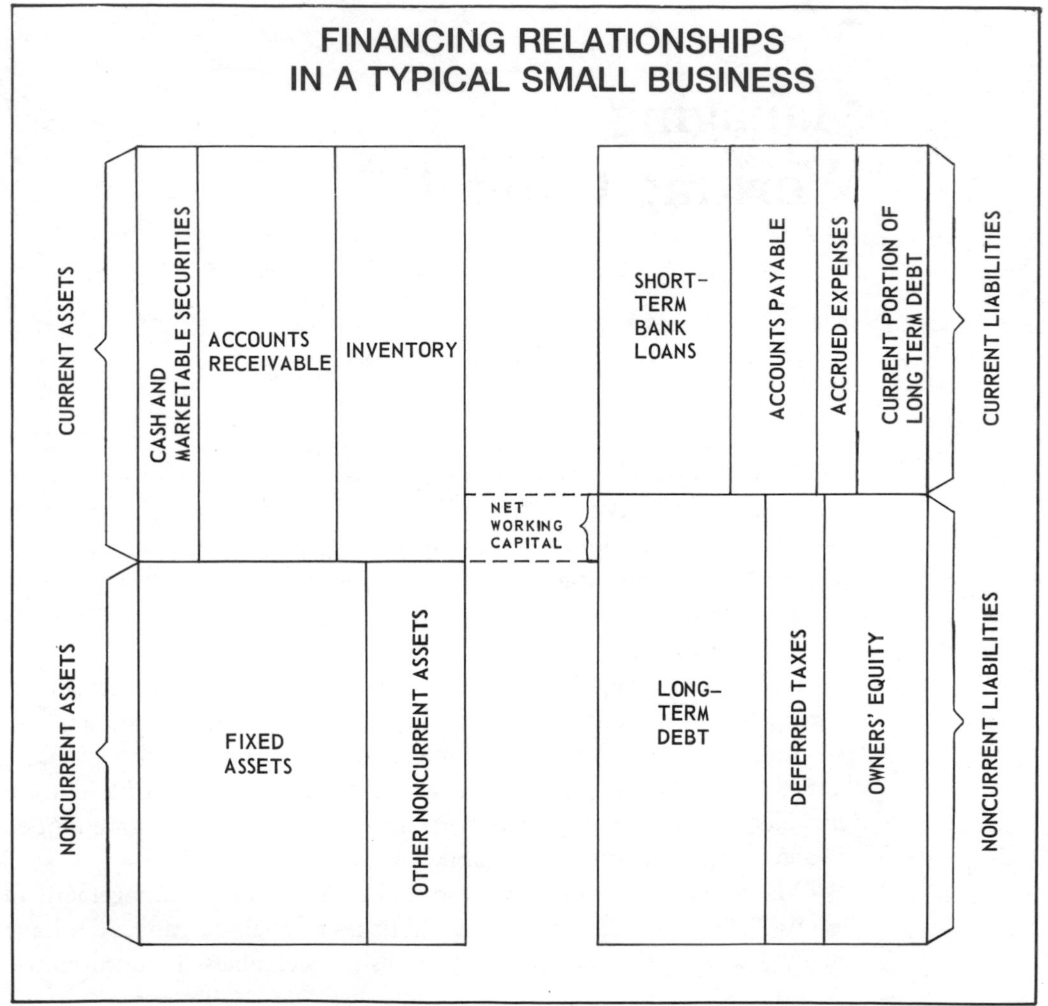

the relationships of current assets to noncurrent assets and of current liabilities to noncurrent liabilities. The figure shows that the net working capital of the business is funded by the owner's equity and a certain amount of long-term debt.

WHY WORRY ABOUT WORKING CAPITAL?

Working capital is important to you as an entrepreneur for the following reasons:

1. Very often, current assets can represent 50% or more of the total assets of a company. In this case, controlling your working capital means controlling the business.
2. There is a direct relationship between increases in sales volume and increases in working capital requirements. Increased sales mean increased receivables that have to be financed and increased inventories that have to be purchased to use in the production of sales. A sudden or unexpected increase in sales volume can overstrain your company's working capital; you may then have to obtain additional working capital quickly.
3. Your working capital must be managed carefully so that you will be able to meet your current obligations as they become due. If you do not have access to funds through a line of credit with your bank or another short-term debt source, and if you cannot collect your receivables or manufacture and sell your inventories quickly, then you could run out of cash and not be able to pay your payroll.
4. Careful management of working capital can significantly reduce your interest expense by releasing dollars invested in receivables and in raw materials and work-in-process inventories. Figure 24.1 shows that current assets are largely funded by short-term bank loans and the current portion of long-term debt, both of which bear interest. Some companies have estimated that the total carrying costs for receivables and inventory can be as much as 25% of their value when this interest is added to storage, handling, and other charges. Therefore, a reduction in the level of receivables and inventories can result in a reduction in debt and a reduction in interest costs and other carrying costs.

How to Improve Your Management of Working Capital

You can make substantial improvements in managing your working capital by using a few simple techniques described in this chapter. One of the first steps is to develop your own working capital improvement target, such as a 10% increase in sales without any additional inventory or receivables and thus no additional bank financing. Another goal could be a 10% reduction in receivables or inventories and bank financing, while maintaining sales at their current level. Before starting on the offense, however, it is wise to have a sound defense. One good defensive move is to *construct a formal contingency plan for a working capital shortage* that might happen unexpectedly. A sample contingency plan might include the following:

1. *Develop a list of vendors who may be willing to grant you more liberal terms in a credit crunch*. The more important you are as a customer and the longer your business relationship, the more likely the vendor is to say yes.
2. *Develop a list of customers who may be willing to accept prebilling or progress billing arrangements.* The customers most likely to be cooperative are those to whom you represent an important supplier or with whom you have a long-standing relationship.
3. *Notify your banker and work closely with him or her*. If you are borrowing from your bank on an unsecured basis, develop a list of available collateral that might cause the banker to be willing to advance more funds. Also list any fixed assets available for a sale-and-leaseback transaction.
4. *Evaluate and list your personal resources that may be available to be used in the short run.*
5. *Develop a list of inventory, either raw materials or finished goods, that could be sold to raise cash quickly.*

How Much Working Capital Do You Need?

How much should you invest in working capital? In each of the various categories of current assets? To answer these questions, it is important first to know the following about your business:

- The cash-to-cash cycle.
- The seasonal and permanent working capital needs.
- The trade-off between liquidity and risk.

Cash-to-Cash Cycle

It is important to look at working capital as a continuous flow of funds. Consider, for example, The Schooltime Company, which manufactures school clothes for children between the ages of six and twelve. Schooltime's cash-to-cash cycle (the length of time between its purchase of raw materials and collection of its accounts receivable) is illustrated in Figure 24.2. Notice that on April 1, Schooltime orders its raw materials—

FIGURE 24.2
The Schooltime Company Cash-to-Cash Cycle

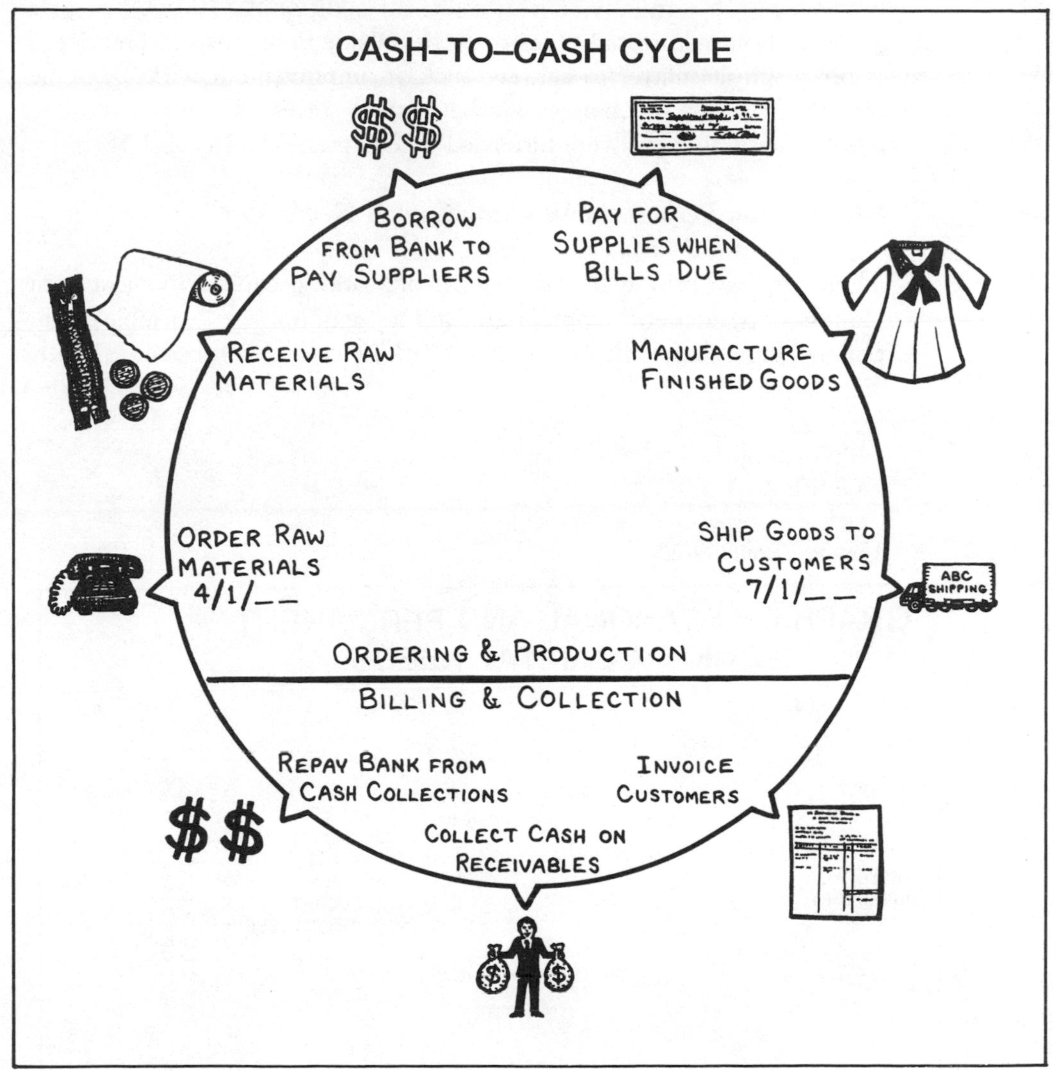

fabric, zippers, buttons, and so on. After receiving these materials, it borrows from its bank to finance its inventories, and pays its suppliers. It begins manufacturing and builds up a substantial finished goods inventory, which it ships to stores on July 1 for the back-to-school season. Schooltime then bills its customers, receives cash from customers, repays its loan, and deposits the remainder in the bank.

A key to successful working capital management is to increase the number of cash-to-cash cycles the business can achieve each year. For example, if Schooltime has $1 million in inventory and receivables that it can turn over four times a year and if it earns 10% on each turn, its gross profit will be $400,000. If the company can speed up the process by one more turn annually, it can make an additional $100,000 of gross profit without additional investment or outside financing. In practice, it is not a simple matter to achieve such an improvement without implementing a series of changes at the critical stages in the cash-to-cash cycle. These changes were discussed in Chapters 15, 16, and 18.

Seasonal and Permanent Working Capital Needs

There are two principal components of working capital in most companies: a "permanent" component and a "seasonal" or "variable" component. Figure 24.3 illustrates these working capital components for the

FIGURE 24.3
Graph of Seasonal and Permanent Working Capital Needs

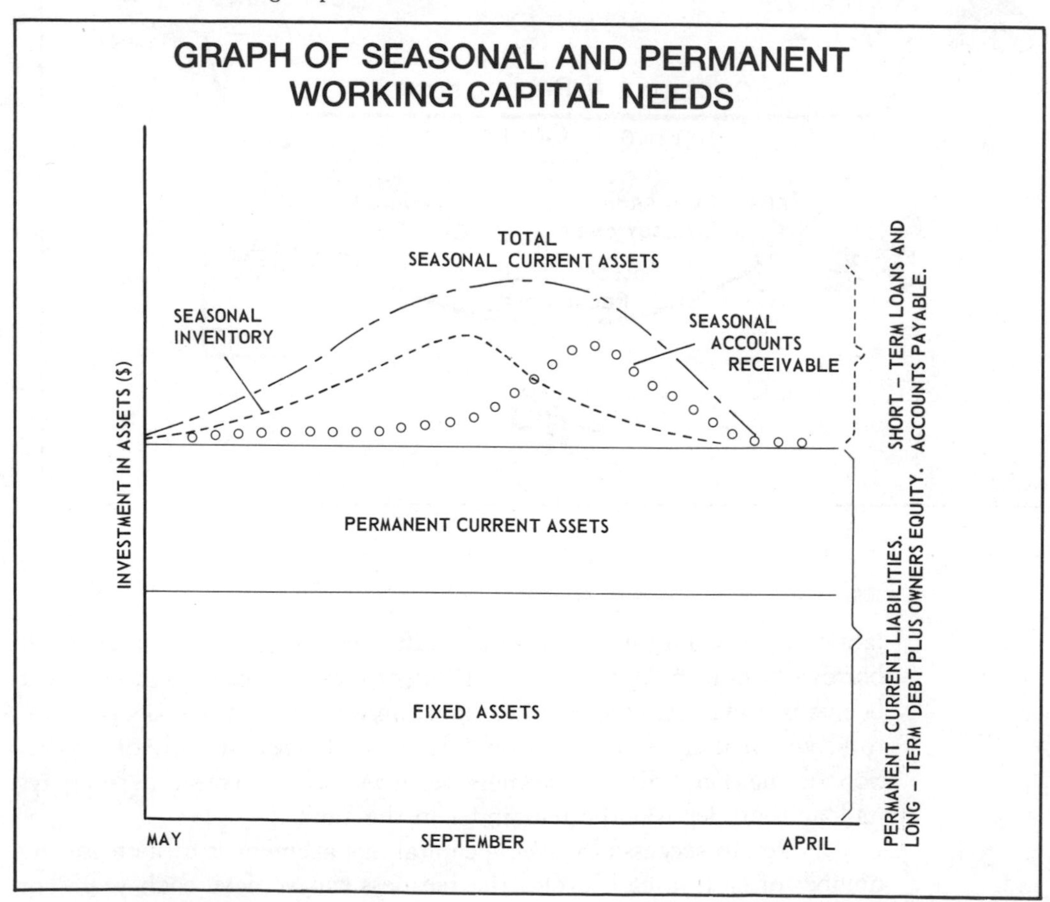

Schooltime Company. In the cash-to-cash cycle for Schooltime, a major portion of the activity occurs in the spring and summer months where there is a build-up in inventories for the back-to-school season. Therefore, in addition to the normal level of receivables and inventories, there is a periodic increase in raw material and work-in-process inventories in the late spring or early summer and a corresponding increase in accounts receivable in the late summer or early fall. The normal level of receivables and inventories during the rest of the year can be referred to as the permanent component of working capital, whereas the periodic increases in accounts receivable and inventories represent the seasonal working capital requirements. The figure also indicates that the fixed assets and permanent current assets of the company are financed by permanent current liabilities (the normal level of accounts payable and accrued expenses, as well as the current portion of long-term debt plus long-term debt and owner's equity. The seasonal working capital needs are financed by additional short-term loans and seasonal increases in accounts payable.

Because the need for working capital increases as sales volume increases, permanent working capital really represents the minimum level below which working capital should never drop unless the company begins to reduce its overall operations or begins permanently to manage its working capital more effectively.

The Trade-off Between Risk and Return

Another important concept in the management of working capital is the trade-off between the risk and the return on investment in current assets. An investment in inventory and accounts receivable generally provides more gross profit to the business than an investment in short-term financial securities, such as Treasury bills (T-bills) or negotiable certificates of deposit. If the business is generating a profit of 15 to 20% (calculated as income before taxes divided by total sales), then it is better to invest your funds in inventory and receivables that contribute to this gross profit instead of investing in short-term financial securities. T-bills currently yield somewhere in the range of 8 to 11%. Therefore, theoretically, your investments in such financial securities should be minimized and your investments in the business or in noncash assets maximized. (If you cannot earn more, on average, on business assets than on financial assets, there is the legitimate question of why you do not sell your business and simply invest the funds. See Chapter 25, which discusses the concept of capital budgeting and illustrates how to calculate a rate of return on your investment in your business).

On the other hand, there is a greater risk associated with an investment in receivables and inventories, because receivables must be collected and inventories must be manufactured and sold. Investments in government securities are considered to be highly liquid, which means that you can convert them into cash quickly. Therefore, keep in mind that the higher return associated with an investment in receivables and inventories is tempered by the increased risk and the reduced liquidity.

HOW TO DETERMINE YOUR WORKING CAPITAL REQUIREMENTS

The answer to the basic question of determining working capital requirements cannot be resolved by using a simple formula. Businesses differ in terms of their products and services, seasonal factors, and various other characteristics. Analyzing how much working capital is appropriate is a matter of analyzing these individual characteristics and how they affect the business. Consider the following important factors:

The length of your manufacturing process or your cash-to-cash cycle. It is important to know how long an item of your inventory will be on the balance sheet before it is used in production, sold, and converted into cash. For example, a manufacturer of heavy construction equipment has a far longer cash-to-cash cycle than does a manufacturer of nuts and bolts.

The seasonality of your business. The seasonal peaks in the operations of your company have an impact on the level of seasonal working capital required.

The unit cost of your product or service. The greater the unit cost of your product or service, the higher your working capital requirements will be. This is because the greater the number of units you have to maintain, the higher will be overall value of your inventories. In addition, the higher the value of the product, the greater the value of receivables. (In a service business, people are your "inventory.")

Your inventory turnover. This is the time between the purchase and the sale of an item of inventory. It represents the production portion of the cash-to-cash cycle. Working capital requirements will be significantly affected by your industry and company practices with respect to inventory turnover, and by the success that your company has in keeping its inventory turning at a quick pace.

Your receivables turnover. This is the time between the sale of an item and the collection of cash (the billing and collection portion of the cash-to-cash cycle). The level of working capital that you require will be directly affected by how quickly your accounts receivable are converted to cash.

This is also a function of management and industry practices. For example, the garment and textile industries, which have 60-day credit terms or longer, require much more working capital than a company with 10- to 30-day terms. The credit terms of a small business cannot usually vary significantly from industry practice.

Your purchases, or payables, turnover. Working capital loan requirements can be dramatically affected by changes in your suppliers' demands for funds payable. A tightening of purchase terms, such as reduction from 45 days to 30 days in accounts payable turnover, would, by reducing the funds provided by current liabilities, significantly increase the amount of working capital loans required from other sources. Similarly, an extension of credit terms by your suppliers from 30 days to 45 days would reduce your working capital loan requirements because it would increase accounts payable.

Risks and hazards inherent in the business. In a risky business, which could mean a new and unfamiliar field of endeavor for your company, you should establish a working capital reserve. Such a reserve, or cushion, would consist of working capital sources that could be accessed quickly to minimize the potential disturbance from unexpected swings in the business.

Your banking relationships for lines of credit. A company can prudently reduce its risk of insolvency (inability to meet current obligations as they become due) by arranging in advance for a bank line of credit to meet unexpected demands for working capital. The line of credit allows the business to borrow funds when needed. This eliminates having to maintain a surplus in cash in anticipation of unexpected changes in working capital requirements.

The growth rate of your business. The rate at which a company is expanding has an impact on its working capital requirements. In most cases, small and medium-sized businesses that are growing quickly find that their working capital needs are always slightly outpacing their ability to provide such capital from operations and trade creditors.

Current business conditions. These conditions include the current and anticipated state of the economy, interest rates, industry trends, and the nature of your business. Rising interest rates mean that it will be more costly for you to fund receivables and inventories. Therefore, smart management of working capital increases the emphasis on reducing inventories, collecting receivables, and arranging for working capital sources if a recession is anticipated.

It is difficult to quantify the impact of each of these factors on the working capital of a particular business. However, it is important to be aware of their impact and to make sure that you consider them when establishing working capital requirements with your banker.

Financing Current Assets

As discussed, seasonal working capital requirements are generally funded through lines of credit, short-term debt, and increases in accounts payable. "Permanent" working capital is funded, in part, by "permanent" current liabilities and by long-term debt and owner's equity.

An important concept to remember is to *match the maturity of your source of financing to the maturity of the assets to be financed.* If you borrow short-term, use those funds for assets that will be converted to cash soon enough to repay the loan. Use short-term credit to finance current assets and long-term credit for fixed assets, such as plant and equipment. It is dangerous to use short-term financing for long-term needs, because your creditors may be unwilling to renew your loans when they come due. Also, depending on general economic circumstances, short-term interest rates may be too high to allow you to refinance and still to operate profitably. Long-term financing for seasonal needs would sacrifice flexibility and would increase the overall cost of borrowing because long-term debt does not fluctuate with seasonal demands for funds.

DO YOU SOMETIMES HAVE SURPLUS CASH?

If you never have surplus cash, then you either have an extremely unseasonal business or you have a problem of insufficient capital in your business. Even companies that struggle to manage their finances for most of the year usually have cash surpluses for short periods. When you have a cash surplus, you have the opportunity to earn interest from a wide range of investment alternatives. But do not invest until you define your investment objectives and rank in order of priority the benefits you are seeking. Unless special circumstances prevail, rank your priorities as follows:

1. *Security* should be the top priority. Can you afford to lose the investment? How risky is it? U.S. Treasury bonds and notes are generally rated as the most secure investments, having virtually no risk of default.
2. *Maturity* should be the second priority. Will you have your cash back when you need it?
3. *Liquidity* is the third priority. Can you turn the investment into cash quickly and without penalties if you need cash sooner than the maturity date?

4. *Yield* should be your fourth and lowest priority because it is less critical than security and liquidity. Also, interest rates on short-term risky investments are generally not high enough to justify the risk. For example, the interest on a risky $100,000 investment for one month at 20% would be $1,666. A safe investment at 10% would yield $833 over the same period. Why risk the $100,000 principal for an extra $833 in taxable interest income?

You must carefully analyze the trade-off between risk and return before investing surplus cash.

Where to Invest Surplus Cash

Eight important investment options are discussed in this section. They differ to some extent in denomination, safety, maturity, and various other ways, as summarized in Figure 24.4. All these investments, known as money market instruments, are highly marketable and relatively low in risk, however.

U.S. Treasury bills. Treasury bills (T-bills) account for the largest fraction of the money market—the market for short-term credit instruments. They are popular because of their safety, high trading volume, and variety of maturities. The bills are sold in denominations of $10,000 and up and are traded in a broad secondary market handled by registered securities dealers and banks. However, if you sell them before maturity, you may suffer from temporary market fluctuations. The Treasury auctions its T-bills weekly, offering standard maturities of *91 days* and *182 days*. One-year bills are sold periodically. Subsequently, these T-bills are traded. Because of the broad secondary market and the weekly auctions, you can purchase T-bills to mature in almost any week you want during the coming months.

T-bills do not pay interest. Instead, they are sold at a discount from their par value. At maturity, the holder collects the full face value. In this way, you earn a return on your investment. For example, you may purchase a 91-day T-bill now for $9,650 and receive $10,000 in 91 days. This $350 profit for 91 days (one quarter of a year) is roughly equivalent to $1,400 ($350 multiplied by 4) annually, or 14½% interest ($1,400 divided by $9,650).

Federal agency issues. Various federal agencies also issue securities. Like T-bills, most of these securities are sold at a discount price, but agency issues give an effective return slightly higher than T-bills. Government security dealers and banks who maintain secondary markets in T-bills also maintain secondary markets in federal agency securities. Agency issues, however, are not a legal debt of the U.S. Treasury and are not

FIGURE 24.4
Selected Surplus Cash Investment Vehicles For the Smaller Business

Investment	Description	Denominations	Safety	Maturity	Liquidity	Yield	State Taxation	Basis
U.S. Treasury Bills	U.S. government obligations	$10,000 to $1 million	Virtually complete	3 and 6 months, sold weekly; 1 year, sold monthly	Large active market	Varying recently from 8% to 12%	No	Sold at discount: traded at market value
Federal Agency Issues	Bonds, notes, and debentures from 6 major federal agencies	Most are $10,000 and up	Considered to be government guaranteed	6 months to 10 years	Large active market	10 to 40 basis points (0.1% to 0.4%) above T-bills	Varies	Either discounted or interest-bearing
Commercial Paper	Unsecured interest-bearing notes of large corporations	$25,000 to $5 million	Very high; backed by financially strong corporations	3 to 270 days	Lack of Liquidity	Above T-bills and below bank's prime rate	Yes	Sold at discount
Certificates of Deposit	Interest-bearing obligations of banks; similar to time-deposits, but negotiable	$100,000 to $1 million	High to very high; backed by large banks	3 months to 1 year	Active market for large denominations and major banks	Above T-bills Wide variation between different CDs	Yes	Sold at par; interest-bearing; traded at market value
Bankers' Acceptances	Draft instructing bank to pay acceptance holder	$25,000 to $1 million	Very high; backed by 2 or 3 financially strong parties	30 to 270 days	Market centered in New York	20 to 50 basis points (0.2% to 0.5%) above T-bills	Yes	Discounted
Repurchase Agreements	Agreement by government securities dealer to sell and repurchase securities	$100,000 and up	Very high; government security collateral	1 day or more	The repurchase date can be set in advance to meet the investor's needs.	Low but a flexible investment	Yes	Contract
Tax-exempt Obligations	Bonds and notes from state and city governments; exempt from federal income tax	$1,000 and up	Ranges from excellent to unacceptable	2 months to several years	Ranges from high to none	Tax exemption can lead to effective yield	No, if issued in own state	Usually interest-bearing
Money Market	Private funds pooling investors' money to purchase money market securities	$1,000 to $5,000 minimum	Usually high; depends on fund's investments	All investments 1 year or less	Often completely liquid without prior notice	Typically 0 to 0.5% below commercial paper yields	Yes	Sold and redeemed at par; interest-bearing

guaranteed by the government. Because of their slightly higher risk, the short-term issues of federal agencies usually offer a yield that is 10 to 40 basis points higher than the current T-bill rate. A basis point is equal to 1/100 of a percentage point on an interest rate; therefore, 10,000 basis points equal 100%. The term is used to simplify the comparison of rates of return on different investments. Therefore, federal agency issues yield a return 0.1% to 0.4% higher than T-bills. Federal agency securities are generally sold in denominations of $10,000 and up.

Six principal federal agencies issue short-term securities:

- *The Federal National Mortgage Association* (FNMA or "Fannie Mae") buys and sells mortgages guaranteed by the Federal Housing Administration (FHA) and the Veterans Administration (VA).
- *The Government National Mortgage Association* (GNMA or "Ginnie Mae") provides conventional mortgage money for homeowners.
- *Federal Land Bank* (FLB) extends long-term credit to Federal Land Bank associations. These associations then make long-term loans to farmers. Typical FLB bonds mature in about ten years.
- *Federal Home Loan Bank* (FHLB) sells notes with 9- and 12-month maturities, as well as bonds with 3- to 5-year maturities. The FHLB then lends these funds to their member savings and loan associations.
- *The Federal Intermediate Credit Bank* (FICB) sells nine-month debentures each month and then lends the funds to credit associations and agricultural credit corporations.
- *The Banks for Cooperatives* (BC) issue six-month debentures once or twice a month.

Money market funds. In 1973 and 1974, interest rates on 90-day commercial paper and negotiable certificates of deposit (discussed later) rose substantially above 10%. Many smaller investors wanted to obtain these high yields but did not have the $100,000 minimum investment necessary to purchase most of these investments. To meet this need, several investment companies formed money market funds that pooled the small investments of thousands of investors and then purchased short-term money market instruments. The money market funds offer several advantages:

- *Low minimum investment*—typically $1,000 to $5,000.
- *Liquidity*—In most funds, investors can withdraw at will, subject to processing delays.
- *Relatively high safety*—Most funds invest in a wide variety of very safe securities. The variety of investments also helps to decrease risk by eliminating the investors' dependence on a small number of securities.

- *High yield*—The money market funds can afford to buy the high denomination ($1 million and up) investments that offer the highest yields. In addition, by buying in large quantities, dealer commissions as a percentage of transaction size are reduced. The fund itself, however, adds its own service charge that offsets some of these savings.
- *Convenience*—Professional money managers make the investment decisions, thus relieving the individual investor or company cash manager of this job.

In this way, money market funds allow you to conveniently earn a high return on your surplus funds. Most money market funds advertise extensively in financial periodicals.

Bankers' acceptances. A bankers' acceptance is a draft that instructs a bank to pay a specified amount of money to the owner of the acceptance at a specified future date. The bank signs the draft in acceptance of its obligation to make this payment. Bankers' acceptances arise out of the following types of transactions:

- To finance exports or imports.
- To finance the storage of goods in international trade.
- To finance the storage of goods in domestic trade.
- To facilitate foreign currency exchange.

Bankers' acceptances are considered very safe, because almost everyone connected with them is responsible for their ultimate payment. Primary responsibility rests with the accepting bank. However, the original drawer, often a foreign trader, is also responsible. Furthermore, if a dealer buys the acceptance from the bank and later sells it to an investor, the dealer is also responsible in case of default by the bank or the original drawer.

The standard maturity on bankers' acceptances is 90 days, and denominations begin at $25,000. Because acceptances are actively marketed, an investor can usually purchase an acceptance on the open market with a maturity of less than 90 days. Bond dealers and many large banks maintain a market in bankers' acceptances; this provides greater liquidity. Bankers' acceptances typically yield 20 to 50 *basis points* (0.2 to 0.5%) above the T-bill rate.

Commercial paper. Commercial paper is the popular name for short-term, unsecured promissory notes issued by industrial, commercial, financial, and banking corporations. Because commercial paper is unsecured, only the largest and most creditworthy corporations can successfully sell these notes. Maturities on corporate paper range from a few days to nine months, but the most popular maturities are three to six or nine months. Most commercial paper is sold at a discount and offers an effective interest rate somewhat higher than the current T-bill rate. Corporations occasionally issue commercial paper in denominations as small as $25,000. However, the denominations for most commercial paper range from $100,000 and up. Moody's and Standard & Poor's, which are bond-rating agencies, also rate commercial paper.

Corporations sell their commercial paper either directly to the buyer or to dealers. Only the most financially sound corporations can sell their paper directly, but this route accounts for the largest dollar volume of transactions. Smaller corporations sell their paper through dealers who investigate carefully the financial strength of all potential issuers. They select only issuers who meet their high standards of financial condition, reputation, and size.

Because of the large percentage of commercial paper placed directly, there is a very small secondary market. Therefore, those who buy commercial paper should generally expect to hold it to maturity. This makes it less satisfactory for the small business than more readily marketable securities.

Negotiable certificates of deposit (CDs). A negotiable certificate of deposit (CD) is an interest-bearing obligation of a commercial bank. It is similar to a time deposit except that it is negotiable—that is, the original buyer can sell the CD to a third party. A CD proves that the owner has a specified amount of money on deposit in a bank for a specific period of time and at a specified rate of interest. Generally, the maturity of CDs ranges from 30 to 360 days.

Certificates of deposit offer higher yields than T-bills and roughly the same yields as commercial paper. However, the interest-rate range from the lowest quality to the highest quality CD can be as much as 75 basis points (three quarters of 1%). Three factors determine the quality of a CD:

- The size and reputation of the issuing bank.
- The maturity date. Companies prefer CDs that mature just before monthly and quarterly tax payment dates. Because the demand is higher for these CDs, the yield on them is lower.
- The denomination; the most popular denomination is $1 million.

There is a large, secondary market for CDs. Therefore, substantial holdings may be traded in a single transaction. This makes CDs of large denomination relatively more liquid but decreases the liquidity of smaller CDs. Some dealers will not buy CDs in denominations under $500,000, nor will they buy the CDs of smaller banks. Banks initially sell their certificates of deposit at par or face value and offer to pay interest at maturity. If the original buyer then decides to sell the CD, market forces determine the price, which can be at a discount on a surplus over par.

Repurchase agreements. A repurchase agreement (a "Repo") is a contract between a government security dealer, often a bank, and an investor, usually a corporation. The dealer sells U.S. Treasury or other securities to the investor and agrees to repurchase those securities for a specified price on a specified future date. In this way, the dealer can finance his large inventory of government securities, and you as the investor can get an essentially risk-free investment with any maturity you choose and with a yield approximately equal to the yield on negotiable CDs. In most cases, the repurchase agreement specifies the repurchase date in advance; it can even be an overnight transaction. Therefore, you should enter into repurchase agreements only when you can plan your cash needs accurately and in advance.

Tax-exempt obligations. City and state governments and their agencies can issue bonds on which the interest is exempt from U.S. income tax. *If your company has an effective* 50% tax rate, tax-exempt interest is worth double its stated value. For instance, if you invest $100,000 in a 10% taxable bond, you earn $10,000 in a year and must pay $5,000 tax, leaving $5,000 net profit. On the other hand, if you invest the same $100,000 in a 5% tax-exempt security, you receive $5,000 in one year but pay no federal tax. Therefore, you are left with the full $5,000. In this case, the 5% tax-exempt security supplies the same after-tax income as the 10% taxable security.

To calculate the taxable-equivalent rate for a tax-exempt security, multiply the rate on the security by the factor: 1 ÷ (1 − Your Effective Tax Rate). You can then compare the result with the rate offered on taxable securities. In the foregoing example, multiplying 5% by $1 \div (1 - 0.50) = 5\% \times (1 \div 0.5) = 5\% \times 2 = 10\%$.

The creditworthiness of tax-exempt securities ranges from excellent to completely unacceptable. You can find estimates of the credit risk of tax-exempt obligations in standard bond-rating tables such as those prepared by Moody's or Standard & Poor's. The liquidity of tax-exempt obligations ranges from very good to none at all. Therefore, get expert advice before purchasing such securities.

Shopping in the Money Market

The easiest way for you to buy money market securities, T-bills, and federal agency securities is through the investment department of your bank, although you can buy these securities directly. You can purchase commercial paper directly from a number of large corporations and finance companies. For example, General Motors Acceptance Corporation and Household Finance Corporation both issue commercial paper directly. In addition, you can purchase certificates of deposit and bankers' acceptances directly from the issuing bank.

CONCLUSION

The purpose of this chapter has been to define working capital and explain how it relates to your business. The chapter has described:

1. How understanding your company's cash-to-cash cycle is fundamental to management of working capital.
2. The difference between "seasonal" and "permanent" working capital and the trade-off between risk and return in your investment in current assets.
3. How working capital is financed.
4. Those factors to consider in determining the working capital requirements for your business.
5. Where to find working capital funds.
6. Where to invest surplus cash.

Essentially, the chapter has dealt with the concept of working capital in general terms. The amount of working capital that your business requires depends on many factors, including the seasonality of the business, receivables, inventory and payables turnover, the unit cost of your product, your growth rate, the degree of risk in the business, and your current business conditions. The chapter has provided some areas to consider, but only you can determine the right amount of working capital for your business and only you can find the sources of funding.

25

Your Long-Term Use of Capital

Chapter 24 covered your effective use of short-term assets or working capital investments. This chapter considers your effective use of capital invested in long-term assets or projects on which returns are expected to extend beyond one year—for example, new plant and equipment, advertising campaigns, or research and development programs. These investments require your careful consideration because they are important to the growth of your company and because they generally require large capital outlays in anticipation of high investment returns. This chapter shows you how to use the techniques of *capital budgeting*—the process that will help you to make important decisions regarding alternative long-term investments.

You will often be faced with alternatives for the use of your capital. Sometimes, these alternatives will be mutually exclusive—that is, if you decide to expand your plant, you may have to forgo an enhanced advertising campaign, or if you invest heavily in research and development, you may not be able also to buy a computer to improve your record keeping. You will probably have to make choices. If one of your major objectives is to maximize your investment in your business (your equity), then you will choose the long-term investment alternative or project that will provide the greatest return to your business and to you. The process of choosing, referred to as capital budgeting, is not easy because projects or investments differ in size (dollars involved), duration, and timing of the return on the investment. Therefore it is hard to compare them on a consistent basis—to compare apples to apples. But there are some simple techniques that can help you. This chapter describes three of those techniques, including a discussion of their related strengths and limitations. They are:

- The payback method.
- The internal rate of return (IRR) method.
- The net present value (NPV) method.

WHAT ARE CASH FLOWS?

Before describing techniques for capital budgeting, we must establish some ground rules. The discussion of each technique will refer to *cash flows*. It is important to understand just what is meant by this term. For each project or investment, there will be a cash outflow—money spent to fund the investment. If you buy equipment or add to your plant, the money will flow out in large amounts, either to pay the invoice for the equipment or to finance construction of the plant. If you invest in a research and development program, you may pay out money over an extended period of time—for the salaries and benefits of the researchers to buy supplies and miscellaneous equipment.

Cash outflow, therefore, includes all payments associated with the project or investment, with one exception—the payments made to finance the investment. If you purchase a machine or other major piece of equipment, borrow the money to do so at the bank, and then pay off the loan, consider that you pay for the item in one lump sum when you pay the invoice. If you were to count the loan principal payments as outflows, too, then you would be double counting. And do not count the interest payments on the loan either because, as you will see later in the chapter, the techniques will have already considered your cost of capital. To consider the interest payments as additional outflows would also be double counting.

After you have calculated the amount of your investment (your cash outflow), you must estimate the return on that investment, often referred to as the cash inflow, or simply the "cash flow" from the investment. As a practical matter, the cash flow from the investment may be one of two types: (1) an additional inflow, or (2) a reduction in outflow.

An advertising program, a research and development program, or the purchase of a machine designed to increase efficiency or productivity illustrates the first type of cash flow because each would be undertaken to increase sales or revenues. The acquisition of a computer, a move to a less expensive location, or the acquisition of machinery and equipment to replace labor are all intended to reduce costs by substituting cheaper processing modes for more expensive ones or by allowing for growth without commensurate increases in costs.

The calculation of cash outflows and inflows is made more complex by income tax laws. For example, depreciation on plant and equipment is deductible as a noncash expense for tax purposes. An investment tax credit is another noncash item that reduces your tax liability. The tax savings from both should be considered as cash inflows in calculating the return on your investments.

A simple example illustrates cash outflows and inflows. Suppose you are considering the purchase of a new machine at $15,000 to replace an older machine that initially cost $11,000. You have taken $5,000 depreciation on the old machine, so its present book value is $6,000. In addition, assume that you can sell the old machine for $2,000, which means that you will lose $4,000 on the sale. This loss, however, is deductible for tax purposes. So if your marginal tax rate is 46%, you have a tax benefit of $1,840 ($4,000 × 0.46). Assume also that you can take an investment credit on the new machine of 10% of its value, or $1,500. This is an additional cash inflow. Therefore, your net outflow is as follows:

Cost of new machine	$15,000
Less: proceeds from sale of old machine	(2,000)
Tax effect of loss on sale	(1,840)
Investment tax credit on new machine	(1,500)
Net cash outflow	$ 9,660

Consider two points. You will not realize this tax saving until it is time to pay your taxes, but you "incur" that saving when you buy the new machine. Also, even though you lost money on the sale of the old machine, the amount of the loss is independent of this new investment decision, with the exception of the tax benefit indicated.

Presumably, this new machine will increase your sales (or reduce your costs); in addition, it will provide a deduction from taxable income for depreciation. Offsetting these additional cash inflows are the costs of the additional sales, the tax effect of additional profits, and possibly the additional working capital required to finance larger inventories and receivables.

Therefore, if you can increase production by 2,500 units with the new machine and if you can sell the product for $2.00 each, then your sales will increase by $5,000. If your total cost is $2,700, the net income from these additional sales is $2,300. Consider that the additional tax on this increased revenue is 46% × $2,300, or $1,058. Finally, assume that your annual depreciation on the machine, on a straight-line basis, is $1,000 ($15,000 − $3,000 salvage value ÷ 12 years); the related tax effect is a saving of $460 (46% × $1,000). In sum, your cash inflows for the next 12 years would be as follows:

Increase in cash collections from sales (2,500 × $2)	$5,000
Increase in operating expenses	2,700
Net operating cash flow	$2,300
Less: additional income tax	1,058
After tax operating cash flow	1,242
Plus: tax savings from depreciation	460
Net cash inflow	$1,702

The numbers used in this example may be affected by the tax legislation of 1986. With respect to cash flow, however, the principle remains the same.

The techniques discussed in the following sections compare the net cash inflows and outflows to evaluate the return on your investments. Comparisons among these returns can help you to select among alternative investment opportunities.

PAYBACK: A QUICK AND EASY METHOD

The payback method (or the payback period) is the simplest capital budgeting tool to use. The payback period is the number of years it will take to recover your original investment. It can be calculated in one of two ways:

- *Method 1*. The payback period equals the dollars you intend to invest divided by the annual cash flow into the business that results from that investment. This method is useful when the cash flow is expected to be level over a period of years.

initial value of the investment. This method is used when the cash flow from the investment is expected to fluctuate—to be low in early years and higher in later years, or vice versa.

The following two examples help to illustrate the concept.

Example 1: How Prince Automotive Parts Figured Its Payback On Buying a Minicomputer

Prince Automotive Parts, Inc., a distributor of automotive replacement parts, is considering acquiring a minicomputer for $50,000 to assist in monitoring and controlling its inventory. The president of the company believes that the minicomputer will generate cost savings of $12,500, after taxes, per year, which would represent the salary of the one clerk to be replaced by the automation. He figures that these net cash savings will extend for approximately seven years, which is roughly the effective useful life of the minicomputer in his business. As a practical matter, he knows he will be able to use the minicomputer for many more years, although after seven years he may wish to replace it with a newer, more efficient piece of equipment. What is the payback on the minicomputer? The formula is as follows:

$$\text{Payback} = \frac{\text{Investment (\$)}}{\text{Annual cash flow (\$)}}$$

$$\text{Payback} = \frac{\text{\$50,000 (Investment)}}{\text{\$12,500 (Annual savings)}} = 4 \text{ years}$$

Comments. In this example, Prince Automotive Parts, Inc. receives three years' benefit after recovering its original investment (seven years minus four years payback). This illustrates one of the drawbacks of the payback method: namely, its calculation does not take into account the expected useful life of the investment. The payback calculation simply tells the president how fast he will recover his investment. The result would be the same if the computer were useful for five years or ten years.

Example 2: How Prince Automotive Parts Recalculated Its Payback Using Method 2

Because there will be certain inefficiencies in the start-up of the computerization process, the president has recalculated the expected cost savings, and he now believes they will be only $6,000 and $7,000 in the first two years, respectively, and $9,000 for each year thereafter. What is the payback?

Year	Cash flow	Cumulative Cash Flow
0	($50,000)	($50,000)[a]
1	6,000	(44,000)
2	7,000	(37,000)
3	9,000	(28,000)
4	9,000	(19,000)
5	9,000	(10,000)
6	9,000	(1,000)
7	9,000	8,000

[a] Year 0 is the time when the initial investment is made.

The *formula* is: Payback equals the point at which the cumulative positive cash flow is equal to the initial investment. Therefore, payback is slightly more than six years, or approximately six years and 1½ months as a result of the change in the cash flow assumptions.

Comments. This method requires a more detailed year-by-year analysis of cash flows.

BAIL-OUT: A VARIATION OF THE PAYBACK METHOD

There is a variation of the payback method, called the *bail-out method*, that addresses some of the weaknesses of payback. It answers the question: "At what point will I have all of my money out of the project?" The calculation of bail-out is basically the same as the second payback method, except that it calculates the point at which cash inflows *plus the salvage value* of the investment (the actual or estimated value at which the used asset can be sold) equals the initial investment. This technique may be used to make a choice between two or more investments—for example, between acquisition of a special purpose machine or a general purpose machine. The general purpose equipment may have a higher salvage value because the market for resale may be broader. Therefore, a bail-out analysis might tip the scales in favor of this alternative.

Conclusions on Payback

The payback method is easy to calculate and understand, but it can lead to the *wrong decisions*. It ignores the timing of cash flows, the useful life of the investment, and the generation of cash flows beyond the payback period. The discussions that follow, relating to the time value of money, further illustrate the limitations of the payback method.

Because the deficiencies of this method outweigh the advantage of its simplicity, it should not be used independently in capital budgeting. It may, however, be used in conjunction with either the net present value or internal rate of return method (to be discussed) to determine *how quickly* you will recover the funds that you invest. Even used in this way, however, payback should not be used to determine profitability of an investment; one of the other two methods provides a better approach to that analysis.

PRESENT VALUE: THE TIME VALUE OF MONEY

As we have seen, a major shortcoming of the payback method is that it ignores the timing of cash flows. Timing is important because the value of money changes over time. For example, if someone were to offer you $909 now or $909 a year from now, which would you take? You would probably take the funds now. Why? Because you could take that $909 now and put it into the bank, a money market fund, or some other similar investment opportunity at, for example, 10% interest. A year from now you would have (to the nearest dollar) $1,000 (the future value of that $909). Money is worth more to you now than later because *if you have it now, you can put it to work*. If you get it later, you lose the return

FIGURE 25.1
The Present Value of $1 Due at the End of N Years

N(period)	*5%*	*7%*	*10%*	*12%*	*15%*	*17%*	*20%*	*22%*	*25%*
1	0.952	0.935	0.909	0.893	0.870	0.855	0.833	0.820	0.800
2	0.907	0.873	0.826	0.797	0.756	0.731	0.694	0.672	0.640
3	0.864	0.816	0.751	0.712	0.658	0.624	0.579	0.551	0.512
4	0.823	0.763	0.683	0.636	0.572	0.534	0.482	0.451	0.410
5	0.784	0.713	0.621	0.567	0.497	0.456	0.402	0.370	0.328
6	0.746	0.666	0.564	0.507	0.432	0.390	0.335	0.303	0.262
7	0.711	0.623	0.513	0.452	0.376	0.333	0.279	0.249	0.210
8	0.677	0.582	0.467	0.404	0.327	0.285	0.233	0.204	0.168
9	0.645	0.544	0.424	0.361	0.284	0.243	0.194	0.167	0.134
10	0.614	0.508	0.386	0.322	0.247	0.208	0.162	0.137	0.107
12	0.557	0.444	0.319	0.257	0.187	0.152	0.112	0.092	0.069
14	0.505	0.388	0.263	0.205	0.141	0.111	0.078	0.062	0.044
16	0.458	0.339	0.218	0.163	0.107	0.081	0.054	0.042	0.028
18	0.416	0.296	0.180	0.130	0.081	0.059	0.038	0.028	0.018
20	0.317	0.258	0.149	0.104	0.061	0.043	0.026	0.019	0.012

that you would have had if you had put it to work immediately. Therefore, it is important to know the timing of cash flows because the faster cash flows in from an investment, the faster you can put it to work and the greater your potential return will be.

Looking at this from the opposite perspective, to compare the future value of dollars with today's dollars, you must reduce those future dollars back to their present value. This means that $1,000 received a year from now is equivalent to $909 received today. Generally, the present value of a stream of cash flows is computed as follows:

Present value = Future value of cash flows × Present value interest factor (PVIFs)

The appropriate PVIF can be found in a table that represents the present value of a dollar received at various times in the future. Figure 25.1 is a sample of such a table. More detailed tables are available in finance and accounting textbooks or through your local banker.

HOW CAN YOU USE THE PRESENT VALUE TABLE?

The present value table in Figure 25.1 displays interest rates across the top and years down the left-hand side. The various present value interest factors (PVIFs) form the body of the table; the appropriate PVIF can be found by finding the intersection of the relevant interest rate and the number of years. For example, assume that you can invest money at an interest rate of 15% and that the project you are considering returns $10,000 in year 1, $20,000 in year 2, and $30,000 in year 3. Then the appropriate PVIF is 0.870 in year 1, 0.756 in year 2, and 0.658 in year 3. The present value is calculated as follows:

Present value (PV) = Cash flow for year 1 × PVIF for year 1 + Cash flow for year 2 × PVIF for year 2 + Cash flow for year 3 × PVIF for year 3

PV = $10,000 (0.870) + $20,000 (0.756) + $30,000 (0.658)
PV = $8,700 + $15,120 + $19,740
PV = $43,560

Even if you are trying to calculate a present value and do not have a table available, you can easily calculate the present value by using the following formula:

$$PV = \frac{\text{Cash flow for year 1}}{1 + r} + \frac{\text{Cash flow for year 2}}{(1 + r)^2} + \frac{\text{Cash flow for year 3}}{(1 + r)^3} + \text{etc.}$$

• *Method 2*. The payback period equals the point at which the cumulative positive cash flow resulting from the investment is equal to the

Where r = the rate at which you can invest the cash flow. Using the example just developed:

r = 15%
Cash flow for year 1 = $10,000
Cash flow for year 2 = $20,000
Cash flow for year 3 = $30,000

$$PV = \frac{\$10{,}000}{1.15} + \frac{\$20{,}000}{(1.15)^2} + \frac{\$30{,}000}{(1.15)^3}$$

PV = $ 8,695.65 + $15,122.87 + $19,725.49
PV = $43,544.01*

*There are minor differences due to rounding of the factors used in the table.

If you wish to find the present value of *monthly* cash flows, you can make r equal the *monthly* interest rate (annual rate divided by 12) and use monthly rather than annual cash flows.

Therefore, your conclusion will be that, if you can invest money at 15%, you will be as well off taking $43,560 now as you will be taking $10,000 in year 1, $20,000 in year 2, and $30,000 in year 3. Without this analysis, you might think that $60,000 received over three years was a better deal than $43,560 received right now. However, the analysis indicates that they are essentially equivalent, *provided you can invest the cash inflows at 15%.*

This present value analysis, often referred to as *discounting* is basic to the net present value and internal rate of return methods of capital budgeting. These techniques convert all expected cash inflows from investment projects into time-adjusted, equivalent dollars. Therefore, they make it possible for you to compare and rank alternative investment opportunities, *using the same basis of comparison.*

COMPARISON OF PRESENT VALUE TO PAYBACK

As discussed, a major criticism of the payback method is that it does not take into account the time value of money. For example, the payback method would not distinguish between the following two projects, each having a cost of $5,000 and total returns of $6,000. The payback in either case would be three years. Yet, using the present value technique, Project B would be preferable because its cash flows are higher in the early years. These early incremental cash flows could then be reinvested to earn additional income.

Year	Project A	Project B
1	$1,000	$2,000
2	1,000	2,000
3	3,000	1,000
4	1,000	1,000
	$6,000	$6,000

Another criticism of the payback method is that it ignores the useful life of the investment and the generation of cash flows beyond the payback period. For example, the payback method cannot distinguish between the following two projects that both cost $7,000 and have the following cash flows:

Year	Project C	Project D
1	$2,000	$2,000
2	2,000	2,000
3	3,000	3,000
4	3,000	
5	3,000	

In either case, the payback period would be three years.

And if the cash flows for Project C were instead as follows, the payback method would favor Project D, which has a shorter payback period.

Year	Project C	Project D
1	$2,000	$2,000
2	2,000	2,000
3	2,000	3,000
4	4,000	
5	3,000	

However, use of the present value calculation shows Project C to be the more profitable investment in either instance. Assuming that these cash flows can be reinvested at an interest rate of 15%, the present value (PV) calculations are as follows:

$$\text{PV (Project C)} = \$2{,}000\ (0.870) + \$2{,}000\ (0.756) + \$2{,}000\ (0.658) + \$4{,}000\ (0.572) + \$3{,}000\ (0.497)$$

$$\text{PV} = \$1{,}740 + \$1{,}512 + \$1{,}316 + \$2{,}288 + \$1{,}491$$

$$\text{PV} = \underline{\underline{\$8{,}347}}$$

or, using the formula:

$$PV = \frac{\$2{,}000}{1.15} + \frac{\$2{,}000}{1.323} + \frac{\$2{,}000}{1.521} + \frac{\$4{,}000}{1.749} + \frac{\$3{,}000}{2.011}$$

$$PV = \$1{,}739.13 + \$1{,}511.72 + \$1{,}314.92 + \$2{,}287.02 + \$1{,}491.80$$
$$= \$8{,}344.59$$

Whereas:

$$PV\ (\text{Project D}) = \$2{,}000\ (0.870) + \$2{,}000\ (0.756) + \$3{,}000\ (0.658)$$
$$PV = \$1{,}740 + \$1{,}512 + \$1{,}974$$
$$PV = \underline{\underline{\$5{,}226}}$$

or, using the formula:

$$PV = \frac{\$2{,}000}{1.15} + \frac{\$2{,}000}{1.323} + \frac{\$3{,}000}{1.521}$$

$$PV = \$1{,}739.13 + \$1{,}511.71 + \$1{,}972.39$$

$$PV = \underline{\underline{\$5{,}223.24}}$$

Clearly, Project C is preferable to Project D ($8,347 vs. 5,226).

Why Does Money Have a Time Value?

Why is money worth more today than later? As illustrated, it is worth more because *you can invest it at some rate of interest.* (This concept should not be confused with the fact that your money may be worth less in the future due to inflation; money has a time value whether or not the economy experiences inflation.) However, the interest rate that you receive for a particular investment will depend on the general level of interest rates and the supply and demand for money in the economy. Another factor that affects the interest rate is the level of risk associated with the investment. The risk relates to the probability that the actual returns in the future will be lower than expected. The interest rate on U.S. Treasury bills is often referred to as a risk-free rate. All other investments carry higher rates because they include a risk premium for their increased levels of risk.

The present value changes with the assumed interest rate. Generally, the present value of money received at some future time *decreases as the interest rate increases*, given a certain payment date or period. The present value changes with the assumed interest rate because these rates include a

FIGURE 25.2
The Relationship of Discount Factors and the Time Value of Money

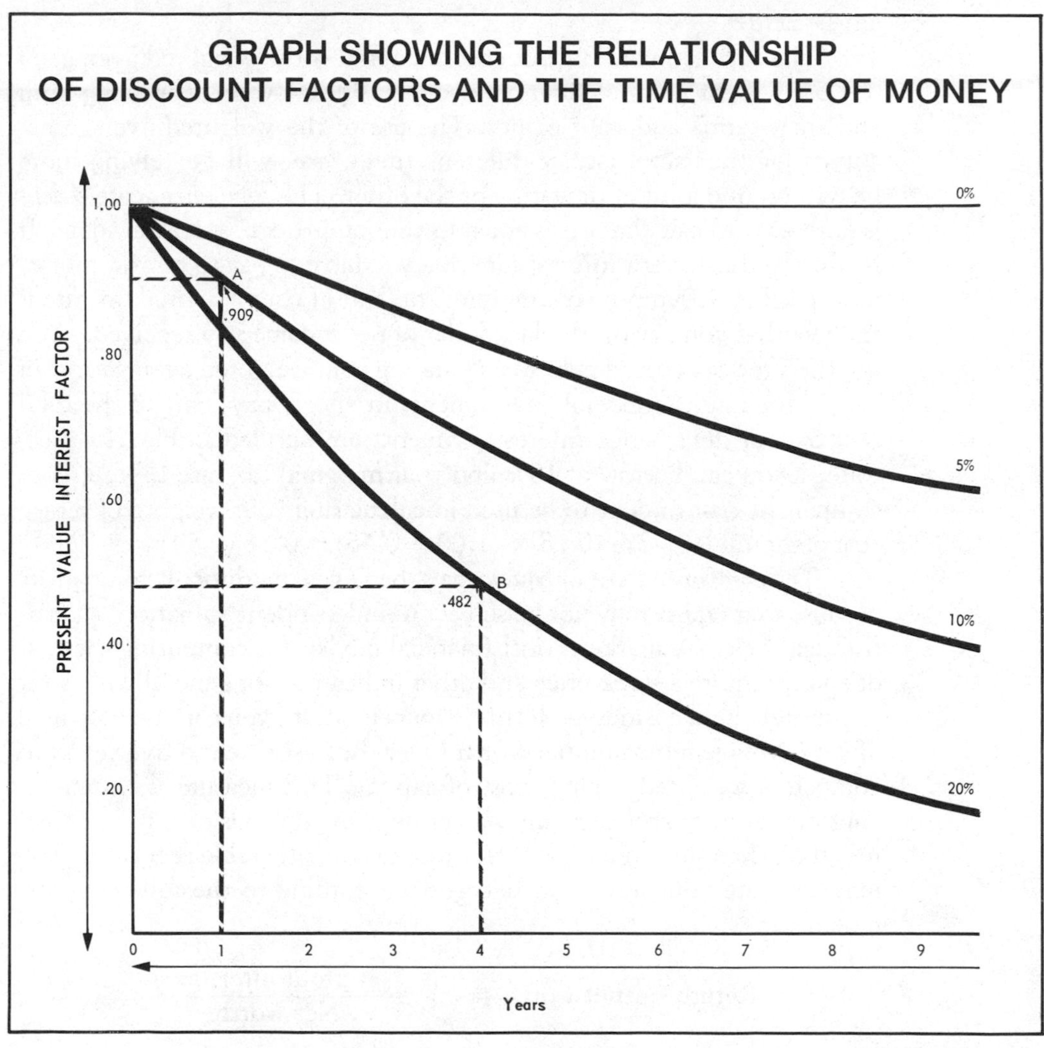

risk premium for their increased levels of risk. Figure 25.2 shows that at a zero interest rate, there is no difference between receiving a dollar four years from now or receiving a dollar now. Yet, with a 20% interest rate, a dollar received four years from now would be worth the equivalent of only $0.482 in today's terms.

Selecting a hurdle rate. What is the appropriate interest rate for you to use in your present value analyses of capital investment opportunities? Basically, it is your *hurdle rate*—the minimum rate of return that you feel you must earn on an investment. At the very least, your hurdle rate should equal *your marginal cost of capital*—what it costs you to acquire the funds you want to invest. If you accept an investment that offers you a rate of return that is *less than* your cost of capital, you are losing money on that investment.

The best estimate of your cost of capital is the weighted average of the component costs of financing your business—your debt (long-term and short-term) and your equity. The use of the weighted average accounts for the fact that, at different times, you will be relying more heavily on one form of financing or the other. The *component cost of debt* is fairly easy to calculate. It is equal to your after-tax cost for new debt. It is equal to the current interest rate that you have to pay to borrow money multiplied by 1.0 minus your marginal tax rate. (Your marginal tax rate is the rate that you pay on the last dollar of net income you received.) You use the after-tax cost of debt in calculating your weighted average cost of capital because the federal government, in effect, pays part of the total cost of your debt, since interest payments are tax deductible. To illustrate, if you can borrow at 18% and your marginal tax rate is 46%, your component cost of debt to be used in calculating your weighted average cost of capital is 9.72% (0.18 × (1.00 − 0.46) = 0.18 (0.54) = 9.72%).

The *component cost of equity* may, however, be difficult to quantify because your equity may not be subject to independent valuation, such as through the stock market. Most financial models for computing the cost of equity require a stock price and other indicators not generally relevant to privately held businesses. If this is your situation, you can use the value of your average return on net worth (over the past three to five years) to compute a weighted average cost of capital. This measure is, in effect, your opportunity cost of retaining earnings in your business rather than investing them in some other enterprise or in marketable securities. You may compute your return on net worth according to the following formula:

$$\text{Return on net worth} = \frac{\text{Net profit after taxes}}{\text{Net worth}}$$

Typically, this component cost of equity is higher than your component cost of debt, because there is additional risk, and therefore an additional risk premium, associated with equity financing. This relates to the fact that in the event of liquidation, creditors have a priority claim, above the owners, on the assets of the business.

Once you have computed your component costs of both debt and equity, you may calculate your weighted average cost of capital by multiplying the cost of debt by the percentage (or weight) of debt in the financing of your business and the cost of equity by the percentage of equity.

For example, assume that your cost of debt is 9.72%, as computed above, and your cost of equity is 17%. And consider that your financing structure is composed of 60% debt and 40% equity. Then your weighted average cost of capital (WACC), to be used in capital budgeting, can be calculated as follows:

Weighted average cost of capital

$$\text{(WACC)} = \text{Cost of debt} \times \text{\% of debt} + \text{cost of equity} \times \text{\% of equity}$$

$$\text{WACC} = (0.0972)(0.6) + (0.17)(0.4)$$
$$\text{WACC} = 0.05832 + 0.068$$
$$\text{WACC} = 0.12632 \text{ or } 12.6\%$$

NET PRESENT VALUE METHOD

Net present value is the first of the two capital budgeting methods discussed in this chapter which take into account the time value of money. To implement this technique, you can use the following formula:

> The *net present value* of a project (NPV) = (the sum of the present value of its future cash inflows and outflows)

The interest rate (or hurdle rate) that you use to determine the present value of the future cash flows should be your weighted average cost of capital or your minimum hurdle rate. Therefore, if the *net present value* is zero or greater, your project will yield a rate of return that is equal to or greater than your hurdle rate. However, if the net present value is negative, the project will return less than the hurdle rate and you should probably seek a better alternative.

The net present value method and the internal rate of return method (discussed in the next section) are superior to the payback method, even though they are a bit more time-consuming to calculate, but it is important to recognize when using these techniques that particular projects do not necessarily have to be evaluated against other projects. They can be evaluated individually to determine whether they measure up to your company's hurdle rate. If the net present value is positive, then you may undertake the project (if you have the money to fund it, of course). In the case of two alternative projects, the one with the greater net present value is preferable. A sample calculation of the net present value is provided in Example 3.

Example 3: How Fashion Garment Decided to Invest in a New Product Line

Fashion Garment Co., Inc. (Fashion) is considering manufacturing and marketing a line of knitted tops and sweaters. The company anticipates that this undertaking will result in additional sales of 4,250,000. The new line will require a permanent working capital investment of $40,000 to fund inventory and receivables. Also, the necessary machinery, which must be purchased, will cost $50,000. Fashion's hurdle rate is 15%. Fashion believes the after-tax net cash flow in the new line will be $20,000 for each of the first six years and $15,000 for each of the following four years. There will be no salvage value on the machinery. Should Fashion invest in the new product line? The following calculation of the net present value provides the answer:

Year	Cash Flow ×	Present Value Interest Factor	=	Cumulative Time-Adjusted Cash Flow	Time-Adjusted Cash Flow
0	($50,000) [a]	1.000		($50,000)	($50,000)
1	(40,000) [b]	0.870		(34,800)	(84,800)
1	20,000	0.870		17,400	(67,400)
2	20,000	0.756		15,120	(52,280)
3	20,000	0.658		13,160	(39,120)
4	20,000	0.572		11,440	(27,680)
5	20,000	0.497		9,940	(17,740)
6	20,000	0.423		8,640	(9,100)
7	15,000	0.376		5,640	(3,460)
8	15,000	0.327		4,905	1,445
9	15,000	0.284		4,260	5,705
10	15,000	0.247		3,705	9,410
	$90,000	Net Present Value =			$ 9,410

[a] Machinery cost.
[b] Permanent working capital investment in year 1.

Cash flow column. This column presents the cash flows described in Example 3. The working capital investment is shown as an outflow in year 1, rather than in year 0, since the build-up of inventory and accounts receivable will not actually take place until the manufacturing process begins in year 1. The working capital estimate is based on previous turnover rates for receivables and inventories, which are multiplied by the incremental sales.

Present value interest factor column. The figures in this column are taken from the present value table at Fashion's hurdle rate of 15%. The example is calculated assuming all cash flows are received at the end of the year. (Tables are also available to determine present value interest factors for monthly, weekly, and even "continuous" cash flows.)

Time-adjusted cash flow column. This column is the product of the cash flows multiplied by the present value interest factor. The cumulative total, $9,410, is the project's net present value. Notice that Fashion reaches a break-even point for the investment—where the net present value after the investment is zero—somewhere in the seventh year. In addition, it is important not to lose sight of the following assumptions that have been built into this analysis:

1. That anticipated cash flows, in fact, will be realized.
2. That those cash flows can be *reinvested* at a rate of 15%.

This analysis does not show what would happen if the hurdle rate were 10% or 20%, or what would happen if the cash flows totaled only $50,000 instead of $90,000. The latter might be the case if the start-up of the new machinery or the new product line took longer to implement than anticipated. Therefore, it is important to remember that although this analysis can help you to make a decision about investing in a particular project, *it is based on certain assumptions that actual experience may show to be incorrect.*

Comments. Fashion should invest in the new product line because the net present value, at Fashion's 15% hurdle rate, is positive. This result indicates that the time-adjusted rate of return on the project is somewhat greater than 15%. It does not tell you what the rate of return is; however, the following discussion will.

INTERNAL RATE OF RETURN METHOD

The internal rate of return (IRR) method also takes the time value of money into account. Unlike the net present value method, which assumes an interest or hurdle rate, *the internal rate of return method seeks to determine the precise hurdle rate at which the net present value will be equal to zero*. In other words, it seeks the break-even cash flow *rate*, the *rate* that causes the time-adjusted cash inflows to equal exactly the time-adjusted cash outflows, or the yield on the investment. It is calculated in part by trial and error. You can first approximate this rate of return by calculating what is known as the *simple return on investment*. This simple return is calculated by dividing the average annual cash flow by the net investment. The simple rate is actually the reciprocal of the payback method discussed earlier. Once you have calculated the simple rate, the quickest way to find the internal rate of return is to use the *straddle* technique. This involves trying rates on both sides of the simple rate. If you initially choose a rate that causes the project to show a positive net present value, you should next choose a higher rate. If you choose a rate that shows the project to have a negative net present value, you should next choose a lower rate. Once you have come very close, you can estimate the exact rate. Remember, projects should be accepted when the calculated internal rate of return meets or, more appropriately, exceeds the company's *hurdle rate*. Example 4 shows you how to compute the internal rate of return.

Example 4: Sound Systems, Inc. Wonders Whether to Move to Larger Quarters

Sound Systems, Inc., which assembles high-quality audio equipment for sale to dealers, is considering moving into larger quarters. The moving costs and leasehold improvements will total approximately $100,000. The net cash benefits to the company will be: $50,000, $40,000, $30,000, $20,000, and $20,000, respectively, over the first five years. What is the internal rate of return of the proposed move?

Year	*Cash Flow*	*At 20% Rate*		*At 23% Rate*		*At 22% Rate*	
		PVIF[a]	*PV*[b]	*PVIF*	*PV*	*PVIF*	*PV*
0	($100,000)	1.000	($100,000)	1.000	($100,000)	1.000	($100,000)
1	50,000	0.833	41,650	0.813	40,650	0.820	41,000
2	40,000	0.694	27,760	0.661	26,440	0.672	26,880
3	30,000	0.579	17,370	0.537	16,110	0.551	16,530
4	20,000	0.482	9,640	0.437	8,740	0.451	9,020
5	20,000	0.402	8,040	0.355	7,100	0.370	7,400
	$ 60,000		$ 4,460		($ 960)		$ 830

[a] PVIF = present value interest factor.
[b] PV = present value.

Comments. The internal rate of return is between 22% and 23%. For purposes of illustration let us assume the rate is 22½%. This rate of return must be compared with the firm's hurdle rate, or alternative uses for these funds. If Sound Systems' hurdle rate is 25%, it should *not* make this move (unless it has no alternative) because the internal rate of return (yield) on the investment is less than 25%. If its hurdle rate is 20%, the company *should invest* because the 22½% return is greater than 20%.

If the company is considering two alternative investments and if they both have rates of return greater than the company's hurdle rate, the one with the higher internal rate of return (yield) is preferable.

There are two other considerations regarding the internal rate of return. First, unlike the net present value method, the IRR method does not calculate the magnitude of the return to the company, only the rate of return. That is, it does not distinguish between a $10,000 investment that returns 20% and a $200,000 investment that has the same yield. Clearly, the latter is preferable because it maximizes the cash flow to the company.

Another characteristic of the internal rate of return method must be taken into account. It assumes, unlike the net present value method, that cash flows *can be reinvested at the internal rate of return*. (The net present value method assumes only that you can invest cash flows at the *hurdle rate*.) In the example of Sound Systems, the calculated rate was equal to 22½%. This calculation assumed that the $50,000 positive cash flow in year 1, as well as all later inflows, could be reinvested at 22½% for the duration of the project. If this is not the case and you can reinvest the funds at only 15%, then the actual rate of return of the project would be lower than the calculated rate. Following is a listing of the significant conditions under which the net present value and internal rate of return methods may rank projects differently because of these different underlying assumptions.

1. Project characteristics:
   - The cash flow of one project increases over time, while that of the other project decreases.
   - The projects have different expected lives.
   - The cost of one project is significantly higher than that of the other.
   - The cash flow of one project is very irregular.
2. Company characteristics:
   - The company is making investments so quickly that its "marginal cost of capital" (or hurdle rate) is increasing rapidly.
   - Capital is scarce and the business is operating under conditions of capital rationing.

A Handy Rule of Thumb

There is a handy rule of thumb for effectively using the simple return on investment method. If the actual useful life of an investment is more than twice the payback period, then the simple return on investment approximates the internal rate of return. Figure 25.3 shows, for example, that if an investment has a 20% simple return on investment, or a five-year payback (point A), and the useful life is 10 years, then the actual rate of return will be 16% (point B) (this can be obtained from Figure 25.4). The 20% simple return on investment is actually too high an approximation, but as the useful life extends beyond 10 years, the

FIGURE 25.3
Simple Return on Investment
Compared with Time-Adjusted Rate of Return

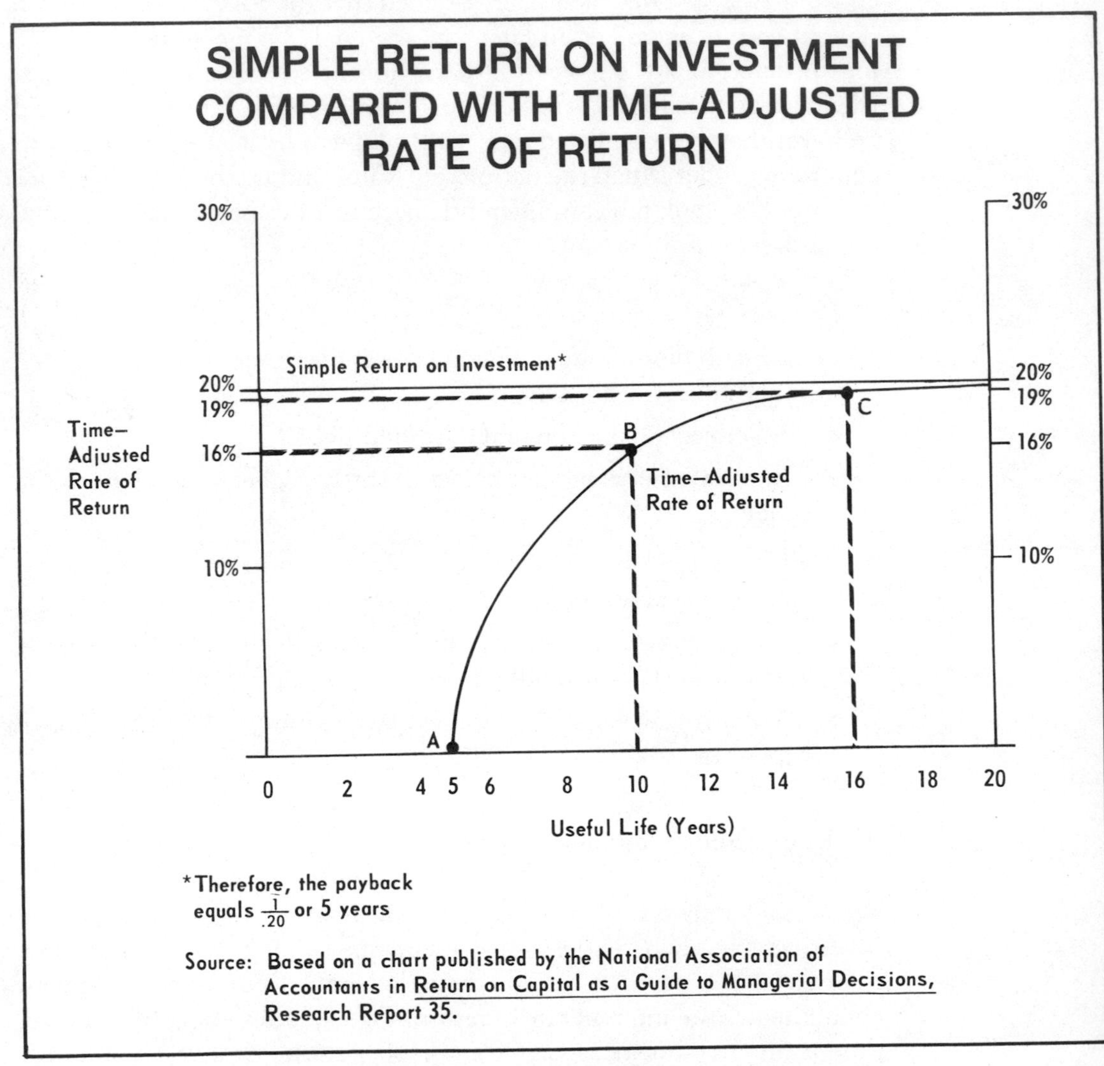

FIGURE 25.4

TABLE FOR APPROXIMATING RATE OF RETURN

NUMBER OF YEARS SAVINGS WILL LAST	¼	½	¾	1	1¼	1½	1¾	2	2¼	2½	2¾	3	3¼	3½	3¾	4	4¼	4½	4¾	5	5½	6	6½	7	7½	8	9	10	12	14	16	18	20	30
1	390	155	60	0																														
2	400	196	122	80	52	30	13	0																										
3	400	198	133	92	70	53	40	29	20	12	6	0																						
4	400	199	133	94	76	60	49	40	32	26	20	15	11	7	3	0																		
5	400	200	133	96	78	64	53	44	37	32	27	23	19	15	12	9	6	4	2	0														
6	400	200	133	97	79	66	55	47	41	35	31	27	23	20	17	15	12	10	8	6	3	0												
7	400	200	133	97	80	67	56	48	42	37	33	29	26	23	20	18	15	13	11	10	7	4	2	0										
8	400	200	133	98	80	67	57	49	43	38	34	30	27	25	22	20	18	16	14	13	10	8	5	3	1	0								
9	400	200	133	98	80	68	58	50	44	39	35	31	28	26	23	21	19	18	16	15	12	10	8	6	4	3	0							
→ 10	400	200	133	99	80	68	58	50	44	39	36	32	29	27	24	22	21	19	18	(16)	14	11	9	8	6	5	2	0						
→ 15	400	200	133	99	80	68	58	50	44	40	36	33	30	28	25	25	23	22	20	(19)	16	15	13	12	11	10	8	6	3	1	0			
20	400	200	133	99	80	68	58	50	44	40	36	33	30	28	26	25	23	22	20	19	18	16	15	13	12	11	10	8	6	4	2	1	0	
OVER 20	400	200	133	100	81	69	59	51	45	41	37	34	31	29	27	26	24	23	21	20	19	17	16	14	13	12	11	10	8	7	6	5	4	2

PAY-BACK PERIOD IN YEARS

EXAMPLE

PROJECT SAVINGS EXPECTED TO LAST 12 YEARS. COMPUTED PAY-BACK PERIOD IS 4.7 YEARS. ENTER TABLE USING NEAREST VALUES, I.E. USE 10 YEARS FOR SAVINGS AND 4¾ YEARS FOR PAY-BACK PERIOD. TABLE SHOWS 18% RATE-OF-RETURN.

actual rate and the approximate rate become closer. Notice that the rate is 19% when the useful life is 15 years.

In summary, the payback method has significant drawbacks because it fails to consider the timing and duration of cash flows. The internal rate of return method does not consider the magnitude of the investment and assumes reinvestment of cash flows at the internal rate of return, which may be unrealistic. *The net present value method*, despite the assumption that the inflows are invested at the company's hurdle rate (the weighted average cost of capital), *is perhaps the most reliable method to use.*

NET PRESENT VALUE (NPV) UNDER CONDITIONS OF UNCERTAINTY

When you project cash flows associated with a particular capital project, it is usually wise to use your most realistic guess. Sometimes it might make more sense to develop alternative assumptions (e.g., an "optimistic-realistic-pessimistic" type of analysis), to attach probabilities to each alternative cash flow, and to multiply the calculated net present value of that cash flow by the probability associated with it.

Assume, for example, that you must decide between Projects A and B, which have the following characteristics:

	Project A			*Project B*		
	Probability	*NPV*	*Expected Value*	*Probability*	*NPV*	*Expected Value*
Optimistic	25%	$150,000	$ 37,500	75%	$150,000	$112,500
Middle Ground	50%	90,000	45,000	0%	—	—
Pessimistic	25%	75,000	18,750	25%	25,000	6,250
			$101,250			$118,750

- In each case, the net present value is based on the cash flow assumed and discounted at the company's hurdle rate.
- All alternative cash flows are discounted at the same rate.
- The NPV is multiplied by the related probability factor to arrive at the expected value.
- The expected values for each project are totaled.
- These totals are the expected net present values and would be compared as in the other examples.
- Based on the given characteristics, *you would choose Project B.*

ARE YOU MAKING THE RIGHT CAPITAL INVESTMENT DECISION?

You can answer this question by monitoring and evaluating the capital investments you have made. It is important to review and evaluate your investments in this way because it:

1. Gives you feedback to evaluate the effectiveness of your capital budgeting and planning process.
2. Points out weaknesses in your forecasting techniques that may result from either habitual optimism or pessimism.
3. Enables you to compare actual results with expected results and to identify areas for improvement.
4. Alerts you to unanticipated problems in other areas of your business being caused by the new project.

Few if any major projects turn out exactly as planned for a variety of reasons (e.g., interest rate changes, the economy, energy costs), many of which are not within your control. A review of how your key assumptions turn out will help you to fine tune your capital investment planning process, however.

PRECAUTIONS AND OTHER CONSIDERATIONS

Remember the following points in your capital budgeting process:

Do not confuse the investment and financing decisions. You finance your entire business, but you invest in specific opportunities. For example, if you are considering buying a forklift, the way you intend to finance it should not affect your capital budgeting analysis. You should not consider loan repayments (principal and interest) as cash outflows over the life of the investment. Consider the purchase price as an outflow in year zero, and the benefits as inflows over the useful life.

Take into consideration different levels of risk when comparing investments. If you are considering investing $100,000 in either a new plant for your current line of business or in an entirely new and exotic line of business, the additional risk of the second project must be worked into the evaluation process. You can do this in a number of ways. You can adjust your hurdle rate to reflect the fact that one project is riskier than another. That is, the riskier the project, the higher your hurdle rate should be. Or you can use a much more sophisticated technique that involves the calculation of probable cash flows that represent the various possible outcomes for different levels of risk. You will probably find the first method sufficient for most purposes.

FIGURE 25.5

Comparison of Advantages and Disadvantages Among Various Capital Budgeting Analysis Tools and Techniques

Techniques	*Payback*	*Simple Return on Investment*	*Net Present Value*	*Internal Rate of Return*
ADVANTAGES	1. The payback method is easy to calculate and easy to understand. The analysis can be done quickly, with minimal management time. 2. The payback method emphasizes liquidity in the recovery of an investment. This could be especially important to a small business, where liquidity is a prime consideration. Payback emphasizes how long it will take to recover the initial investment. 3. In some senses, payback is a measure of risk because, relatively speaking, the quicker the return on the investment, the lower the risk to the company, since risk increases with time. 4. Payback, with its short time frame, ties in more easily with the general planning horizon of small and medium-sized businesses, where it is often difficult to project more than three or four years into the future.	1. The simple return on investment is quickly calculated and easily understood. 2. When the useful life of the investment is more than twice the payback period, the simple return on investment approaches the time-adjusted rate of return. 3. The simple return on investment facilitates the ranking of alternative projects and can be compared with the company's hurdle rate.	1. The net present value method will indicate the correct choice of investments between mutually exclusive projects if the hurdle rate is appropriate to all the projects being considered. 2. Net present value avoids the problem of multiple rates of return, which are encountered in the internal rate of return method, when projects have unusual or irregular cash flows. 3. It reflects the timing and the time value of the cash flows.	1. It is sensitive to the time patterns of the cash flows. 2. It is intuitively easier to understand and to explain than the concept of net present value. 3. It makes the precision of distant cash flows less critical, but considers the entire life of the investment. 4. It can be used to rank proposals or projects. 5. It does not require the predetermination of a value factor (hurdle rate) as does net present value.

FIGURE 25.5 (cont'd.)

Comparison of Advantages and Disadvantages Among Various Capital Budgeting Analysis Tools and Techniques

Techniques	*Payback*	*Simple Return on Investment*	*Net Present Value*	*Internal Rate of Return*
DISADVANTAGES	1. Payback completely ignores the concept of the time value of money. Everyone would agree that he or she would rather have a dollar today versus a dollar a year from now. 2. Payback does not reflect events after the end of the payback period. 3. The payback method does not make a comparison with the company's hurdle rate. 4. The payback method does not factor in equipment salvage value. 5. Payback does not measure profitability or net income from investment.	1. The simple return on investment method ignores the concept of the time value of money. 2. It does not measure profitability or net income from the investment. 3. There is no reference to economic life.	1. The net present value method requires an estimate of the hurdle rate or cost of capital. 2. The net present value only identifies whether a project exceeds the cost of capital. 3. The net present value method does not measure profitability. 4. It does not distinguish between projects that have equivalent net present values but different costs and cash flows.	1. It requires a trial and error computation method to find the appropriate discount rate, although this disadvantage can be minimized by the use of financial or programmable calculators or minicomputers. 2. Because of the way the internal rate of return is calculated, it can have several values for a project.

FIGURE 25.6
Sample Investments and Suggested Type(s) of Capital Budgeting Analysis

Sample Investment	*Hunch*	*Payback*	*Simple Return on Investment*	*Net Present Value*	*Internal Rate of Return*	*Comments*
Advertising campaign	X	X	X			Benefits difficult to forecast precisely. No salvage value to consider.
Major preventive maintenance to existing equipment		X				Risk is relatively low, useful life relatively long.
Routine replacements (for relatively small amounts)		X	X			Risk and amount of capital invested are relatively small.
Replacements (for larger amounts)	X*	X*		X	X	*If a broken machine is being replaced.
New product line			X	X	X	Risk and amount of capital invested are (generally) relatively large.
Consultants	X	X				Risk is relatively low, benefits sometimes difficult to quantify specifically.
In-house computer		X	X	X	X	Also consider subjective factors, such as improved, more timely information.
Expansion		X	X	X	X	Depends upon level of risk and level of investment.
Acquisition			X	X	X	Risk and amount of capital invested are generally quite large.
New labor-saving (or energy-saving) investment	X		X	X	X	Depends upon level of investment.
New investment in working capital necessary for sales volume expansion			X	X	X	Highly dependent on timing, and therefore, a serious candidate for time-adjusted analysis.

FIGURE 25.7

"Don'ts" Checklist, or When Not to Use a Particular Method

Characteristics of Investment Under Consideration	*Don't Use This Method in This Circumstance* [a]	*Use This Method in This Circumstance*	*Reasons*
1. Very irregular or periodically negative cash flows	1. Payback Internal Rate of Return	1. Net Present Value Simple Return on Investment	1. Under these circumstances, the internal rate of return will be equal to two or more different rates.
2. Very significant investment relative to the size of company (e.g., greater than $5,000 or 10% of net worth)	2. Payback	2. Net Present Value Internal Rate of Return	2. Projects of substantial size should be evaluated using the most accurate method available—therefore use NPV or IRR.
3. Significant residual or salvage value in project	3. Payback Simple Return on Investment	3. Net Present Value Internal Rate of Return	3. Payback does not take residual value into account.
4. Long economic life	4. Payback	4. Net Present Value Internal Rate of Return	4. Payback can distort evaluation of those projects with a long economic life.
5. Investment with high potential of technological obsolescence	5. Payback	5. Net Present Value Internal Rate of Return	5. High risk projects should be evaluated using the most accurate method available.
6. "Strategic" investments or investments made to meet competition	6. Payback	6. Net Present Value Internal Rate of Return	6. Strategic investments (of great importance to the company) should be evaluated using the most accurate method available.

[a] The payback method is contraindicated in all circumstances due to its inherent weaknesses, as noted in the text.

FIGURE 25.8

Ten Components of a Capital-Expenditure Management Program

A realistic way to see how these elements tie together is to trace the biography of a single project, such as a proposal to invest $10,000 in a fork-lift truck and pallets for mechanizing materials handling in a warehouse.

1. *Creative Search for Profitable Opportunities.* The first stage is conception of the underlying profit-making idea which is to be embodied in the capital facility, in this case the fork-lift truck. Turning up profitable opportunities for investing the company's capital is in part a by-product of good management. But this cannot be depended on to provide the plethora of enticing capital proposals that constitute the raw material for good management of capital expenditures. Inadvertent opportunities should be supplemented by an active program of seeking out and investigating such opportunities.

Competition is a great creator of investment opportunities, as when equipment manufacturers vie with one another to make facilities obsolete. Comparisons of costs, earnings, and facilities with those of rivals often suggest productive avenues for investment. One company has for several years been going over its entire product line with a comprehensive survey of product design and product components pointed at reducing costs by changing design, substituting materials and processes, and reconsidering past buy-or-make decisions.

2. *Long-Range Capital Plans.* The second stage in the life cycle of our fork-lift truck proposal is to see whether it conforms with long-range dreams of company development as embodied in future facilities plans.

Because today's capital expenditures make the bed that the company must lie in tomorrow, today's decisions must be based on definite assumptions as to what tomorrow will be like. For example, decisions on warehouse facilities need to be made in the light of an over-all long-range plan for the number and general location of distribution facilities needed for the future. Based on projections of future economic conditions, some companies have prepared detailed plant and equipment targets, toward which their entire capital-expenditure program is oriented. Others have been content to draw up their future facilities plans in broad brush strokes, leaving the details to be worked out and adapted as the program is implemented.

To provide consistent bench marks for proposals originating in all parts of the organization, it is necessary to have *some kind of plan* sketched out for the future, no matter how tentative.

3. *Short-Range Capital Budget.* The next hurdle our fork-lift truck project must take is that of getting onto the one-year capital budget. Listing a project in this budget should not mean that the expenditure is authorized but only that it is approved — such *approval* indicating that the project is considered sufficiently timely and promising to warrant careful study for the coming year.

The short-run budget has several purposes. One is to force operating management to submit the bulk of its capital proposals early enough to give top management an indication of the company's aggregate demand for funds. A comparison of the capital requested with the available supply of funds will help management in weighing the desirability of outside financing or the need for cutbacks. Another purpose is to stimulate creative thinking about the capital-facilities program early in the game, so that there will be a reasonable amount of time for analysis.

4. *Measurement of Project Worth.* The next stage is *justification* of the fork-lift project on the basis of a financial and economic analysis of its investment worth to the company. In order to permit an objective ranking of projects, this analysis needs to be summarized in a single measure of the productivity of the proposed outlay. This is the critical component of capital management and, as our central concern, will be discussed fully below.

5. *Screening and Selection.* Next, our project must pass the screening tests set up by the company to compare this fork-lift truck proposal with rival projects. Screening standards should be set in the light of the supply of cash available for capital expenditures, the cost of money to the company, and the attractiveness of alternative investment opportunities. If our project survives these rejection tests, the capital expenditure is *authorized.*

6. *Control of Authorized Outlays.* The next stage is *control* of the outlays authorized for acquisition (or construction). Controls are needed by top management at this life stage in order to assure that the facility conforms to specifications and that the outlay does not exceed the amount authorized. A system for the prevention of overages will keep estimates of investment amount "honest."

7. *Post-Mortems.* Capital-expenditure management cannot stop when our facility goes into operation. In order to preserve the integrity of the estimates of projected earnings and to provide an experience base for improving such estimates in the future, a post-completion audit of the earnings performance of our fork-lift truck is needed.

One company recently instituted a profit audit of all major projects that had been put into service in the preceding year. On a third of these projects it was found that the earnings had been overestimated by an average of 25%, including one new product investment aggregating several hundred thousands of dollars which was rendered obsolete by a competitive development two weeks after it went into production. On another one-third of the audited projects, the available data were found to be inadequate to the task of checking on the original estimates. This points up the need for a system of record keeping which will permit competent post-completion audits.

A sound program of post-mortems can do much to make earnings estimates more conscientious and realistic. Without some comparison of projections with actual performance, estimates might be inflated to the point of making a joke of the entire capital-rationing system.

8. *Retirement and Disposal.* Management's responsibility for an investment project ceases only when the facilities have been disposed of. The usual expectation is that the asset will be retained throughout its economic life so that it will be virtually worthless at the time of disposal. In a dynamic economy, however, economic life projections are necessarily imprecise. One impact of change is that the specialized assets may come to have more value to others than to the company itself. To find out and take proper action when the future earnings' value falls below the asset's market value requires an investment analysis focused on the desirability of disposal.

9. *Forms and Procedures.* At many stages in our project's life it will have to tangle with forms and procedures. An effective system of capital-expenditure control must in any large company be implemented by specialized forms, written project analyses, and routines of approval, which are tailored to the company's needs. This paper work, though a nuisance, is essential to smooth operation.

10. *Economics of Capital Budgeting.* Good estimates of the rate of return on capital-expenditure projects require an understanding of the economic concepts that underlie sound investment decisions, as well as ability in estimating techniques. Such understanding can be achieved only through special training. To assure a good job and to underscore the importance of education for capital expenditures, the financial vice president of one company personally conducted a training course for head-office executives and then took the show on the road to all plants.

SUMMARY EXHIBITS

The following illustrations will be helpful in summarizing some of the major concepts of capital budgeting:

- Figure 25.5: A summary of advantages and disadvantages among various capital budgeting tools and techniques.
- Figure 25.6: Situations in which to use a particular capital budgeting tool, or a "do's" checklist.
- Figure 25.7: Situations in which a particular capital budgeting method should not be used, or a "don'ts" checklist.

A Model Capital Expenditure Management Program

Joel Dean, in an article published in the *Harvard Business Review* (January/February 1954) discusses the 10 components of a model capital expenditure management program. A copy of the summary page to this article is included as Figure 25.8. It can be used as a reference if you are particularly interested in studying this area further.

CONCLUSION

As an entrepreneur, you are constantly making difficult decisions regarding allocation of scarce resources—time and capital. The purpose of this chapter has been to help you to choose your effective use of long-term capital. We have discussed:

1. Cash flow, which is defined as an additional inflow or a reduction in outflow.
2. Payback and bail-out payback, which are quick and easy but conceptually unsound methods of making capital investment decisions.
3. Time value of money, which is the reason $1.00 today is worth more than $1.00 a year from now.
4. Hurdle rate, which is the minimum rate of return you believe you must earn on an investment and which should be calculated using your component cost of debt and your component cost of equity capital.
5. Net present value and internal rate of return, which are conceptually sound methods of making capital investment decisions because they take the time value of money into account.
6. Capital expenditure management methodology, which helps standardize your analysis guidelines and procedures to help you improve your decision-making process.

PART IV CONTROLLING YOUR BUSINESS

Now that you have the money to start or build your business and are managing that money well, are you certain that you are taking adequate precautions to keep your money in your business? The purpose of Part IV is to help you make sure that money is not leaving your business due to careless errors *(like paying the same bill twice or not charging a customer)* or *to the* willful acts *of your employees or others. It does not include a description of all possible control procedures, but it does include many control procedures considered significant to a small business.*

As an entrepreneur, you know that you cannot afford to simply lose $5,000, $10,000, or $20,000. For example, Jim Barnes, a hardware manufacturer in Massachusetts, lost $40,000 one year because there was an 18-inch snowfall in January that closed his plant for a week. The loss came because he had to pay his labor force, heat the building, pay the rent, and so forth regardless of having absolutely no production. The loss hurt his profits, hurt his cash flow, and set back his production schedule so that he even lost some orders. There was nothing Jim could have done about the snow, but there was something he could have done about controlling the business. You can do it, too.

Part IV begins with a chapter containing a brief discussion of the objectives of financial or accounting control. It then describes the three traditional methods of control: segregation of duties, procedural controls, and managerial controls. It distinguishes between "preventive" and "detective" controls. And it emphasizes the use of your financial statements and the analysis of budget to actual variances *contained therein, which is* the best overall control for the small business.

Part IV discusses controls that should be applied to specific financial resources or areas of your business. Each chapter begins with a brief discussion of the objectives of controlling a particular area of your business; it describes the risks of not controlling this segment and it contains a self-assessment checklist that you can use to test the controls over your own business. At the end of the chapter, the intent and nature of each question contained in each checklist is discussed and many of the control points are illustrated.

26
Objectives and Methods of Control

The responsibility for controlling your business starts and ends with you. It is your responsibility to define your organization's control objectives and to establish the system of procedures and records necessary to achieve those objectives. In addition, you must supervise these systems to determine that they are functioning properly, and you must modify them to reflect changes in operating conditions.

OBJECTIVES OF CONTROL

There are two major objectives of a control system: (1) to ensure that access to valuable company assets is permitted only in accordance with specific authorization and (2) to ensure that all authorized transactions are processed as intended, no authorized transactions are omitted, and no unauthorized transactions are processed.

One way to achieve these objectives is to *separate responsibility for controlling physical assets from the responsibility of recording transactions relat-*

ing to those assets. For example, the people who handle cash should not also be responsible for recording cash transactions. Similarly, the people who have physical control over raw materials or finished goods inventories should not also be responsible for the actual record keeping for those inventories. Your control objectives can be compromised if the same individual performs both these functions. You must have an appropriate segregation of duties.

Controlling Access to Assets

Although some access to assets is necessary in the course of doing business, you must limit it to authorized personnel. Access can be both direct and indirect. Direct access relates to physical accessibility; indirect access is the ability to initiate or process documents that authorize the use or disposition of assets. An example of indirect access is the ability of an employee deliberately to misdirect a shipment of goods to an unauthorized location.

Controlling Execution of Transactions

To obtain reasonable assurance that transactions are executed as authorized, you must require an independent verification process—for example, a procedure whereby a second employee checks the work of the originator of the transaction. In other instances, the verification can be performed by a computer. For example, a computer may be programmed to check that the price entered on a customer invoice by a sales employee agrees with an authorized price list maintained in the computer.

Controlling Recording of Transactions

Controls aimed at ensuring that only authorized transactions are recorded, and that they are recorded accurately, have a two-fold purpose. First, they serve to ensure that valuable assets are not lost due to error or neglect. Second, accurate recording enables you to produce reliable financial statements to summarize the transactions of the business for a period (month, quarter, or year). It is obviously important that your financial statements be accurate. You cannot reach proper conclusions or take appropriate actions in the best interests of your company on the basis of inaccurate data.

Practical Limitations of an Effective Control System

No set of accounting controls is foolproof. Not even the largest corporations can guarantee that errors will not occur. The practical limitation for the small business is to develop the best possible set of controls for a reasonable cost. Inherent limitations on the effectiveness of any control system arise from the following factors:

- Errors can result from misunderstanding of instructions, mistakes in judgement, carelessness, or other personal factors.
- Control procedures that depend on segregation of duties for effectiveness can be circumvented by collusion.

It is management's responsibility to monitor the control systems continually in order to determine that the controls are functioning as intended and to modify these controls as necessary.

METHODS OF CONTROL

Preventive Versus Detective Controls

The distinction between preventive and detective controls is clear. Preventive controls are intended to prevent something from happening, such as the loss of a valuable asset or the improper recording of transactions. Detective controls, on the other hand, are intended to determine *after the fact* whether something has happened that management would not condone. As a practical matter, preventive controls are more effective than detective controls, because it may be too late to do any good if you find a sizeable error after the fact.

The Components of an Effective Control System

Experience has shown that there is no one formula for an effective control system. In general, the control system should be a function of the company's size, the dispersion of its operating locations, and its management philosophy. Large companies require more formal documentation and communication of policies, procedures, and control systems than do small businesses. Large companies have many employees and numerous transactions so that one employee's activities can be confined to a small number of types of transaction. In a small business, employees must frequently perform many functions with the result that the traditional components of a control system are not easily applied. The small business is *heavily dependent on the day-to-day personal involvement of management to ensure effective controls*. The components of the traditional control system consist of segregation of duties, procedural controls, and managerial controls.

Segregation of duties. Segregation of duties involves the separation of the responsibility for the custody of assets from the responsibility for the recording of transactions relating to those assets. It also involves the separation of activities that may compromise control objectives such as processing time cards for an employee and also preparing the payroll. Segregation of duties is a preventive control.

Procedural controls. Procedural controls are documented activities that must be performed to ensure that transactions are executed as authorized and that appropriate supporting evidence is gathered. Procedural controls can be preventive or detective.

Managerial controls. Managerial controls are provided by the involvement of the entrepreneur in the day-to-day activities of the business. Managerial controls can be preventive or detective.

Small businesses are more heavily dependent on procedural controls and on the day-to-day involvement of management to ensure that controls are effective. As a manager of an organization, you should seek to establish an environment that creates the appropriate awareness, attitude, and discipline. And you should develop a system of controls that:

- Fits your company and its management philosophy;
- Focuses on the major areas of risk inherent in your particular type of business; and
- Achieves a thoughtful balance between the costs and the benefits of controls.

THE NATURE OF YOUR BUSINESS AND THE KINDS OF CONTROL YOU USE

There are factors that work both for and against you in establishing your company's control system. On the positive side, your company is likely to be of a size to permit you to understand it fully. Even if you did not start the company, you know what makes it tick. Because you know your business thoroughly, you can readily identify where the major areas of risk lie. This same familiarity provides you with the ability to assess the costs and benefits associated with a particular control mechanism. In sum, your expertise in your business will enable you to establish an effective control system.

Segregation of Duties

Although the small size of your business can work in your favor, it can also work against you. Your administrative staff is probably not large enough to allow you to establish complete segregation of conflicting duties. Where you can institute segregation of duties, it is wise to do so because it is an inexpensive and effective control mechanism. Where you cannot, you will have to rely on procedural and managerial controls. The chapters that follow suggest those functions that should be separate.

Procedural Controls

As stated earlier, procedural controls involve defining the procedures to be followed by employees in such a way as to ensure that your assets are protected and that your transactions are recorded properly.

The first step in establishing a system of procedural controls is to identify the actions or the results that you believe should be prevented or detected. Next, you must develop procedures and activities designed to prevent or detect any weaknesses in control. In each of the following chapters, there are self-assessment checklists that will help you to identify the activities or the events that can be prevented or detected by a well-functioning control system. The explanatory comments accompanying the self-assessment checklists will help you to develop basic procedural controls.

Take a look at several examples of procedural controls within a small business:

Case 1—A procedural control exercised by the manager of the company. The president of a small publishing house wanted to be informed of all commitments to purchase goods or services by his organization. Although he signed all disbursement checks, he wanted to review, *in advance*, all purchase orders. His objective was to prevent the ordering of any goods or services in the name of the company without his approval. He wanted to eliminate the need for subsequent justification or approval when it may have been too late to cancel the purchase. To achieve this management objective, the organization established a procedure that required all purchase orders for goods or services to be approved by the president before their release to vendors.

Case 2—A preventive control provided by a procedure. The president of a wholesale distributing company wished to maintain control over cash disbursements to his vendors. Procedures were established in the accounting department to compare vendor invoices in terms of price, quantity, and the description of the goods received to internally generated purchase orders and receiving reports. The company was trying to prevent paying for more or less goods than ordered, for goods received but billed at a different price, or simply for goods different from those ordered. The objective was to safeguard the cash of the organization.

Case 3—A procedural control performed by an automated data processing system. An electrical parts manufacturer uses a minicomputer to process his cash disbursements. Invoice data, including the vendor name and address, are entered into the system. A master file of authorized vendors is stored within the system. The invoice data are compared to the master file, and invoices pertaining to vendors not on the authorized list are rejected. Because only management can update the vendor master list, invoices from new vendors are immediately brought to management's attention. This procedural control is both a preventive and a detective control—preventive in that it highlights transactions with new or unusual vendors before cash can be disbursed to those vendors, yet detective in that it is triggered after the goods or services have been received.

Case 4—A detective control provided by a procedure. In a mail order business, all incoming mail is opened by the receptionist. In preparation for the daily deposit, checks and cash payments are segregated, the checks are restrictively endorsed, and a two-copy adding machine tape of the checks and the cash is prepared by the receptionist. The receptionist delivers the money and the original of the tapes to the accounting department for further processing and sends the duplicate tape to the president's office. The president subsequently compares the tape total to the daily validated deposit ticket. Any discrepancies are investigated immediately.

Case 5—A detective procedural control provided by an automated data processing system. A small manufacturing company uses its minicomputer to process its payroll. Each week, the payroll clerk enters into the computer system the time card information for each hourly employee, generates the gross to net pay calculations, and prepares an authorized payroll report before a check is prepared. The report is scanned to be certain that all payments are, in fact, authorized and will be made as intended. The computer system also prepares a listing of any changes to the employee master file. All such changes can be reviewed to be certain that they were prepared as intended.

Managerial Controls

As has been stressed throughout this chapter, your participation in the day-to-day operations of your company plays the most important role in your control system. Your role in developing and monitoring the control system involves the following three major functions:

1. Establishing the policies under which the employees of the organization will function.
2. Designing procedures for the processing of transactions and the handling of valuable assets.
3. Monitoring your financial results.

In the discussion on procedural controls, you saw how the president of a small publishing company established control over purchase orders issued by his organization. He exercised this control by requiring formal purchase orders and by approving all purchase orders before they were sent to potential vendors. This example clearly demonstrated how this president exercised control through direct managerial involvement in the day-to-day operations of his business.

The importance of policy and procedures manuals. As the overall manager of your company, safeguarding the resources of the company is only one of your many duties. Not all of your time can be consumed by involvement in the control process. Therefore, you must maximize the value of the limited time that you can devote. You can do this not only by defining the policies under which you wish your employees to operate but by *documenting* those policies and distributing them in the form of a policy manual. In addition, you can (and should) document the procedures for processing transactions and for handling physical assets. This documentation can take the form of *an accounting procedures and controls manual.*

An accounting procedures and controls manual can resolve any questions regarding the way transactions should be processed. Documentation of policies and procedures also minimizes the amount of time necessary to train new or otherwise inexperienced employees. It can provide you with some assurance that transactions can be processed if trained employees leave unexpectedly. It also provides a tangible means of resolving questions when differences arise as to how a particular transaction should be handled. Finally, the documentation of procedures is the first step in the consideration of computerizing any of your accounting functions.

MANAGERIAL CONTROL BY USE OF FINANCIAL STATEMENTS

Perhaps *the best overall control mechanism* for a small business is a *detailed set of financial statements* that can be *compared to* either the *prior year* or *to a well-developed budget. Detailed* financial statements are not only helpful in providing a control mechanism; they also provide insight into the impact of day-to-day transactions on the business. Therefore, they can be used to direct the course of the business in the future.

The way in which financial statements become valuable is through the comparison of actual results to the results of a prior year or to an effectively developed budget, with a following analysis of the resulting variances. A review of the resulting variances will help you to determine if they have arisen because you have not achieved the level of sales that you had hoped for or if you have not been able to control your costs, or both. If there are *no logical explanations* for the variances, they may result from errors or even from the willful misappropriation of funds.

The Management Control Cycle

The process of developing plans and budgets, recording actual transactions, and analyzing the variances between actual results and the budget is referred to as the *management control cycle*. The starting point is your expertise in the business. This knowledge will help you to develop both profit and loss and cash flow forecasts for the upcoming operating period. As actual operating results are obtained, they can be compared to your forecasts. Variances between the two should be analyzed and explained. This same expertise enables you to determine the types of corrective actions, if any, that will minimize further variances. Implement the corrective actions, and modify your forecast for the remaining periods as necessary. Now the cycle is complete.

The following paragraphs describe each component of the cycle in greater detail and show how Bill Cosgrove, the owner of the GMG Tire Company, makes the cycle work for him.

The Role of Your Financial Reporting System

Your financial and management reporting system should provide you with meaningful and timely information. Your information needs should dictate the format and content of these reports and statements. Many managers of small businesses, particularly those who do not have a strong background in finance, delegate decisions on report content and format to their bookkeeper. However, your bookkeeper may not be aware of your reporting objectives and may select a format solely on the basis of ease of preparation.

Bill Cosgrove receives a detailed income statement and balance sheet monthly. His income statement is a summary of the departmental statements for his two operating departments. Samples of his financial statements are shown in Figures 26.1 and 26.2. Bill's income statement and balance sheet include a comparison of current year to date results to prior year to date results and to budgeted year to date results. Variances of current results from prior year and budgeted results are expressed in dollars. Also, variances of current results from budget are expressed as a percentage of the budgeted amount for analysis purposes.

In late summer, Bill develops his budget for the next 12 months. In the wholesale tire business, the summer months are the slack period. Armed with years of experience and the prior year's financial statements, Bill and his departmental managers prepare their respective portions of the annual budget by estimating the monthly activity of the business for the year. The managers review their departmental budgets with Bill, who modifies their plans on the basis of his broader knowledge of the industry and the company. Figure 26.3 shows a detailed listing of the steps involved in preparing the annual budget. It is critical that the budget be cast in the same format and embody the same accounting principles as the internal financial statements in order to facilitate review and subsequent comparison. It is also useful to follow Bill's example and involve your employees in the planning process. Their involvement in developing the plan strengthens their commitment to achieving goals embodied in the plan.

Analysis of Variances

As the monthly financial statements are prepared, the bookkeeper compares the actual results to the plan and indicates all variances in dollars and as a percentage of the budget. Copies of this comparison are given to Bill and the department managers. Bill reviews the significant variances and calls on the respective department managers for explanations of their departmental variances. Together, they determine an appropriate course of action to modify the results for the rest of the year, if necessary, and take the necessary steps to implement their corrective actions.

Timeliness of reporting. One of the key factors at this stage of the cycle is the timeliness of reporting. A financial statement prepared six weeks after the date to which it refers is of little use in the control process of a small business. It may be too late to do anything about any adverse conditions brought to light by the analysis of variances. In Bill's case, for example, 40% of his total sales volume is concentrated in September, October, and November. If Bill receives his September statement in December and if it shows a major variance in sales or costs, it may be too late to take corrective action. In effect, his selling season is about over. If his pricing system did not generate sufficient gross margin, correcting it in December is too late to improve his results for the year. However, there are factors in his business that make it difficult for Bill to receive timely financial statements. In fact, he has a genuine "Catch-22" situation on his hands. When volume is the heaviest, his need for timely financial data is the greatest. However, when the daily transaction volume is the heaviest, the bookkeeper has less time to devote to preparing the reports, and thus the reports may be generated even later than usual.

Use of key economic indicators. Bill has been able to compensate for this weakness. He has identified what are referred to as *key economic indicators* for his business. The objective of a key economic indicator for any business is to provide, at a glance, a sort of barometric reading on the

FIGURE 26.1
GMG Tire Company
Comparative Balance Sheet
December 31, 19X0

Current Year	*Prior Year*	*Variance $*		*% of Total Assets*	*Current Year*	*Budget*	*Variance $*	*Variance %*
			Assets:					
			Current Assets					
$ 6,901	$ 4,839	$ 2,062	Cash	.1%	$ 6,901	$ 5,500	$ 1,401	25.47%
2,619,057	2,554,892	64,165	Accounts Receivable—Net	32.1%	2,619,057	2,528,197	90,860	3.59
169,218	90,300	78,918	Other Receivables	2.1	169,218	158,349	10,869	6.86
1,316,451	2,358,205	(1,041,754)	Inventory	16.1	1,316,451	1,750,500	(434,049)	(24.80)
231,346	248,188	(16,842)	Prepaid Expenses	2.8	231,346	174,558	56,788	32.53
25,330		25,330	Income Taxes Receivable	.3	25,330	26,440	(1,110)	(4.20)
4,368,303	5,256,424	(888,121)	Total Current Assets	53.5	4,368,303	4,643,544	(275,241)	(5.93)
3,495,969	3,253,780	241,916	Property, Plant & Equipment—Net	42.8	3,495,696	3,496,978	(1,282)	(.04)
263,444	191,496	71,948	Organizational Costs—Net	3.3	263,444	265,350	(1,906)	(.72)
32,303	27,933	4,370	Other Assets	.4	32,303	34,853	(2,550)	(7.32)
$8,159,746	$8,729,633	$ (569,887)	Total Assets	100%	$8,159,746	$8,440,725	$ (280,979)	(3.33)%
			Liabilities and Shareholders' Equity					
			Current Liabilities					
$2,681,277	$2,336,914	$344,363	Accounts Payable	32.9%	$2,681,277	$2,679,028	$ 2,249	.08%
908,293	1,055,676	(147,383)	Accrued Expenses	11.1	908,293	958,483	(50,190)	(5.24)
686,869	864,814	(177,945)	Advances under Revolving Loan Agreement	8.4	686,869	675,964	10,905	1.61
595,714	480,000	115,714	Current Portion of Long-Term Debt	7.3	595,714	595,900	(186)	(.03)
50,000	110,286	(60,286)	Income Taxes Payable	.6	50,000	75,000	(25,000)	(33.33)
4,922,153	4,847,690	74,463	Total Current Liabilities	60.3	4,922,153	4,984,375	(62,222)	(1.25)

FIGURE 26.1 (Cont.)
GMG Tire Company
Comparative Balance Sheet
December 31, 19X0

Current Year	Prior Year	Variance $		% of Total Assets	Current Year	Budget	Variance $	Variance %
			Long-Term Liabilities					
1,520,000	2,300,000	(480,000)	Long-Term Portion of Term Loan	21.1	1,520,000	1,520,000		
765,000	850,000	(85,000)	Subordinated Debenture	9.4	765,000	750,000	15,000	.02
184,286		184,286	Mortgage Note Payable	2.3	184,286	186,000	(1,714)	(.92)
39,660	89,786	(50,126)	Deferred Taxes	.5	39,660	40,900	(1,240)	(3.03)
7,431,099	8,087,476	(656,377)	Total Liabilities	93.6	7,431,099	7,481,275	(50,176)	(.67)
			Shareholders' Equity					
1,000	1,000	—	Common Stock		1,000	1,000	—	—
499,500	499,500	—	Capital in Excess of Par	6.1	499,500	499,500	—	—
228,147	141,657	86,490	Retained Earnings	.3	228,147	258,950	(30,803)	(11.89)
728,647	642,157	86,490	Total Shareholders' Equity	6.4	728,647	759,450	(30,803)	(4.06)
$8,159,746	$8,729,633	$ (569,887)	Total Liabilities and Shareholders' Equity	100%	$8,159,746	$8,440,725	$(280,979)	(3.33)%
			Financial Ratios[a]					
$553,850	$408,734		Working Capital					
.89	1.08		Current Ratio					
.53	.53		Quick Ratio					
10.20	12.59		Debt to Equity Ratio					
17.94	8.65		Inventory Turnover Ratio					
10.02	8.87		Accounts Receivable Turnover Ratio					
35.93	40.59		Days Sales Outstanding					
.127	.110		Return on Assets					

[a] Based upon December operating results

FIGURE 26.2
GMG Tire Company
Summary Income Statement
December, 19X0

Current Year-to-Date	Prior Year-to-Date	Variance $		Current Year-to-Date	Budget Year-to-Date	Variance $ over/(under)	Variance %
			Sales:				
$1,835,490	$1,560,395	$275,095	Tire Department	$1,835,490	$1,795,660	$ 39,830	2.22%
351,377	327,932	23,445	Sporting Goods Department	351,377	360,875	(9,498)	(2.63)
2,186,867	1,888,327	298,540		2,186,867	2,156,535	30,332	1.41
			Cost of Goods Sold:				
1,692,853	1,443,860	248,993	Tire Department	1,692,853	1,650,196	42,657	2.58
274,840	256,198	18,642	Sporting Goods Department	274,840	279,970	(5,130)	(1.83)
1,967,693	1,700,058	267,635		1,967,693	1,930,166	37,527	1.94
			Gross Margin:				
142,637	116,535	26,102	Tire Department	142,637	145,464	(2,827)	1.94
76,537	71,734	4,803	Sporting Goods Department	76,537	80,905	(4,368)	(5.40)
219,174	188,269	30,905		219,174	226,369	(7,195)	(3.18)
			Selling and Administrative Expenses:				
31,614	26,837	4,777	Tire Department	31,614	28,090	3,524	12.54
18,026	16,098	1,928	Sporting Goods Department	18,026	17,125	901	5.26
8,263	7,192	1,071	Other	8,263	8,035	228	2.84
57,903	50,127	7,776		57,903	53,250	4,653	8.74
(44,471)	(34,879)	(9,592)	Other, net	(44,471)	(39,128)	(5,343)	13.65
116,800	103,263	13,537	Income (Loss) Before Taxes	116,800	133,991	(17,191)	(12.83)
(30,310)	(23,192)	(7,118)	Income Tax Benefit (Provision)	(30,310)	(32,420)	2,110	(6.51)
$ 86,490	$ 80,071	$ 6,419	Net Income (Loss)	$ 86,490	$ 101,571	$ (15,081)	(14.85)%
$ 141,657	$ 61,586	$ 80,071	Retained Earnings at Beginning of Period	$ 141,657	$ 157,379	$ (15,722)	(9.99)%
$ 228,147	$ 141,657	$ 86,490	Retained Earnings at End of Period	$ 228,147	$ 258,950	$ (30,803)	(11.89)%

FIGURE 26.3

GMG *Tire Company*

Tire Department Operating Statement

One Month Ended December 31, 19X0

Current Year-to-Date	*Prior Year-to-Date*	*Variance $*		*Current Year-to-Date*	*Budget Year-to-Date*	*Variance $ over/(under)*	*Variance %*
$1,835,490	$1,560,395	$ 275,095	Sales	$1,835,490	$1,795,660	$ 39,830	2.22 %
			Less: Cost of Goods Sold				
936,211	1,858,823	(922,612)	Inventory, December 1, 19X0	936,211	1,244,864	(308,653)	(24.79)
1,782,483	1,526,378	256,105	Cost of Goods Purchased	1,782,483	1,750,832	31,651	1.81
2,718,694	3,385,201	(666,507)	Cost of Goods Available for Sale	2,718,694	2,995,696	(277,002)	(9.25)
1,025,841	1,941,341	(915,500)	Inventory, December 31, 19X0	1,025,841	1,345,500	(319,659)	(23.76)
1,692,853	1,433,860	248,993	Cost of Goods Sold	1,692,853	1,650,196	42,657	2.58
142,637	116,535	26,102	Gross Margin	142,637	145,464	(2,827)	1.94
			Less: Selling and Administrative Expenses:				
12,387	10,627	1,760	Advertising	12,387	10,898	1,489	13.66
5,398	4,793	605	Office Salaries	5,398	5,010	388	7.74
1,952	1,726	226	Office Supplies	1,952	2,234	(282)	12.62
5,650	5,253	397	Rent Expense	5,650	5,125	525	10.24
31,614	26,837	4,777	Total Selling and Administrative Expenses	31,614	28,090	3,524	12.54
$ 111,023	$ 89,698	$ 21,325	Net Profit or (Loss)	$ 111,023	$ 117,374	$ (6,351)	(5.41)%

economic status of the business. Bill monitors on a daily basis the *types of products sold*, the *average selling price* versus the *cost of the product*, *inventory levels*, and his *accounts receivable aging*. These statistics give him an overall indication of how his business is doing. Although Bill uses these indicators as a substitute for timely financial reporting, the true value of key economic indicators is that they provide up-to-the-minute data on critical operating statistics without the burden of generating a full financial report. Key economic indicators enable you to stay on top of the vital areas of your business where your tolerance for error is very small.

Update of the Remaining Forecast Periods

Bill completes this management control cycle, after he has received his financial information and analyzed his variances, by updating his forecast for the remaining months if necessary. Each year the cycle begins again. The management control cycle is a pervasive method of exercising managerial control over your company. You may find that the cycle you establish for your company will have several more steps or may incorporate a greater time span than Bill Cosgrove's. The underlying objective is the same: control of the organization through expertise and managerial involvement.

CONCLUSION

This discussion on controlling the resources of your business has identified the objectives of an internal control system, which are:

1. Access to assets is permitted only in accordance with specific authorization.
2. Authorized transactions are processed as intended.

This chapter has focused on the general types of controls available to small businesses, the components of a control system, and the limitations of such controls. The chapter has discussed specific control techniques actually used in real small businesses and the ways financial statements and a business plan can be useful control techniques.

FIGURE 26.4
GMG Tire Company
Sporting Goods Department Operating Statement
One Month Ended December 31, 19X0

Current Year-to-Date	*Prior Year-to-Date*	*Variance $*		*Current Year-to-Date*	*Budget Year-to-Date*	*Variance $ over/(under)*	*Variance %*
$351,377	$327,932	$ 23,445	Sales	$351,377	$360,875	$ (9,498)	(2.63)%
			Less: Cost of Goods Sold				
190,807	315,817	(125,010)	Inventory, December 1, 19X0	190,807	312,295	(121,488)	(38.90)
374,643	357,245	17,398	Cost of Goods Purchased	374,643	372,675	1,968	.53
565,450	673,062	(107,612)	Cost of Goods Available for Sale	565,450	684,970	(119,520)	(17.45)
290,610	416,864	(126,254)	Inventory, December 31, 19X0	290,610	405,000	(114,390)	(28.24)
274,840	256,198	18,642	Cost of Goods Sold	274,840	279,970	(5,130)	(1.83)
76,537	71,734	4,803	Gross Margin	76,537	80,905	(4,368)	(5.40)
			Less: Selling and Administrative Expenses:				
9,532	8,193	1,339	Advertising	9,532	9,325	207	2.22
3,465	2,985	480	Office Salaries	3,465	3,245	220	6.78
2,380	2,193	187	Rent Expense	2,380	2,545	(165)	6.48
18,026	16,098	1,928	Total Selling and Administrative Expenses:	18,026	17,125	901	5.26
$ 58,511	$ 55,636	$ 2,875	Net Profit or (Loss)	$ 58,511	$ 63,780	$ (5,269)	(8.26)%

FIGURE 26.5
Detailed Listing of the Steps Involved in Preparing the Annual Forecast

Step	Responsibility of Dept. Mgr.	Owner Mgr.
1. Review historical data for trends or seasonal patterns	________	________
2. Consider anticipated business conditions, for example:		
—change in volume	________	________
—change in price	________	________
—change in cost components	________	________
3. Develop and document underlying assumptions	________	________
4. Prepare budget in dollars for the year by month	________	________
5. Review and coordinate with overall business plan	________	________
6. Modify the actual budget and the underlying assumptions, for any changes arising from Step 5.	________	________

27 Controlling Your Cash

OBJECTIVES AND RISK CONSIDERATIONS

In controlling your company's cash, make certain that you establish procedures to accomplish the following objectives. These objectives are addressed by the questions in the Self-Assessment Questionnaire indicated by the numbers in parentheses.

- All collections must be properly identified, totaled, and forwarded intact for deposit (Q4).
- All collections must be deposited promptly and intact (Q4).
- All collections must be promptly and accurately recorded (Q3).
- All checks must be prepared on the basis of adequate and approved documentation (Q8).
- All checks must be compared with supporting data and properly approved, signed, and mailed (Q8).
- All checks issued must be promptly and accurately recorded (Q1).

- All general ledger entries for collections and disbursements must be properly and accurately accumulated, classified, and summarized; general ledger balances must be reconciled with bank statement balances (Q1).

The risk considerations associated with cash are as follows:

- Withholding or delaying recording of collections (Q1, Q3, Q4, Q5).
- Misappropriating cash proceeds (Q1, Q3, Q4, Q5).
- Issuing checks drawn to other than the intended payee (Q6, Q7, Q10, Q11, Q12).
- Diverting checks prepared for legitimate purposes (Q3).
- Recording fictitious cash or other discounts (Q4).
- Understating cash receipt totals (Q4).
- Overstating cash disbursement totals (Q3).
- Processing duplicate or incorrect payments (Q8, Q9).
- Falsifying bank reconciliations (Q1, Q2, Q5).

SELF-ASSESSMENT QUESTIONNAIRE

	Yes	*No*	*Not Applicable*	*Comment*
Control Procedures				
1. Are monthly bank statement balances reconciled to general ledger account balances?	___	___	___	________
2. Are bank reconciliations prepared promptly?	___	___	___	________
Segregation of Duties				
3. Is the recording of cash receipts and the signing of disbursement checks performed by different individuals?	___	___	___	________
4. Is the preparation of the cash deposit separated from the recording of the cash receipt?	___	___	___	________

	Yes	No	Not Applicable	Comment
Management Controls				
5. Do you review bank account reconciliations monthly?	___	___	___	___
6. Do you or does someone you trust sign all checks?	___	___	___	___
7. Are the payee and the amount recorded on the face of the check before you sign the check?	___	___	___	___
8. Do you review the documentation supporting the cash disbursement at the time of the check signing?	___	___	___	___
9. Do you clearly cancel the supporting documentation at the time of the check signing?	___	___	___	___
10. Do you control the number of authorized check signers?	___	___	___	___
11. Do you have the sole authority to open new bank accounts?	___	___	___	___
12. If a check-signing machine is used, do you control the signature plates and log their use?	___	___	___	___

RECOMMENDATIONS FOR CONTROLS ON CASH

Control Procedures

Q1. Are monthly bank statement balances reconciled to general ledger account balances? General ledger balances represent summaries of approved and valid transactions. By comparing the bank statement balance to the general ledger balance, you are afforded some degree of assurance that only authorized and valid transactions have passed through the cash accounts. Refer to Figure 27.1 for an example of a bank reconciliation that reconciles the bank statement balance to the general ledger balance.

FIGURE 27.1
The Standard Company
Bank Reconciliation

THE STANDARD COMPANY
BANK RECONCILIATION A/C 29-12003
MARCH 31, 198X

Balance per Bank Statement	3/31/81	$19,642.00
Less: Outstanding Checks:		- 9,218.00
Plus: Deposit in Transit:	3/31/81	+ 3,492.00

Miscellaneous:

Less:

Debit Memo 3/31/81 (wire transfer from XYZ Company)	- 6,321.00

Plus:

Credit Memo - Bank service charge	+ 25.00

Balance per General Ledger Account	$ 7,620.00

Outstanding Checks:

Check No.	Amount
1342	4631.00
1354	254.00
1401	3125.00
1431	1208.00
	9218.00

Q2. Are bank reconciliations prepared promptly? Bank reconciliations should be prepared promptly and accurately to highlight any discrepancies. The reconciliation is a detective control; like all detective controls, it can identify a problem only after it has occurred. The prompt preparation of the reconciliation helps to minimize the lag between the occurrence and the correction of the error. A misunderstanding as to a bank balance is a serious matter. It can result in an embarrassing situation where you have insufficient funds to pay your bills, or it can lead to a possible violation of a compensating balance agreement.

Segregation of Duties

Q3. Are the recording of cash receipts and the signing of disbursement checks performed by different individuals? It is imperative that these two functions be separated. Access to both the cash receipt and disbursement functions provides the opportunity for concealing defalcations. For example, a diverted cash receipt, offset by recording a fictitious disbursement of the same amount, will have no noticeable effect on the overall cash balance. Where segregation is not feasible, it is important to establish control over cash receipts before their delivery to the accounting department. At this point, your expertise can assist. Your careful scrutiny of profit and loss statements in relation to budget or forecast should reveal any unusual disbursement amounts that you should investigate further.

Q4. Is the preparation of the cash deposit separated from the recording of the cash receipts? It is important that the process of preparing the cash deposit be separate from the process of recording cash receipts data. Access to the deposit and to the accounting records can allow the concealment of misappropriated funds. In certain companies, where this segregation cannot be effected, a second individual, typically a receptionist or a secretary, should open the mail, restrictively endorse the checks, and prepare an adding machine tape of the total remittances. This control total should be forwarded to a supervisory individual not involved in the accounting process. The checks and other remittance data should be forwarded to the bookkeeper who prepares the deposit and records the receipts. The receipted deposit ticket from the bank should be given to the supervisory individual, who has retained the control total of the remittances. The supervisor should compare the control tape to the receipted deposit ticket.

Another method for offsetting lack of segregation of duties is to use a lockbox, a service offered by a bank. Your customers can mail their remittances to the lockbox account at the bank. The bank deposits the amounts directly into your account, forwarding to your company any remittance data included in the payment envelope, or photocopies of the checks.

Management Controls

Q5. Do you review bank account reconciliations monthly? To detect irregularities, your review of the bank reconciliation should include the following steps:

- Compare the balance per bank to the actual bank statement.
- Compare the balance per general ledger to the period-end general ledger balance.
- Compare deposits in transit to actual receipted deposit tickets, investigating delays in processing.
- Trace a selected number of outstanding checks to the disbursement records.
- Review debit and credit memoranda and the support for any other reconciling items, as well as the accounting treatment of such items.

Again, look at the example of a bank reconciliation in Figure 27.1. Prepared in this format, the reconciliation provides you with the data you need to test the reconciliation process, using the foregoing steps. In addition to reviewing the reconciliation, you, as general manager of the Standard Company, should review the accounting treatment of and subsequent processing to the general ledger of any debit and credit memoranda appearing as reconciling items. Debit and credit memos are often included in the monthly bank statement. These memos serve to notify you that a transaction involving your company has occurred through the banking process. If the debit and credit memos enclosed in the bank statement are your first notification of the transaction, then the transactions would not have been included in your general ledger as of the statement date.

For instance, in Figure 27.1, the Standard Company has received a credit memo in its March bank statement that informs them that on March 31, 19X1, the XYZ Company, a customer, has paid its obligations to the Standard Company via wire transfer to Standard Company's bank. Because the remittance amount has been included in the bank statement balance of March 31, 19X1, it must be deducted from the bank statement balance at that date in order to reconcile the bank statement balance to the general ledger balance. Similarly, from a debit memo included in the bank statement, the Standard Company has learned that the bank has levied a service charge on Standard's account and has removed $25 from their account. Because this transaction has been reflected on the bank statement but not in Standard's general ledger, the amount of the transaction must be added in the process of reconciling from the bank statement balance to the general ledger balance. In both cases, you should ascertain that entries have been made to reflect these transactions in your accounting records.

Q6. Do you or does someone you trust sign all checks? One of the strongest controls in smaller organizations without a segregation of duties is that all disbursement checks are signed by the owner/manager. Your expertise in the business often affords you the ability to assess the validity of a disbursement. In certain instances, it may be impractical for you to sign all checks. If your situation requires that numerous checks of low dollar values be written, you may need to sign only those checks over a certain dollar amount.

Q7. Are the payee and the amount recorded on the face of the check before you sign the check? You should not sign any checks unless the payee and amount have been recorded on the face of the check. Also, never sign blank checks for use in your absence, despite apparent safeguards.

Q8. Do you review the documentation supporting the cash disbursement at the time of the check signing? You should have available for your review, at the time of the check signing, the documentation supporting the disbursement. The supporting documentation, which is likely to include a vendor invoice, receiving report, and purchase order, or invoice for service approved by the recipient of the service, should be assembled by the bookkeeper. Compare the check data to the supporting documentation. Never sign a check because the expenditure sounds reasonable; require supporting documentation.

Q9. Do you clearly cancel the supporting documentation at the time of the check signing? Cancellation of the supporting documents at the time of payment prevents an item from being presented for payment more than once. Cancellation may take several forms. You can place your initials on the supporting documents. The documents can be perforated using a perforation device. In some businesses, the bookkeeper in preparing the supporting documents will enter the check date and check number on the documents before these items are presented for signing. Having the preparer of the payment mark "paid" on the document before your review, or assuming that the preparer will cancel the documents after you sign the check, is unsatisfactory. If the word "paid" is written on the invoice prior to its presentation to you, how can you know whether you were signing a disbursement check for a valid invoice or for an invoice that you have paid previously? Likewise, if the invoice is cancelled out of your presence after you sign the check, can you be certain that the cancellation is actually performed? Making payment on duplicates or copies of invoices and, in certain instances, on statements, subverts the control of cancellation of supporting documentation upon payment. How can you ascertain that you have not already made payment on this invoice if a copy, rather than an original, is presented as back-up for payment? How can you determine whether or not you have already paid

FIGURE 27.2
Check Signing Machine Control Log

CHECK SIGNING MATCHING CONTROL LOG

Date	(1) Meter Beginning Number	(2) Meter Ending Number	(2)−(1)=(3) Checks Signed Per Machine	(4) Physical Count of Checks Signed	(3) − (4) Difference*
2/24	38431	38691	260	260	0
2/25	38691	39043	352	352	0
2/26	39043	39204	161	161	0

* Any difference must be explained.

for an item listed on the statement? It is possible that your payment for an item was not processed by the vendor prior to the preparation of the statement of the open items on your account.

Q10. Do you control the number of authorized check signers? Be aware at all times which individuals have the authority to sign checks within your organization. Minimize the number of check signers to the greatest extent possible. Be certain that the bank is aware that a new check signer may be authorized only on your notification.

Q11. Do you have the sole authority to open new bank accounts? As in the case of check signers, be aware of all bank accounts in your company's name. Limit the number of accounts to the extent possible. As in the case of check signers, instruct the bank to open additional accounts only on your specific authorization. By limiting the number of accounts, you diminish the possibility of an undetected diversion of funds.

Q12. If a check-signing machine is used, do you control the signature plates and log their use? In some companies a check-signing machine is employed. You should retain custody over the signature plates when they are not in use. Each time the machine is used, ascertain the number of checks to be signed and compare this quantity to the machine's usage meter. Control is further strengthened by maintaining a log of machine usage, that is, starting meter number, ending meter number, and quantity signed per machine versus quantity of checks authorized to be signed.

Figure 27.2 provides an example of a control log for a check-signing machine. The objective of this log, which compares the number of checks signed according to the meter device to your count of the checks signed, is to highlight any unauthorized use of the machine and the signature plates.

28

Controlling Your Accounts Receivable

OBJECTIVES AND RISK CONSIDERATIONS

In controlling your company's accounts receivable make certain that you establish procedures to accomplish the following objectives. These objectives are addressed by the questions in the Self-Assessment Questionnaire indicated by the numbers in parentheses.

- Sales orders or orders for service must be accepted only if they meet management's authorized criteria (Q13, Q21).
- Orders must be appropriately approved for acceptance of credit risk (Q13).
- Make sure that goods shipped or services provided have been authorized (Q13).
- All shipments must be billed, and at authorized prices and terms. Billing adjustments for allowances, discounts, and returned merchandise must have been authorized (Q14, Q15, Q17, Q18).

- Billings, adjustments, and collections must be properly recorded in individual customer accounts (Q16, Q23).
- Revenues, collections, and receivables must be properly accumulated, classified, and summarized in the accounts (Q20).

The risk considerations associated with accounts receivable are the following:

- Shipments in excess of quantities ordered (Q14).
- Failure to bill (Q14).
- Failure to record billings (Q17).
- Billing at less than full price (Q18).
- False credits in sales adjustment entries (Q20).
- False credits to receivable accounts (Q20).
- Failure to record cash receipts (Q20).
- Diverting cash receipts after recording (Q20).
- Substituting unsupported credits or fictitious write-offs to cover misappropriated collections of receivables (Q22).
- Lack of follow-up on overdue accounts (Q19, Q24).

SELF-ASSESSMENT QUESTIONNAIRE

	Yes	*No*	*Not Applicable*	*Comment*
Control Procedures				
13. Before your company delivers goods or performs services on credit for a customer, does an employee compare the customer's existing balance owed to the customer's approved credit limit?	___	___	___	___________
14. Does someone regularly match shipping records to billed invoices?	___	___	___	___________
15. Does someone review and update credit limits for customers on an ongoing basis?	___	___	___	___________

	Yes	No	Not Applicable	Comment
16. Is the accounts receivable subsidiary ledger trial balance total matched to the general ledger accounts receivable balance?	____	____	____	__________
17. Does the account department use and account for prenumbered billing invoices?	____	____	____	__________
18. Are billing invoices reviewed with regard to pricing and mathematical accuracy?	____	____	____	__________
19. Is an employee responsible for the review and follow-up of delinquent accounts?	____	____	____	__________
Segregation of Duties				
20. Are the cash receipt and recording functions separated from other revenue and receivable functions?	____	____	____	__________
Management Controls				
21. Do you develop and review, on an ongoing basis, your credit policies?	____	____	____	__________
22. Do you review and approve all write-offs?	____	____	____	__________
23. Do you review and match the accounts receivable subsidiary ledger trial balance total to the general ledger accounts receivable balance?	____	____	____	__________
24. Do you review the aged accounts receivable subsidiary ledger trial balance on a regular basis?	____	____	____	__________

RECOMMENDATIONS FOR CONTROLS ON ACCOUNTS RECEIVABLE

Control Procedures

Q13. Before your company delivers goods or performs services on credit for a customer, does an employee compare the customer's existing balance owed to the customer's approved credit limit? An employee should review the existing amount owed to you by the customer before goods are delivered or before services are rendered on credit. It may be that the customer is on the edge of insolvency and that the extension of further credit will only increase the bad debt you will incur. The trade credit you offer to other businesses can have a significant impact on the success of your own organization.

Q14. Does someone regularly match shipping records to billed invoices? Shipping records should be matched to billing invoices on a regular basis to ensure that all goods shipped have been billed. You cannot recognize revenues on a shipment unless you bill it; moreover, if you neglect to bill it, you suffer a loss because you have incurred the costs of obtaining or manufacturing the inventory items in question. You have been saddled with the costs of producing the item without having received the anticipated benefits of the revenues.

Q15. Does someone review and update credit limits for customers on an ongoing basis? Because businesses operate in a dynamic environment, you should review and update your customers' credit limits on an ongoing basis. Perhaps your customer has grown significantly and is capable of sustaining a larger debt balance. By levying an unnecessarily conservative credit limit on the customer, you may be unintentionally driving your customer to your competitors, who may be willing to establish a credit limit more in line with the customer's size and ability to repay. On the other hand, be on the watch for the customer who is experiencing a business downturn. If his ability to pay appears to be weakening, lower his limit. Do not get stuck with a large receivable balance when the customer "goes under" simply because the customer was once strong and profitable.

Q16. Is the accounts receivable subsidiary ledger trial balance total matched to the general ledger accounts receivable balance? The accounts receivable balance in the general ledger represents the summary of all approved and valid transactions to that account. The accounts receivable subledger captures these individual transactions and summarizes them by individual customer account. Therefore, these two records should be in agreement. Differences may indicate a breakdown in the posting of data to the individual customer accounts. This breakdown may result in revenues foregone from invoices not posted to customer accounts, or it may create poor customer relations as a result of dunning on items already paid. Your subsidiary ledger of customer receivable balances represents your claims against your customers; therefore, you would be well advised to keep it in order.

Figure 28.1 is an example of an accounts receivable subsidiary ledger trial balance. In this example detailed information is presented by customer with a subtotal by aging category for each customer. The grand total of all customer accounts, which in this example is $98,234.00, should agree with the general ledger balance for accounts receivable.

Q17. Does the accounting department use and account for prenumbered billing invoices? Prenumbered invoices are of particular control importance when the billing invoice is not mailed directly to the client on preparation. For instance, in an electrical parts warehouse, a multicopy billing invoice is prepared, and a copy of the invoice is forwarded to the inventory stockkeeper to initiate the shipment. On shipment, the invoice copy is returned to the billing clerk, who then mails the original of the invoice to the customer. The prenumbering allows the clerk to determine that all items have been shipped, billed, and recorded.

Q18. Are billing invoices reviewed with regard to pricing and mathematical accuracy? To be sure that you are billing your customers for the amounts to which you are rightfully entitled, the prices charged should be checked by an individual who is responsible for maintaining up-to-date price lists. Also, it is important that the mathematical accuracy of the invoice be checked. Do not expect your customers to inform you that your company has made an error in their favor!

Q19. Is an employee responsible for the review and follow-up of delinquent accounts? Although it is important that you establish policies regarding the follow-up of delinquent accounts, the actual review and follow-up can be delegated to an employee. This process must be treated as a regular duty to be performed diligently and not as a "time-permitting" project. Remember, the longer a balance remains outstanding, the harder it is to collect.

The accounts receivable subsidiary ledger trial balance can be used in this review process. Figure 15.1 of Chapter 15, "Managing Accounts Receivable," shows an accounts receivable subsidiary ledger trial balance that has been reviewed for delinquent accounts. Notice that follow-up actions on delinquent accounts have been documented on the actual report to facilitate your subsequent review.

FIGURE 28.1
Bonsignore Products, Inc.
Aged Accounts Receivable Trial Balance
As of March 31, 19X1

Customer Name/Number	*Limit*	*Transaction Code*	*Transaction Date*	*Invoice Number*	*Current*	*Over 30 Days*	*Over 60 Days*	*Over 90 Days*	*Over 120 Days*
Kelm-Ware Inc.	10,000.00	INV	11/18/X0	5006					320.00
6442		INV	12/10/X0	5427				1,020.00	
		INV	12/30/X0	5480				628.00	
		PAY	3/12/X1					(1,648.00)	(320.00)
		INV	3/18/X1	5634	508.00				
CUSTOMER TOTALS				508.00	508.00	.00	.00	.00	.00
Pottery Land Co.	5,000.00	INV	1/21/X1	5521			340.00		
6521		INV	2/12/X1	5584		460.00			
		INV	2/26/X1	5601		290.00			
CUSTOMER TOTALS				1,090.00	.00	750.00	340.00	.00	.00
GRAND TOTAL				$98,234.00	$45,296.00	$23,490.00	$15,208.00	$10,960.00	$3,280.00

Segregation of Duties

Q20. Are the cash receipt and recording functions separated from other revenue and receivable functions? As discussed in Chapter 27, "Controlling Your Cash," the cash processing functions should be separated from the revenue and receivable functions. Access to the cash as well as to the accounts receivable records permits a fraudulent practice known as "lapping" to go undetected. To describe "lapping" briefly, cash is retained by an employee before the deposit is prepared. A record is retained of the amount and the name of the customer to whom it pertains. Several days before a statement or dunning notice is prepared for this customer, a cash remittance from some other customer is applied to satisfy the account of the first customer. The cycle continues, while the retained funds are used outside of the business. If segregation of duties is not feasible in your company, consider the procedures for offsetting this control weakness described in the response to Question 4 in Chapter 27, "Controlling Your Cash."

Management Controls

Q21. Do you develop and review your credit policies on an ongoing basis? Your expertise in your business is critical in establishing credit policies and subsequently modifying those policies for changing conditions. You are familiar with industry practices and the credit that your company can sustain. See Chapter 22, "Ratio Analysis," and Chapter 24, "Managing Working Capital," for assistance in analyzing your business's credit limit.

Q22. Do you review and approve all write-offs? Your review and approval of proposed write-offs of your customers' accounts should serve as a check that all possible efforts at collection have been exhausted. Many companies, after in-house attempts to collect an overdue account have failed, turn the accounts over to a professional collection bureau. If you choose this route, take time to determine which bureau can offer the best service at the lowest rates.

Q23. Do you review and match the accounts receivable subsidiary ledger trial balance total to the general ledger accounts receivable balance? In a brief time, you can assure yourself that your employee has carried out this important function. Compare the general ledger accounts receivable balance to the total of the accounts receivable subsidiary ledger trial balance. If the amounts agree, your testing is complete. If there is a difference, ask your employee to explain the difference.

Q24. Do you review the aged accounts receivable subsidiary ledger trial balance on a regular basis? Review the aged accounts receivable subsidiary ledger trial balance to gain an understanding of your company's overdue accounts. Question the individual who is responsible for the follow-up on delinquent accounts to know what actions are being taken. If an increasing number of accounts are falling into the overdue category, a revision in your credit and collection policies may be necessary.

29

Controlling Your Inventory

OBJECTIVES AND RISK CONSIDERATIONS

In controlling your company's inventory make certain that you establish procedures to accomplish the following objectives. These objectives are addressed by the questions in the Self-Assessment Questionnaire indicated by the numbers in parentheses.

- All production activity must be authorized and inventories maintained at prescribed levels (Q25, Q26, Q33, Q34).
- All production activities and costs must be properly and accurately reported (Q32).
- All inventory items must be subject to effective custodial accountability procedures and physical safeguards (Q27, Q28).
- All receipts, transfers, and withdrawals of stock must be properly recorded and the records must reflect actual quantities on hand (Q29, Q30, Q31).

- All production and inventory transactions must be properly accumulated, classified, and summarized in the accounts (Q32, Q37).

The risk considerations associated with inventory are the following:

- Loss through theft (Q27, Q28).
- Cash drain and potential obsolescence through maintenance of excess levels of inventory (Q25, Q26, Q33, Q34).
- Production inefficiencies resulting from imbalanced inventory levels (Q25, Q26, Q33, Q34).
- Financial statements improperly presented (Q30, Q31, Q32, Q35, Q36).

SELF-ASSESSMENT QUESTIONNAIRE

	Yes	*No*	*Not Applicable*	*Comment*
Control Procedures				
25. Is production coordinated with sales planning?	___	___	___	___
26. Are all inventories subject to continuing review for excess stock, obsolescence, damage, or other factors regarding their ultimate use in production or sales?	___	___	___	___
27. Are inventories, particularly finished goods and raw materials, physically safeguarded?	___	___	___	___
28. Is responsibility for the safeguarding of all inventories assigned to specific employees?	___	___	___	___
29. Are withdrawals from inventory areas supported by approved work orders, requisitions, or shipping orders?	___	___	___	___

	Yes	No	Not Applicable	Comment
30. Are materials or goods stored off-premises (for example, in warehouses and at consignees) confirmed on a regular basis with the holders and counted at least once a year?	____	____	____	____________
31. Are physical inventories conducted periodically, and are necessary adjustments made to the accounting records?	____	____	____	____________
Segregation of Duties				
32. Are responsibilities for maintaining inventory records and general ledger records separated?	____	____	____	____________
Managerial Controls				
33. Do you review and authorize major inventory purchases?	____	____	____	____________
34. Do you review inventory levels periodically?	____	____	____	____________
35. Do you review and approve the instructions for the physical inventory counting?	____	____	____	____________
36. Do you supervise the physical inventory counting and review any adjustments to the accounting records arising from inventory counts?	____	____	____	____________
37. Do you review and approve salvage sales and the write-off of obsolete inventory items?	____	____	____	____________

RECOMMENDATIONS FOR CONTROLS ON INVENTORY

Control Procedures

Q25. Is production coordinated with sales planning? Depending on the nature of your business and your production process, production should typically be based on either existing customer orders or forecasted sales levels. Your objective is to minimize the amount of capital tied up in inventories. The longer the time that products remain in inventory, the longer the gap between your payment for the products and your receipt of revenue from the sale of products.

Q26. Are all inventories subject to continuing review for excess stock, obsolescence, damage, or other factors regarding their ultimate use in production or sales? Your inventory levels should be watched for excess stock levels and potentially obsolete or useless items. Minimize your risk of having your funds invested in products that have become obsolete or useless. This procedure is of particular importance if you operate in an industry that is influenced by trends, such as the fashion industry, or characterized by rapid technological advances, such as the semiconductor industry.

Q27. Are inventories, particularly finished goods and raw materials, physically safeguarded? It is important that your inventories be physically protected. Finished goods and raw materials inventories are particularly vulnerable to theft because they tend to be more readily salable than in-process inventories. They should be kept in locked storerooms with restricted accessibility. In addition to safeguards from theft, you should consider protection from the elements. Is your product susceptible to damage from water, excessive heat, or vermin? Maybe your stockroom is well protected from the external elements, but think about this: If a water pipe breaks and your stockroom is flooded with water three inches deep, how much of your inventory would be ruined?

Q28. Is responsibility for the safeguarding of all inventories assigned to specific employees? Responsibility for protecting inventory should be assigned to specific individuals. Protection from theft from outsiders after working hours is not sufficient. Inventories should be protected during working hours from theft occurring within the organization. Access to inventory areas should be restricted to those employees who have been assigned responsibility for safeguarding those areas.

Q29. *Are withdrawals from inventory areas supported by approved work orders, requisitions, or shipping orders?* You must establish procedures for keeping track of raw materials or finished goods after they have left the inventory areas. The documents supporting the withdrawals, such as production work orders or requisition forms in the case of raw materials, or shipping instructions in the case of finished goods, should be approved by the appropriate supervisory employees. An example of a raw materials requisition form is shown in Figure 29.1. Notice that the form includes the type and quantity of the item requested, the job for which the item has been requested, and an identification of the individuals involved in approving the issuance, dispensing the items, and receiving the items. Before releasing the inventory items, storeroom clerks should observe the approval on the form and maintain a log of inventory issued, noting description and quantity. The individual receiving the materials or products should sign the log. Figure 29.2 provides an example of a raw materials issues log. Notice that the log summarizes the data contained on the individual materials requisition forms. Likewise, movement of materials between processes or work stations should be documented in a log, identifying quantity and description. A unique identification number can be assigned to a batch or lot of materials to identify it as it

FIGURE 29.1
Raw Materials Requisition Form

REQUISITION #2416

RAW MATERIALS REQUISITION FORM

Job No.	Part No.	Quantity
342-1	RJ63	24

Authorized by: RL Watkins Issued by: DRL Received by: DLS

Date 2/24/81

FIGURE 29.2
Raw Materials Issues Log

RAW MATERIALS ISSUES LOG

Date	Job No.	Part No.	Quantity	Raw Materials Requisition No.	Received By
2/24	342-1	RJ63	24	2416	DLS
2/24	532-4	D091	12	2417	RNB

passes through the various production processes. Your goal is the ability to identify and trace the whereabouts of inventory items after their release from the protected inventory areas.

Q30. Are materials or goods that are stored off-premises (for example, in warehouses and at consignees) confirmed on a regular basis with the holders and counted at least once a year? If any of your inventory is held off-premises, it is important that you confirm your records of this inventory on a regular basis with the records of the keeper of the inventory. You want to identify any differences as soon as possible in order to correct the existing imbalance and prevent further occurrences. A difference may be merely a bookkeeping error, or it can mean that inventory is being lost or stolen.

Q31. Are physical inventories conducted periodically and are necessary adjustments made to the accounting records? The inventory balances in the general ledger consist of the sum of the cost of purchased materials and parts, the labor and overhead associated with work in process, and the total cost (material, labor, and overhead) of any finished goods, less the cost of products manufactured and sold. If the universe were perfect, the

FIGURE 29.3
Wright Bros.
Raw Material/Purchased Parts
Inventory Reconciliation
March 31, 19X1

Raw Material		*Units*	*Std.*	*Physical*
			Cost/	*at*
Description	*Code*	*Physical*	*Unit*	*Std. Cost*
½″ Tubular Aluminum	R1154	30,000 lbs.	$1.27	$ 38,100
½″ Tubular Magnesium	R1155	4,000 lbs.	2.97	11,880
½″ Tubular Steel	R1156	20,000 lbs.	1.15	23,000
Lock Washers	PP1519	620	1.65	1,023
Butterfly Nuts	PP1527	653	1.83	1,195
				398,164
		Balance Per General Ledger		(396,560)
		Inventory Adjustment		$ 1,604

physical inventory counts, when valued in dollars, would equal the general ledger balances. However, because of differences in the quantities according to the physical count due to waste, pilferage, and other shrinkage, the physical inventory is likely to differ from the general ledger balance for inventory. Since the physical inventory represents the actual inventory, the general ledger inventory balance must be adjusted to equal the balance rendered by the physical inventory. Large differences may be indicative of weaknesses in the inventory accounting system or of theft and waste in the production process.

Figure 29.3 shows a reconciliation of the physical inventory counts to the general ledger balance for inventory. The actual counts of items have been multiplied by their respective values. These values are added, and the sum is compared to the balance in the related inventory account in the general ledger. The difference represents the adjustment necessary to bring the inventory balance in the general ledger into agreement with the actual inventory balance.

Segregation of Duties

Q32. Are responsibilities for maintaining inventory records and general ledger records separated? Access to both the detailed inventory records and the general ledger records would permit an employee to conceal an error or fraudulent action. The inventory balance in the general ledger is the summary of entries from areas external to the production and inventory areas. Thus, you can use the general ledger balance as a check on the accuracy of the detailed inventory records.

Management Controls

Q33. Do you review and authorize major inventory purchases? Your review of major inventory purchases can serve several important purposes. It will inform you of potentially large inventory balances that will soon be on hand and enable you to answer such questions as: Do you need such a large balance at one time? Is there a possibility that these items will become obsolete before all of them are used? Is there adequate protected storage space for these materials? Also, with your expertise in the business you may be able to negotiate a better price or better terms for this large purchase if you know about it in advance.

Q34. Do you review inventory levels periodically? You should review inventory levels periodically to be sure that your employees are performing their duties adequately. Inventory is likely to represent a key item to your business—stockouts can cause interruptions in production and possibly lost orders, yet the cost of carrying excess inventory is high. Inventory requires your attention and expertise. Since it is likely that your knowledge of the business is more extensive than that of your employees, you will probably be able to give them some useful pointers after you have conducted your review. A word of caution—detailed inventory records that are used as "memo" records and that do not tie directly to the general ledger are often not compiled with the same degree of accuracy as your general ledger or other accounting records. Therefore, complement your use of the detailed inventory records with a brief physical inspection of key items.

Q35. Do you review and approve the instructions for the physical inventory counting? The physical inventory count is an important function, yet it interrupts operations and requires an extensive commitment of manpower. It is important that you review the instructions for the physical inventory process carefully to ensure that the counting will be conducted efficiently and effectively.

A set of instructions for a physical inventory should address the following three major questions:

1. Most importantly, *will the counts be accurate?* Can items be excluded from the count without detection? Is it possible that the same item

can be included twice? Will management-level employees oversee and test the counts?

2. *How will inventory movements between departments be controlled?* Is it possible that an item can be counted in one department, be moved to another department, and be included in the counting a second time? In general, you should seek to minimize all movement of inventory items during a physical count.
3. And finally, *has there been an appropriate cutoff of the shipping and receiving functions?* Is the cutoff for the accounting records consistent with the cutoff for inventory items received into or shipped from inventory? Is it possible that inventory items received or shipped after the accounting records are closed will affect the physical counts adversely, or, conversely, that items shipped or received after the physical count will affect the accounting records before the count?

In order to minimize interruption to shipping and receiving caused by a physical inventory, segregate items received after the cutoff in the receiving area for subsequent transfer to stock areas. Similarly, for items to be shipped immediately after the cutoff (next period per accounting records), assemble these items in the shipping area, count the items, and test the counts as necessary. After approval of the counts, release the items for shipment.

Q36. Do you supervise the physical inventory counting and review any adjustments to the accounting records arising from inventory counts? The physical inventory process is an important function. You should supervise the counters to be sure that your approved instructions are being followed. After the count has been completed, review the accounting adjustments arising from the physical inventory. The adjustments arising from the physical inventory will affect your income statement; therefore, you should investigate the necessity for any adjustment and understand thoroughly the resulting accounting entry.

Q37. Do you review and approve salvage sales and the write-off of obsolete inventory items? Your review and approval of salvage sales and the write-off of obsolete inventory items serves as a check that valuable products are not being sold at less than their true value or that useful inventory items will no longer be recorded in your general ledger. Furthermore, your knowledge of the business may tell you that an otherwise obsolete material has an alternative application in your product line or that it is of value to another company in the industry.

30

Controlling Your Investments

OBJECTIVES AND RISK CONSIDERATIONS

In controlling your company's investments make certain that you establish procedures to accomplish the following objectives. These objectives are addressed by the questions in the Self-Assessment Questionnaire indicated by the numbers in parentheses.

- All purchase or sale transactions must be initiated by authorized individuals and properly documented (Q38, Q46, Q47).
- All proposed transactions must conform to company investment objectives and be supported by appropriate written justification (Q41, Q46, Q47).
- Approval of the allocation of company resources must be obtained before investments are made (Q41, Q46).
- All securities must be subject to effective custodial accountability procedures and physical safeguards (Q39, Q40, Q50).

- All security transactions must be properly recorded in adequate detailed records and appropriate reports issued (Q42, Q43, Q45, Q48).
- All transactions must be properly accumulated, classified, and summarized in the accounts (Q44).

The risk considerations associated with investments are the following:

- Using corporate securities as collateral for personal loans (Q38, Q44, Q45, Q46, Q47, Q48, Q49, Q50).
- Sale or purchase of securities at an improper price for personal gain (Q46, Q47).
- Simple theft of corporate securities (Q39, Q40, Q44, Q45, Q46, Q47, Q48, Q49, Q50).
- Failure to record purchases, sales, or income from securities (Q42, Q43, Q44, Q48, Q49).

SELF-ASSESSMENT QUESTIONNAIRE

	Yes	*No*	*Not Applicable*	*Comment*
Control Procedures				
38. Are securities executed in the name of the company or restrictively endorsed in the name of the company?	____	____	____	____________
39. Are investment securities and other negotiable instruments held by an independent custodian?	____	____	____	____________
40. If the answer to question 39 is no, then are they kept in a safe deposit box or under lock and key?	____	____	____	____________
41. If an independent custodian is used, does the custodian receive and deliver securities only on your written authorization?	____	____	____	____________

	Yes	No	Not Appli-cable	Comment
42. If an independent custodian is used, does an employee match the custodian's monthly listing of securities held to the company's record of securities held by the custodian?	____	____	____	__________
43. Is an employee responsible for promptly and accurately recording dividend and interest income?	____	____	____	__________
Segregation of Duties				
44. Is the investment subsidiary ledger maintained by someone other than the employee who maintains the general ledger?	____	____	____	__________
Management Controls				
45. Do you match the subsidiary ledger balance to the general ledger investment account balance?	____	____	____	__________
46. Do you authorize all purchase, sale, renewal, and extension transactions?	____	____	____	__________
47. If you instruct an employee to perform the purchase and sale activities, do you check the prices involved in the transaction?	____	____	____	__________
48. Do you maintain a separate detailed listing of securities, in addition to the detailed listing maintained by your accounting department?	____	____	____	__________

	Yes	No	Not Appli-cable	Comment
49. On a regular basis, do you compare your listing of securities to the one maintained by the accounting department and/or to the report from the independent custodian, if one is employed?	____	____	____	____________
50. If an independent custodian is not used, do you periodically take a surprise count of the securities?	____	____	____	____________

RECOMMENDATIONS FOR CONTROLS ON INVESTMENTS

Control Procedures

Q38. Are securities executed in the name of the company or restrictively endorsed in the name of the company? Securities are often readily negotiable instruments. As such, they must be closely protected from theft. By executing the securities in the company's name, or by restrictively endorsing them in the company's name, you limit their negotiability to a certain extent. Although these actions enhance the safeguarding of securities, they must be supplemented by other procedures for protection.

Q39. Are investment securities and other negotiable instruments held by an independent custodian? Use of an independent custodian assists in the ongoing protection of securities owned by your company. Because protection of securities is the custodian's business, he can provide the facilities needed for the safeguarding function.

Q40. If the answer to question 39 is no, then are they kept in a safe deposit box or under lock and key? A safe deposit box provides physical protection for securities. Day-to-day access to the securities is likely to be unnecessary so long as all pertinent data on the securities have been recorded. If a safe deposit box is not used and the securities are maintained on the premises, they should be kept under lock and key away from everyday access.

Q41. If an independent custodian is used, does the custodian receive and deliver securities only on your written authorization? Because of the negotiable nature of most securities, it is imperative that the custodian receive and deliver securities only on your written authorization.

Q42. If an independent custodian is used, does an employee match the custodian's monthly listing of securities held to the company's record of securities held by the custodian? Your company must maintain a record of all securities delivered to and held by the independent custodian. Although it is his function to provide accurate recordkeeping for the securities he holds in his custody, do not rely solely upon his report of the securities held. Assign an employee the responsibility of comparing the custodian's monthly report to your company's detailed listing of securities held by him. Any differences between the two lists should be investigated and brought to your attention immediately.

Q43. Is an employee responsible for promptly and accurately recording dividend and interest income? An employee should be charged with the responsibility of monitoring and promptly recording all dividend and interest income in the accounting records. The objective of this procedure is to maintain up-to-date records on the income generated by your securities. You can test these income amounts by comparing the per share or percentage amounts to independent records of dividend or interest income, such as those provided in Moody's Dividend Record. To test the completeness of your accounting records, trace amounts *from* the independent source *to* the accounting records.

Segregation of Duties

Q44. Is the investment subsidiary ledger maintained by someone other than the employee who maintains the general ledger? It is important that these functions be performed by separate employees. Access to both the general ledger and the investment subsidiary ledger may allow an employee to conceal an error or fraudulent action. If this segregation of duties is not feasible in your organization, you must increase your personal participation in the safeguarding process.

Management Controls

Q45. Do you match the subsidiary ledger balance to the general ledger investment account balance? As a check on the detailed investment recordkeeping, it is important that you or an employee not involved in the detailed investment recordkeeping process match the total balance from the detailed records to the general ledger balance. The general ledger balance is used as the benchmark because the general ledger balance represents the summary of approved and valid transactions.

Q46. Do you authorize all purchase, sale, renewal, and extension transactions? Because securities are readily negotiable, it is important that all securities transactions receive your authorization.

Q47. If you instruct an employee to perform the purchase and sale activities, do you check the prices involved in the transaction? Documents provided by the broker regarding the transaction are likely to satisfy your information needs for the checking process. Advise your broker to forward the transaction documents directly to you. It is important to check the prices involved in a securities transaction to ascertain that the transaction has been executed as you authorized.

Q48. Do you maintain a separate detailed listing of securities, in addition to the listing maintained by your accounting department? If you do not use a custodian to hold your securities, you may wish to keep your own listing as a check on your accounting group.

Q49. On a regular basis, do you compare your listing of securities to the one maintained by the accounting department and/or to the report from the independent custodian if one is employed? To be sure that all securities transactions have taken place as authorized by you and that no unauthorized transactions have been processed, compare your list to the list maintained by the accounting department and/or to the general ledger investment account balance for agreement. You should also compare your lists to the independent custodian's report.

Q50. If an independent custodian is not used, do you periodically take a surprise count of the securities? If a safe deposit box is used or if the securities are maintained on premises under lock and key, you should periodically perform a surprise count of the securities. Compare your count of your detailed listing of securities to the custodian's list or to the general ledger.

31

Controlling Your Fixed Assets

OBJECTIVES AND RISK CONSIDERATIONS

In controlling your company's fixed assets make certain that you establish procedures to accomplish the following objectives. These objectives are addressed by the questions in the Self-Assessment Questionnaire indicated by the numbers in parentheses.

- All productive asset transactions must be initiated by authorized individuals in accordance with management's criteria (Q58).
- Advance approval must be obtained for all significant productive asset transactions (Q58).
- Adequate project cost records must be maintained, and in-progress and completed project reports must be issued (Q59).
- All productive assets must be accurately recorded in detailed records that are compared with existing assets at reasonable intervals (Q53, Q54, Q56).

- All productive assets must be adequately safeguarded (Q52).
- All productive asset transactions must be properly accumulated, classified, and summarized in the accounts (Q55, Q57).

The risk considerations associated with fixed assets are the following:

- Fictitious or excessive purchases or payments (Q58).
- Kickbacks to company employees (Q58).
- Purchase of assets that fail to meet company needs (Q58).
- Improper or erroneous recording of productive asset transactions (Q57).
- Theft of tools, equipment, or supplies (Q52).
- Unauthorized use of productive assets (Q52).
- Misappropriation of proceeds from sales of assets (Q58).
- Loss of uninsured assets (Q51, Q60).

SELF-ASSESSMENT QUESTIONNAIRE

	Yes	*No*	*Not Applicable*	*Comment*
Control Procedures				
51. Is an employee responsible for monitoring the insurance coverage over fixed assets, including fixed asset additions?	____	____	____	__________
52. Are fixed assets adequately safeguarded?	____	____	____	__________
53. Are physical inventories of fixed assets taken periodically?	____	____	____	__________
54. Are detailed records maintained for individual fixed assets?	____	____	____	__________
55. Are the detailed records matched at least annually with the general ledger fixed asset balances?	____	____	____	__________

	Yes	No	Not Applicable	Comment
Segregation of Duties				
56. Are the periodic physical inventories of fixed assets conducted by individuals other than those responsible for the physical assets?	___	___	___	___
57. Are the detailed fixed asset records maintained by persons other than those responsible for the fixed assets?	___	___	___	___
Management Controls				
58. Do you personally authorize major fixed asset purchases and dispositions?	___	___	___	___
59. Do you review fixed asset construction projects on an ongoing basis?	___	___	___	___
60. Do you periodically review insurance coverage and negotiate policy renewals?	___	___	___	___

RECOMMENDATIONS FOR CONTROLS ON FIXED ASSETS

Control Procedures

Q51. Is an employee responsible for monitoring the insurance coverage over fixed assets, including fixed asset additions? It is important that you assign to an employee the responsibility of monitoring insurance coverage on fixed assets. The employee must make sure that premiums are paid when required and that policies do not expire without renewal. It is of particular importance that the employee obtain coverage on a timely basis for fixed asset additions. Conversely, the employee should notify the insurer of fixed asset dispositions for appropriate cancellation of coverage and termination of premium expense.

Q52. Are fixed assets adequately safeguarded? Fixed assets should be safeguarded. When possible, try to anchor your fixed assets to your building structure. All fixed assets should be tagged with a unique identifying number and separately listed in a detailed record. Instruct your security personnel to question any removal of fixed assets from company premises. Require that a log or other direct order be signed by the individual removing the property from the premises. Included in the log should be a description of the asset, any identifying numbers on the asset, and the identification of the individual removing the property. This log should then be reviewed by you or a management-level employee not responsible for the purchase or sale of fixed assets.

Q53. Are physical inventories of fixed assets taken periodically? Physical inventories of fixed assets should be taken periodically to ensure that there has been no unauthorized removal of assets from the company's premises.

Q54. Are detailed records maintained for individual fixed asset items? It is important that detailed records be maintained in order to provide specific identification of fixed assets held, to support depreciation calculations, and to provide a record of asset cost to calculate gain or loss when the asset is disposed of. If fixed assets have been assigned unique identifying numbers, these numbers should be included in the records. The fixed asset records provide the basis for your fixed asset physical inventory.

Q55. Are the detailed records matched at least annually with the general ledger fixed asset balances? The general ledger balance for fixed assets represents the summary of approved and valid transactions. Matching the total of the detailed fixed asset records to the general ledger proves the accuracy of the detailed records. Any discrepancies noted should be investigated.

Segregation of Duties

Q56. Are the periodic physical inventories of fixed assets conducted by individuals other than those responsible for the physical assets? The physical inventories of fixed assets should not be conducted by the individuals who are responsible for the physical properties. The objective of the physical inventory is to serve as an independent check on the performance of the individuals who are responsible for the property.

Q57. Are the detailed fixed asset records maintained by persons other than those responsible for the fixed assets? Because the fixed asset records serve as a source for checking on the performance of the individuals who are responsible for the fixed assets, it is imperative that these individuals do not maintain or have access to the detailed records.

Management Controls

Q58. Do you personally authorize purchases and dispositions of major fixed assets? Because of the typical high value of a major fixed asset purchase, it is likely to have a significant impact on your cash flow position. It represents a major commitment on the part of your company; therefore, it should receive your careful review and approval. Likewise, you should approve fixed asset dispositions. Your expertise allows you to judge whether a fair selling price has been reached. Your knowledge of the industry may help you to identify a ready market for an asset no longer needed in your operations.

Q59. Do you review on an ongoing basis construction of fixed assets? You should review fixed asset construction projects on an ongoing basis. The objective of your review is to ascertain that the progress timetable is being met, that specifications are being followed, and that costs are in line with initial estimates. Deviations in any of these areas can seriously affect your operations, if not interrupt them completely.

Q60. Do you periodically review insurance coverage and negotiate policy renewals? You should monitor insurance coverage for adequacy on a periodic basis, keeping in mind the impact of inflation on the market value of assets. Professional advice to determine the appropriate level of coverage for your company can be obtained from an independent insurance consultant. It is important that you take an active role in negotiating policy renewals. Seek to obtain the coverage you deem adequate at the lowest possible price.

32

Controlling Your Purchasing and Accounts Payable

OBJECTIVES AND RISK CONSIDERATIONS

In controlling your company's purchases and accounts payable make certain that you establish procedures to accomplish the following objectives. These objectives are addressed by the questions in the Self-Assessment Questionnaire indicated by the numbers in the parentheses.

- All requests for goods and services must be initiated and approved by authorized individuals (Q69).
- All purchase orders must be on valid, approved requests and properly executed as to price, quantity, quality, and vendor (Q61, Q62, Q69).
- All materials and services received must agree with the original purchase orders (Q64).
- All invoices processed for payment must represent goods and services received and be accurate as to terms, quantities, prices, and extensions. Account distributions must be accurate and agree with established account classifications (Q63, Q64, Q65, Q72).

- All checks must be prepared on the basis of adequate and approved documentation, compared with supporting data, and properly approved, signed, and mailed (Q64, Q66).
- All invoices and disbursements must be promptly and accurately recorded as to payee and amount (Q67, Q68).
- All entries to accounts payable, asset and expense accounts, and cash disbursements must be properly accumulated, classified, and summarized in the accounts (Q68, Q71, Q72).

The risk considerations associated with purchasing and accounts payable are the following:

- Purchases from unauthorized vendors (Q72).
- Purchases that are not timely (Q62).
- Purchases in violation of conflict of interest policies or business practice (Q70).
- Payments in excess of optimum price (Q69).
- Quantities not adequate or in excess of need (Q62).
- Substandard quality of goods purchased or services received (Q63).
- Damaged or missing goods not reported (Q63).
- Payment for goods or services not received (Q64).
- Payments based on improper price or terms (Q64).
- Transactions improperly reflected in the accounts (Q72).
- Alteration of checks (Q77).
- Improper cash and accounts payable general ledger balances (Q67, Q68, Q71).
- Misstated financial statements (Q67, Q71, Q72).
- Misleading internal financial reports (Q72).

SELF-ASSESSMENT QUESTIONNAIRE

	Yes	*No*	*Not Applicable*	*Comment*
Control Procedures				
61. Are purchase orders based on approved requests?	___	___	___	___

	Yes	No	Not Applicable	Comment
62. Do purchase orders completely specify quantity, quality, price, terms of payment, and expected date of delivery?	___	___	___	___
63. Are receiving reports prepared for all purchased goods?	___	___	___	___
64. Is the vendor invoice compared to the purchase order and receiving report for quantity, quality, price, and terms of payment?	___	___	___	___
65. Are invoices checked for mathematical accuracy?				
66. Are payments made only on the basis of original invoices?				
67. Are trial balances of accounts payable regularly reconciled to the general ledger?	___	___	___	___
Segregation of Duties				
68. Are responsibilities for the requisitioning, purchasing, and receiving functions separated from the invoice processing, accounts payable, and general ledger functions?	___	___	___	___
69. Do you review purchase prices on a periodic basis?	___	___	___	___
70. Do you approve major purchase orders?	___	___	___	___
71. Do you review the reconciliation of the accounts payable trial balance to the general ledger?	___	___	___	___

	Yes	No	Not Appli-cable	Comment
72. Do you review the general ledger account distribution on vendor invoice amounts?				

RECOMMENDATIONS FOR CONTROLS ON PURCHASING AND ACCOUNTS PAYABLE

Control Procedures

Q61. Are purchase orders based on approved requests? Chapter 26 "Objectives and Methods of Control," described the need to control direct and indirect access to assets. The purchasing process is an example of indirect access to assets in that it gives instructions to a vendor to provide goods or services to your company. It commits the resources of your company. By limiting the issuance of purchase orders to authorized employees only, you limit indirect access to your company's assets.

Q62. Do purchase orders completely specify quantity, quality, price, terms of payment, and expected date of delivery? Specification of quantity, quality, price, terms of payment, and expected date of delivery is essential in purchase transactions with vendors. These items outline the conditions under which you are willing to do business. By documenting your intended transaction in a definitive purchase order, you minimize subsequent misunderstandings between your company and the vendor. A misunderstanding regarding any of these conditions could potentially disrupt the intended flow of your operations. In addition, a well-defined purchase order is a source for evaluating the validity of the vendor invoice. Figure 32.1 is an example of a completed purchase order. Notice that it clearly specifies the due date for the items ordered, the shipping instructions, the quantity, the type of item required, and the unit price of the item ordered.

If the price cannot be established at the time of the preparation of the purchase order, a "not to exceed," or a ceiling, price should be specified; however, you should minimize the issuance of purchase orders that are not price-specific.

Q63. Are receiving reports prepared for all purchased goods? The receipt of purchased goods should be fully documented in a receiving report that

FIGURE 32.1
Example of a Purchase Order

PURCHASE ORDER

XYZ Co.
1 Federal Street
Boston, MA 02110

NO. 212153

DATE 1/3/8X **DATE REQUIRED** 2/15/8X

SHIP VIA Train **F.O.B.** S.P.

TERMS

TO • ABC Co.
Route 9
• Framingham, MA 20125
•

SHIP TO XYZ
1 Federal Street
Boston, MA 02110

QUANTITY	√	STOCK NUMBER/DESCRIPTION	PRICE		PER		
20		Standard Office Chairs (Catalogue #517-58914) (A/C 01-1510-000) Office Eq. Capital Expense	23	95	ea	479	00

OUR ORDER NUMBERS MUST APPEAR ON INVOICES,
PACKAGES AND CORRESPONDENCE.
ACKNOWLEDGE IF UNABLE TO DELIVERY BY DATE REQUIRED.

Finance Dept.

By RE Butler, Treas.

notes the vendor, quantity, quality, and condition of the goods. To be sure that the receiving report gives an accurate description and count of the goods received, it is necessary that the report be prepared by the employee who is responsible for receiving goods from outside parties. Packing slips enclosed in vendor shipments should not be relied on. An independent count should be performed by the employee who is responsible for receiving purchased goods.

Typically, a copy of the purchase order is forwarded to the receiving department. The receiving department should be instructed to reject any items not supported by a purchase order. The purchase order quantity should not be relied on by the receiving department; instead, an independent count should be made by the receiver. If possible, the receiving department copy of the purchase order should not include the quantity ordered.

Q64. Is the vendor invoice compared to the purchase order and receiving report for quantity, quality, price, and terms of payment? To establish the validity of a vendor invoice, your accounting department should compare it to the purchase order and the receiving report. The purchase order should include data on price, quality, quantity requested, and terms of payment. The receiving report should provide data on the description, condition, and count of goods actually received. The "ship to" address or location of service should be reviewed to be sure that the goods or services were delivered or rendered to bona fide operating units of the organization. Procedures should be established to investigate any discrepancies noted between the vendor invoice and the purchase order and receiving report.

Q65. Are invoices checked for mathematical accuracy? To prevent the payment of excess amounts on vendor invoices, an employee should fully test the mathematical accuracy of the invoice.

Q66. Are payments made only on the basis of original invoices? As discussed in Chapter 27, "Controlling Your Cash," one control objective is to prevent duplicate payments to vendors. One of the procedures identified for attaining this objective was the cancellation of the vendor invoice concurrently with the signing of the related disbursement check. Payment based on duplicate invoices or photocopies of original invoices subverts this control because, as the check signer, you have no immediate means for determining if payment has already been made on this vendor claim.

Q67. Are trial balances of accounts payable regularly reconciled to the general ledger? To ensure that accounts payable records have been accurately maintained, a listing of unpaid vendor invoices (trial balance) should be prepared and compared to the general ledger balance for accounts payable. Agreement between the trial balance and the general ledger balance provides assurance that transactions have been accurately entered into the accounting system. Any discrepancies should be investigated and appropriately resolved.

Segregation of Duties

Q68. Are responsibilities for the requisitioning, purchasing, and receiving functions separated from the invoice processing, accounts payable, and general ledger functions? From the standpoint of the segregation of duties, these activities are incompatible. Unless separated, these activities provide the potential for the concealment of an error or an unauthorized transaction. In this situation, you are seeking to control the direct and indirect access to your company's assets. In terms of direct access, your objective is to prevent the outright theft of your company's purchased goods. In terms of indirect access, your objective is to prevent arrangements between your employees and your vendors, whereby unjustified and inappropriate transactions take place between your company and your vendors for personal profit to your employees. For example, do not allow goods to be shipped to your purchasing agent, and do not allow your purchasing agent to approve vendor invoices for payment.

Management Controls

Q69. Do you review purchase prices on a periodic basis? Use your industry expertise and general business knowledge to test the reasonableness of prices charged by vendors. You can perform this review as a formal step in the invoice approval process or when the check to pay the invoice is given to you to sign.

Q70. Do you approve major purchase orders? You should review and approve all major purchase orders before their release to vendors. The purchase is likely to represent a major commitment of your company's resources. Can you obtain a better price? Can you obtain more favorable terms of payment? Will your cash flow be sufficient to pay for the purchase? It is likely that you are the best qualified, if not the only, individual in your organization to provide answers to these questions.

Q71. Do you review the reconciliation of the accounts payable trial balance to the general ledger? The reconciliation of the accounts payable trial balance to the general ledger balance for accounts payable provides a good indication of the accuracy of the maintenance of accounts payable records. With a minimal amount of time and effort you can review and test the reconciliation prepared by your employees. Note the appropriate accounting disposition of any reconciling items specified.

Q72. Do you review the general ledger account distribution on vendor invoice amounts? On a test basis, at the time of check signing, review the account distribution assigned to a vendor invoice. Transactions should be classified accurately and consistently to permit subsequent comparison of financial statements and management reports to prior period or budgeted amounts.

33

Controlling Your Payroll

OBJECTIVES AND RISK CONSIDERATIONS

In controlling your company's payroll make certain to establish procedures to accomplish the following objectives. These objectives are addressed by the questions in the Self-Assessment Questionnaire indicated by the numbers in the parentheses.

- Additions, separations, wage rates, salaries, and deductions must be authorized (Q73, Q78).
- Employees' time and attendance data must be properly reviewed and approved (Q74).
- Employees' time and attendance data must be properly processed and documented and accurately coded for accounting distribution (Q81).
- Computations for gross pay, deductions, and net pay must be accurate and based on authorized time and amounts; the recording and summarizing of payments to be made and costs to be distributed must be

accurate and agree with established account classifications (Q74, Q81).

- Payments for employee compensation and benefits must be made to or on behalf of only bona fide employees for services performed as authorized by management (Q74, Q75, Q79, Q80).
- Employee compensation and benefit costs must be properly accumulated, classified, and summarized in the accounts (Q81).

The risk considerations associated with payroll are the following:

- Fictitious payroll additions or unreported severances (Q78, Q80, Q82).
- Overstated rates, hours, extensions, piecework, or totals (Q74).
- Misappropriation of unclaimed wages (Q76, Q77).
- Erroneous recording of compensation costs (Q81).

SELF-ASSESSMENT QUESTIONNAIRE

	Yes	No	Not Applicable	Comment
Control Procedures				
73. Are all changes in employment (additions and terminations), in salary and wage rates, and in amounts of payroll deductions adequately documented?	___	___	___	___________
74. Are all time reports reviewed and approved by the employee's supervisor?	___	___	___	___________
75. Does all overtime work require advance authorization by the employee's supervisor?	___	___	___	___________
Segregation of Duties				
76. Is the distribution of payroll checks made by employees who are not involved in the payroll preparation process?	___	___	___	___________

	Yes	No	Not Appli- cable	Comment
77. Is the distribution of payroll checks made by employees who are not involved in the time re- port approval process?	___	___	___	___
Management Controls				
78. Do you approve all hirings and terminations and changes in salary and wage rates?	___	___	___	___
79. Do you sign the payroll checks and/or review the payroll register?	___	___	___	___
80. Do you distribute the payroll checks periodi- cally?	___	___	___	___
81. Do you compare current payroll expense to prior year levels or to bud- geted payroll expense?	___	___	___	___
82. Do you use the annual W-2 form issuance pro- cess to contribute to payroll control?	___	___	___	___

RECOMMENDATIONS FOR CONTROLS ON PAYROLL

Control Procedures

Q73. Are all changes in employment (additions and terminations), in salary and wage rates, and in amounts of payroll deductions adequately documented? All changes in employment status and the authorizations of such changes should be documented and maintained on file for each employee. Many small businesses prepare a standardized form to document hirings, terminations, and salary and wage changes. Figure 33.1 is an example of this type of form.

Q74. Are all time reports reviewed and approved by the employee's supervisor? To be sure that wages are paid only for hours actually worked, you should require your supervisors to review and approve their respective employees' time reports. This control, however, presupposes that you in

FIGURE 33-1
Payroll notification.

PAYROLL NOTIFICATION

Effective date ____________________

Employee name ____________________

Social Security Number ____________________

Employee Number ____________________

Addition/Termination

Check applicable activity — Reason

________ Addition

________ Termination

The Change(s)

Check applicable activity		From	To
________	Department	_____	_____
________	Job	_____	_____
________	Shift	_____	_____
________	Rate	_____	_____

Reason for the Changes(s)

________	Promotion	________	Probationary period completed
________	Demotion	________	Length of service increase
________	Transfer	________	Reevaluation of existing job
________	Merit increase	________	Union scale

________ Leave of absence from ________ until ________

Change authorized by ______________________________ Date ________

Change approved by ______________________________ Date ________

turn are evaluating your supervisors in terms of their departments' payroll charges.

Q75. Does all overtime work require advance authorization by the employee's supervisor? Overtime typically arises from unplanned events and results in premium labor charges. To protect your company from excessive labor charges, you should establish that the overtime charges have been incurred for a sound business purpose and that the decision to incur the overtime charges has been based on experienced judgment. Requiring the advance approval from departmental supervisors before any overtime charges are incurred limits unnecessary or fraudulent time charges. Again, this control procedure presupposes that the supervisors are evaluated on their departments' total labor costs compared to budget.

Segregation of Duties

Q76. Is the distribution of payroll checks made by employees who are not involved in the payroll preparation process? Barring collusion, there is little or no incentive for the preparer to falsify the payroll data unless access to the paychecks or pay envelopes can be obtained. After the payroll checks have been signed, they should be given to an employee not involved in the payroll preparation process for distribution. Checks for absent employees should not be returned to the preparer of the payroll. An individual not involved in the payroll preparation process should have custody over unclaimed wages.

Q77. Is the distribution of payroll checks made by employees who are not involved in the time report approval process? An employee who both approves time reports and distributes payroll checks potentially has the ability to create a fraudulent time report and gain possession of the resulting payroll check. The payroll checks should be distributed by an employee not involved in the time report approval process; for example, the foremen should not distribute paychecks. Likewise, unclaimed checks for absent employees should not be held by those who approved the payroll, despite their proximity in the working area to the employee.

Management Controls

Q78. Do you approve all hirings and terminations and changes in salary and wage rates? Payroll charges represent a disposition of the assets of your company. By requiring that all hirings, terminations, and changes in salary and wage rates receive your prior approval, you limit accessibility to the assets of your company.

Q79. Do you sign the payroll checks and/or review the payroll register? You should sign all payroll checks and/or review the payroll register to be sure that individual employee amounts appear to be in line with your understanding of the wage and salary structures of your company. See Figure 33.2 for an example of a payroll register. You will see that it includes information on each employee who is receiving a paycheck. It identifies the number of hours worked, the gross wage amount, deductions for tax, insurance, and other items, and the net amount of the payroll check.

Watch for excessive overtime payments. Not only is this a drain on the resources of your company, but it may also adversely affect the morale of your employees. An hourly employee with overtime may be receiving more pay than his salaried supervisor for the same number of hours worked.

Q80. *Do you distribute the payroll checks on a periodic basis?* On a surprise basis, distribute your company's payroll checks. Request identification from employees with whom you are not familiar. Investigate the authenticity of employees who are "absent" at the time of the distribution.

Q81. *Do you compare current payroll expense to prior year levels or to budgeted payroll expense?* Labor expense is likely to represent one of the largest outflows of resources from your company. Therefore, it deserves a careful and frequent review. Comparison to prior year levels is likely to highlight any unfavorable trends. Comparison to budgeted amounts will indicate variances from the business plan. Identify the causes of any variances, determine the necessary actions to minimize further occurrence of the variances, and take steps to implement corrective actions.

Q82. *Do you use the annual W-2 form issuance process to contribute to payroll control?* The annual issuance of W-2 forms, required by federal statute, can serve as a payroll control mechanism for your company. Require a reconciliation of the total of the W-2 form amounts to the total labor expense per the general ledger for the year. Instruct an employee independent of the preparer of the payroll to maintain control over the W-2 forms and to test the reconciliation to the general ledger accounts. This same employee should perform the mailing of the W-2s. W-2 forms should not be manually distributed. Require any undeliverable W-2 forms to be returned directly to you. Investigate undeliverable W-2 forms for payments to fictitious employees.

Index

A

B

C

G

H

I

M

N

O

P

Q

R

T

V

W

Z